New Perspectives in Community Development

New Perspectives in Community Development

Edited by

Sanjoy Roy
Bishnu Mohan Dash

ATLANTIC
PUBLISHERS & DISTRIBUTORS (P) LTD

ATLANTIC
PUBLISHERS & DISTRIBUTORS (P) LTD

7/22, Ansari Road, Darya Ganj, New Delhi
Tel.: +91-11-4077 5252, 2327 3880
E-mail: orders@atlanticbooks.com
Web: www.atlanticbooks.com

Reprint 2026

Published by Atlantic Publishers & Distributors (P) Ltd.

Printed & bound in India by Atlantic Print Services

Preface

The book, *New Perspectives in Community Development* presents a critical analysis on the important emerging issues on community development. It aims to help the readers understand the issues involved in the process of community development. In the opening chapter, "Rural Community Development in India: Emerging Issues, Challenges and Strategies", Suresh Pathare and Jaimon Varghese have described that the basic approach of rural community development has shifted from the centralised planning to people's planning. The strategies and methods of rural development have undergone dramatic changes over the past six decades. Self-Help Group strategy has evolved as a powerful means for rural development. Ecological concern, natural and organic farming, water harvesting, management of non conventional energy sources, etc. have become essential aspects of rural development. Participation of the corporate enterprises in rural development is also a growing trend. There are a number of innovative models of rural development across the country like Tilonia, Ralegaon Sidhi, Hiware Bazar and many more. New methods and strategies to work with rural communities with innovative participatory approach such as micro-planning, people planning, etc. are emerging. Social work as a profession is finding new roles and responsibilities in the changed rural scenario.

Guljit K. Arora in his paper, "Women Empowerment, Globalization and Cooperatives: Role of Women Fisheries Cooperatives in Sri Lanka", raises the issue of women empowerment and its importance in the country. He has made an attempt to explore how the cooperative model of development can empower and enable powerless women to compete the world and make sustainable human development possible. He suggests that the young women must be provided the right environment to feel motivated to develop knowledge, competence, determination and perseverance to work for women cooperative fisheries because these cooperatives offer at least two keys of strength which no other enterprise can fully match: one, it gives an opportunity to each person to help themselves by cooperating with others, and two, it provides strength to an individual to acquire and control private property while preserving individual freedom, dignity and responsibility. National development is a daunting task, in which young women can play a leading role.

In his chapter, "Gender-based Development in India: Social Provisions, Failures and Interventions", Asok Kumar Sarkar states that 'gender inequality' is one of the major obstacles in fulfilling the Millennium Development Goals in most of the Third World countries including India. Thus, arguments for gender equity to go beyond equal opportunity require the transformation of basic rules, hierarchies and practices of public institutions. This calls for more involvement and participation of women in politics to challenge the existing marginalization (Priyam et al., 2008). The paper has forwarded various social work interventions to challenge the patriarchy at grassroots level, and can play a gigantic role to accelerate gender-based development in India. G. Ram in his article, "The Emerging Power Structure in Rural India: Democracy, Development and Decentralization", highlights that the Panchayati Raj institutions were set up to accelerate the arrested process of change and development to enable rural people to participate and contribute in national rural reconstruction and development, and to redistribute land among the poor with a view to transforming the agrarian structure. However, these measures could not bring about much of desired results. In concrete terms, the political response with regard to major structural changes has not been satisfactory, and indifference has prevailed among political workers at the grassroots level.

Heena K. Bijli's paper, "Extension and Corporate Social Responsibility: New Paradigms and Linkages for Community Development", contextualizes CSR strategies that can be leveraged through emerging paradigms and practices of extension. These are achievable by fostering corporate linkages with R&D and S&T institutes, voluntary organizations, and in promoting employee volunteerism and corporate social entrepreneurship for encouraging more robust forms of corporate citizenship. Integrated studies in extension education and corporate citizenship will emphasize the need for socially responsible behaviour. Heena has highlighted that there is need to build platforms where public and private entities can converge and contribute to the resolution of social causes. To meet the challenges of the new millennium with respect to corporate social responsibility and partnerships, extension services will have to be given a serious thought.

Y.S. Siddegowda in his article, "Sustainable Development", suggests as to how the sustainable development and higher education, sustainable development and social work, and need for development play an effective role in managing the boundaries between knowledge and action in ways that simultaneously enhance the salience, credibility, and legitimacy of the information they produce. Effective systems apply a variety of institutional mechanisms that facilitate communication, translation and development across boundaries. D.P. Singh and Ritu in their paper, "Community Ownership of School Education: A Pre-requisite for Development", have examined the process of communitization of education at the village level by evaluating the functioning of the committees that provide a platform for the people to own the school-related activities at the community level, thereby accelerating the process of social development. Manushi in her paper, "ICT Development in Rural India", has highlighted that India carries great disparity between users of ICT as there is a social and economic divide, disparities exist between urban and rural area. Limitations in electricity, telephony, Internet connectivity and other kinds of basic infrastructure in India's rural areas are key challenges. The country is going through an ICT revolution and this has become an enabling force for those living in rural India to become active participants in the growth of the country.

Manju Panwar in her paper, "Self-Help Groups and Rural Development", has highlighted that despite efforts made over the past few decades, rural poverty in India continues to be significant. In recent years, the SHGs have become a very important tool for reducing poverty. In economic literature, credit has been assigned a docile and a passive role. It has been accepted as a lubricant or facilitator of trade, commerce and industry. But in reality credit plays a far more powerful, social and political role than is generally admitted. It is, in fact, a powerful weapon. With appropriate credit institutions and credit policies, it is possible to drive the society towards a desired shape. In order to develop our villages, need of the hour is that banks and other institutions which are involved in the promotion of SHGs should understand their responsibility towards society. They should participate in SHGs bank linkage programme with greater enthusiasm and dedication. The success of every programme depends upon the collective efforts. Hence, it is imperative that there is proper coordination and cooperation to fulfill the objectives of a rural development.

Rakesh Dwivedi in his paper, "Role of Indian Women in Agriculture: An Overview", has explored the participation of women in agriculture and its allied fields. The major obstacles faced by women have been highlighted and provisions for upliftment of women in agriculture suggested. Chittaranjan Das Adhikary in the paper, "Wither Away Panchayats: Two Narratives of Embedded Development", has captured two contrasting styles of governance in Odisha, described as liberal, democratic, socialist and developmental models of democratic decentralization. His studies have pointed out different ways in which these institutions are embedded in the colonial history, deficient political will and innovative use and misuse of power. Pradipta Dubey and Atonu Chatterjee in their paper, "Marketing the Products of Self-Help Group—A Study of North 24 Parganas, West Bengal", has explored the efforts and procedures adopted by a specific district in West Bengal in marketing the products of SHGs operative under Swarna Jayanti Gram Swarojgar Yojana (SGSY). In course of discussion, the paper also traces the importance of group-based microfinancing and explains how SGSY programme is different in terms of ensuring forward linkage and imparting entrepreneurial skill and expertise among the SHG members. V. Naveen Kumar and V. Venkateswarlu in their paper, "Participation of Non-Governmental Organizations in Rural Development—A Social Work Perspective", have stated that NGOs are organizations within the civil society that work on the "not-for-profit" approach in the space which exists between the family (household), markets and state. It is made up of several types of formal voluntary organizations, where people based on community, neighbourhood, workplace and other connections form their association to participate in actions for their own collective interests or for larger social good. A.V.V.S. Swamy, V. Subhashini and Ch. Rani in their paper, "Eco-Feminism and Dynamics of Gender Development in Rural India" have emphasized that women are no longer viewed as mere victims, and it is increasingly recognized that women can play a key role in natural resources management as they have the knowledge and experience gained from working closely with their environment. To maintain sustainable development, it is necessary to educate women regarding environmental problems and environmental degradation and there impact on human health. Environment education should include the whole spectrum of women-nature relationships.

Noorbasha Abdul, V. Tulasi Das and Ch. V. Krishna Reddy in their paper, "Watershed Development Programme in Andhra Pradesh—A Study on Income and Employment Generation", have reported that SHGs formed and established under WDP have provided more benefits and facilities to the members to improve their economic standards resulting in the improvement of their living standards. Besides, WDP has motivated all the communities in villages regarding credit and thrift. The respondents in the study have stated that SHGs under WDP have been helping them by facilitating with required loan for dairy development and management and other tiny business like establishment of *pan* shops, laundries, etc. They have also stated that after the implementation of WDP, the respondents have been getting employment (labour) for more days with good remuneration. V. Venkateswarlu in his paper, "A Study on Micro-Credit through Self-Help Groups and its Impact on Rural Development", has concluded that SHGs are able to generate savings and recycle the funds due to prompt repayment by members. The default rate in repayment has been very low. Among the different activities, tiffin centers, petty shops, laundry shops and tailoring units are high income-fetching and some other activities generate low incomes. But, on the whole, SHGs and micro-credit through self-help groups have a positive impact on poverty reduction. K. Madhu Babu and P. Srinivasulu in their article, "Mahatma Gandhi National Rural Employment Guarantee Programme in Andhra Pradesh: Its Social Audits", have presented the view that the National Rural Employment Guarantee Scheme (NREGS) is one of the major landmarks in the process of formulation, and adopting the rights-based approach. In Andhra Pradesh, women have been major beneficiaries of this scheme since its inception as the scheme guarantees work for all those who demand it. The study has revealed various limitations of NREGS. Misappropriation of funds, incomplete works and lack of follow-up, leakages, poor quality of physical assets created under this scheme, and poor wages are the important lacunas in the working and implementing the process of the NREGS.

Brajesh Kumar and Mintu Gogoi in their study, "Fast Moving Consumer Goods Industry in Rural Market of India: A Case of Mutual Reinvigoration", have made an assessment of the growing eminence of FMCG industry in the rural markets in India. Manish Dwivedi and Surendra Singh in their paper, "Participatory Watershed Planning", have mentioned that participatory approaches are also a reverse of the conventional approaches in which technocrats and administrators control decision-making participatory rural appraisal and goal-oriented project planning. These tools would facilitate local communities to undertake appraisal, make decisions and prepare plans on their own using their knowledge and wisdom. Village communities have their own understanding of the problems, solutions for them, and importantly, a vision for their village. The staff would be willing to learn from the local communities. Adoption for participatory approaches and tools would require changes in the attitude and outlook of the project authorities and technocrats, and in the systems and procedures they have established to control decision-making changes in behaviour in project staff; thus, it is a critical prerequisite. "Ownership" by the local community and their taking over responsibility for the project management are critical prerequisites for project sustainability, and this condition could be achieved only when an authentic process of participation takes place. This is not an 'ideal' situation to hope for; rather it is a minimum condition to be achieved. Jaimon Varghese in his paper, "Contemporary Models of Gandhian Gramswaraj—The Story of Ralegaon Sidhi and Hiware Bazar, the Ideal Villages in Ahmednagar", has described about two model villages in Ahmednagar district which can provide several lessons, particularly for social workers, and especially the community development professionals to learn from these contemporary models of Gandhian gramswaraj. Sameeksha Sharma in her paper, "Satisfaction Motives of Pilgrim Community", has examined the key conceptualizations and gaps in the scholarship on satisfaction motives of pilgrim community. The paper is based on the review of researches on motives of pilgrim satisfaction. By understanding the trend and changes that have taken place in research work in the subject, it analyses the concepts, theories and paradigms within the ongoing pilgrim motivation and satisfaction issue. Simultaneously, the gaps and issues for the future researches have also been put forth.

Kumar Satyam in his paper, "Mainstreaming Mal Paharia Primitive Tribal Groups of India", has attempted to understand the consequences the tribals have been facing in their different domain of life. Despite making so many measures for fortifying and enriching their social, economic, and political states, the Mal Paharia primitive tribal group still remains underdeveloped and underprivileged in every walk of life. He has forwarded various suggestions for their empowerment. Nagaraju Battu in his article, "Revisiting Women's Participation" has presented the view that women are the backbone of agricultural workforce, and a vital part of Indian economy. The purpose of the study was to evaluate the activities of women and their participation in agricultural production to fulfill the food security of their families, and more specifically, to answer the question: "What is the role of women in agriculture"? In view of the current agrarian crisis facing the country, it is important to recognize women's role in agriculture to ensure agricultural growth so as to (a) eradicate poverty, (b) ensure food security for the majority, and (c) promote the well-being of women themselves. Over the years, there has been a gradual realization of the key role of women in agricultural development and their contribution in the field of agriculture, food security, horticulture, dairy, nutrition, sericulture, fisheries, and other allied sectors. Lastly, Mukul Srivastava in his paper, "An Analysis of Theoretical Context of Implications of Development Discourses", has discussed development theories, comparative development history, and implications of development theories.

We acknowledge the contribution, cooperation and suggestions of the contributors in the preparation of the book. It is hoped that the book will be very useful to the students, researchers and academicians in the field of social work, rural development, sociology, public administration and allied disciplines. It will also be very useful for the development practitioners and policy-makers.

Sanjoy Roy
Bishnu Mohan Dash

Contents

Contributors

Suresh Pathare. Director, CSRD, Ahmednagar, Maharashtra.

Jaimon Varghese. Assistant Professor, CSRD, Maharashtra.

Guljit K. Arora. Principal, Bhim Rao Ambedkar College, University of Delhi, Delhi.

Asok Kumar Sarkar. Professor & Head, Department of Social Work, Visva-Bharati, West Bengal.

G. Ram. Professor, Department of Sociology, Assam University, Silchar, Assam.

Heena K. Bijli. Associate Professor in Home Science, (Community Resource Management & Extension), School of Continuing Education, Indira Gandhi National Open University, Maidan Garhi, New Delhi.

Y.S. Siddegowda. Professor, Department of Social Work, University of Mysore, Mysore.

D.P. Singh. Professor & Head, Department of Social Work, Punjabi University Patiala, Punjab.

Ritu. Senior Secondary Model School, Punjabi University Patiala, Punjab.

Manushi. Research Department, Indian Institute of Mass Communication, New Delhi.

Manju Panwar. Head, Department of Social Work, B.P.S. Mahila Vshwavidhalaya, Sonipat, Haryana.

Rakesh Dwivedi. Assistant Professor, Department of Social Work, University of Lucknow, Uttar Pradesh.

Chitta Ranjan Das Adhikary. Assistant Professor (senior scale), Department of Sociology, Banaras Hindu University, Varanasi, Uttar Pradesh.

Pradipta Dubey. Research Scholar, Rural Development and Management Department, University of Kalyani, West Bengal.

Atonu Chatterjee. is a member of West Bengal Civil Service.

V. Naveen Kumar. Research Scholar, Department of Sociology and Social Work, Acharya Nagarjuna University, Guntur, Andhra Pradesh.

V. Venkateswarlu. Assistant Professor, Department of Sociology and Social Work, Acharya Nagarjuna University, Guntur, Andhra Pradesh.

A.V.V.S. Swamy. Department of Environmental Sciences, Acharya Nagarjuna University, Nagarjunanagar, Guntur, Andhra Pradesh.

V. Subhashini. Department of Environmental Sciences, Acharya Nagarjuna University, Nagarjunanagar, Guntur, Andhra Pradesh.

Ch. Rani. Department of Environmental Sciences, Acharya Nagarjuna University, Nagarjunanagar, Guntur, Andhra Pradesh.

Noorbasha Abdul. Professor & Head, Department of Commerce, Acharya Nagarjuna University, Guntur, Andhra Pradesh.

V. Tulasi Das. Assistant Professor, Department of Commerce, Acharya Nagarjuna University, Guntur, Andhra Pradesh.

Ch. V. Krishna Reddy. Research Scholar, Department of Commerce, Acharya Nagarjuna University, Guntur, Andhra Pradesh.

K. Madhu Babu. Assistant Professor, Dept. of Economics, Acharya Nagarjuna University, Nagarjunanagar, Guntur. Andhra Pradesh.

P. Srinivasulu. Lecturer, V.K.R. College, Buddavaram, Gannavaram, Andhra Pradesh.

Brajesh Kumar. Assistant Professor (senior scale), Department of Commerce, Assam University, Silchar, Assam.

Mintu Gogoi. Research Scholar, Department of Commerce, Assam University, Silchar, Assam.

Manish Dwivedi. Regional Director, Rajashri Tondon Open University, Uttar Pradesh.

Surendra Singh. Ex Vice Chancellor, Mahatma Gandhi Kashi Vidyapeeth, Varanasi, Uttar Pradesh.

Sameeksha Sharma. FPM, Indian Institute of Management, Indore, Madhya Pradesh.

Kumar Satyam. Assistant Professor, Department of Social Work, Bhim Rao Ambedkar College, University of Delhi, Delhi.

Nagaraju Battu. Assistant Professor, Acharya Nagarjuna University, Nagarjunanagar, Guntur, Andhra Pradesh.

Mukul Srivastava. Department of Social Work, Institute of Social Sciences, Agra, Uttar Pradesh.

1

Rural Community Development in India: Emerging Issues, Challenges and Strategies

Suresh Pathare and *Jaimon Varghese*

ABSTRACT

Community development programme was launched by the Government of India in 1952. Rural Community Development has been the chief focus of several Five-Year Plans in India. Governmental and non-governmental agencies have been implementing varied community development programmes since then. It has been commented by scholars that community development and extension works of the government have not yielded the desired results. Lack of people's participation has been cited as the major reason for this failure. Therefore, periodical evaluation, revision and modifications have been made to the policies and rural development programmes over the time. The basic approach has shifted from the domain of centralised planning to people's planning. The strategies and methods of rural development have undergone dramatic changes over the past six decades. SHG strategy has been evolved as a powerful means for rural development. Ecological concern, natural and organic farming, water harvesting, management of non-conventional energy sources, etc. have become essential aspects of rural development. Participation of the corporate enterprises in rural development is also a growing trend. There are a number of innovative model concepts of rural development across the country such as Tilonia, Ralegon Sidhi, Hiware Bazar and many more. New methods and strategies to work with rural communities with innovative participatory approach are emerging such as micro-planning, people planning, etc. Social work profession is finding new roles and responsibilities in the changed rural scenario.

In view of the emerging trends of rural development, are the conventional social work methods relevant to accommodate the modern trends in rural development in the country? Do the social work professionals get adequate training in the participatory approaches that are relevant in professional practice in the rural context? Are the social work professionals able to participate effectively in the national agenda for rural development? Is the profession equipped enough to give the much felt leadership in the field of social development in rural context? Do the social work professionals have enough expertise to handle the emerging trends in rural development such as ecological and energy concerns? These are some of the significant questions to be answered by rural development professionals today. In this paper, a critical review of rural community development programmes in India is undertaken with the objective of deriving certain guidelines for the future interventions in this field of social work.

Rural Community Programmes in India

Being the nodal ministry for most of the development and welfare activities in the rural areas, the Ministry of Rural Development plays a pivotal role in the overall development strategy of the country. The Ministry of Rural Development consists of two departments, viz. (i) Department of Rural Development, (ii) Department of Land Resources. The vision and mission of the Ministry is sustainable and inclusive growth of rural India through a multi-pronged strategy for eradication of poverty by increasing livelihoods opportunities, providing social safety net and developing infrastructure for growth. This is expected to improve quality of life in rural India and to correct the developmental imbalances, aiming in the process, to reach out to most disadvantaged sections of the society. Over the years, the Ministry of Rural Development has been monitoring several schemes and programmes. Table 1 lists out the major schemes of the Ministry of Rural Development in India.

Table 1: Rural Development Programmes in India

S.No.	Programmes	Date	Priorities	Partner Group	Strategy
1.	Land Reforms	Since 1947	Land to the tiller	Landless rural poor	Ceiling, abolition of intermediary
2.	Drought Prone Areas Programme	1972-73	Check draught	Village communities	Watershed development
3.	Rajiv Gandhi National Drinking Water Mission	1972-73	Safe drinking water	Rural Population	Supplement to the state missions
4.	Desert Development Programme	1977-78	Combat desertification	Village communities	Water-shed development
5.	Extension Training Centres (ETCs)	6th Plan	Training	RD functionaries, district level	Training
6.	National Institute of Rural Development	6th Plan	Training, research	RD functionaries	Training
7.	State Institutes of Rural Development (SIRDs)	6th Plan	Training	RD functionaries, state level	Training
8.	Rural Building Centres	1985	Housing technology	States and NGOs	Grant
9.	Indira Awaas Yojana	1985	Housing	SC/ST of BPL	Grant for construction

S.No.	Programmes	Date	Priorities	Partner Group	Strategy
10.	Council for Advancement of People's Action and Rural Technology (CAPART)	1 September 1986	Assistance, coordination	NGOs	Grants
11.	Centrally Sponsored Rural Sanitation Programme	1986	Rural Sanitation	Rural Population	Supplement to the state missions
12.	Integrated Wastelands Development Project (IWDP) Scheme	1989-90	Employment generation, waste land dev.	Village communities	Watershed development
13.	Wastelands Development Task Force (WOTF)	1992	Chambal ravine dev., Empl. for ex-servicemen	Ex-service men	Afforestation, watershed
14.	Investment Promotional Scheme (IPS)	1992-93	Dev. of Non-forest waste land	Farmers	25-50% subsidy on farm dev. projects
15.	Support to NGOs/VAs (Grant-in-Aid) Scheme	8th Plan	Afforestation, awareness	NGOs, SHGs	Grants for waste land development
16.	Technology Development Extension and Training Scheme	8th Plan	Technology for reclamation of waste land, Sust. Dev.	Gos/NGOs	Research, demonstration
17.	Employment Assurance Scheme	2 October 1993	Employment, asset building	Unemployed from backward blocks	Manual work

S.No.	Programmes	Date	Priorities	Partner Group	Strategy
18.	National Family Benefit Scheme (NFBS)	15 August 1995	Family benefit	Families BPL	Lumpsum grant (₹ 10000)
19.	National Maternity Benefit Scheme (NFBS)	15 August 1995	Maternity	Families BPL	Lumpsum grant (₹ 500)
20.	National Old Age Pension Scheme (NOAPS)	15 August 1995	Old age pension	Citizens above 65	Monthly pension
21.	Credit-cum-Subsidy Scheme for Rural Housing	1 April 1999	Housing	Rural Poor	Subsidy and Loan
22.	Innovative Stream for Rural Housing and Habitat Development	1 April 1999	Housing technology	States and NGOs	Grant
23.	Jawahar Gram Samridhi Yojana	1 April 1999	Durable rural assets, employment	Unemployed poor	Manual work
24.	Swarnjayanti Gram Swarozgar Yojana	1 April 1999	Poverty alleviation	BPL families	Self Help Groups
25.	Samagra Awaas Yojana	1 April 2002	Housing	Rural Poor	Convergence of schemes
26.	National Rural Employment Guarantee Act	5 September 2005	Employment	Rural Poor	100 days' job or allowance
27.	Aajeevika-National Rural Livelihoods Mission (NRLM)	3 June 2011	Rural Livelihood	Rural Poor	Livelihoods Options, building skills; nurturing self-employed entrepreneurs

Performance Highlights of Rural Community Programmes in India

Annual report of the Ministry of Rural Development (2012-13) has given the performance highlights of various rural community development programmes in India (*www.rdmin.nic.in*). The major programmes and their achievements of the Ministry of Rural Development are given below.

Mahatma Gandhi NREGA: In 2012-13, 4.16 crore households were provided employment and 141 crore person days of employment were generated. Self-targeting in nature, the programme had high work participation from marginalized groups like SC/ST (38%), women (53%). In 2012-13, 70 lakh works were undertaken, of which 60 per cent for water conservation, 12 per cent for the provision of irrigation facility on land owned by SC/ST/BPL and IAY beneficiaries, 17 per cent for rural connectivity and 8 per cent for land development. With a view to universalise the system of wage payments through institutional accounts, it has been recommended to all states to disburse wages through Post Offices and Bank Accounts. Around 8.54 crore Mahatma Gandhi NREGA bank and post office accounts have been opened to disburse wages. An Electronic Fund Monitoring System (eFMS) has been set up to speed up payment of wages to workers employed on schemes under the Mahatma Gandhi National Rural Employment Guarantee Act. Electronic Muster Measurement System (eMMS) has been introduced using NREGA-soft and mobile based software wherein every day the attendance is taken in the mobiles and put in the public domain. "Aadhar enabled" direct electronics crediting of accounts payments for workers in MGNREGA is being implemented in 51 districts, in its pilot phase. Aadhar has the potential to be superior to other biometric solutions for various reasons (*Annual Report 2012-13: www.rdmin.nic.in*).

SGSY: Since the inception of the programme, 43.96 lakh SHGs have been formed. During 2011-12, a total of 16.77 lakh Swarojgaris were assisted out of which 11.03 lakh (68.63%) were women Swarojgaris. In 2012-13, till December, 4.38 lakh Swarojgaris have been assisted out of which 3.49 lakh (79.68%) are women (*Annual Report 2012-13: www.rdmin.nic.in*).

IAY: Since inception of the scheme, about 300.83 lakh houses have been constructed with an expenditure of ₹ 94086.61 crore (upto December 2012). For the financial year of 2012-13, ₹ 11075 crore has been provided for Rural Housing. Out of this ₹ 10513.20 crore has been allocated under IAY for release to the various districts of various states for construction of 30.10 lakh houses. Besides this, ₹ 500 crore has been kept for homestead scheme. Under Bharat Nirman Programme Phase-I, 60 lakh houses were envisaged, 71.76 lakh houses were constructed with an expenditure of ₹ 21720.39 crore. The target for the Bharat Nirman Phase-II for five years period starting from the year 2009-10 approximately 85.72 lakh houses have been constructed (*Annual Report 2012-13: www.rdmin.nic.in*).

PMGSY: Up to December 2012, a total of 87382 habitations have been connected out of 164849 habitations to be connected and works for 126179 habitations sanctioned. In 2012-13, a target of 4000 habitation is set to be covered and 30,000 kms of road length is to be constructed. Till December 2012, a total of 4968 habitations have been covered and 1628712 kms of road has been constructed (*Annual Report 2012-13: www.rdmin.nic.in*).

IWMP: Since launching of IWMP (i.e. 2009-10), 5830 projects covering an area of 27.815 m ha have been sanctioned (as on 31-12-2012). Central funds to the tune of ₹ 6092.27 crore have been released upto 31.12.2012 (*Annual Report 2012-13: www.rdmin.nic.in*).

Rural Development in India: Issues and Challenges

The first issue concerning rural development is about the concept of development itself. There are varied ideas concerning development especially the rural development. The best accepted aspect of development is that it should be sustainable. Development refers to positive changes in the society. Unless there is a harmony in the qualitative and quantitative changes, the development would not be sustainable. Therefore, sustainable development is related with the value system of the people. "Development is a process of change involves various economic, cultural, social, political and physical dimensions of the society. The harmony between the qualitative and quantitative achievements of such development in a given context determines its sustainability. Lack of such harmony in the dynamics of developmental efforts is largely due to improper understanding of peoples need and value system, based on economic and socio-cultural properties of the communities" (Dash, 2000: 9).

The concept of development has to consider the most important stakeholder of development—the human persons. Human beings are better defined as collective entities. Individual persons hardly ever exist in this world in isolation. Livelihood is the prime concern of human beings. In the words of Katar Singh, "Human beings are both the cause and consequence of development: it is the human factor that is the pivot of the process of development. Though the study of a human being is basic to the study of development, it cannot be of a human being in isolation, but rather of human beings in relation to their fellows or of humans in society and in their environment. It is the creation of conditions, both material and spiritual, which enable the human being as an individual, and the human being as a species, to be at her/his best. Those who control a human being's livelihood, control a human being. A person's freedom is illusory when he/she depends upon others for the right to work and the right to eat. Equally, a nation is not independent if its economic resources are controlled by another nation" (Singh, 1999: 25). It can be concluded that the concept of development is closely associated with social justice especially with freedom and equality.

Concept of rural development is a sub-domain of the concept of development. Development is often considered be an urban phenomenon. Therefore, urbanisation is sometimes considered as synonymous to development especially economic development. However, we need to state that there are significant differences between urban and rural living. Hence, rural development cannot be measured as per the urban parameters. Rural development cannot underestimate the rural characteristics. According to Samantary, "Rural development is economic development under rural setting. It is an area concept. The term rural essentially means an area, characterised by non-urban style of life. Occupational structure, social organisation and settlement pattern or it is essentially agricultural, homestead settlements, independent social life and slow moving rhythm of life built around nature" (Samantary, 2000: 106).

Rural development is essentially concerned with development of the rural infrastructure and implementation of poverty reduction measures to pull out the families from below poverty line to above poverty line. In that process, additional employment opportunities shall be created in the rural sector, the quality of rural living might improve. "In nutshell, the objectives of rural development are as under: (i) providing certain social goods and services in terms of social and economic infrastructure, (ii) increasing the income of every rural family and to see that those who are below the poverty line are enabled to come above that line in coming years, (iii) improving the quality of the rural poor, and (iv) creation of additional employment opportunities in rural areas" (*ibid.*). Employment and livelihood are key components of rural development.

Rural development is essentially the capacity building of rural communities. Urban-based planning cannot satisfy the rural development needs. This is another issue worth mentioning. There is a need to sit with the rural folk and decide the area and scope of the type of development people want in their village. "Rural development as a strategy to enable the rural people for gain of more economic values, improvement of production system and social justice aims at planning with the people for their development" (Dash, 2000: 10). The recent government strategies put emphasis on people's level planning for rural development.

As mentioned in the previous section, there are a number of rural development programmes launched by the Ministry of Rural Development. Another set of programmes are in the pipeline. There are both area focused and people-oriented programmes. They are not exclusive categories, rather mutually inclusive and complementary. "Rural development programmes are often classified into two categories—area development-oriented programme and beneficiary-oriented programmes. Despite their complementary nature, the distinction is made on the basis of the target of the programme. Land reforms belong to the second category and give more direct benefits to individuals and to the household economy" (Beera, 2000: 81). Livelihood mission is a people-oriented programme. Recent trend is investing more on people than the area. The empowered community finds its own ways and means for area development.

One of the key issues of rural development is inadequacy of basic infrastructure in the rural sector. Without adequate and proper infrastructure, no development can take place. In fact, development in terms of modernisation begins with infrastructural development. Poor infrastructure affects the production, distribution and trade (domestic as well as international). "Adequate quantity, quality and reliability of infrastructure are important pre-conditions to determine a country's success or failure in diversifying production, expanding trade, coping with population growth and reducing poverty" (Bishoyi and Sahu, 2006: 103-04). "Unsatisfactory basic rural infrastructure in India in terms of its roads, irrigation, education and health services, telecommunications, electricity supply, sanitation, etc. has become a serious menace for sustainable growth of the village-based economy. Realising the significance of rural infrastructure as the driver of the nation's future prosperity, the government has recently initiated a number of policy measures to balance the growth process and bridge divides between Bharat and India by strengthening rural infrastructure services which are now way behind the urban services" (Prasad, 2008: 267). Bharat Nirman is the Central Government-sponsored strategy for infrastructural development. Government has also been trying public-private partnership with regard to the improvement of infrastructure.

After infrastructure, availability of adequate credit is another key issue concerned with rural development. The rural communities of our country are characterised by constraints of occupational and skill specialisation, underemployment and lack of capital resources. There is readiness on the part of the rural households, for initiating different productive enterprises, but find themselves helpless for want of rural credit. "A large segment of rural population who are socio-economically backward are unable to raise adequate funds from their own resources to replace the traditional farming practices with scientific and modern practices which is reflected by the use of high yielding variety seeds, chemical fertilisers, pesticides, irrigation, machinery and equipment, etc. Similarly, the rural households who are engaged in different non-farm productive activities like small business, retail shops, transport operations, etc. are also economically backward and their limited resources is quite insufficient to put their productive activities on sound footing" (Patra, 2000: 90). In this context, micro-finance enterprises have been a path-breaking step forward.

Self-help groups (SHG) are the micro-finance models in India. Self-help group campaigns or SHG movements are often sponsored by the formal banking system that has a vast branch network in rural areas. SHGs have already proved to be informal means to improve the access of rural poor to the existing banking network. The provision of financial services through self-help groups has further encouraged the growth of grassroots level institutions in the rural development sector for socio-economic development of the poor. "Drawing lessons from experiments carried out in various parts of the world, particularly by the well-known Grameen Bank of Bangladesh, an attempt was made to build financial relationship between informal groups of people and formal agencies like banks for catering to the financial service requirements of the poor, especially belonging to the marginal downtrodden category and women. Over the years, this linkage model has emerged in India as a core strategy for the banking system to extend their outreach to the poorest among the poor" (Swain, 2008: 144). The future strategy for poverty alleviation has been envisaged in the SHG model of community organisation.

There is yet another issue in rural development which is the consideration for locally viable technology for community development. There are experiments and exploration for discovering locally relevant, reliable and viable measures of resource management. Sudhakara Reddy's investigation reveals that "the natural resource management by the rural people provides considerable inputs for policy and planning. The evidence that emerged from the eight case studies suggests that sustainable tree plantation programmes on a cooperative basis are financially viable, if opportunity cost of land and wages low and do not rise in future in real terms above the general interest rate" (Reddy, 2008: 128). There is a growing need to identify more and more rural as well as tribal development models to substitute the so-called globalisation model of rural development.

Globalisation, the Major Challenge to Rural Development

Globalisation started in the year 1991 in India has posed several challenges in the rural development sector. There are mixed responses among the scholars regarding the impacts of globalisation upon community development in India. There are views that support globalisation as a key strategy for overall development of the nation. "Reform measures initiated by the government in 1991, have varieties of steps ranging from fiscal, monetary, price reform, opening of economy for foreign investors, liberalisation of trade, de-licensing, privatisation to agriculture policy. Impact of these reform measures on most of the macro variables is satisfactory. From nearly stagnant economy during 1991-92, Indian economy has moved to a growth path comparable to the East Asian miracles. Indian achievements can be attributed as one of the swiftest recovery during the reform process" (Kumar and Sharma, 2005: 2). Globalisation has certainly given visibility of Indian economy in the world scenario. It has brought some positive changes to the Indian economy. "From economic point of view the reforms and globalisation have brought in lot of dynamism in Indian economy and the growth rates are very high. While it is a welcoming feature for economic stability which is being experienced in India, vast majority of the population are not able to get benefits out of the promising economic development" (Rao, 2008: 6). This is only one of many views on globalisation in India.

Majority of the scholars have shown their interest to highlight the drawbacks of globalisation. Globalisation is said to lead our economy into confusion and instability. "As an impact of globalisation, there is less capital investment in rural development sector. Globalisation is considered as an economic reformation in India. Indian Government introduced many reform measures in the form of globalisation, liberalisation and privatisation in July 1991. As a result of these measures, subsidies to agriculture were reduced, fiscal deficit was controlled, economy was opened up to the global market, restrictions and controls were reduced, private sector had to grow and public sector had to shrink. In the wake of reform measures, rural sector of our country has faced uncertain future" (Subramanian, 2000: 1).

Globalisation is often alleged that the poor segments of the population have systematically been bypassed from every reform strategies. Scholars have supported their view quoting productivity statistics of the country. "A critical analysis of development scenario over the past two decades has posed a serious concern that whether the reform-led growth has bypassed the rural sector, especially the rural poor. In India, agriculture growth was about 3.2 per cent per annum during 1981-95, which dropped to 1.5 per cent during 1996-2003. The deceleration in agriculture growth during the post-reform period could be primarily attributed to cumulative effect of the sharp decline in public investment in agriculture sector over the past two decades" (Janaiah, 2008: 67). Agricultural productivity has been adversely affected by globalisation.

Globalisation has also posed another serious challenge in the social security sector of rural development. Social security concerns are more crucial in the lives of rural poor than their urban counterpart. Globalisation has set such competitive fields in the world of work, that the unskilled and illiterate workforce is more exposed to occupational hazards. The poor unskilled workforce is exposed to greater risks in terms of dangerous working conditions, lack of preventive healthcare and exposure to environmental contaminants. "What is more, the poor are less able to manage shocks successfully, e.g. they possess fewer cushions in the form of savings and insurance. When a shock occurs, poor households may be pushed deeper into poverty and ultimately become destitute. Once destitute, it is difficult if not impossible for the afflicted household to recover or regain basic economic security" (Shyam Sunder, 2008: 73). Once lost the economic control, the poor households seldom find ways and means to recover from the shock.

Globalisation has set another challenge to the rural development sector. It has exposed rural non-farm enterprises to the impact of liberalisation placing stress on equipping the working poor and micro-enterprises with skills, knowledge, access to credit and technology to enable them to operate, compete and survive in the competition against the large multinational and international players. Development support for rural non-farm sector enterprises need to be redesigned in this emerging scenario. "This also requires large scale state investment for modernisation and expansion of infrastructure in terms of power, transport, communications, and cold storage facilities. This is necessary to equip these industries with the requisite capability to face international competition" (Nagayya, 2005: 76-77). This further re-emphasises the need for improvement in the rural infrastructure.

Globalisation is considered to be a dangerous economic system as far as the poor sections of the country are concerned. Globalisation is reckoned as a successor in the lineage of feudalism, imperialism, colonialism and capitalism. It is a system for formalised exploitation of the indigenous and the marginalised sections of the community—economically, socially, culturally, politically and militarily. The rich and the elite have always been the beneficiary of all the systems preceding globalisation, viz. capitalism, colonialism and imperialism. Today's world is in the grip of the so-called imperialist globalisation. In the words of Ramanjaneyulu, "the imperialist globalisation has been attacking the people of poor countries economically, socially, culturally, politically and militarily. It has affected negatively all the sections of economy including agriculture, industry, infrastructure, service, etc. and all the sections of population, particularly peasants, agricultural labour, artisans, dalits, tribals, women, etc. in the rural areas and also poor and middle class population and workers in the towns and cities. The comprador rich classes of population are the beneficiaries of globalisation. It is necessary to chalk out an action programme against imperialist gloabalisation" (Ramanjaneyulu, 2005: 338). This is going to be a challenge before the government machinery in India as well as other developing and underdeveloped countries.

The criticism against globalisation is so severe that it is just equated with capitalism. "To conclude, historically speaking, globalisation is the product of the development of capitalism; therefore, as long as capitalism reigns supreme in the world, globalisation runs like a juggernaut to widen the scope of capitalist exploitation is space and time. And the only solution to the present globalisation is to end capitalism itself and replace it by another system, free of exploitation, economic and social disparities and a system that recognises human beings as human beings" (Reddy, 2005: 350). Will the government succeed in finding a substitute for globalisation or are there any ways and means to modify globalisation so that the challenges posed by globalisation in the field of rural development may be overcome? What would be the role of rural development professionals in the changed rural development scenario?

Rural Development Strategies for the Future

In the recent past, certain policies and programme initiatives have been implemented by the Government of India that highlight the role of rural development professionals. Prime Minister's Rural Development (PMRD) fellows are the young development professionals who carry the development message directly from the district headquarters to the remote villages. This fellowship scheme has the scope to harness the young and creative youth power for the cause of rural community development. Certain government schemes and legislations like National Rural Livelihood Mission, Food Security Act, Right to Information Act and Adarsh Gram Yojana are other prospective provisions having scope for effective rural development interventions. "Studies across rural India aptly reveal the fact that in spite of initiating a large number of legislations aimed at securing legally guaranteed rights to rural population through the Right to Information Act, the Forest Rights Act, the Right to Education Act, the Mahatma Gandhi National Rural Employment Guarantee Act and the National Food Security

Act—the weaker sections of the rural society, for whom different rural development schemes are primarily designed and intended, are still not aware or empowered enough to access the benefits out of these developmental policies" (Hazra, 2012: 6). In this context, PMRD fellows have a significant role to play.

In the recent past, Mahatma Gandhi National Rural Employment Guarantee Scheme (MGNREGS) has emerged as the most successful strategy as far as rural employment in the unorganised sector is concerned. However, studies conducted by Tata Institute of Social Sciences, Mumbai have revealed certain flaws in its implementation. "MGNREGS is powerful because it gives the right to work that is demand driven and has an inbuilt targeting mechanism. To ensure that the benefits of MGNREGS reach the poor, checks and balances are introduced in the design of the scheme. Available literature shows that despite checks and balances in the issue of job cards, payment of wages, implementation of work, MGNREGS funds have been embezzled because of the capture of the programme by the rural elite with political backing and official support, lack of voices from below, and the absence of civil society agencies backing the rural poor" (Rajasekhar, Devendra Babu and Manjula, 2012: 574). Once these shortcomings are rectified, MGNREGS could be an effective strategy for delivering employment services to the unskilled and illiterate rural masses of the country.

Indian history has witnessed the women empowerment campaign in the form of Self-help Group (SHG) movement during past two decades. "As per the recent microfinance report released by NABARD as in March 2012, a total number of 79.6 lakh SHGs with active bank-linkages are operating in India which have been able to ensure involvement of around 9.7 crore people of this nation, with an aggregate bank balance of ₹ 6,551 crores; simultaneously latest statistics also indicate that over 90 per cent of SHGs in India consist exclusively of women. So it seems that in recent years, SHG approach has emerged to be one of the most aggressive strategies for empowering rural women and alleviating rural poverty" (Hazra, 2013: 4). Taking lessons from SHG strategy of Swarna Jayanti Gram Swarozgar Yojana, the rural livelihood mission has been launched and this movement has a long way to go in the holistic aspect of rural development. This is indeed the effective rural development strategy for the future.

Rural infrastructure has undoubtedly an irreplaceable role in rural development sector. "Infrastructure is the biggest issue for India's future growth. Population growth and worse infrastructure are challenges for India" (Mahore, 2008: 218). Prime Minister's Gram Sadak Yojana has made an impact in the creation of rural infrastructure. However, the present status of infrastructure is far from the ever-growing demand and requirement. Investment in infrastructure is essential for growth and development of the every sector.

There is an often unnoticed section of the rural population that is neglected from the mainstream development process. It is the elderly section of the society. While the women's empowerment as well as the Scheduled castes and Scheduled tribes' empowerment issues are addressed in several government schemes, the empowerment of elderly is seldom addressed. Recently, Senior Citizens Act (2007) was passed to protect the rights of the elderly. However, the real problems of the elderly are not sufficiently addressed. According to Lekshmi Nair, "Social engagement fulfils the mind and body of the aged and thus we could bring an improvement in the life of the elderly of today and tomorrow" (Nair, 2012: 21). There is a need to engage the elderly in social and cultural life of the community. Suitable measures need to be formulated.

Conclusion

The discussions hitherto bring light in the role of professional social workers in the field of rural development. While the government, corporate and non-government agencies increase their outlay in the development sector, there emerges the need for development professionals to efficiently manage the proper utilisation of the same. When the corporate social responsibility (CSR) sector is increasingly investing in the rural development fields, the role of professionals becomes highly significant. The core competencies required for rural development professionals are varied and specific. Professional social workers need to develop such type of skills that make them effective in working with every section of the communities such as self-help groups of women, elderly, the youth and the farmers. Rural development professionals need to develop the skills of micro-planning and social auditing while working with local bodies. They need to improve their research skills while critically evaluating the effectiveness of the implementation strategies of the various government-sponsored schemes and programmes, so that they might suggest timely improvement for the future. Participatory monitoring skills are another set of competencies required for rural development professionals.

REFERENCES

B. Sudhakara Reddy (2008). Natural Resource Management through Rural Cooperatives in Vinayak Reddy A. and Yadagira Charyulu M. (Eds.), *Rural Development in India—Policies and Initiatives,* New Delhi: New Century Publications.

Beera, Surendra Nath (2000). Land Reforms: A Key to Rural Uplift—Need and Reorientation of Policies in Tripathy S.N. (Ed.), *Rural Development,* New Delhi: Discovery Publishing House.

Bishoyi, Deepak and Ananta Bashudev Sahu (2006). Role of Infrastructure in Rural Development in Tripathy S.N. (Ed.) (2006), *Rural Development for Social Change,* New Delhi: Sonali Publications.

Dash, Chita Ranjan (2000). Rural Development and Dairying in Orissa in Tripathy S.N. (Ed.) (2000), *Rural Development,* New Delhi: Discovery Publishing House.

Gopala Rao, T. (2008). Dimensions of Economic Reforms in India in Vinayak Reddy A. and Yadagira Charyulu M. (Eds.) (2008). *Rural Development in India—Policies and Initiatives,* New Delhi: New Century Publications.

Hazra, Anupam (2012). Development—Demography of Rural India in *Kurukshetra—A Journal on Rural Development,* 60(9) July, New Delhi: Publication Division, Ministry of I&B, Govt. of India.

Hazra, Anupam (2013). Adding New Dimensions to Sustainable Rural Growth in *Kurukshetra—A Journal on Rural Development,*

61(9) July, New Delhi: Publication Division, Ministry of I&B, Govt. of India.

Janaiah, Aldas (2008). Have the Economic Reforms Bypassed the Rural Poor? in Vinayak Reddy A. and Yadagira Charyulu M. (Eds.) (2008). *Rural Development in India—Policies and Initiatives,* New Delhi: New Century Publications.

Kumar, Vijaya T. and Sharma, S.S.P. (2005). Economic Reforms and Rural Poverty in India: Some Emerging Issues in Narasimha Rao C. (Ed.), *Rural Development in India—A Multi-Disciplinary Analysis,* New Delhi: Serials Publications.

Mahore, R.Y. (2008). Infrastructure and Rural Development in Vinayak Reddy A. and Yadagira Charyulu M. (Eds.), *Rural Development in India—Policies and Initiatives,* New Delhi: New Century Publications.

Nagayya, D. (2005). Enhancing Competitiveness Among Rural Non-Farm Small Enterprises in Narasimha Rao C. (Ed.), *Rural Development in India—A Multi-Disciplinary Analysis,* New Delhi: Serials Publications.

Nair, Lekshmi V. (2012). Elderly in Rural India: A Sociological Analysis in *Rajagiri Journal of Social Development,* 4(2) December, Kochi: Rajagiri College of Social Sciences.

Patra, Sudhakar (2000). Demand-Supply Mismatch of Credit and Role of Cooperative Bank in the Rural Development in Tripathy S.N. (Ed.) (2000). *Rural Development,* New Delhi: Discovery Publishing House.

Pothal, Siba Prasad (2008). Reinforcing Rural Infrastructure in India in Vinayak Reddy A. and Yadagira Charyulu M. (Eds.), *Rural Development in India—Policies and Initiatives,* New Delhi: New Century Publications.

Rajasekhar, D., Devendra Babu, M. and Manjula, R. (2012). Are Checks and Balances in MGNREGS Effective? in *The Indian Journal of Social Work,* 73(4) October, Mumbai: Tata Institute of Social Sciences.

Ramanjaneyulu, M. (2005). Impact of Globalisation on Rural Development in India in Narasimha Rao, C. (Ed.), *Rural*

Development in India—A Multi-Disciplinary Analysis, New Delhi: Serials Publications.

Reddy, V.V. (2005). Globalisation and Rural Development in Narasimha Rao C. (Ed.), *Rural Development in India—A Multi-Disciplinary Analysis,* New Delhi: Serials Publications.

Samantary, P.C. (2000). The Role of Cooperative for Rural Development in Tripathy S.N. (Ed.) (2000), *Rural Development,* New Delhi: Discovery Publishing House.

Sharma, Shyam Sunder Pd. (2008). Poverty, Environment and Sustainable Freedom: Evidence from Villages in Vinayak Reddy A. and Yadagira Charyulu M. (Eds.), *Rural Development in India—Policies and Initiatives,* New Delhi: New Century Publications.

Singh, Katar (1999). *Rural Development—Principles, Policies and Management* (second edition), New Delhi: Sage Publications.

Subramanian, M.S. (2000). Economic Reforms and Rural Development in Tripathy S.N. (Ed.), *Rural Development,* New Delhi: Discovery Publishing House.

Swain, B.K. (2008). Micro Finance and Emerging Trends in Rural Economy in Vinayak Reddy A. and Yadagira Charyulu M. (Eds.), *Rural Development in India—Policies and Initiatives,* New Delhi: New Century Publications.

www.rdmin.nic.in

2

Women Empowerment, Globalization and Cooperatives: Role of Women Fisheries Cooperatives in Sri Lanka*

Guljit K. Arora

ABSTRACT

It is generally said that men dominate in all spheres of life, though women are equally important and have a far more responsible role to play particularly at the grassroot and household levels. The research studies have further shown that countries which have (i) performed well towards achieving gender equity have also done better in economic growth and social well-being;[1] (ii) invested in reducing gender inequality in literacy, education, health and survival have effectively reduced hunger.[2] Thus, the question of women empowerment and its further enhancement assumes a crucial importance before the country. An attempt is made here to explore how the cooperative model of development can empower and enable powerless women to compete the world, and make the sustainable human development possible.

The entire discussion is divided into seven sections. Section I gives a brief background of Sri Lanka as placed

---

* This is the revised version of the paper presented at Symposium on Community Empowerment through Social Enterprise Development in Fishing and Farming Communities in Sri Lanka, during 21-25 December, organized by Small Fishers Federation of Lanka.

in the context of world development. Section II highlights the cooperative model of development and its features as a social development enterprise. Section III deals with the role of cooperatives in the international perspective, and the role of cooperatives in developed countries is discussed in Section IV. Section V briefly reviews the Indian cooperative sector along with some lessons to be drawn out that experience. The role of women fisheries cooperatives in women empowerment in view of sustainable human development in Sri Lanka is brought out in Section VI. Section VII draws broad conclusions, challenges and outlook for women fisheries cooperatives.

I. Sri Lanka: "The Pearl of Indian Ocean"

The Democratic Socialist Republic of Sri Lanka is a beautiful country, laden with lush tropical forests, white beaches and diverse landscapes. The natural beauty has earned the country the title of, "the pearl of the Indian ocean". It has got one of the longest documented histories in the world. Its reference is found in the Indian epic *Ramayana*. Sri Lanka shows a continuous history of Buddhism, and also a land of the historical "Bodhi tree"—considered to be oldest tree in the world, under which the great Gautama Buddha became enlightened. Let us also recall that Sri Lanka was the first Asian country to have a female ruler, Queen Anula from 47-42 BC. UNESCO also found the 8th wonder of the world, i.e. Sigiviya, the so-called "Fortress in the Sky" in Sri Lanka. Sri Lanka was the first country in the world to have established a dedicated hospital in the 4th century. It is also the oldest democracy in South Asia.

After achieving independence on 4 February 1948, Sri Lanka passed through different phases of socio-economic and political developments. Besides, it witnessed devastating 2004 Asian tsunami and ethnic tensions. Today, Sri Lanka with 9 provinces and 25 districts has come a long way. Thanks to the market economy measures introduced way back in 1977 and the forward looking moves of the people of Sri Lanka, the country is one of the fast growing economics of the world.

As per the Global Competitiveness Report,[3] Sri Lanka is ranked 52nd in global competitiveness, 45th in health and primary education, 32nd in business sophistication, 42nd in innovation and 41st in goods market efficiency out of 142 countries. The country ranks far above as compared to other developing and SAARC countries in HDI with 0.691 points in 2011. Placed at number 1 position in 31 places to visit in 2010 by the *New York Times*, Sri Lanka is also ranked 8th in the World Giving Index. This implies the Sri Lankan society has got a high level of contentment and charitable behaviour, and the people of Sri Lanka must feel proud of this.

But this should not make the countrymen lazy and complacent for further growth and development. Sri Lanka faces serious problems related to malnutrition, underweight and anemia among children; infectious and non-communicable diseases; poverty and underdevelopment in the rural areas; and macroeconomic imbalances in internal and external accounts and so on. The country is vulnerable to natural disasters and climate change. It has to make constant efforts for achieving an enduring peace. Sri Lanka, thus, has got a long way to go to achieve inclusive development and economic transformation comparable to the developed countries.

It is, in this context, the women empowerment through cooperatives in the fishery sector is conceived. How cooperatives can do that is discussed in the next section.

II. Cooperative Model: People-Centred Social Development Enterprise

A cooperative is defined as an "...autonomous association of persons united voluntarily to meet their common economic, social and cultural needs and aspirations through a jointly owned and democratically controlled enterprise".[4] It is based on values such as self-help, honesty, self-responsibility, care and cooperation, democracy, equality and solidarity. Given these values, a cooperative as an enterprise or organization endeavours to empower the weak and isolated individuals to come together to achieve the desired common economic interests, which may not have been possible otherwise.

In general, all the cooperative societies with marginal variations supposedly adhere to some principles. They are open, democratic, independent and voluntary organizations, wherein all persons willingly accept responsibilities and remain accountable, have voting rights and participate in decision-making. They democratically control the cooperatives, maintain the cooperative autonomy, and allocate surpluses. Cooperatives serve their members by providing education and training and ensuring sustainable development of their communities. People being at the centre as the owners, controllers, and beneficiaries, cooperatives are benefit-driven rather than profit-driven.

Given these principles and practices, cooperatives have a great potential and thrived in many parts of the world despite the combined effects of the food and financial crises. They can be used as social development enterprise for community empowerment, promote economic development, political democracy and social responsibility.[5] They can venture into any business ranging from consumer to producer cooperative to worker or employee-owned cooperatives. They encourage people and not the capital, and further build communal harmony, and promote tolerance and solidarity. Their shareholders are guided by satisfaction not by remuneration. They are dependent on their capital base and its accumulation rather on financial markets. They are governed by a long-term strategy and horizontal democratic control rather than short-term strategy and vertical control. As 'schools of democracy', they promote the rights of each individual and respond to the social needs of their members, whether it is to provide literacy or technical training, or to take action against the HIV/AIDS pandemic. Since members expect a fair play and quick economic returns, honesty, transparency and respect for others become the hallmarks of cooperatives. Giving its members a feeling of rightful owners, cooperatives can go a long way in building goodwill and harmony among the community members of various factions. This ultimately leads to national development and promotes social integration. Open, honest and regular dialogues between the leaders, managers and members can enlighten members, community and ultimately the nation.

Cooperatives can be the strong alternative models of business and institutional diversity, and a potent institution for inclusive growth by involving millions of people in economic activities who fall outside the purview of the formal economy. They undoubtedly are the most legitimate socially responsible institutions imbibing values of good and effective corporate governance in multiple spheres of economy.[6] With clearly defined objectives and a set of values, and given the professionally trained and sensitive management and operational policies framed in the competitive perspective, cooperatives can enhance significantly the social cohesion. The ignorance, misinformation, indifference, and corruption in management ultimately spell the doom of a well-intentioned cooperative often leading to social conflicts. Therefore, a cooperative once formed should not subordinate its members.

Cooperatives, thus, can prove to be "the preferred form of organization and perhaps the only organization with which rural people are familiar with". The United Nations has already recognized that the cooperative movement being people-controlled is an important partner in the implementation of the development agenda. It limits the role of governments to create an enabling environment and level playing field so that cooperatives grow in a sustainable manner. The ILO underscores the need to raise the business potential of cooperatives so as to create employment opportunities and contribute to sustainable development.

Many have raised serious doubts over the functioning of the cooperatives as an institution and enterprise. They have viewed cooperatives as state instruments; and less concerned about the genuine needs of their members. Their ability to quickly respond to market changes and raise capital is found limited. Many vested interests emerge in the process when members make deals during procuring supplies, marketing, and obtaining credit and advice from the government. Social welfare is questioned when such management opportunism creeps in and large producer cooperatives behave as monopolies in the market place. Examples in this regard include cases where members elected into official positions grant large loans for themselves in violation of the rules or take arbitrary decisions in hiring and firing of staff or take strategic decisions with private interest in mind.

To allay those fears, cooperatives have to constantly work and innovate to ensure universal acceptability, least dependence, self-regulation and their due enforcement by best standards of internal management, compliance to better values, principles and guidelines through effective supervision, education, training and capacity building, strategies for awareness campaigns for the community so as to give informed choices to the non-members. The favourable legal frameworks and least regulated like private entities adhering to the broad government regulatory frameworks can play an important role. Cooperatives can be better harnessed in the pursuit of socio-economic development, if the youth and women are actively involved as partners of development. Lessons should also be drawn from a number of shining stars of the cooperatives from all over the world including the Indian examples such as IFFCO; AMUL; Warna Coop Sugar factory and so on. Cooperatives have further to ensure a capable management, governance, the ability to innovate and adapt to prevailing business conditions and the vision of the government.

III. After Effects of Globalization: Cooperatives Offer a Solution

Globalization further facilitated by information and communication technologies (ICT) has led to an obsessive love for market values through creating global mindset while subordinating the interests of common people, the dignity of work and the social considerations. The full impact of the on-going process of liberalization, privatization and globalization (LPG) though not yet very clear particularly in developing countries, yet the broad message in the context of the developing countries is loud and clear as under:

(i) LPG has come to be accepted as more or less the *necessary foundation* for productivity, growth and development. (ii) The business environment has to be changed by making conscious efforts towards market orientation at all levels. (iii) The business environment has made the *comparative advantage* in the world of work as the condition of business sustenance. (iv) The pattern of competitiveness has undergone a sea-change with *non-price factors* like product quality, brand name, packaging, delivery, after-sale services, etc. assuming equally important consideration like that of price. (v) Business is constantly under *strong pressures*—to acquire competitive capabilities, cut down costs, achieve price competitiveness, improve quality, efficiency, productivity and services—all to be accounted simultaneously in an interconnected manner. (vi) The change in business environment has brought transformation in the 'world of work': (a) competition has become intense; (b) "time-to-market" has become the most important "competitive asset"; (c) reliance on worker has increased for his creativity, knowledge and ability to acquire new knowledge; and (d) pressure to rely on the external labour markets for inputs of temporary duration requiring highly sophisticated skills has increased. This is clear from the increased number of call centers, data conversions, medical transcription, back office operations, content-development, insurance claims processing, etc. Thus, there would be a change in the structure of labour sector. (vii) It is likely to penetrate deep into all the socio-economic political structures of the country by forcing a change in the mindset of all the decision-makers. It is because globalisation induced economic pressures do not work in vacuum and go hand in hand with administrative decentralization, federal restructuring, and fiscal devolution, while influencing the ways in which the different levels of government conduct their business and interact with the private sector, and also the civil society.

Globalization and global governance characterized by unfair agenda, non-transparent negotiations and unfair compliance have led to a number of social and economic ills the world over. The fundamental problems of poverty, unemployment, exclusion, inequality and corruption are serious. Environmental degradation is widespread. The socio-economic inequalities between the rich and poor countries, and also between the urban and rural areas within countries have deepened. The most recent economic and financial crisis (2007-08) has not only destabilized the world, but has also produced a crisis of social values marked by uncertainty and a loss of confidence in the future.

Micro and small and medium enterprises (MSMEs) are going to face much tougher challenges in the future with consumers becoming more demanding; competition getting more intensified; compliance to non-trade measures relating to TRIMs, TRIPs, and standards with respect to sanitary, phyto-sanitary, environment and labour is enforced; and trade through illegal channels unchecked. The labour sector has started feeling its pinch with respect to creation and loss of jobs, the nature of employment and the skills required the worker-employers relations, etc. The job market would become tough with the declining job-creating capacity of growth and agriculture failing to absorb any more labour.

In the era of globalization and economic downturn, cooperatives can find unparalleled opportunity to broaden their scope by venturing into non-conventional sectors together with the conventional ones, to handle economic ills and prosperity. As a business model, they are independent of external influences like stocks. Instead of profit maximizing, they focus on people by aggregating the market power. They, to a large extent, have successfully managed the socio-economic and political changes and competitive pressures induced by globalization and the implications emerging from global economic and financial crises engulfing a large number of countries of the world from time to time.

During the most recent crisis, the cooperative banks and credit union sector expanded their lending when other financial institutions had to cut back, thereby, easing the impact of the credit freeze on the most vulnerable sectors of the economy and sections of the society.[7] A recent ILO study demonstrates that financial cooperatives have remained financially sound; agricultural cooperatives in many parts of the world are showing surpluses; consumer cooperatives are reporting increased turnover; and worker cooperatives are seeing growth. People are increasingly choosing the cooperative form of enterprise to respond to the new economic realities. Many governments are now considering the cooperative option in this new economic environment.[8]

Globalization also poses a threat to cooperatives. Competitive pressures from MNCs pose a serious challenge to the resource base of these cooperatives. It will further hinder the growth and development of healthy and self-reliant cooperatives. The new economic scenario, of course, can also be effectively utilized by learning from the international experiences. Simultaneously, cooperatives need serious reorientation in terms of functioning and management by enhancing their competitive strength through merger and division; liquidating non-viable societies; ensuring active, honest and enlightened management and membership in their day-to-day business, and to enter the capital market by mobilizing funds with cost-effectiveness; further popularizing the cooperative model by launching intensified enrolment drives in rural areas and sectors where competitive advantage is established and linkages at all levels including NGOs, self-help groups, Panchayats, the government and international organization are established.

The existing cooperative model as seen in the above background, thus, has the potential to be the powerful social development enterprise to withstand all challenges and pressures emerging from globalization. They, in particular, can truly empower women by creating enabling environment by giving powers, resources and their ownership, strength, competence and capabilities required for achieving substantive freedoms. Some countries have evolved non-cooperative business structures like private limited companies for their associate or subsidiary entities into the cooperative sector. These 'new generation co-operatives' enable cooperatives to expand their capital base while still retaining some cooperative characteristics. This is an important challenge for the cooperative movement which has to be handled with innovation.

IV. Cooperative Sector in Developed Countries: Some Features

The world of cooperatives has come a long way starting from 1844, when the first cooperative business (Rochdale Equitable

Pioneers Society) emerged with a group of 28 artisans working in the cotton mills in the town of Rochdale (north England) living in miserable conditions. However, the basic principles of openness, democracy, honesty, autonomy and respect though revised and updated continue to be the same.

In international perspective, cooperatives have assumed the role of significant economic and social actors. Over 800 million of people in over 100 countries have chosen the cooperative model of business enterprise to achieve their personal and community development goals. The countries, with the most cooperatives include France, the U.S., Japan, Germany, and the Netherlands. Some of the important lessons to be learnt and remembered are as under:

1. Cooperatives and competition can go together. The first Global 300 list reveals, the cooperative groups that contribute most to their national GDP (Finland, New Zealand, Switzerland, Netherlands and Norway), are also the countries that rank as the world's most competitive economies (based on 2004 data published by the World Economic Forum 2006). The world's 5th most competitive economy, Singapore boasts of a vibrant and growing cooperative movement. The countries with the largest per cent of GDP from Global 300 turnover (2004) are: Finland 16 per cent; New Zealand 14 per cent; Switzerland 11 per cent; Netherlands 10 per cent; and Norway 9 per cent.

2. Cooperatives are popular among people in the developed world. In Canada, four of every ten Canadians are members of at least one cooperative (Cooperative Secretariat, Government of Canada). In Germany, 1 out of 4 people are members of co-operatives. In Japan, 1 out of every 3 families is a member of cooperatives. In Malaysia, 24 per cent of the total populations are members of cooperatives. In New Zealand, 40 per cent of the adult populations are members of cooperatives. In Singapore, 50 per cent of the populations are members of a cooperative. In the United States, about 25 per cent individuals are a member of a cooperative.

3. Cooperatives are dominant and diverse economic actors in national economies. Three groups of cooperatives represent nearly 80 per cent of the Global 300 turnover: Food and Agriculture about 33 per cent; Retailing about 25 per cent; and Insurance about 22 per cent. Agricultural cooperatives account for 80 to 99 per cent of milk production in Norway, New Zealand and the United States of America. They account for 71 per cent of fishery production in the Republic of Korea; and 40 per cent of agriculture in Brazil. In the United States, 900 rural electric cooperatives serve 37 million people and own almost half of the electric distribution lines in the country.

Finnish cooperative groups within Pellervo were responsible for 74 per cent of the meat products, 96 per cent of dairy products; 50 per cent of the egg production, 34 per cent of forestry products and handled 34.2 per cent of the total deposits in Finnish banks. In France, 9 out of 10 farmers are members of agricultural cooperatives; cooperative banks handle 60 per cent of the total deposits; and 25 per cent of all retailers are cooperatives [*GNC Newsletter*, No. 348, June 2007]. In New Zealand, 22 per cent of the gross domestic product (GDP) is generated by cooperative enterprise. Cooperatives are responsible for 95 per cent of the dairy market and 95 per cent of the dairy exports. They hold 70 per cent of the meat market, 50 per cent of the farm supply market, 70 per cent of the fertilizer market, 75 per cent of the wholesale pharmaceuticals, and 62 per cent of the grocery market (New Zealand Co-operative Association, 2007). In Norway, dairy cooperatives are responsible for 99 per cent of the milk production; consumer cooperatives hold 24.1 per cent of the market. In Sweden, consumer cooperatives held 17.5 per cent of the market in 2004. In the United States approximately 30 per cent of farmers' products are marketed through 3,400 farmer-owned cooperatives.

4. Cooperatives create employment and enhance social inclusion. Co-operatives account for more than 100 million jobs (20 per cent more than the MNCs). In addition of creating incomes for billions of people worldwide, cooperatives produce and supply safe and quality food and services to their members and communities. In Canada, the Desjardins movement (savings and credit cooperatives) is the largest employer in the province of Quebec.

5. The cooperative sector is vibrant, widespread and continues to grow. The study by International Co-operative Alliance (ICA) in its Global 300 list for 2008 shows that the 300 top cooperatives are responsible for an aggregate turnover of 1.1 trillion USD, which makes it the size of the 10th economy of the world. The largest share of revenue from the Global 300 is generated in France, which turns out to be around 28 per cent. This is followed by the United States (16 per cent); Germany (14 per cent); Japan (8 per cent); Netherlands (7 per cent); and so on.

Thus, strength of cooperatives must be harnessed to bring socio-economic transformation of a country.

V. Cooperatives in India: A Quick Survey of Lessons

The cooperation, though a worldwide movement, was introduced in India about 105 years ago in the wake of famines resulting into economic hardships and a rapid increase in the indebtedness of the farmers. Thanks to the vision of leaders like Pandit Nehru, who wanted "to make the cooperative approach the common thinking of India", cooperatives recorded a significant growth. The number of cooperatives in India has increased to about five lakh, and the total membership of cooperative societies 20 crore covering 100 per cent villages and 71 per cent rural households. Though they cover a wide range of commercial activities, nearly 50 per cent of them are engaged in agriculture and agricultural-related sectors. Agricultural cooperatives have strong linkages with cooperative banks and marketing unions. A large chunk of food segment is supplied by them. It includes food grains, milk, sugar, fruits and vegetables, edible oil, etc. The cooperative sector stands along with the private and public sectors.

Cooperatives contribute about 43 per cent of total agricultural credit; distribute 36 per cent of total fertilizer consumption in the country and produce 51 per cent of total sugar output. The edible oil marketed through cooperative channels is estimated around 50 per cent, and hand looms around 54 per cent of the total. Their share in wheat production turns out to be around 34 per cent. About 64 per cent of storage facility is in cooperative sector. In addition of employing 1.2 million persons they account for self-employment for about 15 million persons (NCUI, Coop Vision-2015: 2-3). They play a crucial role in the agro-processing sector which includes processing of sugarcane, milk, cotton and oilseeds, etc. Dairy cooperatives have excelled and have enabled India to attain top position in milk production in the world.

A scrutiny of the cooperative societies highlights the following problems: (i) the cooperative structure at the primary level continues to be weak; (ii) the response from the federal organizations towards the needs of their member organizations has not been encouraging; (iii) cooperatives continue to be working in isolation rather as a unified system; (iv) participation of user members is lacking; and (v) many state governments have yet to amend the State Cooperative Societies Act in line with the Multi-State Cooperative Societies Act, which will provide autonomy and independence to cooperatives.

These problems get compounded with lack of professional management, inadequate infrastructure, and lack of capability to withstand competition; overdependence on government and its agencies for financial assistance; restrictive provisions of cooperative law; mismanagement, inefficiency and corruption at the financing level. Questions related to legal basis, age and membership, participation and leadership, training, awareness and appreciation, financial resources, people to implement programmes, etc. remain serious and unanswered at many levels.

Fisheries sector in India, though plays an important role in socio-economic life of India, remains unorganized and scattered. About 14 million people are estimated to be employed in fisheries, and it contributes about 1 per cent of India's GDP. Indian share in global production has reached above 4 per cent with about 10 per cent share in inland and about 3 per cent in marine. For inland sector, India is ranked second after China. Other major producer countries are China, Japan, the United States, the Russian Federation and Indonesia.

VI. Women Empowerment: Role of Fisheries Cooperatives

In Sri Lanka, nearly half of the population comprises women. The literacy rate for women, though quite high, is little less than the men. The labour force participation rate for women is nearly half the rate for men (65.3 per cent). About 41 per cent of the employed women engaged in agriculture and allied sectors are more than those employed men. Women are not only directly affected by different socio-economic problems related to poverty, unemployment and inequity, but also have to perform a dual role. They undertake home maintenance. In addition, women generate production both at the farm and household levels by working in livestock production, forest resource use and fishery processing. About two-third of the women employed in agriculture, work in plantations and subsistence production. Women despite contributing to household income through farm and non-farm activities and saving on account of house maintenance, and by taking employment in non-farm sector continue to be powerless.

Women are active in both artisan fisheries and the commercial fishery sectors. They are likely to constitute a larger proportion of the poor within the fisheries sector, fisheries governance and resource management. Their activities range from shallow water wishing in artisan fisheries to waged labour in the commercial fisheries sector. Fisherwomen market fish as a retailer, auctioneers or as agents of merchants; make and repair nets; collect prawn seeds or fish seeds from back waters to supply to fish farmers; work as labourers for shrimp processing firms; and prepare a variety of fish products.

The fisheries sector plays a key role in Sri Lanka's social and economic life. It contributes about 2 per cent of GDP, brings substantial export earnings and employs more than a million people. It is directly linked with the lives of approximately 50 per cent of the population who resides in the coastal belt. Of the total fish landings of the country, about 95 per cent is handled by the private sector; and more than two-third of that is transported to urban markets. A small percentage (less than 3 per cent) is handled by the Ceylon Fisheries Corporation (CFC)—a government entity. Established with the aim of offering competition to private fish traders and thereby ensuring better producer prices for fish, it was never able to compete fully with private traders of this sector.

Nearly half of the fishers are in the 35 to 54 year age group, and about 40% of the fisher population has completed primary school education. This shows that Sri Lanka's fishers are active and literate communities. On 26 Dec. 2004, the fisheries sector was severely affected by Tsunami tidal waves that hit two-thirds of the coastline of the island. It is estimated that nearly 80 per cent of active fishers were affected and more than 75 per cent of the fishing fleet was destroyed or damaged by the tsunami in addition, of a large number of small-scale fishing crafts.

The world experience shows that women support, complement and subsidize men's small-scale fishing activities in many ways as given below:

Women's involvement in fisheries is much more significant than often assumed. The nine major fish producing countries show that they constitute about 46 per cent of the labour force in small scale capture fisheries-related activities.

- Women's work remains under-enumerated, hidden and undervalued.
- Women subsidize men's fishing efforts in many ways, but are rarely involved in decision-making related to fishing at the household, community, regional or national level.
- Members of fishing households in general are less educated and have less access to health and infrastructure services than those of the neighbouring communities such as farmers.
- Women's access to and outcomes in education and health are generally less than that of men in fishing communities.
- There is a need to ensure gender equitable outcomes in the pursuit of livelihood strategies leading to the well-being of households engaged in small-scale fisheries.

It is in this background, women have to be encouraged, socially mobilized and organized into women fisheries cooperatives to achieve the collective socio-economic development goals and the livelihood security. The government, community organizations as well as other donor agencies have shown some interest in expanding this model. Such cooperatives can diversify and help in improving the existing levels of contribution from this sector by increasing output, raising the value addition and import substitution. It is more so because there is a vast coastal area of Sri Lanka and a great scope exists for diversification, and untapped huge export potential with the world demand increasing.

Such a cooperative project can financially and socially empower fishing communities by promoting collective ownership of assets and transfer of land rights, savings for welfare, managing fee and funds for education, creating awareness of basic human and legal rights related to land, voting, marriage age of girls and boys, etc. The movement of women communities, through parents' meetings in schools, government offices, NGO offices and other marketplaces will create social bonding and confidence to meet relatives, and attending culture events, clinics/hospitals, crises of others. Their general confidence level in day-to-day life and decision-making capabilities regarding general marketing will rise with the participation of women in various activities such as fish standardization, processing and sale, wet and dried fish trading, fish meal production, fish vending, sale, net making and repairing, grocery/shopping, ferry, livestock/poultry rearing, etc. and other non-income activities like social and religious events, shouldering household responsibilities, family planning, and so on.

Women fisheries cooperatives being people-centered rather than capital-centered organizations can substantially contribute to the overall development needs of the nation by providing food security generating employment, economic gains for the optimum utilization of resource and finally improving the socio-economically status for those who are directly and indirectly connected with exploitation, production and processing of fish.

But that requires the application of best practices learnt from the well-known cooperative models. These include: (i) the formulation, operation, implementation, and management should be well thought of and cover all stages of project and post-project development activities; (ii) factors such as social mobilization, health, education, disaster preparedness, alternative income-generating activities, legal aid, awareness and adaptation, project management and policy, etc. have to be given due weightage at different stages; (iii) the project staff, service providers, government and the beneficiaries should be sensitized towards needs of the members and the region; (iv) the management must adopt a participatory and interactive approach at all levels particularly for planning and budgeting of project activities, their implementation, monitoring and evaluation; (v) constant innovation and openness and adaptation to new ideas of diversification, etc., evidence-based international practices, cooperation with the R&D institutions, agriculture universities, governments, fisheries departments and marketing agencies and so on.

The scope of women cooperatives can further be enlarged by involving the women at the early age by inculcating the cooperative ideology to bring them into the desired fold of cooperatives. The present education and social system must therefore be geared and so structured to make youth capable to come together to form cooperatives. There is no substitute for involving youth as they can build up value-based strong economy and cohesive society. This can lead to positive outcomes for people, communities and the national and international cooperative movement. This is not possible without building up the important cooperative skills which require significant investment in teachers, research, resources, technology and students' development and designing suitable priorities for maximizing the contribution of cooperatives to national development.

In many developed countries, cooperative education and resources are provided along with financial resources to those who want to get involved in or start their own cooperatives. A good example of this is the Wood Craft Folk in the United Kingdom. Around the world, one notices students have formed cooperative bookstores, computer stores, housing associations and food outlets to benefit others. Cooperative studies can motivate the youth to form cooperatives.

Thus, women fisheries cooperatives particularly with relatively young minds adapted to cooperative behaviour has the potential to build strong economy and create a cohesive society that can also influence the government and public behaviour. However, their success is determined how much it involves and concentrates, among other things, on education, awareness and innovation; training and employment; health and family welfare; preservation of environment; arts, culture and sports; science and technology; and civics and good citizenship.

VII. Conclusions, Challenges and Outlook

Sri Lanka is a beautiful country with high growth potential and developed human resources to lead the country to be at par with the developed world. This is a difficult work. The dynamics of the interconnected process of ongoing liberalization, privatization and globalization backed by information and communication technologies, highlights both the challenges and opportunities. The fisheries sector in Sri Lanka plays an important role in the economy by contributing more than 1 per cent of GDP besides providing employment and contributing to export earnings. The fisherwomen by organizing themselves into cooperatives, given their diverse and versatile role, can play a leading role in further developing the fisheries sector and achieving sustainable human development.

Fishwomen farmers constitute the backbone of Sri Lanka fisheries industry. Fisherwomen come from relatively weaker sections of the society; they are economically, politically, educationally and socially weak. Fisherwomen cooperatives can engage in variety of productive activities, in the field of education, health, public distribution system, social reform and charity in normal and abnormal times, and during natural or manmade calamities in the interest of members. Sri Lanka despite having enormous resources for fishery development activities, records a very low contribution of fisheries sector in GDP. Therefore, women fisheries cooperatives should be encouraged as they are expected to contribute substantially to the national economy.

However, lessons from the successful cooperatives particularly from India as is evident from IFFCO, KRIBHCO,

AMUL, Warnanagar and Indore Projects point out many preconditions: (1) local leaders must be "models of responsible and responsive factor" having honesty, integrity, vision and professional management skills to mobilize the people under the fold of cooperatives; (2) continuous innovations and adaptations; (3) enabling environment be created by government; (4) open membership irrespective of gender, religion, caste and creed; (5) members' cooperative efforts put in to build up the most essential infrastructure including irrigation dams, roads, electricity generation, cooking gas supply, plant nurseries, agricultural research centres, etc.; (6) extending the most needed social benefits and care to youth and women through better healthcare, education services; (7) creating additional income-generation opportunities through voluntary organizations established simultaneously; (8) encouraging members to take initiatives to improve management, increase productivity levels by making use of improved farm inputs and crop care; (9) facilitating transfer of the technology from the urban to the rural areas; and (10) continuously giving a feeling to the members to take pride in owning and managing large cooperatives.

Women fisheries cooperatives since are based on values like economic democracy, social responsibility and unity, can play a vital role in Sri Lanka. They are member-driven rather than investor-driven and focus on providing benefits to their members. Cooperatives have proved that they are capable of handling all issues of development. It is not the size of a firm or the networks that determine the success. Rather, it is the attitude of cooperation that acts as the software which runs the system, and measures the success. The future of cooperatives as social development enterprise for generating productive employment and income would depend on how communities are involved in the cooperative movement.

The young women must be provided the right environment to feel motivated to develop the knowledge, competence, determination, perseverance, etc. to work for women cooperative fisheries. Let us not forget that (i) youth is our next generation of workers, entrepreneurs, parents, citizens and leaders; (ii) women fisheries cooperatives offer at least two keys of strength which no other enterprise can fully match: one, it gives an opportunity to each and everybody to help themselves by cooperating with others, and two, it provides strength to an individual to acquire and control private property while preserving individual freedom, dignity and responsibility; and (iii) the national development is a daunting task, in which young women can play a leading role.

NOTES

1. World Economic Forum 2008.
2. IFPRI 2009.
3. World Economic Forum 2009.
4. International Cooperative Alliance, for details, see website, http://www.ica.coop. Also see, J. Birchall, paper presented at the expert group meeting on cooperatives, United Nations, New York, 28-30 April 2009.
5. Asia-Pacific Agriculture Committee. Message from the International Co-operative Alliance: 87th ICA International Co-operative Day, 4 July 2009.
6. Jakhar, S.K. an International Conference: "Enhanced Role of Cooperatives in the Recovery from Economic Crisis" held at Bangkok from 2 to 4 July 2009, under the auspices of ICA.
7. Message from the Secretary General (U.N.) on the International Day of Cooperatives, 4 July 2009.
8. Message from ILO on the International Day of Cooperatives, 4 July 2009.

REFERENCES

Arora, G.K. (2002). *Globalisation, Federalism and Decentralisation, Implications for India.* Delhi: Bookwell.

Arora, G.K. (2009). Globalisation, Global, Governance and Developing Countries: A Special Focus on India, *Indian Journal of Social Enquiry*, New Delhi.

Arora, G.K. (2012). "Globalizing India: Need for Inclusive Sustainable Human Development" (November 7, 2012). *OIDA International Journal of Sustainable Development*, Vol. 05, No. 03, 115-28,

Available at SSRN: http://ssrn.com/abstract=2172550 (jointly with Ashug).

Arora, G.K. and A. Gumber (2009). "Globalisation and Health Sector in India: Some Emerging Issues in India". *Indian Eco Journal* (Vol. 53, No. 4), Jan.-March 2006.

Dubash I, P.R. (2002). Cooperatives in the Next Millennium, *The Cooperator*, Vol. XXXVII, No. 9.

FAO, World Fish, World Bank 2008.

Government of India—Reports of the Ministry of Finance, New Delhi, 1993-1998.

ILO Recommendation No. 193 of 2002 and UN Guidelines on Cooperatives 2 of 2001.

Message from the Food and Agriculture Organization of the United Nations on the occasion of the 15th UN International Day of Cooperatives Driving global recovery through cooperatives. "Recommendations of the Cooperative Societies Forum, Saudi Arabia" Jun. 12, 2009.

NCUI (2009). 56th Guidelines Indian Cooperative Week, 14-20 Nov. 2009.

Patel, Kandarp. Universal Value Based Youth Cooperative for Wealthy Economy in Healthy Society: A Dream in Indian Context, Institute of Rural Management, Anand, India.

Prakash, Daman. Paper Prepared for Inclusion in the Publication of the National Cooperative Union of India in connection with the Centenary Celebrations of the Indian Cooperative Movement 1904-2004.

Ramesh, R. S. (2000), Challenges Before Cooperatives under Liberalized Economic Regime, *The Cooperator*, Vol. XXXVII, No. 10.

RBI Bulletin, Oct. 2009: 1725-46.

Some Essential Factors for Strengthening Co-operatives—20 Points to Consider Dr Daman Prakash Senior Consultant, IFFCO Foundation, New Delhi (former Project Director, ICA ROAP, New Delhi).

Special Address during the National Symposium to Commemorate 60th year of Independence 'Agriculture cannot wait: New Horizons',

President of India's, NASC Complex, New Delhi, 05-06-2007: New Delhi.

Speech in ICA Assembly on 18 October 2007 by V. Balakrishnan (Speech No. 50/2007).

Stiglitz Joseph (2006). *Making Globlisation Work*, Penguin Books, England.

Subramanyam, B. (1998). Cooperative Credit Structure: A Perspective for 2000 A.D., Cooperative Perspective, pp. 6-14, July-Sept. 1998.

World Bank Institute: Development Outreach, June 2007, Oct. 2009.

World Fish Centre, 2010.

3

Gender-based Development in India: Social Provisions, Failures and Interventions

Ashok Kumar Sarkar

ABSTRACT

Women continue to suffer from fewer rights, less income, limited access to resources and opportunities, lower educational and health status, vulnerability to violence and conflict, and so on. This inequality or 'gender inequality' is one of the major obstacles to fulfill the MDGs in most of the Third World countries including India. Thus, arguments for gender equity to go beyond equal opportunity require the transformation of basic rules, hierarchies and practices of public institutions. This calls for more involvement and participation of women in politics to challenge the existing marginalization (Priyam et al., 2008). The paper has forwarded various social work interventions to challenge the patriarchy at grassroots level and can play gigantic role to accelerate gender-based development in India.

Introduction

Women constitute half of the world's population but perform two-thirds of the world's working hours (www.wvasiapacific.org/gender.and.development.html). Despite of this fact, they are poorer than men. They continue to suffer from fewer rights, less income, limited access to resources and opportunities, lower educational and health status, vulnerability to violence and conflict, and so on. This inequality or 'gender inequality' is one of the major obstacles to fulfill the MDGs in most of the Third World countries including India. Moving towards gender equality, hence, is one among the key paths to development (UN OSAGI, 2001). But only equality of opportunity would not suffice because all opportunities are institutionalized into structures that have evolved in a gendered way. These might require the creation of special provisions for women; some of the examples are separate toilets for women, facilities for breast feeding, crèche, etc. Thus, arguments for gender equity to go beyond equal opportunity require the transformation of basic rules, hierarchies and practices of public institutions. This calls for more involvement and participation of women in politics to challenge the existing marginalization (Priyam et al., 2008). Implicitly, involvement of women in politics indicates that gender and governance is interrelated for development. It also relates capabilities perspective that directs us to look at conditions that influence women's internal development and also at conditions of the material and social development that influence their ability to turn their ideas into action (Nussbaum, 2005). Truly speaking, this kind of gender-based development approach would be suitable to achieve sustainable progress.

Social Provisions

In India, in order to carry out gender-based development, there are many social provisions enunciated in the constitution, national policies, legislations, five-year plans and development programmes. In the Constitution of India, apart from the *Preamble*, articles 14, 15 and 16 regarding *Fundamental Rights* under Part III; articles 39 and 42 about the *Directive Principles* under Part IV; and article 51(A) on *Fundamental Duties* of the citizens under Part IVA ensure rights and interests of women. The *73rd* and *74th Amendments* (1993) to this Constitution have provided provision for reservation of seats in the local bodies of Panchayats and municipalities for women. The *National Policy for the Empowerment of Women 2001* (Government of India) ensures mainstreaming of women's perspectives in all developmental processes as catalysts, participants, and recipients. The government has *enacted almost 42 legislations* related to women. All are not gender specific but each one has special provisions to safeguard women. Regarding Five-year Plans, from First to Fourth Plan, women were treated as subjects of 'welfare' and clubbed together under the category of disadvantaged groups such as destitute, disabled, aged, etc. From the Fifth Five-year Plan (1974-78) onwards, there has been a marked shift in the approach to women's issues, i.e. from 'welfare approach' to 'development approach'. Apart from the above social provisions, there are also several *special initiatives* such as National Commission for Women, Rashtriya Mahila Kosh, Legal Literacy Manuals, National Plan of Action for the Girl Child, National Resource Centre for Women, and Mahila Samriddhi Yojana; several *support services* through VOs/NGOs such as hostels for working women, creches for children, scheme for adolescent girls, and gender sensitization and awareness generation; and several *employment and income generation programmes* such as STEP, NORAD, SEP, and CCE&VT (NIPCCD, 2007).

Failures

The above-cited social provisions are still a far-reaching reality for Indian women which can lead to have an equitable society with the attitudinal change of man. The influx of foreign and modern culture has put them in exploitable situation. Women in India are ill-treated everyday. Many a time, they face violence at the hands of their protectors. They encounter physical violence, sexual violence, verbal violence, social violence, emotional violence, financial violence, intellectual violence and so on (Nigam, 2002). Though many complaints are unreported, police records show an increase in the incidence of crime against women during the last decade (2002-11). As per Table 1, total incidents of reported crime reached from 1,43,034 in 2002 to 2,28,650 in 2011.

The trend continued to rise in 2002, fell during 2003, and again rose from 2004 to 2011. Table 1 also gives incidence of the various types of reported crimes against women in India. It is found, cruelty at home by husband and relatives ranks first, molestation second, rape third, kidnapping and abduction of women and girls fourth, sexual harassments fifth and dowry

Table 1: Crime against Women in India (2002-11)

Nature of Crime	Incidence of Crime									
	2002	2003	2004	2005	2006	2007	2008	2009	2010	2011
Rape	16373	15847	18233	18359	19348	20737	21,467	21,397	22,172	24,206
Kidnapping and abduction	14506	13296	15578	15750	17414	20416	22,939	25,741	29,795	35,565
Dowry deaths	6822	6208	7026	6787	7618	8093	8,172	8,383	8,391	8,618
Cruelty at home	49237	50703	58121	58319	63128	75930	81,344	89,546	94,041	99,135
Molestation	33943	32939	34567	34175	36617	38734	40,413	38,711	40,613	42,968
Sexual harassments	10155	12325	10001	9984	9966	10950	12,214	11,009	9,961	8,570
Importation of girls	76	46	89	149	67	61	67	48	36	80
Other crimes	11922	9237	10718	12030	10607	10391	9240	8969	8576	9508
Total reported incidence	143034	140601	154333	155553	164765	185312	195856	203804	213585	228650

Source: Crime in India, National Crime Records Bureau, 2004, 2005, 2006, 2007, 2008, 2009, 2010 and 2011.

deaths sixth. The other crimes include sati practice, immoral trafficking, indecent representation, dowry harassment, etc. It has been observed that crimes like rape, kidnapping, dowry deaths, cruelty at home and molestation have increased during last eight years.

These crimes or violence affect some of the fundamental human rights of women such as right to freedom from torture and right to health, etc. In true sense, violence has direct impact on health. It causes *physical health problems* such as injuries, headaches, back pain, abdominal pain, fibromyalgia, gastrointestinal disorders, poor health status, etc.; *sexual and reproductive health problems* such as unintended pregnancies, gynaecological problems, induced abortions, adverse pregnancy outcomes including miscarriage, low birth weight and fetal death, etc.; *mental illnesses* such as increasing the risk of depression, post-traumatic stress disorder, sleep difficulties, eating disorders, emotional distress and so on; *risky behaviours* such as sex at early age, multiple partners, unprotected sex, substance use, etc.; and so on. Crimes or violence also put off women from access to resources, ability to continue daily work, education, travel, community meeting, care for themselves and children, etc. In fact, violence does not allow women to have full participation in the society and bear the economic costs for both individual and society. Thus, crime or violence against women constitutes a major obstacle to development, peace and security.

Factors Responsible for Gender-based Violence

Who is responsible or what factors are responsible for this gender-based violence that causes individual as well as social loss? Ironically speaking, it is *patriarchal notion of superiority* or *men's idea of ownership over women* which plays important role. Physically, woman is weaker than man. Along with this biological reason, man has also socially constructed the idea of superiority which is deeply rooted in the structures and functions of society for hundreds of years. Hence, man wants to control woman's body, sexuality, labour, mobility and autonomy. He uses cultural norms, military tactics, negative media images, social pressures and so on. Violence is thus a means that men use persistently to control women as a result of superiority (Sharma and Gupta, 2004). The other important factor is *consumerism* that has become gradually prominent since 1970s with the emergence of liberalization at the global level. New technology, more earning, easy accessibility of goods and new modes of advertisements have made people materialistic to have more comforts. This selfish acquisitive culture increases violence in the family (Sharma et al., 2003; Sharma et al., 2002a, b, c). *Unrealistic expectations,* to become rich quickly, influenced by consumerist culture and media industries affect the thinking processes and behaviour of masses. The inability to meet unrealistic expectations leads to frustrations and increasing violence against women. *New style of advertisement and media portrayal* almost in every TV channel use women's body openly and the same leads to erosion of social values as well as develop the thinking process to entertain violence against women. Apart from the above reasons, *individual factors* like women's level of education and financial autonomy; *partner factors* like male partner's level of communication with her, use of alcohol and drugs, employment status, etc. and *factors related to immediate social context* such as degree of female mobility, attitude towards gender roles, the extent to which extended family or neighbours and friends intervene in domestic violence incidents, male-male aggression, and so on are accountable for crime against women.

Interventions Require

In the preceding discussion, it is found, despite of having many social provisions, that there are incongruities in gender-based development. Crimes against women have been increasing every year. In fact, social work profession can take initiative to challenge the patriarchy at grassroots level and can play gigantic role to accelerate gender-based development in India. It applies principles of social justice and human rights to bring change in the gender blind communities. Like generalist social work, ecological social work, ethnic-sensitive social work, social work profession uses feminist or gender aware social work. Gender aware social work advocates for understanding and combating women's unfavourable placement in society. According to McMohan (1996), "Gender aware social work is expected to communicate with women and with men in a manner that reflects an understanding of and responsiveness to their distinctive problems and experiences." Here social workers comprehend and respond to political, economic, social, cultural, familial and individual factors that work in tandem to construct inequalities between sexes in a given society in which they operate (Gandhi, 1998). Gender aware or feminist model of social work suggests the following measures to reinforce the gender-based development in India:

(a) Social work practitioners must be aware of and provide services to the people as men and women and not merely treating and perceiving the women in terms of social role—housewife, widow, wife or mother or young girl.

(b) Social workers must recognize the powerful impact of cultural context on the lives of women. In a patriarchal culture where women have less power than men, women should be assertive and attempt to adopt relationships that are non-mutual so that inequality does not perpetuate in invisible or unnoticed form.

(c) Social workers should help women to share similar problems with other women in the group so that they can feel less isolated. Working with group in this manner enables women to see that problems which they thought were exclusively theirs are not so and that they can work out joint solutions.

(d) Social workers should increase gender awareness getting involved in the campaign or propagation through government or non-government agencies and should change perception of society towards the dignity of women treating them at par with their male counterpart.

(e) Resource centers should be developed under NGOs where social workers should work to provide legal education to the girls studying in secondary and higher secondary schools to fight for their rights, to guide women suffering from violence for legal action, to motivate poor women to avail facilities from government programmes, to provide vocational training for economic empowerment, to provide counseling and family planning services for strengthening family, and to mobilize civil society organizations to put pressure on government agencies for strict implementation of legislations pertaining to women's rights and interests.

REFERENCES

Gandhi, A. (1998). "Gender Aware Social Work: From Theory to Field Instruction", *The Indian Journal of Social Work*, Vol. 59, No. 4, pp. 981-97.

Government of India (2001). *National Policy for the Empowerment of Women 2001*, Ministry of Women and Child Development: New Delhi.

http://www.wvasiapacific.org/gender.and.development.html, for details read 'Why Gender Development is the Key'.

McMohan, M.O. (1996). *The General Method of Social Work Practice: A Generalist Perspective*, Allyn and Bacon: Boston.

NIPCCD (2007). Statistics on Women in India 2007, National Institute of Public Co-operation and Child Development (NIPCCD): New Delhi.

Nigam, S. (2002). "Silent Enemy in the Home", *Social Welfare*, 49(4), pp. 12-16.

Nussbaum, M. (2005). "Gender and Governance: An Introduction", HDRC, UNDP's ed., *Essays on Gender and Governance*, MacMillion India Ltd., New Delhi.

Priyam et al. (2008). *Human Rights, Gender and the Environment*, Pearson (Longman), Delhi.

Sharma et al. (2002a). "Poisoning Scenario in Northern India—Challenges and Suggestions", *Journal of Mahatma Gandhi Institute of Medica Sciences*, Vol. 7, pp. 37-42.

Sharma et al. (2002b). "Poisoning in Northern India—Changing Trends, Causes and Prevention Thereof", *Med. Sci. Law,* Vol. 42, pp. 251-57.

Sharma et al. (2002c). "Epidemiology of Poisoning—An Indian Viewpoint", *Journal of Forensic Medicine Toxicology,* Vol. 19, pp. 5-11.

Sharma et al. (2003). "Suicides in Northern India—Causes, Methods Used and Prevention Thereof", *Med. Sci. Law,* Vol. 43, pp. 221-29.

Sharma, B.R. and Gupta, M. (2004). "Gender Based Violence in India—A Never Ending Phenomenon", *Journal of International Women's Studies*, Vol. 6, No. 1, pp. 114-23.

United Nations Office of the Special Advisor on Gender Issues and the Advancement of Women (UN OSAGI), 2001, *Joint Workshop on Governance, Poverty Reduction and Gender Equality,* Vienna, 23-25 April 2001.

4

The Emerging Power Structure in Rural India: Democracy, Development and Decentralization

G. Ram

ABSTRACT

In sociological sense, power is an integral part of social structure and a patterned power-interrelationship refers to a power structure. Power structure in India's rural setting has historically undergone significant changes, especially in the post-Independence period. The traditional rural power structure was basically a feudal system of rights and privileges embedded in landed property, which reflected through institutions, values, religion, culture and ideology in the society. The Panchayati Raj institutions were set up to accelerate the arrested process of change and development, to enable the rural people to participate and contribute in the national rural reconstruction and development and to redistribute land among the poor with a view to transform the agrarian structure. However, these measures could not bring about much of desired results. In concrete terms, the political response with regard to major structural changes has not been satisfactory, and indifference has prevailed among political workers at the grassroots level. There is perceived policy-gap in the party politics at the national, state and local levels. Ignorance, poverty, illiteracy and inegalitarian (caste-based) social system have, all favoured the political intentions of the parties which easily sway the ignorant voters on desired political lines. This rural power structure is subjected to two models of explanation; namely, dominant caste and rich peasant models. These models are complementary to each other. According to these models, a single power resource is not sufficient. A group with power in a village must control some supra-village power resource. Control of various power resources in a village places a minority (caste or elite individuals) ahead of others in possession of at least most resources and, therefore, many of the traditional attributes continue in the changed context as well.

There have been various perceptions and conceptions of power among social scientists such as political scientists, psychologists and sociologists. Ancient socio-political thinkers like Plato and Aristotle have analysed power in relation to state while sociologists have considered it an integral part of social structure. In Max Weber's sociological conception, power is the fundamental factor to social stratification which comprises three dimensions; namely, class, status and party. According to him, class is the outcome of distribution of economic power; status is a kind of normatively defined social power and party is a group having concern for political power. Weber (1947: 152) defines power as "...the probability that one actor within a social relationship will be in a position to carry out his own will despite resistance, regardless of the basis on which this probability rests". In this sense, power is merely a factual relation that involves use of force or coercion which may or may not be carrying social approval. Since Weber's time, many sociologists have assumed power as an action involving subordinates' resistance and super-ordinates' enforcement. In this sense, Alvin Gouldner (1970) has noted: "Power is, among other things, the ability to enforce one's moral claims. The powerful can, thus, conventionalize their moral defaults." Similarly, David Lockwood has recognized power as a latent force. He viewed that power must only refer to the capacity to realize one's ends in conflict situations against the will of others, and it must also include the capacity to prevent opposition arising in the first place. Robert Dahl (1961) has conceptualized power as the ability to make and implement decisions. Here, the powerful are those whose decisions consistently match the outcomes. This, all, makes the concept of power complex. Since there is found a huge variety of socio-cultural set-ups in the world in its contemporary and historical existence one perceives various facets of power. That is, power may be formal or informal; it may be modern or traditional and there may be discerned macro or micro form of power. Social structure has been mostly conceptualized in anthropological and sociological literature by drawing its analogy from organic structure of human body in Biology where structure is taken as a set of interrelated organs. Therefore, in anthropology and sociology social structure has usually been conceived as a relatively stable social relationship, a pattern of interactions and, as such, a social relationship which involves power is a power relationship. The nature of a power relationship is determined by the way power is distributed between two individuals or groups which are related to each other. Thus, power structure refers to a pattern of relationships involving power, whatever forms these relationships take—they may be arranged tightly or loosely or in many other ways. Sometimes, sociologists and political scientists seem to be differing in their perception of power structure as the elements of power structure, with which each discipline is concerned, are perceived differently. Besides, power relations are structured differently in different location settings of people. As rural society consists of characteristically distinct relationships, institutions and groups as compared with urban society, one finds a distinct pattern of power distribution among individuals and groups, and distinct elements that constitute rural power structure. Rural power structure thus refers to a pattern of the relationships which are based on power distribution among individuals or/and groups in rural setting. Analysis of power structure occupies a central place to understand the Indian rural society which has historically undergone significant changes, especially in the post-Independence period. To initiate a thorough discussion on rural power structure in India, the attainment of Independence is to be used here as a watermark. Here, a discussion is taken up to analyse the traditional power structure, democratization of power and emergent power structure in rural India.

The Traditional Power Structure in Rural India

Traditional India is generally referred to India's pre-British era. The British established, strengthened and expanded their rule in India after the Battle of Plassey in 1757 AD. They introduced a new settlement of land revenue, in 1772, which became a useful instrument for them for a systematic collection of land revenue (Grover and Grover, 1986: 101-04). However, on the whole, the traditional land system superimposed with the British commercial interests in land continued till India's Independence. By that time, there prevailed a feudal political system in India, consisting of hundreds of the British-ruled areas and princely states and chieftaincies which were replicated by the Zamindari and Jagirdari systems in the rural areas. This feudal system was basically a system of rights and privileges embedded in landed property, which reflected through institutions, values, religion, culture and ideology in the society. Therefore, rural social structure as a whole and rural power structure in particular was, then, greatly influenced by the Zamindari and Jagirdari systems in the society. Primarily, this system represented economic interests of Zamindars and Jagirdars and it manifested through the institutions of caste and panchayat. Agriculture being the primary occupation, ownership of land and monopoly on economic activities influenced and controlled rural power structure. The Zamindars had a monopoly in the selection of rural leaders and functioning of village panchayats and caste panchayats. Combined with the Zamindari system had been another fundamental element of rural social structure, i.e. caste system and even village panchayats were constituted mostly by representatives of caste panchayats. In pre-Independence India, both the systems had given rise to a unique rural power structure, in which the Zamindari and Jagirdari systems, caste panchayats and the village panchayats had monopoly of power. Besides these, there also lived different religious and tribal communities which had no notion of caste. Such communities had their own community panchayats and they also participated in village panchayats. However, tribal communities which were more or less isolated and lived out of the Zamindari and Jagirdari systems had their own village panchayats. Literacy was very low or totally absent and modern democracy was alien to the masses in the rural areas. Thus, it was the landed gentry or the illiterate elderly of upper castes or communities which assumed power in the traditional rural India.

During the British regime, there was first initiated a change in the traditional rural power structure. As in the beginning the caste and village panchayats were very effective in various parts of the country, the British in the early times established a highly centralized administration in the country, introduced the Zamindari system of separate property rights along with administrative and judicial functions and gave autonomy to the government's nominees such as headmen, Patwaris and Lambardars. These changes set in motion the real decay of traditional village panchayats. However, there was also constantly felt a need for statutory revival of rural local government as a link between the British administration and the villagers. On 18 May 1882, Lord Rippon, the then Viceroy of India, announced setting up of local self-government bodies as an instrument of political education as well as an outlet for the people's ambitions and aspirations engendered by Western ideas. It is remarkable that Rippon proposed a network of rural local bodies, forming a two-tier system of boards at district or sub-district and sub-division or tehsil levels. The district boards which composed of officials and elected members could evoke only a lukewarm response from the Indians who were mainly in the village panchayat bodies. Deploring the disappearance of village autonomy in the Zamindari system under the British regime as against the ryotwari system the Royal Commission in 1909 proposed a separate department of panchayats and also proposed village panchayats consisting of five elected members, each with the headman as ex-officio chairman which were to be endowed with civil and criminal jurisdiction in petty cases and responsibility for minor developmental works under control of the district authorities. Under the Government of India Act 1919, the provincial governments passed several acts to render local self-government a fully representative character. There followed the period of the historic non-cooperation movement which encouraged settlement of disputes through informal panchayats and also boycott of the Government courts. As a result, there sprang-up numerous panchayats in various parts of the country. The Government of India Act 1935 provided an opportunity to the provinces for furtherance of democratization, financial powers and developmental functions of village panchayats. However, the village panchayats still worked as small *darbars* (courts) and petty courts of the British regime. Besides, the emerging opportunity for local government appeared to be short-lived in the wake of intensified freedom struggle, emergent important national and international questions and resignation of the popular provincial governments at the outbreak of the World War II throwing the administrative responsibility on the governors. The indifference to these bodies continued till 1946 when the Constituent Assembly debated the draft Constitution to a great length and included a provision in the Directive Principles of State Policy for decentralization of power and establishment of panchayats at all levels of rural self-government. Need for review of the structure of panchayats continued in different states of Independent India and it was specially felt while implementing the Community Development Programme in the early 1950s. Therefore, Balwant Rai Mehta Committee was constituted to study a proposal for setting up viable units of rural self-government. The committee recommended a three-tier system called Panchayati Raj which was enacted into a legislative act by various states under the Parliament's authorization. However, the traditional panchayats were allowed to continue in the tribal majority states and districts in North-East India. In 1992, the Mehta model of Panchayati Raj finally attained constitutional status through the Constitution (seventy-third) Amendment Act enacted by the Indian Parliament. Significantly, in the 1950s, the government abolished the Zamindari and Jagirdari systems and introduced land reforms by enacting laws. Public land such as village ponds, grazing grounds, village streets, etc., which were used by the Zamindars as personal property, were declared as community property. The abolition of Zamindari system disarmed the Zamindars of economic exploitation and political dominance over the villagers and it paved the way for a more democratic system in the changed socio-economic circumstances and the emerging Panchayati Raj institutions in the rural areas. As a result, the rural power structure has undergone a transformation.

There have been various factors contributing to the change that has occurred in the traditional rural power structure and their contribution also varies in terms of magnitude of each factor at different stages of the change and in different regions of rural India. These factors are as follows:

(i) As the British administration extended it adversely affected the existing traditional village panchayats because the British administration gave autonomy to the government officials.

(ii) The British made efforts to set up rural local government, though in a limited way, and this helped in evoking political consciousness among the rural people.

(iii) Mahatma Gandhi had insisted for autonomy of village panchayats in the Independent India and this inspired the Indian leadership to set up rural local self-government as well as added importance to it.

(iv) Inclusion of panchayats under the Directive Principles of State Policy in the Indian Constitution paved the way for decentralization of power and people's participation in the decision-making in rural areas.

(v) Abolition of the Zamindari and Jagirdari systems and land reforms in the post-Independence period changed the socio-economic context of the power structure in the rural areas. With the abolition of the feudal system, participation of common people increased in the Panchayati Raj institutions as well as political decision-making in the rural areas.

(vi) After Independence, it was felt that rural development was essential for removal of poverty of rural masses and rural development was possible only through people's participation. Therefore, in the Community Development Programme, statutory panchayats were made the instrument of change and development in rural India.

(vii) Working of party politics and regular holding of general elections for electing people's representatives for governance at national and state levels have provided significant political education to the rural people. The people's political education has been further strengthened in the process of formation and working of Panchayati Raj institutions at district, block and village levels in most of the parts of the country.

(viii) Green revolution ushered in the 1970s, which increased farm production through the use of new farm technology and gave rise to middle-class farmers in the rural areas. As a result these farmers made their entry into the existing rural power structure and significantly influenced the decision-making process in the rural areas.

(ix) Various legislations enacted and implemented in the country for security of people, specially for protection of the weaker sections, have instilled confidence in the poor people for political participation as well as provided them opportunity to organize against their exploitation.

(x) Constitution (seventy-third) Amendment ensured the representation of weaker sections such as the Scheduled Castes, Scheduled Tribes, Other Backward Castes/ Classes and women and as a result the presence of the representatives of these sections at every level of rural self-government has rendered more democratic character to the rural power structure.

The Democratization of Power in Rural India

The concept of Panchayati Raj derives itself from Gandhiji's vision of future India of self-reliant villages. It assumes powers for political and economic decentralization on the principle: The greater the power of the panchayat, the better for the people. The Constituent Assembly while framing Indian Constitution was concerned more with a centralized government for stability, unity and economic progress of the nation. Therefore, it failed to accept Gandhiji's proposal of autonomous panchayats in

Independent India. But it was his insistence that the panchayats could find a place in the Directive Principles of State Policy under Part IV of the Constitution. Though non-judiciable, the Part IV lays down fundamental and binding reference points for the state in the matter of legislation. Its Article 40 makes a provision that the state shall take steps to organize village panchayats and endow them with such powers and authority as may be necessary to enable them to function as units of self-government.

Originally, the Panchayati Raj was conceived as a means for the Community Development Programme (CDP) which itself is seeded into the recommendations of the Grow More Food Enquiry Committee. The Grow More Food Enquiry Committee recommended that food production should form the part of a wider plan for all-round village development and that the administrative machinery of the government should be organized and equipped for efficient discharge of its duties for India as a welfare state. The CDP started on 2 October 1952 in 55 Community Development Projects, each, covering three development blocks of 300 villages with the population of about three lakhs. It aimed at four objectives: (i) transformation of the people's outlook, (ii) inculcation of the spirit of self-reliance, (iii) generation of the habit of cooperative action through popular bodies and (iv) these three objectives leading to new enlightenment, strength and cooperation. In view of the people's demand for increase in the number of blocks as well as the stress of the Grow More Food Enquiry Committee on improving the people's socio-economic conditions as a means to succeed in agricultural development, the Government of India introduced National Extension Service (NES) on 2 October 1953 as immediate extension of the CDP was not possible. Originally, CDP aimed to mark an intensive phase of rural development lasting for three years and NES was a permanent multi-functional extension agency in a block. CDP was the method and NES was the agency to cover the entire country within the following 10 years or till 1963. During the First Five-Year Plan (1951-56), various development activities such as animal husbandry, construction of roads and buildings, health programmes, etc.

were launched by dividing the country into development blocks, each, under a Block Development Officer—assisted by a team of extension officers, gram sevaks and gram sevikas. The people's participation was sought through the village panchayats with a view to limit the role of government in advice as well as financial assistance. Expert committees were constituted at the block and district levels (Ram 2001: 36-37).

However, after the initial momentum of 3-4 years, the people's participation declined and CDP grew more as a government programme. This decline ushered in due to (i) lack of consciousness among the rural masses, (ii) too much emphasis on *shramdan* (free-labour), (iii) lack of financial resources, (iv) wrong approach in the training process, (v) absence of proper local leadership, (vi) neglect by political parties and (vii) lack of proper propaganda. Therefore, Planning Commission urged National Development Council (NDC) for investigation of the whole issue of rural development by a team of experts. Early in 1956, NDC appointed a study team headed by the rural specialist, Balwantrai G. Mehta, to identify the problems emergent in the rural community development work and, also, to assess the proposal to set up viable units of local self-governance in the rural areas, thus, initiating democratic decentralization of authority in favour of villages and groupings of villages. In 1957, the team recommended a three-tier system of rural local self-government, indirect elections and a genuine transfer of power to the bodies for planning and implementing developmental activities at the levels of village, block and district. The middle tier, i.e. block level body was conceived as the main agency for rural development with vast administrative and financial powers whereas the district body was given the advisory-cum-supervisory role. After NDC's approval of the report in January 1958, the Parliament enacted the act and the states also passed legislative acts to suit special needs of their respective regions. In August 1958, the scheme was implemented in some areas of Andhra Pradesh on experimental basis but Rajasthan was the foremost to introduce it on 2 October 1959. While implementing it, majority of the states and union territories followed three-tier system and the remaining adopted either two-tier or one-tier (Jammu and Kashmir) or traditional panchayats (Nagaland and Meghalaya). Andhra Pradesh, Gujarat, Karnataka, Madhya Pradesh, Maharashtra, Punjab, Rajasthan, Tamil Nadu, Uttar Pradesh, West Bengal, Arunachal Pradesh and Chandigarh adopted the three-tier system, out of which three models of Panchayati Raj emerged in the country; namely (i) the Rajasthan model with the central role of the Panchayat Samiti at the block level, (ii) the Maharashtra model with the central role of Zila Parishad at the district level and (iii) the Gujarat model in between the Rajasthan and the Maharashtra model (Ram 2001: 37-38).

There has been a gradual shift-away from the community or area development to a sectorial or professional approach. In 1960, the government initiated Intensive Area Development Programme, following its disappointment with the CDP's performance in raising agricultural production. In the same year, a group headed by Jayaprakash Narayan was appointed to study how far and in what manner the CDP and the three-tier panchayat system could promote economic development and welfare of the weaker sections in the village communities. The group recommended proper delegation of powers to the Panchayati Raj (PR) institutions. Thus, the PR has passed through four phases, in all; namely initial ascendancy, growth and consolidation, phase of decline and phase of resuscitation. The initial phase was concerned with the establishment of NES (agency) for bringing technical services to the villages by CDP (method) for rural reconstruction during the First Five-Year Plan and extended over the bulk of the country during the second plan. The growth and consolidation of the PR institutions took place during the Third Five-Year Plan with an emphasis for realization of developmental potential in various sectors. Legislations defining relations of the PR institutions with the state, coming up in most of the states, laid down for administration of CDP through the Panchayat body at intermediary or block level. The zenith of the Panchayati Raj institutions was seen in the middle of 1960s when CDP along with representation of the weaker sections covered the entire country. The mounting food shortage and crop failure in 1966-

67 forced the reshuffling of priorities in CDP itself resulting in an overriding emphasis on agricultural production. The Ministry of Community Development was reduced to a department in 1966-67 and appended to the Ministry of Food and Agriculture. The Community Development Department intensified the efforts to gain support at the grassroots level. By the arrival of 1970s, the zeal for the PR institutions and CDP was on decline. In 1977, the Ashok Mehta Committee opined that the PR was meant for decentralization of power and increasing people's participation as well as for supporting rural development and strengthening planning process at the micro-level. It recommended a two-tier system of Zila Parishad and Gram Panchayat, along with the Mandal Panchayats of a population of 15,000 to 20,000 as the intermediary linkage between the two. Gram Panchayat was the focal point of decentralization of power. In 1980, R.K. Hegde, the then Chief Minister of Karnataka, implemented the recommendations and introduced a real district government with liberal transfer of powers and resources and effective role of the elected PR office bearers at the local level planning. Andhra Pradesh Government headed by N.T. Rama Rao, also, moved in this direction. During 1980s, the village panchayats were used for implementation of land reforms and distributive justice under Tibhaga Movement in West Bengal. In Maharashtra and Gujarat, the PR system has been functioning in a comparatively better manner. In all these states, the PR institutions have provided the weaker sections and intermediary castes the opportunity to rise up on the political ladder. In 1989, the then Prime Minister, Rajiv Gandhi, attempted to strengthen the PR institutions by bringing the Constitution (Sixty-Fourth Amendment) Act which could not be passed in Rajya Sabha. But with the passing of the Constitution (Seventy-Third) Amendment Act in 1992, inserted as the Part IX of the Constitution, the PR system has attained a constitutional status. The Act makes provisions for regular elections conducted by the State Election Commission of the respective state and ensures representation of weaker sections such as Scheduled Castes, Scheduled Tribes, Other Backward Classes and women through reservations of seats in various

bodies. Various states have enacted acts accordingly with variations suitable to their situations (Ram 2001: 39-41).

Before the Constitution (Seventy-Third) Amendment Act 1992, the PR was not very effective. It had limited powers and had to face various structural constraints, limitations and weaknesses. To strengthen it, the Act of 1992 which came into force from 24 April 1993 has enabled the panchayats to play a very important role in development. This Act has identified the areas of jurisdiction of the panchayats, as mentioned in the Eleventh Schedule (Article 243) of the Constitution, which are: (i) Agriculture, including agricultural extension; (ii) Land improvement, implementation of land reforms, land consolidation and soil conservation; (iii) Minor irrigation, water management and watershed development; (iv) Animal husbandry, dairying and poultry; (v) Fisheries; (vi) Social forestry and farm forestry; (vii) Minor forest produce; (viii) Small scale industries, including food processing industries; (ix) Khadi, village and cottage industries; (x) Rural housing; (xi) Drinking water; (xii) Fuel and fodder; (xiii) Road, culverts, bridges, ferries, waterways and other means of communication; (xiv) Rural electrification, including distribution of electricity; (xv) Non-conventional energy sources; (xvi) Poverty alleviation programmes; (xvii) Education, including primary and secondary schools; (xviii) Technical training and vocational education; (xix) Adult and non-formal education; (xx) Libraries; (xxi) Cultural activities; (xxii) Market and fairs; (xxiii) Health and sanitation, including hospitals, Primary Health Centres and dispensaries; (xxiv) Family welfare; (xxv) Women and child development; (xxvi) Social welfare, including welfare of the handicapped and mentally retarded; (xxvii) Welfare of the weaker sections, and in particular of the Scheduled Castes and Scheduled Tribes; (xxviii) Public Distribution Systems; and (xxix) Maintenance of communication assets (Govt. of India 1993).

As the objective of the PR institutions was to ensure active and meaningful participation of people in the programmes of rural development under the Community Development Programme and National Extension Services, they were expected to accelerate the arrested process of change and development and to enable the rural people, including the deprived sections, to participate and contribute in the national rural reconstruction and development. They were also assigned the task of redistribution of land among the poor with a view to transform the agrarian structure. However, these measures could not bring about any desired results till the 1990s. In concrete terms, the political response with regard to major structural changes has not been satisfactory, and indifference has prevailed among political workers at the grassroots. Power capture at national and state levels has been the main objective of political parties. Political parties generally ignore their manifestoes once the elections are over. There is also a policy-gap in the party-politics at the national, state and local levels. Ignorance, poverty, illiteracy and inegalitarian (caste-based) social system have, all, favoured the political intentions of the parties which easily sway the ignorant voters on desired political lines.

The Emergent Power Structure in Rural India

Historically and in contemporary time, caste has continued to be a main determinant of power in the rural Indian setting where dominant caste has been in the centre of power structure. Besides, the rich peasants, drawn from multiple castes, who emerged as a new class as a result of the land reforms and green revolution, have also later become a main factor to determine the rural power structure. The dominant caste and the class of rich peasants cannot be segregated in all regions or situations: in some situations or regions they may be separate realities in contemporary time or historically these categories might have appeared in subsequent order while in other situations or regions the rich peasants might have historically replaced the dominant caste or both of these appear separately. These two categories offer explanations for the emergent rural power structure and therefore depending on these categories social scientists have used two models; viz. dominant caste model and rich peasant model to analyse the dynamics of the rural power structure in the post-Independence India. These models are discussed below.

The Dominant Caste Model

M.N. Srinivas (1987) has given the concept of dominant caste. He considered it essential to use the concept of dominant caste to analyse hierarchy in a multi-caste village and to settle disputes, at the level of village or caste. Besides, the concept is important to study the process of sanskritization of some caste or other group in an area, its relationship with the locally dominant caste and the kind of dominance the dominant caste enjoys. Occasionally, a caste is dominant in a group of neighbouring villages if not over one or more districts and in such cases local dominance is linked with regional dominance. Such linkage also exists when the locally dominant caste is different from the caste which is regionally dominant. Power of dominant caste emanates from various sources. Srinivas finds that a dominant caste preponderates numerically over the other castes and it also wields preponderant economic and political power. A large and powerful caste group can more easily dominate other groups if its population among the local castes is not too less. Besides, he has also added Western education and modern occupations as the sources of dominance. Using the term 'decisive dominance', he further explains that if a caste enjoys dominance in all the above elements, it becomes decisively dominant. However, this kind of dominance is not common as one finds the power attributes dispersed among the castes in the villages and, therefore, a caste may be ritually high but economically and numerically inferior while a populous caste may be economically poor and ritually low. This model implies that there exists a 'status summation', i.e. high status in one aspect of life helps people acquire the same status in other aspects as well. A caste endowed numerical majority of members in a village along with possession most of the land in the village can be in a position to use the coercive power. The land and the members' strength ensure a caste's success to occupy by election of its members into official positions in PR institutions and make it to claim high ritual status. Thus, attributes, symbolic (ritual) and material (land and office) are the crucial sources of power.

However, various experiences from the countryside have offered several variants and modifications of his model. In many cases, it has been observed that only a segment of a dominant caste actually makes major decisions in villages and derives benefits out of the decisions taken. S.C. Dube (1958, 1968) opines that a caste is dominant when power is diffused in the group and is expressed in the interest of the whole group or at least a sizeable part of it. Pronounced inequalities of wealth, prestige and power found among the members of a so-called dominant caste create the dominant individuals of such caste who exploit non-dominant members of that caste itself as well as the members of non-dominant castes. Similarly, T.K. Oommen (1970a: 73-83, 1970b: 226-39) feels that Srinivas could not discern alternative situations wherein "a numerically weak caste owning most of the land and wealth in a village; or a numerically strong caste which is economically deprived and ritually depressed; or a ritually superior caste which is numerically weak and so on. It seems fairly obvious that in such situations a number of castes will share the community power". According to him, there are 'multiple power structures' in a multi-caste village or region having different layers and levels of leadership. He has also given two other useful concepts; namely 'Power pool' and 'Power dispersion'. According to K.L. Sharma (1976: 45-62), in certain domains a few families and individuals dominate whereas in other domains a caste's near-monopoly of power or dispersion of power is found. Thus, both, caste and individuals are dominant but the areas and aspects of dominance of the two differ to a large extent. According to him, the rural power elites are not a homogenous social group; rather they are only aggregation of differentiated dominant individuals which is not characterized by unity, commonality of interests, equality of status and economic position and so on.

Succinctly, the dominant caste model of the rural power structure assumes that (i) there are dominant castes, dominant caste segments and dominant individuals in the village communities; (ii) there exist multiple power structures in a multi-caste village or region; (iii) there is power pools and power dispersion in the village communities and (iv) elites, usually drawn from the dominant caste or castes, are a heterogeneous lot and therefore they participate in the power structure of rural communities differently. Thus, looking to differential extent of dominance, the dominant caste model admits the possibility that many castes or their caste segments, or individuals or other groups have access to power resources and therefore they share some of the power in a village or group of villages. Moreover, dominance is normally exerted through influence rather than power. At the same time, the tolerable amount of social mobility that occurs in the caste hierarchy certainly aids the recruitment of suitable individuals and groups for the emergent economic and social roles created by industrialization. But in any event the inequality of power is viewed as the general condition for stability of the rural society in India.

The Rich Peasant Model

This model assumes that the rural power structure in contemporary India is based on the control of economic and political resources. Since Independence, command of the economic surplus and formal and informal political institutions in the villages has increasingly passed on to rich peasants who have been able to corner the lion's share of the government's development resources at the cost of low status groups and also to exert major power in state and local governments. At the same time, the rich peasants have been able to protect their control of intra-village economic and political process. This type of development is the consequence of dependence on the so-called 'progressive farmers' as agents of community development project for change and development in Indian villages. According to Wertheim (2000: 894-902), to become a progressive farmer, a peasant has to fulfill certain pre-conditions such as (i) his household possesses at least two acres of land for irrigation and eight acres of land for dry farming, and if irrigation is not possible in any area he should have 16 acres of land for dry farming; (ii) he should have at least one pair of good bullocks; (iii) he should have at least one cow preferably of good Gir breed or of local breed or he should arrange to have it at the earliest, in case he has none; (iv) he should have planted at least five trees on his farm or should have given an assurance of doing so at the earliest; (v) he should have dug at least two systematic compost pits either on his *wadi* of field, or he should give an assurance of doing so at the earliest; (vi) he should have taken all possible measures to prevent erosion of his land; (vii) he should have adopted improved agricultural practice by taking advantage of agricultural research and (viii) he must be a member of any one of the cooperative societies or should enrol himself as such within a year of having been registered as a progressive farmer. These progressive farmers were accorded preferential treatment in the services provided by the government and they were given improved agricultural practices, assuming that by such a scheme the agriculturists would have greater faith and confidence in the results obtained in fields of their fellow-cultivators which they would readily adopt. A smaller group of individuals was expected to function as local agents of change. The persons occupying the existing positions of leadership in the village as well as the traditional leaders were to be used as role-models for dissemination of innovations. The underlying assumption in this approach was that if leaders could first be converted into those who subscribe to the ideology of change, the task of converting the rest of the community into pro-change villagers would be greatly facilitated. Implicit in this assumption was the belief that people would normally look up to this group for guidance and would automatically start emulating their example, once the leaders adopted the new practices. It was also hoped that by making them a link between the officials and the people some of the difficulties in communication would be appreciably reduced. However, these people not only failed to attract people towards development but also they manipulated the available resources and the benefits from the government in their own favour. The rich peasants, besides a section from the descendants of the traditional feudal lords, are mostly the creation of Zamindari abolition, land reforms, democratization and green revolution and they own land as a rule. They perform some manual work in major farm operations whereas generally they hire the labour. According to D.N. Dhanagare (1983), landlords and rich landowners (including non-cultivating urban moneylenders/ owners) belonged to the upper castes such as Brahmin, Thakur, or Bania in Northern India; the Kammas, Reddis and Raos in Andhra; the Vokkaligas and Lingayats in Mysore; the Patidars in the Gujarat region and the Kunbi, Marathas and Deshmukhs in Maharashtra. At the village level, these landowning classes often formed only a small nucleus.

Thus, according to these two models, a single power-resource is not sufficient. A group with power in a village must control some supra-village power resource. Control of various power resources in a village places a minority ahead of others in possession of at least most resources. In the rich peasant model, this minority controls most of the land, credit, agricultural inputs and products whereas in the dominant caste model it controls most of the economic resources, prestige and government positions. Now, the following main features of the emergent power structure in rural India may be drawn: (i) Directly or indirectly, the upper castes have a dominant role in rural power structure. (ii) Power has shifted from crude caste structure to more differentiated structures such as panchayats and political parties. However, there remains the important role of caste. (iii) Due to the process of democratization, the lower castes have become more organized and their empowerment to exert control over rural power structure is clearly visible. (iv) Rural leadership of limited caste groups is being replaced by other caste groups. Caste remains an inseparable part of rural power structure. (v) Quite often informal leaders influence the decisions at the village level. The most important feature of this kind of leadership is that they are men who can get things done, despite the contrary wishes of other less powerful people.

Conclusion

The traditional power structure, consisted of the Zamindari system, the village panchayats and the caste panchayats, has undergone democratization in the post-Independence period. Through democratization new democratic institutions have been introduced at multiple levels of governance. The set of democratic institutions of rural local self-government operating at village, block and district levels is called Panchayati Raj. It is decentralization of power in rural India. In the process of democratization of political institutions, decentralization of power and rural development there emerged dominant castes and individuals as well as rich peasants, operating power in the rural India. As a result, multiple power structures of castes, classes, caste-segments and elites have emerged. However, many of the traditional attributes are continuing in the changed context as well.

REFERENCES

Dhanagare, D.N. (1983). 'The model of agrarian classes in India'. In *Peasant Movements in India, 1920-50*. Delhi: Oxford University Press.

Dahl, Robert A. (1961). *Who Governs? Democracy and Power in an Americancity.* New Haven: Yale University Press.

Dube, S.C. (1958). *India's Changing Villages.* London: Routledge and Kegan Paul.

Dube, S.C. (1968). 'Caste dominance and factionalism'. *Contributions* to *Indian Sociology (n.s.),* Vol. II.

Gouldner, Alvin. (1970). *The Coming Crisis of Western Sociology.* New York: Basic Books Publisher.

Government of India (1993). 'The Constitution (Seventy Third Amendment) Act, 1993'. *The Gazette of India.* New Delhi: Ministry of Law, Justice and Company Affairs.

Grover, B.L. and S. Grover (1984). *A New Look on Modern Indian History.* New Delhi: S Chand and Company Ltd., pp. 101-04.

Oommen, T.K. (1970a). 'The concept of dominant caste: Some queries'. *Contributions* to *Indian Sociology (n.s.),* Vol. IV, pp. 73-83.

Oommen, T.K. (1970b). 'Rural community power structure in India'. *Social Forces,* XXXXIX (2): 226-39.

Ram, G. (2001). *Politics, Development and Modernization in Tribal India*. Delhi: Manak.

Sharma, K.L. (1976). 'Power elite in rural India: Some questions and clarifications'. *Sociological Bulletin,* XXV (1): 45-62.

Srinivas, M.N. (1987). 'The dominant caste in Rampura'. In *The Dominant Caste and Other Essays* (ed.). Delhi: Oxford University Press.

Weber, Max. (1947). *The Theory of Social and Economic Organization.* Glencoe: Free Press, p. 152.

Wertheim, W.F. (2000). 'Betting on the strong'. In A.R. Desai (ed.), *Rural Sociology in India.* Bombay: Popular Prakashan, pp. 894-902.

5

Extension and Corporate Social Responsibility: New Paradigms and Linkages for Community Development

Heena K. Bijli

ABSTRACT

India's economy is on a positive growth trajectory, but the human development indicators continue to present a grim picture and have rather regressed on several fronts. This is posing a challenge to the developmental efforts of a country where one-third of the world's poor resides. The significant contribution in this regard, towards community development through Extension, a science that brings about behavioural changes in people for enhancement of their living standards, cannot be ignored as it dates back to the time when community development programmes were initiated in India in 1952, and are still ongoing. Today, the government, while striving to meet the complexities of the business world and in achieving growth with equity and inclusiveness, is looking at Corporate Social Responsibility (CSR) as a hope in enabling efforts towards human development. The paper talks about the role of CSR, a concept which is again not new to India, and in contemporary times is not just about compliance of human right standards, labour and social sector arrangements, but also about efforts to fight against poverty, hunger, climate change, infant/maternal mortality, promotion of women's empowerment and sustainable management of resources. The paper benchmarks human growth potential, though synergistic linkages and new approaches between CSR and Extension. Many CSR projects in India already prove that they would not have seen the expected outcome, had it not been for suitable extension approaches—through collaborations, private efforts and partnerships. Recently, with the passage of the Companies Act (2013), CSR activities will receive a boost by promoting best practices. The paper contextualizes CSR strategies that can be leveraged through emerging paradigms and practices of Extension. These are achievable by fostering corporate linkages with R&D and S&T institutes, voluntary organizations, and in promoting employee volunteerism and Corporate Social Entrepreneurship for encouraging more robust forms of corporate citizenship. Integrated studies in Extension Education and Corporate Citizenship will emphasize the need for socially responsible behaviour. Building and strengthening suitable platforms to bring the desired social impact are possible, if Extension and CSR are given a serious thought.

Introduction

India is emerging into a robust economy and is gearing up to become the third largest economy in terms of GDP in the next two decades. As a country it is home to almost a sixth of the global population and the buzzword for development today is 'Inclusive Growth'. Although the economy is on a strong positive growth trajectory, we cannot achieve its targets of sustained and inclusive growth until we ensure that all challenges are addressed related to food, education, health, nutrition, gender disparities, and poverty with an attempt to reach the marginalised particularly in the rural areas, tribal areas, and the remotest parts of the country.

A look at some human development indicators reveals that the life expectancy at birth (in years) is at 65.4, the Maternal Mortality Ratio has come down to 230/1,00,000 live births and the under five mortality has come down to 66/1,000 live births since 1980. The Census of India 2011 further reveals that 68.2 per cent of our population lives in rural India. Over 93 per cent of India's labour force is employed in the informal sector, where wages are low and work conditions onerous.

Among India's youth, only 2 per cent have any kind of formal technical training making gainful employment difficult. Women workers make up only 15 per cent of the labour force, a pointer to the immense waste of productive capacities. The largest number and the largest proportion of marginalised children in the world live in India. Of the nearly 400 million children that enrol in primary school, about half drop out by class 8 and just 17 per cent study after class 12. Among tribals and dalits, dropout rates are even higher (*The Times of India*, 2012). Though India has seen three decades of economic growth, this has not been accompanied with societal transformation. Over and above, India has regressed on certain fronts like life expectancy, female literacy, improved sanitation, maternal mortality rate (MMR), infant mortality, child immunisation and mean years of schooling.

India has lagged in improving its Global Hunger Index (GHI) score despite strong economic growth, according to the 2012 Global Hunger Index report released for the seventh year by the International Food Policy Research Institute (IFPRI), Welt Hunger Hilfe, and Concern Worldwide. The report suggests that Bangladesh has overtaken India on a range of social indicators, including how fast it has reduced child mortality. In India, 43.5 per cent of children under five are underweight, which accounts for almost two-thirds of the country's alarmingly high GHI score (Parsai, 2012).

Being predominantly a rural nation, with 70 per cent population residing in rural areas, and a large agrarian community, poverty is still very widespread in India, where one-third of the world's poor resides. There are variations in natural resources endowments, physical and climatic conditions. There are also variations in demographic factors like household size, degree of urbanisation and cultural factors. But the ratio of rural to urban poverty has increased. Economic development fetches significant dividends in the form of changes in the living standards and social life of a population, for the long run. India is striving to keep to the current trends of infrastructure development. Improving the quality of life is an enormous, challenging task in meeting the basic needs of the society by enhancing the quality of life of people. This involves an innovative and holistic approach towards development by providing facilities like clean drinking water and sanitation, inclusive education, irrigation facilities, rural credit institutions like rural banks, rural housing, public health services, microfinance and income generation, facilities for women's empowerment, watershed management, communications services, electrical grids, rural transport and roads, environmental protection and management, farm inputs supply and management, and social and farm forestry.

The government is striving to meet the complexities of today's business world and the challenges of a global society which are also affected by factors like income, prices and the extent of monetisation. This largely means investing in and enriching its communities (Bijli, 2012).

Extension and Community Development Programmes in India

Extension is a subject that helps to bridge to the gap between ignorance and sustainable development. Extension is an education (formal as well as informal) aimed at assisting people (rural as well as urban) to bring about continuous improvement in their physical, economic and social well-being through their individual and cooperative effort. It makes available to the client system scientific and other factual information, training and guidance in application of such information to the solution of their problems (Dahama, 1997).

Scientifically speaking, extension is a two-way process where the problems of the client system (farmers, youth, women, etc.) are brought by the change agents (extension workers, subject matter specialists of the R&D departments and educational institutes) for finding solution in these institutes and taking back the results in the acceptable form to the client system. Popular approaches in extension are: technology transfer approach, participatory approach, empowerment approach and lab to land approach, to name a few. Above all, extension education equips trainers with those skills that bring about the relevant behavioural changes in people, so that they enjoy their new learning experience that is participatory.

The concept of extension is not new. It became visible in India during the early efforts of rural reconstruction through the Gurgaon Attempt (1920), Sevagram Attempt (1920), Shriniketan Attempt (1921), Martandum Attempt (1921), Etawah Attempt (1948). Besides these attempts, some projects were also undertaken at Baroda, Madras, Nilokheri and Faridabad. The Grow More Food Enquiry Committee recommendations triggered the start of 55 community projects across the country in 1952. These initiatives saw extension education evolve as a lifelong process of learning.

The Community Development Programme (1952) marked a beginning in the area of rural development and a network of National Extension Services was established in the villages to create awareness among rural communities regarding their potential and means of development. Several programmes were introduced in successive Five-Year Plans for agricultural development, employment generation, promoting rural, cottage and artisan-based industries, poverty alleviation, special area development and meeting basic/minimum needs towards rural development during pre-reforms period. Earlier extension activities were carried out with the help of farmers' associations, service cooperatives, panchayats, schools, youth clubs, mahila mandals, District Rural Development Agencies, and other rural social groups through community organizations (Bijli and Tewari, 2011).

Programmes for community development today aim to achieve not just growth, but equity, by widening reach through 'inclusiveness'. The launch of Bharat Nirman by the Government of India in 2005, for upgradation of rural infrastructure which covers six components, namely roads, telephone connectivity, irrigation, water supply, housing and electrification, which later got reinforced by Pradhan Mantri Gram Sadak Yojana, to improve accessibility and mobility of rural communities was a significant step towards bringing about inclusive growth. Other significant programmes like the Rajiv Gandhi Rural Drinking Water Mission, the National Rural Drinking Water Quality Monitoring and Surveillance of Drinking Water Sources, Rural Telephony, Pradhan Mantri Adarsh Gram Yojana, Indira Awas Yojana, the Mid-day Meal Scheme, Welfare of Minorities, the Sarva Shiksha Abhiyan, National Food Security Mission and the recently launched Food Security Bill, the National Old Age Pension Scheme, Total Sanitation Campaign, National Rural Livelihood Mission, the National Rural Health Mission, Janani Suraksha Yojana, Integrated Pest Management, ICTs as tools for rural empowerment through the Universal Services Obligation Fund, the Jawaharlal Nehru National Urban Renewal Mission, and the Mahatma Gandhi Rural Employment Guarantee Act that treats employment as a right and is intended to be demand-driven, have been implemented with an attempt to ensure that developmental efforts are successful if made mandatory, and participatory.

Being a developing nation, it can be argued that the role of government, merely, in bringing about development is not enough. To put in place the agenda for development, the government is looking for external support. In the contemporary era of globalization, one such area is Corporate Social Responsibility (CSR). The philosophy of CSR indicates that it is not just public policies, but also the corporates that are responsible for social upliftment.

Corporate Social Responsibility: The Context

CSR as a concept has been linked, traditionally speaking, to philanthropy and community development. In Western societies, CSR was seen as charity rising out of philanthropy. For several decades now, CSR has been a topic of interest among academia and business practitioners alike.

The genesis of CSR sees itself in connotations underlying the ethics of businessmen and corporations, mostly highlighting interest in activities on social welfare. Gary Erickson, a cyclist, a world traveller, and a high-achieving US entrepreneur, reminds organizations that operate solely on profit motive: "Business has a purpose beyond money. We look for meaning in our lives. Business has a meaning too. If it has any meaning, it is public welfare." These words of Erickson foreshadow how social responsibility evolved into the concept of CSR. William J. Bowen in 1953, first mentioned Corporate Social Responsibility in the publication *Social Responsibilities of the Businessman.* In 1990s, the concept of CSR became popularised by a German Betapharm, a generic pharmaceutical company decided to implement CSR. The company adopted CSR as an expression of the company's values and as a part of its corporate strategies, when in 1997 a halt in sales growth led the company to the realization that in the generic drugs market, companies could not differentiate on price or quality. This gave the company a premise to adopt CSR. Betapharm used strategic and social commitment for families with chronically ill children, to its strategic advantage. A consultative paper titled "Promoting a European Framework for Corporate Social Responsibility" was launched by the European Commission in July 2001. This paper aimed to launch a debate on how the European Union could promote CSR at both the European and international levels.

The concept and meaning of CSR differs in terms of its application. CSR cannot only refer to the compliance of human right standards, labour and social security arrangements, but also to the fight against poverty, hunger, climate change, infant and maternal mortality, sustainable management of natural resources, consumer protection and women's empowerment. The larger goals of social value and impact are reflected through an organization's CSR activities. For example, empowerment through education and skill development are thrust areas when it comes to CSR initiatives focusing on the underprivileged youth. Many leading corporate organizations today have made CSR an integral part of the corporate strategy. The CSR teams in companies devise specific policies, strategies and goals for their CSR programmes and set aside budgets to support them. These programmes, in many cases, are based on a clearly defined social philosophy or are closely aligned with the companies' business expertise.

The core principles of CSR are:

1. Each corporate body must operate as a socially responsible market player; and
2. Each entity should take up programmes that address sustainable social welfare and preserve the public and social interest (Muslim, 2012).

The terms—Fundraising, Donations, Corporate Sponsorship, and Philanthropic activities—are associated with Corporate Social Responsibility (CSR). While there is no unanimity direct control, aimed at the simultaneous creation on the definition of CSR, the triple bottomline approach suggesting that business should balance their economic, social and environmental responsibilities (Elkington, 2001), is at the centre of current CSR conceptualisations and activities.

Companies worldwide are facing a combination of push and pull factors that propel them towards more robust forms of CSR. While the social dimension has been present in the world of private business, these tectonic movements are reshaping the landscape and raising the bar of what is expected of businesses in the social realm (Austin et al., 2006).

In India, CSR is seen in the context of community development. A small number of companies in India practice CSR, though India has been rated among the top ten Asian countries that is paying increasing importance to CSR. The Tata and Infosys, taken CSR icons in India, have since long taken the lead in this endeavour. These companies have been deeply involved with social development initiatives in the communities surrounding their facilities. Jamshedpur, one of the prominent cities in the north-eastern state of Jharkhand in India, is also known as Tata Nagar and stands out at a beacon for other companies to follow. Jamshedpur was carved out from the jungle a century ago. TATA's CSR activities in Jamshedpur include the provision of full health and education expenses for all employees and the management of schools and hospitals. Today, Bharati Enterprises, Indian Oil Corporation, ITC Welcome Group, Life Insurance Corporation of India and many other corporate organizations are making notable contributions in CSR. Corporate giants such as the Tata and Birla group companies which have led the way in making corporate social responsibility an intrinsic part of their business plans. India was ranked fourth in the list, according to social enterprise CSR Asia's Asian Sustainability Ranking (ASR) in 2009.

However, most of the Indian enterprises are not engaged in development of education, environment conservation and poverty alleviation. CSR activities lack an understanding about the concepts, philosophy, objectives and method of working with rural people. In the informal sector of economy which contributes to nearly half of the Gross National Product, the application of CSR is rare. This is despite the fact that the informal sector employs 93 per cent of the workforce. Although corporate India is involved in CSR activities, the Central Government is working on a framework for quantifying the CSR initiatives of companies to promote them further. Besides the private sector, the government is also ensuring that the public sector companies participate actively in CSR initiatives (Berad, 2011). The Department of Public Enterprises (DPE) has prepared guidelines for central public sector enterprises to take up important social responsibility projects that are funded by a certain percentage of the company's profits.

There is a dearth of research and motivation in CSR. Few studies suggest that CSR activities lack of community participation; common problems in leveraging CSR by companies is due to insufficient availability of well-organized NGOs who could partner with their CSR activities. There is lack of visibility factor of successful CSR initiatives and lack of employee volunteerism.

The CSR strategies of many companies vary and show major deficiencies. There is a dearth of international guidelines which could be a major reason for these. There are still complaints about multinational companies wasting the environment and NGOs still denouncing human rights abuses in companies. As per some critics, CSR programmes are undertaken by multinational companies to distract the public from ethical questions posed by their core operations. Questions have been raised on the social responsibility programmes and policies of even reputed multinational companies.

Today, there is reason to hope. The Indian Parliament on August 8, 2013, passed the much-awaited Companies Bill which requires companies that meet certain criteria, to spend at least two per cent of the average profits in the last three years towards CSR activities. The Companies Bill would replace the nearly 50-year-old Companies Act. The Bill aims to protect the interest of employees and small investors with the government (PTI, 2013).

CSR and Extension: New Approaches and Synergistic Linkages

The passage of the Companies Bill will give development practitioners a hope towards community development, through CSR activities. It is envisaged that this Bill will give a boost to CSR projects. CSR is reflected in the voluntary community work that the private sector puts in. Business and social commitments are aligned in such a manner that they are mutually reinforcing, and neither is sustainable without the other. With the help of CSR, the private sector can extend support to the NGO sector. In this way, the NGO sector plays a complementary role in the vision and mission of business enterprise. The role of extension, though invisible, is a significant element here.

Verma (2007) has suggested a way of operationalizing CSR through Extension Management. According to him, interventions like these are Extension Services in the realms of Corporate Social Responsibility. This means that the basic tenets of Extension Education are inherent in the CSR concept. In order to operationalize CSR, there can be several alternative organizational systems: (1) Well-structured own foundation, (2) formulation of a trust, (3) separate CSR departments within the organization, (4) building public-private partnership, and (5) sharing CSR efforts and initiatives for a compendium. Although these are workable propositions, these entities often work in isolation without creating a synergy. Hence, there is a need to understand CSR altogether in different frame of reference. The Single Window Area Development (SWAD) Approach can discharge CSR in a befitting manner under the command of a separate Department of Extension Education Services within the structural cadres of the corporate houses. Single Window Area Development Centre (SWAD-Centre) is born out of this approach. The SWAD-Centre is a four-walled boundary building located over one acre of land at a central place around which a cluster of five villages is formed for the delivery of extension interventions. Each SWAD-Centre is equipped with appropriate infrastructures, logistics, manpower, and building blocks. Each SWAD-Centre approximately requires a finance of INR two crores (Verma, 2007). Since the CSR strategies for small business houses is yet to gain momentum, Verma proposes that these business houses can pool up their resources, each one adopting one village in a cluster of five villages. The SWAD-Centre model is relevant to all the developing countries where people live in village communities in densely populated rural areas. In order to encourage the corporate houses to discharge their CSR with commitment, the respective government should give them the rebate in corporate taxes for the entire amount spent in SWAD-Centre.

Development initiatives have been short-lived for decades as they would run out of steam a couple of years after implementation. It is suggested that in order to sustain the development process, every corporate house can establish a SWAD-Centre that can be guided by extension departments at the State and national level, with appropriate linkages with R&D institutes.

Collaboration in Extension Work: Need for New Approaches

Extension educational philosophy is based on the hypothesis that community people are intelligent, are receptive to new information and at the same time have a keen desire to utilize this information for individual and social development. The challenge now is to deal with current concerns.

Collaboration is a tradition of extension work. Application of new knowledge calls for goods and services support. Therefore, extension education while imparting education to target people looks forward to supportive services to take part in the behavioural change process so that people enjoy their new learning experience. Collaborative work provides for experiential learning. It creates a field for one agency to learn the capacity of the other agency and what to do to build up the capacity further for attaining the agreed upon goal in the most befitting manner. The Collaborative Agricultural Extension Programme implemented since 1990 by the Assam Agricultural University (AAU) and the TATA Tea Company is an excellent example. Tea companies that joined the venture were TATA Tea Company and a few companies under Assam Branch of Indian Tea Association (ABITA). Under this programme, AAU provided technical inputs and the tea company supplied the material inputs in order to put the technical inputs into practice by farmers. The collaborative programme was carried out in the light of the "Lab to Land" guidelines where scientists of AAU and the tea company's management cadre made direct contact with the farmers and intervened in farm operations for enhancing farm productivity and income of the farmers (Sarmah, 2001).

Alliance between public extension and research services and private organizations or farmers' associations enhance the prospects of technical effectiveness, cost sharing and cost recovery, thereby increasing the opportunities for collective bargaining, and better impact of extension per unit of expenditure (Soam, 2001).

In today's times, an extension system with business and professional approach is a must. In recent years, there has been an increase in the gross capital formation in agriculture as a proportion of agricultural GDP which has gone up from 14.1 per cent in 2004-05 to 21.3 per cent in 2008-09. Despite these achievements, Indian agriculture continues to face serious challenges because of its ever increasing population, limited land and water availability, and degradation of natural resources. Expertise related to cutting edge technologies, organizational development, market development, legal issues related to farmer's rights, ICT, etc. are very important. The livestock and fisheries sector play an important role in generating income and employment for marginal farmers and landless labourers in meeting nutritional and livelihood security. A suitable example is where a viable partnership among NDRI (National Dairy Research Institute), NDDB (National Dairy Development Board), dairy co-operatives and the state Department of Animal Husbandry in the field of dairying can potentially lead to a successful technology generation, support, transfer and application for dairy development (Venkatasubramanian, 2013).

Privatization of Extension

When the policymakers are thinking of promoting, regulating and trying new innovations in "private extension", Indian context needs to be adequately stressed. A private extension provider is an individual or organization other than government who is providing single service or integrated services to the farmers. These can be scientists, para-technologists, ICT providers, activists, and organizations specializing in R&D, and S&T. Extension techniques have been administered since several years to initiate formation of cooperatives. The most popular example that can be cited here is that of Amul at Anand, the pattern of co-operative dairying which was replicated all across India. Amul, an outcome of the efforts done by Kaira District Co-operative Milk Producers' Union, has demonstrated that farmers' cooperatives can employ professionals, make use of modern technology, and harness market forces to serve their ends without disturbing the agro-system. In co-operative dairying, there is a greater chance of rural development leading to the empowerment of the poor and disadvantaged (Shekara, 2001). Such a successful initiative by the National Dairy Development Board, that was termed the "Operation Flood" dates back to its start in 1970 and went on to carve out the "White Revolution" in India. Today, India has emerged as the largest milk producer in the world and in 2011, Amul paid its farmers approximately INR 380 for every kilogram of fat. The success of Operation Flood has been linking up of rural producers, tribal milkmen, with the urban consumers (Bhattacharya, 2013). Indian corporations can play a significant role in drawing such examples like creating co-operations and drawing inspiration from change agents of the caliber of Varghese Kurien, Chairman of NDDB during Operation Flood, to carry forth their CSR mission.

CSR Practices: A Glimpse

The dominant ideology of CSR is that all corporates build and nurture a social conscience. Some of the biggest names in the industry have now enlisted the challenge of rural transformation prominently in their CSR initiatives focusing on the underprivileged youth. Few of the recent examples can be cited here. Through their 254 schools in rural India, Bharti Foundation, the philanthropic arm of Bharti Enterprises, provides employment to more than 1500 village youth (59 per cent females) and provides them with teaching opportunities. Presently, Bharti Foundation is transforming the lives of 38000 children, of which 49 per cent are girls and 75 per cent belong to SC/ST/OBC category. Ambuja Cement Foundation (ACF) works with rural communities on three broad focus areas—water resource management, livelihood generation for people from the community and social development. Since most of their plants are in rural India, all ACF initiatives include projects and schemes for promoting economic development for communities in and around the manufacturing locations (Shreeram, 2013).

The Hindustan Latex Family Planning Promotion Trust (HLFPPT), set up in 1992, is supporting implementation of the Reproductive and Child Health Programme and HIV prevention and care programmes across 11 States in India. An initiative of public sector HLL Lifecare Ltd., this trust will distribute 1.2 billion pieces of condoms in six States—Uttar Pradesh, Madhya Pradesh, Bihar, Delhi, Andhra Pradesh and Odisha, during the next three years. This distribution is aimed to promote reproductive health and maternal health in the country, under its social marketing initiatives (Dhar, 2013). As accessibility to contraception is a major impediment to sexual and reproductive health, this project is aimed to increase accessibility with the result that access to condom has come down from 30 minutes to 19 minutes. It has established partnership with the Union Ministry of Health and Family Welfare (MOHFW), the governments of Andhra Pradesh, Bihar, Jharkhand, Kerala, Madhya Pradesh, Maharashtra, Odisha, Rajasthan, Uttarakhand, Uttar Pradesh and North-Eastern states for implementing programmes that reach millions of women and families. Besides, HLFPPT programmes are supported by its partners such as Bill and Melinda Gates Foundation, Department for International Development, National AIDS Control Organization, Family Health International 360, UNICEF, CAIRN Energy, Deloitte Consulting, Merck for Mothers, Agency for International Development, OXFAM, and the Norway-India Partnership Initiative.

Another good example of partnership, supported by the participatory model of extension, is the watershed project in the Neduwa-Baraicha village in Uttar Pradesh's Banda district that was supported by Sir Dorabji Tata Trust and implemented by a voluntary organization ABSSS. As in many other villages across the country, Dalit and other weaker section households in this village had received land under the land distribution programme of the government, but the land was highly uneven, prone to soil erosion, lacked rainwater retention capacity and had no irrigation facility. The watershed project was thereby initiated and helped implementation of agriculture in the following four ways: (i) firstly land levelling was taken up, mainly through manual labour but sometimes by machines, (ii) land bunding was then done on the fields of land allottees and other farmers to benefit soil and water conservation, (iii) thirdly, lift irrigation facilities were provided by making arrangements to lift water at five points from a nearby river and *nullah*, and (iv) lastly, and most importantly, the mobilisation of beneficiaries in a watershed committee to properly implement the project helped to increase local participation. The overall impact of these steps was that many villagers who were earlier forced to migrate for sheer survival could now feed their families round the year on the food grown on their fields while also meeting their cash needs. An expansion of the project is a further hope for the villagers so that the village emerges as a model for development (Dogra, 2012).

The CSR projects mentioned above and many similar ones would not have seen the desired outcome without application of extension approaches. Besides this, Public-Private Partnerships (PPPs) have a major role to play in investments, and efficiencies in management and utilisation of resources. PPPs are critical for sustained economic growth and are responsible for equitable development in the country as they impact all strata of the society.

Fostering Women's Empowerment

The need for women's empowerment, being seen as the key aspect of all social development programmes, has seen the administering of policies at the national, state and local (panchayat) levels in the areas of education, employment, political participation, entrepreneurship, microfinance, health and gender-based violence.

Women are responsible for 60 to 80 per cent of the food production in most of the developing countries. Agriculture, the single largest production endeavour in India employs 4/5th of all economically active women in the country and 48 per cent of India's self-employed farmers are women. Women constitute 48.5 per cent of the total population but constitute 70 per cent of the labour force in animal husbandry. These are important stakeholders in farming activities in India constituting 90 per cent of the total marginal workers in India (Kumar, 2013). But till date, gaps exist between policy implementation and actual practice at the community level.

Rural India is witnessing a process which could be described as 'Feminization of Agriculture'. Studies reveal that the working hours of agricultural women a day last for 15 hours whereas her male counterparts work for 7 to 8 hours. In the Indian Himalayas, a pair of bullocks works for 1064 hours, a man 1212 hours and a woman for 3485 hours in a year on a one hectare farm, a figure that illustrates women's significant contribution to agricultural production. In villages, women are overburdened with the three-fold responsibility of home, agriculture and livestock management (Kumar, 2013). Despite their contribution to economy, women's state of malnourishment is high as compared to men. In rural communities, women are found to eat less food as compared to men, particularly at the time of food scarcity such as just before the harvest, or when the workload increases without a corresponding increase in food. The problems of gender inequality are so prominent that they are evident in women's lack of access to resource entitlements, land, credit inputs, and technology and extension services. In the rural development sector, a significant gender issue that needs attention is—gender, extension and research.

Drudgery reduction by introducing capacity building programmes, appropriate tools and technologies, agricultural credits and microfinance can elevate women to the mainstream of development. Globalization has increased opportunities for entrepreneurship and off-farm activities, SHGs, wage employment in non-agricultural sectors and opportunities for participation in grassroots democracy, local political life and networking through ICTs. Studies show that higher levels of gender equality correlate possibility with higher levels of per capita gross national product (Hazra, 2013). Agriculture-related input and other services should be made easily accessible to women farmers or at least a certain percentage of the total advances of the banks under agriculture sector should be exclusively reserved for women farmers.

Some of the significant programmes that aim at the socio-economic empowerment of women and child development in India are the Reproductive and Child Health programme (I and II) and the Integrated Child Development Services of the National Rural Health Mission, the Rajiv Gandhi Scheme for Empowerment of Adolescent Girls (RGSEAG), Women Dairy Development Scheme, the Mahatma Gandhi Rural Employee Guarantee Scheme, the Indira Gandhi Matritva Sahyog Yojana (IGMSY), Rashtriya Mahila Kosh (RMK), the Criminal Law (Amendment) Act 2013, Self-Help Groups for financial inclusion through microfinance, assisted by agencies like Ministry of Rural Development, National Bank for Agriculture and Rural Development and Rashtriya Mahila Kosh (RMK), etc., having nearly 79 per cent of total groups run by women, and the National Mission for Empowerment of Women (NMEW) which has taken up initiatives to address the issue of the declining sex ratio of 914/1000 males, as per Census 2011. Besides the role of groups like Mahila Mandals, it was the NGOs such as the Self-Employed Women's Association (SEWA) and the Working Women's Forum (WWF) that gave a boost to the formation of the SHG women's collective, linked them to credit and gave recognition to the fact that women are bankable and are not defaulters of credit repayment. A cadre of women extension agents should be created to provide timely information to the women farmers regarding agriculture and entrepreneurship. Women empowerment has to be made an integral component of CSR activities.

The Department of Science and Technology has done several projects to leverage the potential of women learners through participatory approaches. Agarwal (2003) talks about one of the successful extension endeavours in leveraging technology package, that was taken up by the Science and Society Division under DST, who launched a coordinated programme at the village-level on low cost processing, preservation and marketing of horticultural produce, for a period of four years. The project was initiated through the systems' approach, in which the trained women who became para-technologists got involved in imparting training and technical know-how to other women for horticultural products, which got requisite FPO licence. Training, an essential element of the programme was designed to be imparted at two levels: at institutional level by resource agency (Indian Agricultural Research Institute—IARI, New Delhi) to the core women group and at field level by trained women core group to network beneficiaries.

The participating field groups were mostly NGOs; for example, Centre for Social Work and Research in Agartala was the field group for Gokulnagar gaon Panchayat in West Tripura District. The States of West Bengal, Odisha, Uttarakhand, Himachal Pradesh and Uttar Pradesh were the other states that were covered by the project. Technological back up/training from IARI, New Delhi, was provided and the success of this programme lay in the "bottom-up approach" and linkages with DST, S&T-based field groups, S&T Institutions and above all the target group (women). From planning to implementation stage, women were involved as partners, carriers and change agents in technology development and transfer, by way of decentralized functioning. Following this successful attempt, a U.N. agency, Asia Pacific Centre for Transfer of Technology, Delhi, took the initiative in collaboration with DST to replicate this technology model for large-scale replication in North Eastern States of India.

Agarwal thus suggests that for effective transfer of technology, various interrelated components of the technology, namely "hardware" (materials such as crop variety), "software" (technical know-how, information), "humanware" (human ability), "orgaware" (organizational and management aspects) and the final products (including marketing) are rendered accessible to people as consumers/end users. This will enable easy adaptability and replicability.

Leveraging the Technology Model and Establishing Suitable Linkages

A systems approach for development that is participatory should have the appropriate coordination, technological back-up and support.

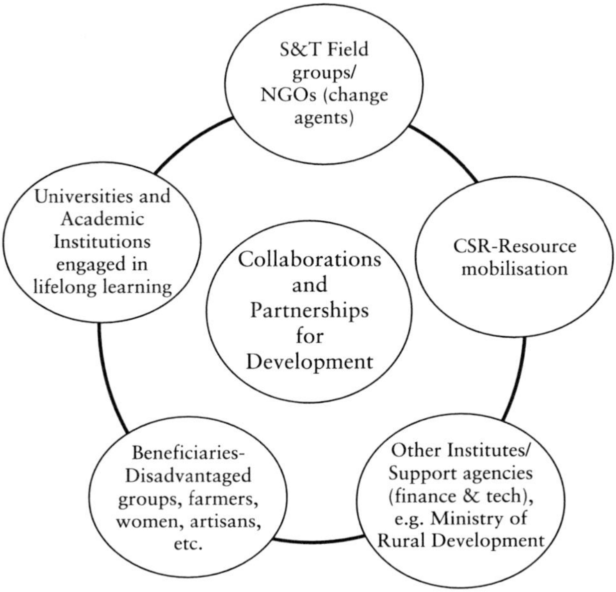

Fig. 1: Linkages and Partnerships for Development

Success of such programmes as described above is due to strong institutional linkages with an extension machinery to disseminate the proven technological package at the grassroots for women's empowerment and social transformation (Fig. 1). A company's social commitment is seen through its strategies and implementing mechanisms to generate sustainable livelihoods and community development. The problem-solving approach at grassroots level involves the following steps (Bijli, 2012):

- Need assessment;
- Identification of technology source (S&T institutions);
- Maximum utilization of local resources for skills and markets;
- Participatory technology modulation/developments which are environmentally compatible and socio-economically sustainable;
- Self-sustaining S&T base in rural areas;
- Setting up of a viable S&T-based micro-enterprise and linking them with national S&T institutions/labs for adopting R&D based on field generated specifications;
- Qualitative shift in production/distribution from household models to collective, networked "industrial" forms for higher productivity, incomes, etc.; and
- Constant interaction between the innovator, the producer and deliverer or technology transfer group for technology assessment and further refinement.

While linking CSR with extension, efforts need to be made in technology targeting, technology production, technology integration, technology dissemination and technology delivery. The extension interventions for technology should be based on:

1. Indigenous knowledge and skills.
2. Availability of human resources for leverage.
3. Optimal use of resources.
4. Techno-economic viability.
5. Ability and aptitude to adapt R&D inputs.
6. Social acceptability.

Science and technology inputs should see the following outcomes:

1. Value addition and quality control.
2. Sustained financial outreach (in microfinance by increasing access to microcredit loan) to potential beneficiaries, for use of technology in microenterprises, through regulated funding.
3. Increased quality, shelf life of products, better hygiene (for those involved in farm products) and little or no nutrient loss.
4. Co-operative-based enterprise development.
5. Capability for organizing production and marketing of processed products.
6. Social and financial inclusion.

For the vast majority of population living in far flung rural and tribal areas, companies having links with organizations having scientific and technological capabilities (R&D and S&T institutions), voluntary organizations, etc. will provide the crucial link between emerging new developments in knowledge and technology and in strengthening rural economy using local resources and material as per people's needs. Initiatives have already been taken in developing of solar energy and wind energy systems, small-scale village industries, village broadcast unit, youth self-employment, etc. Thus, the Technology Model of Extension describes how scientific and technical interventions foster improving the quality of life in rural areas. Adopting a village or a cluster of villages in the region of their establishments is the befitting initiative to fulfil this demand by the corporate houses. Several meaningful interventions, which can directly benefit the rural domains, can be introduced in these villages (Bijli, 2012). Extension specialists possess the required expertise in not just technology transfer strategies, but in diffusion of ideas and adoption of integrated approaches such as watershed management and wasteland development schemes, SHGs formations and public health service linkages, etc. It is here that extension change agents can engage corporates, donors, and government agencies to play a supportive and collaborative role.

Corporate Social Entrepreneurship

Companies need to find a process to respond to the challenges stated, and move their social initiatives to a higher level; Corporate Social Entrepreneurship is that process. The corporate entrepreneurship is aimed at spotting and redefining market opportunities through innovative strategies, processes, and organizations that would generate new competitive advantage. Parallel to this trend, the social sector saw the emergence of the practice of 'social entrepreneurship', which aimed at achieving greater social impact through innovation and adaptation of the discipline and tools from the business world in support of a social mission. CSE here is defined as the process of extending the firm's domain of competence and corresponding opportunity set through innovative leveraging of resources, both within and outside its direct control, aimed at the simultaneous creation of economic and social value. The CSE process takes companies beyond traditional patterns of charitable giving to more robust forms of corporate citizenship (Austin et al., 2006). In today's era of globalization, CSE can be seen as an emerging tool that can be used by companies to achieve CSR goals. The CSE goal of integration implies inserting the social entrepreneurship dimension into the daily operations of the operating units as part of their ongoing responsibilities.

Success is largely attributable to involvement of local people as active "change agents" or "natural carriers" and "consumers" of technology, through the dovetailed approach of motivation. For example, gender-segregated information and gender integrative participatory technology appropriation are effective enablers in carrying on such projects. A catalytic relationship between CSE and extension is the need of the hour. CSE ensures that the company's social actions and impact are adequately shared with the internal and external stakeholders. External communications that envisage mobilizing, extending support and harmonizing action, help companies earn a reputation with external stakeholders. In the extension process, beneficiaries; S&T institutes; CSR arms of companies (that provide funding, change agents and technical support); government bodies,

NGOs and academic institutes are stakeholders to development, based on their involvement.

Towards Sustainable Partnerships and Development

In order to develop a mutually beneficial relationship between extension practices and CSR strategies, we need to shift to a contemporary extension approach rather than the conventional approach of technology design and dissemination that miserably failed to address the needs and priorities of marginal farmers; the rural, tribal and dalit women; who generally operate in complex, diverse and risk-prone production situations. Contemporary extension approach for transfer of technology involves the research and extension managers to shift to more holistic, systematic, client oriented (women/men) and interdisciplinary approach for development and delivery of production technologies appropriate to the small farming and diverse income-generating situations such as wasteland development, rain-fed agriculture, improved seed practices, small-scale production of agricultural produce, handicrafts, etc. These practices hold their roots to the concept of Farming Systems Research and Extension (FSR/E). Any company can adopt FSR/E as mandatory to its CSR strategy.

Putting globalization in the present context, companies are becoming aware that CSR can be of direct economic value. Although a company's primary goal is to generate profits, CSR is being seen as a strategic investment into business strategy by simultaneously contributing to social and environmental objectives. Yet while they recognize their social responsibility, many of them have yet to adopt management practices that reflect it: company employees and managers need training in order to acquire the necessary skills and competence. Pioneering companies can help the fraternity to implement socially responsible practices by guiding the processes. A number of companies with good social and environmental records indicate that CSR activities can result in a better performance and can generate more profits and growth. But the fight against poverty, the development of education, as well as the conservation of the environment are not existent in most of the Indian enterprises

(Bijli, 2012). We need more corporate players who can integrate CSR practices into their business operations. With the passage of the Companies Bill in August 2013, the possibility of CSR practices is expected to increase in the near future.

At present, few CSR initiatives in India are being recognized as best CSR practices in their respective fields. Extension specialists can support other corporates to replicate their project area. This can be done by guiding them in effective project implementation. Corporates are gearing up towards sustainable initiatives, and are targeting effective partnerships with NGOs and government. In collaborative learning, extension creates a field where one agency gets to learn the capacity of the other agency, and how to build up the capacity further. Extension specialists can help the civil society organizations to plan their resource mobilisation strategies and can also help put into motion, the processes for self-regulation of each. The corporations could play a facilitating role in this regard. For example, through CSR outreach strategies, agricultural business companies can specialize in one extension activity with the help of local NGOs such as machineries and technology, soil and water testing, etc.; pharmaceutical companies can focus on promoting women's health by promoting male contraceptives, reaching out to health services and concerns of adolescents, women and child nutrition, etc.

NGOs on the other hand can draw corporations into a dialogue to adopt voluntary codes of conduct. If collaboration means working in partnership, collaboration of extension with supportive services is inherent in the meaning of extension education. Collaborative work provides for experiential learning. And this is the benchmark of sustainable growth (Bijli, 2012).

Of late, educating the farmers through web, on new agricultural technology has been attempted by the government and non-government organizations. The advantages of web education are that of updating its database on weather conditions and the market situation on a frequent basis and in providing access to the farming community from any part of the country or world. Similar attempts can be made in ICTs for women. Rural India is supported by a magnitude of change agency systems, like government departments, quasi-government and autonomous institutions, non-governmental organizations, religious institutions, youth clubs and local voluntary groups. NGOs and local community organizations experiment at the grassroots with development projects and implement them on weaker sections of the population. Their efforts are being linked with extension personnel who are the change agents and CSR strategies of corporations.

Few NGOs are already engaged in successful collaborations such as the Modicare Foundation, with its commitment to prevent HIV/AIDS, has collaborated with NACO, SACS, UNICEF, Delhi Government and reputed corporate houses. Although voluntary organizations working in rural areas have the advantage of better knowledge the felt needs of local people, they have a limited area of operation, limited infrastructure, staff strength, paucity of funds and sometimes lack a dynamic leader. The basic principles of vocational training is "teaching by doing and learning by doing". In extension training programmes, vocational training is provided for imparting new knowledge, to develop skilled manpower, adopt new technologies and building up the desirable scientific attitude among the rural families (Bijli, 2012).

While there has been a serious dearth of organizations that can sustain CSR initiatives, corporations today are working earnestly to strengthen their CSR strategies and earn a reputation. Extension education can motivate young people in corporates into employee volunteerism. In the higher institutions of teaching and research where development studies are taught, formal education and training in CSR could be introduced in core disciplines of Family and Community Sciences (Home Science), Community Resource Management and Extension, Extension Education Systems and Management, Agricultural Extension, Social Work, Economics and other Social Sciences, Resource Mobilisation and Fund Raising, Behavioural Sciences, and Social Entrepreneurship.

Several reputed business schools and management institutes have already introduced corporate citizenship in their curriculum. Some international business schools are in the process of introducing the concept in India. Students often compete for scholarships to realise their academic dreams, but the global community looks at social responsibility as a priority area. For instance, the Hult International Business School is likely to open its local presence in Mumbai, to better serve potential students as well as local corporates with their talent hiring and executive education needs. Add to the fact, many of the corporate clients like Abbot, Deloitte, IBM, KPMG, Microsoft, Oracle and Standard Chartered have substantial operations in Mumbai (Rane, 2013).

Attempts towards development are not new to India. We need to build and strengthen platforms where public and private entities can converge and contribute to sustainable growth. The onus of wealth creation and its consequent usage lies not only with the government, but also private enterprises. Therefore, we need to build platforms where public and private entities can converge and contribute to the resolution of social causes. To meet the challenges of the new millennium with respect to CSR and partnerships, extension services will have to be given a serious thought.

REFERENCES

Agarwal, S. (2003). 'Technology Model for Women's Empowerment: Reaching the Unreached', *Kurukshetra,* May, 51(7): 18-28.

Austin, J.E., Leonard, H.B., Reficco, E. and Wei-Skillern, J. (2006). 'Social Entrepreneurship: It is for Corporations, Too', in Nicholls, A. (ed). *Social Entrepreneurship: New Models of Sustainable Social Change.* New York: Oxford University Press, pp. 169-80.

Berad, N.R. (2011). Corporate Social Responsibility—Issues and Challenges in India, Paper presented in the International Conference on "Technology and Business Management", March 28-30.

Bhattacharyya, K. (2013). 'Milking it Right: The Problems and Prospects of the Dairy Sector in India', *Kurukshetra,* June, 61(8): 36-41.

Bijli, H.K. (2012). 'Role of Extension in Strengthening Corporate Social Responsibility and Leveraging Partnerships', *SR Asia Journal,* pp. 53-61.

Bijli, H.K. and Tewari, R. (2011): 'Extension Education and Its Relevance in Higher Education: Emerging Trends', *University News*, July 04-10, 49(27): 19-24.

Census 2011, available at www.census2011.co.in/

Dahama, O.P. (1997). *Extension and Rural Welfare*, India, Agra: Ram Prasad & Sons.

Dhar, A. (2013). 'Accessibility is the key', *The Hindu,* New Delhi, 12 April, p. 8.

Dogra, B. (2012). 'When the ravines were tamed', *The Hindu*, New Delhi, 30 December, p. 8.

Elkington, J. (2001). 'The Triple Bottom Line for 21st Century Business', in R. Strakley and R. Welford (eds.), *Business and Sustainable Development*. London: Earthscan, pp. 20-43.

Global Hunger Index 2012, by Welt Hunger Hilfe, IFPRI and Concern Wordwide, available at www.ifpri.org/sites/default/files/publications/ghi12.pdf

Hazra, A. (2013). 'Where do women stand in rural India?', *Kurukshetra,* August, 61(10): 13-15.

Indian Brand Equity Foundation, available at www.ibef.org.in.reset.to/knowledge/corporate-social-responsibility-csr—societal-responsibility-companies

Kumar, P. (2013). 'Empowering Women for Food Security', *Kurukshetra,* August, 61(10): 28-31.

Muslim, S.N. (2012). 'Practice of Social Responsibility as a Corporate Value: The Cases of Two Bangladeshi Banks', *SR Asia Journal,* pp. 46-52.

Parsai, G. (2012). 'India lags behind Bangladesh in improving Global Hunger Index despite economic growth', *The Hindu*, New Delhi, 12 October, p. 12.

PTI (2013). 'New rules under Companies bill to be in place by FY '14 end: Ministry of Corporate Affairs', 14 August, available at www.articles.economictimes.indiatimes.com/2013-08-14/news/41409895_1_draft-rules-the-companies-bill-corporate-affairs

Rane, G. (2013). 'Social Scale', *The Times of India—Education Times*, New Delhi, 29 April.

Rao, A.V. (2011). 'Levels of Living of Rural Households,' *Journal of Rural Development*, Oct-Dec, 30(4): 461-72.

Sarmah, R.C. (2001). 'Private-Public Collaborative Extension Programme—Experience of Assam Agricultural University', in P.C. Shekara (ed.), *Private Extension: Indian Experiences*. Hyderabad, India: National Institute of Agricultural Extension Management, pp. 66-80.

Shekara, P.C. (2001). 'Private Extension: Indian Way', in P.C. Shekara (ed.), *Private Extension: Indian Experiences*. Hyderabad, India: National Institute of Agricultural Extension Management, pp. 1-31.

Shreeram, A. (2013). 'CSR: Your Responsibility', *The Times of India-Ascent*, New Delhi, 17 April, p. 1.

Soam, S.K. (2001). 'A Case Study of Extension Services for Organic Farming in UK: Options for Private Extension in India', in P.C. Shekara (ed.), *Private Extension: Indian Experiences*. Hyderabad, India: National Institute of Agricultural Extension Management, pp. 211-21.

Times News Network (2012). 'It's time to salute India's silent heroes again—The Times of India Social Impact Awards', *The Times of India*, New Delhi, 2 October, p. 1.

UNDP (2010). *Asia Pacific Human Development Report: Power, Voice and Rights—A turning point for gender equality in Asia and the Pacific*. Available at: hdr.undp.org/.../reports/regionalreports/featuredregionalreport/RHDR-2010-AsiaPacific.pdf

Venkatasubramanian, V. (2013). 'Framework for Strengthening Technology Application and Delivery System in Agricultural Extension', in H. Phillip, T. Rathakrishnan and R.K. Theodore (eds.), *Extension Management in the Information Age: Initiatives and Impacts*. New Delhi: New India Publishing Agency, pp. 1-41.

Verma, O.S. (2007). 'Corporate Social Responsibility', *Journal of Extension Systems*, December, 23(2): 1.

6
Sustainable Development

Y.S. Siddegowda

ABSTRACT

The challenge of meeting human development needs while protecting the earth's life support systems confront scientists, technologists, policymakers, and communities from local to global levels. Many believe that science and technology must play a more central role in sustainable development, yet little systematic scholarship exists on how to create institutions that effectively sustain the growth of development. This study suggests that how the sustainable development and higher education, sustainable development and social work, and need for development play an effective role in managing the boundaries between knowledge and action in ways that simultaneously enhance the salience, credibility, and legitimacy of the information they produce. Effective systems apply a variety of institutional mechanisms that facilitate communication, translation and development across boundaries.

Introduction

Sustainable development refers to a mode of human development in which resource use aims to meet human needs while preserving the environment so that these needs can be met not only in the present, but also for generations to come. The term 'sustainable development' was used by the Brundtland Commission which coined what has become the most often-quoted definition of sustainable development: "development that meets the needs of the present without compromising the ability of future generations to meet their own needs".

Sustainable development ties together concern for the carrying capacity of natural systems with the social challenges faced by humanity. As early as the 1970s, "sustainability" was employed to describe an economy "in equilibrium with basic ecological support systems". Ecologists have pointed to the Limits to Growth, and presented the alternative of a "economy" in order to address environmental concerns.

The concept of sustainable development has in the past most often been broken out into three constituent parts: environmental sustainability, economic sustainability and socio-political sustainability. More recently, it has been suggested that a more consistent analytical breakdown is to distinguish four domains of economic, ecological, political and cultural sustainability. Thus, sustainable development was made popular by the World Commission on Environment and Development in its reports titled "Our Common Future". The ability to meet the needs is largely determined by human capital.

The sustainable development debate is based on the assumption that societies need to manage three types of capital (economic, social, and natural), which may be non-substitutable and whose consumption might be irreversible. Daly (1991), for example, points to the fact that natural capital cannot necessarily be substituted by economic capital. While it is possible that we can find ways to replace some natural resources, it is much more unlikely that they will ever be able to replace eco-system services such as the protection provided by the ozone layer, or the climate stabilizing function of the Amazonian forest. In fact, natural capital, social capital and economic capital are often complementarities. A further obstacle to substitutability lies also in the multi-functionality of many natural resources. Forests, for example, not only provide the raw material for paper (which can be substituted quite easily), but they also maintain biodiversity, regulate water flow, and absorb CO_2.

Another problem of natural and social capital deterioration lies in their partial irreversibility. The loss in biodiversity, for example, is often definite. The same can be true for cultural diversity. For example, with globalization advancing quickly the number of indigenous languages is dropping at alarming rates. Moreover, the depletion of natural and social capital may have non-linear consequences. Consumption of natural and social capital may have no observable impact until a certain threshold is reached. A lake can, for example, absorb nutrients for a long time while actually increasing its productivity. However, once a certain level of algae is reached lack of oxygen causes the lake's ecosystem to break down suddenly.

Sustainable Development and Social Work

The concept of sustainable development can be interpreted in different ways, but at its core is an approach to social work development that looks to balance different, and often competing, needs against an awareness of the environmental, social and economic limitations we face as a society. The need for keeping view the interests of the future generations has arisen because in the past the benefits of development have often been exaggerated, the cost of development, in particular the costs of environmental loss have been ignored. Apart from natural capital, the term sustainable development, in its wider sense, also refers protection of human capital and physical capital, so that future generations do get, if not more, at least as much as the present generations has inherited from the past. All this involves such a management of resources, natural capital, human capital and physical capital that while we satisfied with present needs, the maintain or enhance quality of these resources.

The ability to meet the needs is largely determined by the accumulation of human capital through education and technological advances and man-made physical capital machines, tools, etc. The accumulation of capital will, however, inevitably involve some depletion change of natural resources. Thus, sustainable development demands that society designs activities to meet human needs while definitely preserving the life support systems to further enhance the quality of resources.

The sustainable development not only includes the human development but it also includes the domains of sustainability such as economics, ecology, politics and culture.

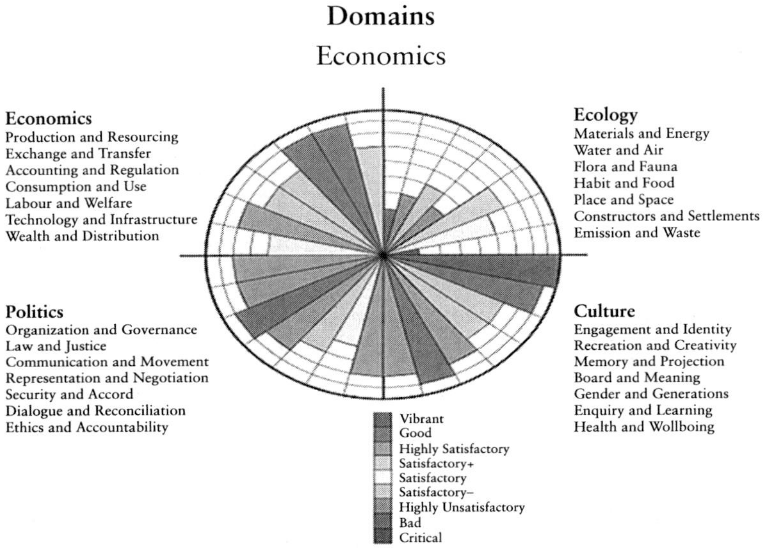

Circles of Sustainability

Source: Circles of Sustainability image (assessment-Melbourne 2011)

The domain of 'economics' is fundamental to considerations of sustainable development, however, there has been considerable criticism of the tendency to use the three-domain model of the triple bottomline: economics, environment and social. This approach is challenged to the extent that it treats the economy as the master domain, or as a domain that exists outside of the social; it treats the environment as a world of natural metrics; and it treats the social as a miscellaneous collection of extra things that do not fit into the economic or environmental domains (see the section on Economic Sustainability below). In the alternative Circles of Sustainability Approach, the economic domain is defined as the practices and meanings associated with the production, use, and management of resources, where the concept of 'resources' is used in the broadest sense of that word.

Ecology

The domain of 'ecology' has been difficult to resolve because it too has a social dimension. Some research activities start from the definition of green development to argue that the environment is a combination of nature and culture. However, this has the effect of making the domain model unwieldy if culture is to be considered a domain in its own right. Others write of ecology as being more broadly at the intersection of the social and the environmental—hence, ecology. This move allows culture to be used as a domain alongside economics and ecology.

Culture

Working with a different emphasis, some researchers and institutions have pointed out that a fourth dimension should be added to the dimensions of sustainable development, since the triple-bottomline dimensions of economic, environmental and social do not seem to be enough to reflect the complexity of contemporary society. In this context, the Agenda 21 for Culture and the United Cities and Local Governments Executive Bureau lead the preparation of the policy statement "Culture: Fourth Pillar of Sustainable Development", passed on 17 November 2010, in the framework of the World Summit of Local and Regional Leaders—3rd World Congress of UCLG, held in Mexico City. This document inaugurates a new perspective and points to the relation between culture and sustainable development through a dual approach: developing a solid cultural policy and advocating a cultural dimension in all public policies. The Network of Excellence "Sustainable Development in a Diverse World", sponsored by the European Union, integrates multidisciplinary capacities and interprets cultural diversity as a key element of a new strategy for sustainable development. The Circles of Sustainability Approach defines the cultural domain as practices, discourses, and material expressions, which, over time, express continuities and discontinuities of social meaning. However, culture falls within the social/socio-political dimension of sustainability, and therefore the proposal for adding a fourth "cultural" dimension has not been widely accepted.

Politics

The United Nations' Global Compact Cities Programme has defined sustainable political development is a way that broadens the usual definition beyond states and governance. The political is defined as the domain of practices and meanings associated with basic issues of social power as they pertain to the organization, authorization, legitimation and regulation of a social life held in common. This definition is in accord with the view that political change is important for responding to economic, ecological and cultural challenges. It also means that the politics of economic change can be addressed. This is particularly true in relation to the controversial concept of 'sustainable enterprise' that frames global needs and risks as 'opportunities' for private enterprise to provide profitable entrepreneurial solutions. This concept is now being taught at many business schools including the Center for Sustainable Global Enterprise at Cornell University and the Erb Institute for Global Sustainable Enterprise at the University of Michigan.

Sustainable development is an eclectic concept and a wide array of political views fall under its umbrella. The concept has included notions of weak sustainability, strong sustainability and deep ecology. Different conceptions also reveal a strong tension between egocentrism and anthropocentrism. Many definitions and images (visualizing sustainability) of sustainable development coexist. Broadly defined, the sustainable development mantra enjoins current generations to take a systems approach to growth and development and to manage natural, produced, and social capital for the welfare of their own and future generations.

During the last ten years, different organizations have tried to measure and monitor the proximity to what they consider sustainability by implementing what has been called sustainability metrics and indices. This has engendered considerable political debate about what is being measured. Sustainable development is said to set limits on the developing world. While current First World countries polluted significantly during their development, the same countries encourage Third World countries to reduce pollution, which sometimes impedes growth. Some consider that the implementation of sustainable development would mean a reversion to pre-modern lifestyles.

Sustainable Development and Education

Education for Sustainable Development (ESD) is simultaneously a sub-field of education and a conceptual tool to aid policymakers in authoring educational policies that take into account the present environmental, societal and economic challenges. According to the UNESCO, it is based on all levels and types of learning—learning to know, learning to be, learning to live together, learning to do and learning to transform oneself and society.

It further says that, "Perhaps ESD can be seen as the total sum of diverse ways to arrive at a 'learning society' in which people learn from and with one another and collectively become more capable of withstanding setbacks and dealing with sustainability-induced insecurity, complexity and risks. From this vantage point, ESD is about—through education and learning—engaging people in sustainable development issues, developing their capacities to give meaning to sustainable development and to contribute to its development and utilizing the diversity represented by all people—including those who have been or feel marginalized—in generating innovative solutions to sustainable development.

The state of the environment is a reminder of what we as humans are capable of inflicting on nature, which by itself, is in perfect harmony with its elements. However, this study highlights the opportunities at hand to reverse the process of environmental decline and work for a present and future built on the principles of environmental justice, equity and humane development. In this regard, the role of education is critical as it is the cornerstone of a modern society. It not only determines the present level of progress of people of a society but also charts out the future course of advancement of the civilization. Therefore, in view of the current environmental crisis, the content of education requires restructuring. This would mean that education systems across the world would be required not only to make a person employment worthy, it would have to capacitate people with values that would help them understand their relationship with the society and environment and empower a person lead a life of contentment and satisfaction. In this context, education will have to go beyond mere transfer of information.

Education for Sustainable Development therefore is an important pedagogical tool as it is based on the fundamental principle of making an individual see and recognize the interdependence between human beings and each and every unit of ecology. The Brundtland Report of 1987 also made a very important point in this context stating, "Sustainable development requires meeting the basic needs of all and extending to all the opportunity to fulfill their aspirations for a better life." The role of ESD, which is based on the three pillars of economy, society and environment, is critical in changing prevalent perceptions and attitudes of people towards self, society and environment.

Traditionally, India has been a sustainable society. A large part of the Indian population still has a lifestyle that is based on the principle of reuse, reduce and recycle. In some cases, it is a matter of personal choice but for a large majority, it is necessitated by economic compulsions.

The Government of India has integrated the principle of 'sustainability' in its various policies and developmental programmes. India's developmental strategic framework is based on a five-year planning system. The First Five-year Plan was rolled out in 1951. Presently, the soon-to-be concluded Eleventh Plan is underway which focuses in a big way on education.

In order to promote the value of sustainable development in education, the Indian Government directed its various education departments to actively work on an Environment Education component as part of the curriculum. This strategy was adopted post Stockholm conference in 1972 by setting up Centers of Excellence for Environment Education under Ministry of Environment and Forests (MoEF) in the early 1980s. For a very long time, most of these activities were restricted to the MoEF but gradually the government realized that the purview of education is very broad in a developing country like India and cannot be limited to the workings of one single ministry. As a result, the GoI recommended Ministry of Human Resource Development to integrate environmental concerns into all aspects and levels of education.

The mandate of ESD is very broad. Therefore, it simultaneously becomes a challenge and an opportunity. ESD provides an excellent doorway to the social, economic and environmental spheres of India and societies elsewhere to trigger awareness, analysis and action on sustainable development.

The path to ESD is an important one and countries that tread it carefully and use it to their advantage would provide its present populace and bequeath its future generations an environment that would empower them to fulfill their needs and aspirations by striking a balance between economy and ecology. Otherwise, the consequences can be mildly termed disastrous. As the noted Indian economist and scholar, Amartya Sen points out, "a fouled environment in which future generations are denied the presence of fresh air...will remain foul even if future generations are so very rich".

Need for Sustainable Development

For a long time and even now at some degree, there are people who believed that sustainable development is an oxymoron because it is impossible to reach development without polluting. Fortunately, there are other people who have proven that there is a way to reach economic development in a sustainable way.

This concept solves the issue on whether those words (development and sustainability or environment) can go together. And solving that issue is important because developing countries can't excuse their unsustainable practices in order to reach development. That was basically China's argument in Copenhagen when they said that the US had its chance to grow up by polluting the world and that is now other countries' turn.

Since the tension between environment and development is not necessarily present all the time, a country, specially a developing country, does not have to choose between growing up economically and preserving the environment. Actually, the other alternative to development is stagnation and that is not sustainable at all.

Sustainable development is the way to reach development without causing a harm or damage to the environment. Having that concept of sustainable development, we understand that pure economic development needs to have some limits because the achievement of sustainable development requires the integration of not only its economic, but also its environmental and social components at all levels. If a society focuses only on the economic component, then it would be a society whose gross domestic product gets higher, but also one that destroy the environment or one that disrespect their population's rights.

Those three components of sustainability have to be present in any decision process relating to development for it to be sustainable development.

Of course, there are people who believe that there is no reason for worrying about saving resources for future generations or stopping any kind of development. They think that our ancestors did not care about us when they developed, otherwise we would not have the standard of living we do now days. They also think that resources we consider crucial now may have no relevance in the future. But recent studies prove that there will be serious consequences if we keep developing the way we have been.

Given that development is not only good but also necessary, the questions remaining would be how to achieve this development in a way that allows future generation to keep using the resources we use today.

Sustainable development should be regulated either by national or international law. But national laws in terms of sustainability are not very well implemented in developing countries yet, and international laws have a severe limitations if not agreed by the parties so there is a need for a new approach on how to achieve the goals of sustainability in developing countries that could make them complain with certain standards to assure that their development is actually sustainable.

One possible solution is certification, a system of certification that assures that companies all over the world comply with international standards on sustainable development. Of course, this system calls for standards: required or agreed levels of quality or attainment. These standards would be minimum requirements that companies will need to meet in order to obtain a certification as a sustainable business.

There will have to be an international institution that gives this certification and that put pressure in the most industrialized countries for requiring their companies to get certificated if they want to take their businesses overseas.

The problem is that in a globalized world it is very hard to come up with standards that are going to fit every country or even every industry (since some industries are more protected than others). Even though it might be possible, and in some cases even recommended, to reach a standard for companies all over the world to become sustainable, there does not seem to be a way of reaching a standard that is going to be applicable for the whole world, considering the different needs existing. It is maybe time to think about developing international standards for areas or even continents.

It seems almost ridiculous to require meeting with the same environmental standards two different companies, one located in Switzerland and the other one in China. How could people agree in a standard of sustainability when the concept of sustainability means many different things to different people in the first place, and a large part of humanity around the world still lives without access to basic necessities? The answer is they probably can't.

The only possible solution would be to have different standards of sustainability for different areas, but all of them being part of the same system for it not to loose strength. The world needs a certification system that sets the standards according on the area where the company is located, because helping will vary depending on the needs of the communities of where the companies are located.

Most of the social responsibility reports from American companies are made thinking about the needs of Americans, but those reports do not always take into consideration that those companies have operations and a great impact in other countries too.

An example of a company that makes efforts to do something for the sustainable development of communities is Nike, but they might not just do what is really needed in a given country. Nike's asserts that the company is helping communities in Honduras by training unemployed workers to upgrade their technical skills so they can compete for jobs. Well maybe that help is not really needed. Maybe the problem is lack of jobs and opportunity instead of lack of technical skills to compete for jobs. Maybe the community does not even have electricity. It just seems like there are many other things that Nike could do with the same resources and some information provided. Of course, Nike does not have any obligation (morality aside) to help people in any different way, but their sustainability policy alone with proper international standards set up could just be enough to canalize their help in a more efficient way. There is a need for international standards on sustainable development then, standards that should focus on specific communities so they take in consideration specific needs and the best way to achieve sustainable development under the specific circumstances.

Sustainability should be measured depending on the characteristics of the community and not forgetting the social, environmental and economic components. If we take the Andean people who live around the mining companies for example, we should take into consideration that they lack electricity, cars, and even proper houses, that they have a high rate of mortality and illiteracy, and that their economic activity is so slow that probably do not pollute at all. The desired standard for the sustainable development projects on those areas have to be more focused on meeting basic necessities.

Conclusion

Sustainable development can be defined simply as a better quality of life for everyone, now and for generations to come. It is a vision of progress that links economic development, protection of the environment and social justice, and its values are recognized by democratic governments and sustainable development for higher education politic movements the world over. So the sustainable development includes the overall concepts of social work, higher education and the need for development.

REFERENCES

Ahmadi, N. (2003). "Globalization of Consciousness and New Challenges for International Social Work". *International Journal of Social Welfare*. 12(1): 14-23.

Alphonse, M., P. George and K. Moffatt (2008). "Redefining Social Work Standards in the Context of Globalization: Lessons from India". *International Social Work*. 51(2): 145-58.

Bhattacharya, Sanjay (2003). *Social Work: An Integrated Approach*. Deep and Deep Publications, New Delhi.

Byres, T.J. (ed.) (1998). *The State, Development, Planning and Liberalization in India*. Oxford University Press.

Carley, M., I. Christie (2000). *Managing Sustainable Development*, London, UK, Taylor & Francis.

Encyclopedia of Social Work, Publication Division, Government of India, New Delhi (1990).

Folke, Carl, Steve Carpenter, Thomas Elmqvist, Lance Gunderson, C.S. Holling, and Brian Walker (2002). "Resilience and sustainable development: Building adaptive capacity in a world of transformations". *AMBIO: A Journal of the Human Environment*, 31(5): 437-40.

Lele, S.M. (1991). "Sustainable development: A critical review". *World Development*, Vol. 19, Issue 6, June 1991, pp. 607-21.

Rosen, M.A., I. Dincer (2001). "Exergy as the confluence of energy, environment and sustainable development". *Exergy, An International Journal*, Vol. 1, Issue 1, pp. 3-13.

http://www.google.co.in/search

www.sd-commission.org.uk/pages/what-is-sustainable-development.html

en.wikipedia.org/wiki/sustainable development sustainability and law. classcaster.net/sustainable development-in

7

Community Ownership of School Education: A Pre-requisite for Development

D.P. Singh and *Ritu*

ABSTRACT

In India, it was only in the initially years of post-independence that centralization was thought to be important. At that time, a notion prevailed that everything that belonged to the government and not the community is sustainable and enduring but this idea could not be carried on for very long. Soon it was realized that there is a vital link between decentralization and development and the community plays a very important role in sustainable and a long-term people-oriented development. Communitisation was thought even more essential in the area of school education and in provisioning basic services to the masses with a view to achieve the mandate of rural development. Decentralization was envisioned as an effective tool for addressing the local needs of the teeming millions residing in the villages. The most basic need, *inter alia*, is the education of the masses, which is, inevitably and essentially very important for bringing a discernible change in the quality of life of the people apart from helping in the successful implementation of any of the welfare programmes. Education remains the central cog in the wheel of development of any nation. Communitisation of Education or in other words participatory management of the schools has always been viewed as important for improving education at the village level thereby improving the development indices in the social sectors of any nation for that matter.

Against this backdrop, the present paper intends to examine the process of communitisation of education at the village level by evaluating the functioning of the committees that provide a platform for the people to own the school-related activities at the community level, thereby, accelerating the process of social development.

Introduction

The need of communitisation of school education or to say that decentralization and participatory management of school education through involvement of local bodies in the school-related processes was spelled out by the First Education Commission in 1966. Community participation as a primary strategy for ensuring decentralization in school education got another major boost with the adoption of National Policy on Education in year 1986. The policy laid primary emphasis on decentralized planning and management of elementary education in the country. The policy visualized direct involvement of the community in the form of Village Education Committees (VECs) for management and improvement of school education. The Programme of Action (POA) 1992 further strengthened the Village Education Committees by providing that the State Government would lay down general guidelines regarding the constitution of village education committees and establish norms of accountability in respect of the Heads of these institutions. The 73rd and 74th constitutional amendments provided for decentralisation of the activities and facilitated the transfer of power and participation of the local self-government institutions or the Panchayati Raj Institutions (PRIs). Sarva Shiksha Abhiyan (SSA) assigned greatest importance to systematic mobilization of the community and creation of an effective system of decentralized decision-making. The Right to Education Act 2009 also recognizes the role of local governance in school education by necessitating the formation of a School Management Committee (SMCs) in each school. Thus, we see that participatory management of school education as a novel and unique approach of development and school governance, have always been emphasized in all the education-related policy documents in India in order to build a synergic relationship between the community and the government with a view to create a sense of ownership, better resource management and overall development at the grassroots level.

Communitisation of School Education in Punjab

The State of Punjab has been accorded a fair amount of importance to education in the major policy initiatives. Over the years promotion of education has been one of the top priority areas for the State Government. A vast network of schools and institutions of education have been set up. A number of schemes and incentives have been launched to motivate the parents so that the children go to school. As regards the school infrastructure, Punjab is considered to be one of the best in school infrastructure in the country. In fact, as per the Educational Development Index (EDI) 2011 prepared by National University of Educational Planning and Administration (NUEPA), Punjab is at the top in infrastructural parameters in the country followed by Puducherry and Andaman and Nicobar Islands. The EDI reflects remarkable gains made by Punjab on parameters of school accessibility, infrastructure and teaching facility outcomes. Giving unqualified priority to school education, the State Government has introduced various innovative approaches like mobilizing community support and introducing decentralized planning to help achieve the goal of universalization of elementary education. The Village Education Committees (VECs) known as Village Education Development Committees (VEDCs) are in place since 2002. The Sarva Shiksha Abhiyan (SSA) which hinges around decentralized planning and community participation is being religiously implemented by the Government of Punjab since 2002. SSA has empowered the local community by their involvement in all aspects of plan formulation. Community-based planning process is being carried out by delegating powers to Panchayati Raj Institutions and constituting the Village Education Development Committees (VEDCs). However, with the implementation of the Right to

Education Act 2009, these committees have been rechristened as School Management Committees (SMCs) with effect from April 1, 2012.

The Study

The above background provides that the link between community participation and equitable quality education is very crucial. Keeping this in view the present paper compiles the findings of a research study carried out for examining the Village Education Development Committees in the state of Punjab in terms of their contribution towards increasing enrollment, improving school result and reducing school drop-out rate. Besides this the paper also takes into account the contribution of VEDC members, conduct of meetings and activities undertaken for improving school infrastructure, for raising funds and provisioning incentives to the school students.

Methodology

The study has been done across the two least literacy districts of Punjab, namely Mansa and Muktsar. For the sample, a total of 52 villages (26 villages from Mansa and 26 villages from Muktsar) as per required indices, were selected. The selection of a village eventually led to the selection of a school and the respective Village Education Development Committee (VEDC). A total of 411 members of the VEDCs comprising the head teachers, panchayat members, members of the PTA, ex-servicemen, retired teacher and philanthropist/NRIs were finally interviewed by a predesigned schedule. The process of formation, composition and functions of VEDCs was studied primarily from the secondary sources largely consisting of the documents, reports, circulars and guidelines of the State as well as the Central Governments.

Village Education Development Committees in Punjab

Village Education Committees (VECs) known as Village Education Development Committees (VEDCs) or in Punjabi addressed as Pendu Sikhiya Vikas Committees (Pasvak) were formally announced in October 2002 in Punjab. After the announcement, VEDCs actually started functioning after the panchayat elections held in June 2003. With the Right to Education Act 2009, these committees have been named as School Management Committees (SMCs) with effect from April 1, 2012. The formation of Village Education Committees has legitimately ensured people's participation in the school-related activities at the village level by involving the teachers, parents, women representatives and social activists. The committees are expected to improve the standard of school education and act as a platform for providing representation to both the elected local bodies like PRIs and the common people. A VEDC consists of eight members. Two members are from the village panchayat, two members are from the PTA, one member each has to be an ex-military personnel, a philanthropist/NRI and a retired teacher of the Government of Punjab. The head teacher of the concerned school is the Secretary of the VEDC. For effective working there has to be chairman elected by majority from amongst the members and head teacher as the secretary. The Panchayat passes a resolution for nominating the PRI members and sends to the head teacher. The nominations of the PTA members are done by the school PTA by passing a resolution. Only those PTA members are made the members of the VEDC whose children study in that particular school. PTA members remain the members of the VEDC till the time they are members of the PTA. The headmaster nominates the ex-serviceman, philanthropist, retired teacher and the seniormost teacher. For ex-serviceman, the highest rank and length of service shall be given preference. As philanthropist such person from amongst the villagers is nominated who has donated the maximum amount to the school. The seniormost teacher from among the school-staff excluding the headmaster shall have to be the member of the VEDC. The seniormost teacher is authorized to act as the secretary of VEDC in the absence of the head teacher. The formation of VEDC is sent to DEO (Elementary Education) by the head teacher for approval. The DEO (Elementary Education) approves the formation and sent it back to the head teacher. The tenure of VEDC shall be three years from the date of approval by the DEO (Elementary Education). By passing a resolution, the VEDC can change any unfit member but such a change can be made only with the approval of the DEO (Elementary Education). In case, any member of the committee remains absent in three consecutive meetings, his membership shall be cancelled and a new member shall be nominated in his place. In any case, the position of any VEDC member shall not remain vacant for more than three months. At least one monthly meeting of VEDC is compulsory. This meeting is to be held in the school as per pre-decided date and time. The notice of the meeting is to be issued by the member secretary. The quorum of the VEDC meeting shall essentially be 1/3 of its total members. The VEDC meeting or any other work of the committee shall not remain interrupted due to the absence of a member. The VEDC is fully authorized to take any appropriate decision in the interest of the school.

The Findings

The Contribution of VEDCs

Increasing Enrollment

It was found that before the formation of VEDCs in the high literacy villages, the gross enrollment increased by 0.51 per cent during the year 2000-01 and 2001-02 and by 2.10 per cent during the second year (2001-02 to 2002-03). After the formation of VEDCs, the gross enrollment increased by 2.25 per cent during 2003-04 and 2004-05 while by 11.46 per cent during 2004-05 and 2005-06. This shows that the rate of increase in the gross enrollment in the high literacy villages was higher after the formation of the VEDCs in comparison to the period of two years when VEDCs were not in place. Thus, it can be said that the Village Education Development Committees contributed positively towards the rate of increase in the gross enrollment in the high literacy regions. Across gender, the VEDCs had a positive contribution towards increasing girls' gross enrollment as well as boys' gross enrollment in the high literacy regions. In the low literacy regions, before the formation of VEDCs, there was a decrease of 5.03 per cent during the year 2000-01 and 2001-02 whereas in the following year (from 2001-02 to 2002-03), the enrollment increased by 3.54 per cent. After the formation of the VEDCs, the gross enrollment dropped by 2.72

per cent during the first year (2003-04 to 2004-05) and by 3.13 per cent in the following year (2004-05 to 2005-06). Thus from the findings it is concluded that the formation of VEDCs did not make any significant contribution with regard to the increase in enrollment of students in the low literacy villages. Across the gender similar pattern was followed. Thus, it is concluded that VEDCs did not have any role across gender of students.

Improving School Results

In high literacy villages, before the formation of VEDCs, the number of failures declined by 42.33 per cent during the year 2000-01 and 2001-02 while the number of failures increased by 62.02 per cent during the year 2001-02 and 2002-03 while after formation of the VEDCs, the number of failures increased by 24.27 per cent in year 2003-04 and 2004-05 while it decreased by 11.7 per cent during 2004-05 and 2005-06. Thus from the findings it is suggested that the VEDCs did not play any role in improving the school results in the high literacy villages. In the low literacy regions, before the formation of VEDCs, the number of failures increased by 1.29 per cent during 2000-01 and 2001-02 and by 5.73 per cent during 2001-02 and 2002-03. After the VEDCs were formed, there was a drop of 56.7 per cent in the number of failures during 2003-04 and 2004-05 and further a drop of 22.89 per cent was witnessed during 2004-05 and 2005-06. Thus, it is suggested that since the school results have improved after the formation of VEDCs in the low literacy regions, the VEDCs has played a positive role towards reducing the number of failures thus improving the school results.

Reducing Dropout

In high literacy villages, before formation of VEDCs, the dropout rate has decreased by 16.67 per cent during 2000-01 and 2001-02 and by 34.28 per cent during 2001-02 and 2002-03. After the formation of the VEDCs, the dropout increased by 196.7 per cent during 2003-04 and 2004-05 and there was a decrease of 65.21 per cent during 2004-05 and 2005-06. This means that the VEDCs did not play any positive role in reduction of dropout rate in the high literacy villages. In the low literacy villages, before the formation of the VEDCs, the dropout rate has witnessed and increase of 57.14 per cent from 2000-01 to 2001-02 whereas the dropout rate decreased by 32.72 per cent during 2001-02 and 2002-03. After the VEDCs were formed, the dropout rate increased by 105.17 per cent during 2003-04 and 2004-05 and it got reduced by 35.25 per cent during 2004-05 and 2005-06. From the findings it is suggested that the VEDCs did not play any significant role in reducing the school dropout rate in the sampled schools situated in the low literacy villages.

Contribution of VEDCs Members in Individual Capacity

The findings revealed that only about one-fifth (20.0 per cent) members discussed the problems of the school with the appropriate officials or the parents while a little more than one-fifth (22.4 per cent) members had paid one or two visits to the school with an aim of monitoring the school environment. As regards the member-teacher interaction on issues relating to school improvement, only 35.8 per cent members gave an affirmative reply. 44.0 per cent members has collected money for organizing sports activities in the school and contributed towards arranging funds/donations for the school. In general, the findings suggest that the contribution of individual members of the VEDCs with regard to school improvement has not been very encouraging except for the head teachers. Thus, the study underlines the need for initiating some programme for morale boosting of the VEDCs members so that they develop a feeling of belongingness towards their school and contribute significantly in their individual capacity.

Conduct of Meetings

The monthly meeting of VEDC is compulsory. If need arises more than one meeting can also be held. This meeting will be held in the school as per pre-decided date and time usually between the 2nd and 7th day of every month. The notice of the meeting is issued by the member secretary. The quorum of the VEDC meeting is essentially be 1/3 of its total members. The meeting or any other work of the committee shall not remain interrupted due to the absence of a member. The present study finds that the meetings of these bodies are not held in accordance with the guidelines laid down by the Sarva Shiksha Abhiyan Authority

Punjab and most of the norms regarding conduct of meetings of these bodies are not followed in letter and spirit. The meetings of the VEDCs are not at all a monthly feature. In fact, no formal meetings of the VEDCs are held. The meetings of the VEDCs are held on papers only. Whenever a grant is received, the head teacher/secretary after recording the minutes of the meeting on his own, sends the register to the residences of the VEDCs members for signatures. This way the paper formality is completed. The VEDC members don't come to the school for meetings in spite of requests from the secretary. It is the primary reason why the VEDC meetings are to be held in circulation. A huge majority (89.5 per cent) of the VEDC members themselves agreed that they don't give any importance to the VEDC meetings as they viewed the meetings of VEDCs just as a formality. As per them, the VEDCs meetings don't serve any purpose; attending or not attending them does not make any difference. The study finds that there is a general lack of interest among the teachers as well as the VEDC members towards VEDCs. Therefore, it is suggested that there is a need to reorient the VEDC members such that they begin to value the importance of VEDC meetings.

Issues Discussed in the Meetings

There are two major issues that always find a place in the minutes of the VEDC meetings. The first relate to making provisions for infrastructural facilities like construction of rooms, repair of buildings, purchase of furniture and other such civil or maintenance jobs while the second is regarding the utilization of grants. The major focus of VEDCs remains on the issues relating to financial matters. An omission in the matters involving money like not discussing them in the VEDCs meetings, etc. entails serious disciplinary action. Therefore, the secretary/head teacher is particularly careful in completing all the paper work in this regard. To escape any reprimand or punishment from the higher authorities, such issues are always recorded in the minutes of the VEDCs meetings. The quality issues like teaching learning material, classroom processes and learning achievements, etc. are not considered of much worth for the meetings as avoidance of these issues don't entail any serious punishment.

Activities Undertaken to Improve Infrastructure

Majority (81.1 per cent) of the VEDC members informed that the main activities undertaken by the VEDCs were about repairing and constructing the classrooms followed by repairing and constructing the toilets and ramps (70.4 per cent). Nearly one-third (28.19 per cent) respondents told that the VEDC repaired/constructed boundary wall of the school whereas a little more than one-tenth (11.1 per cent) of these respondents informed that the committee purchased furniture for teachers and students. The VEDCs don't give any importance to fundraising activities. 87.3 per cent VEDCs members replied in the negative when asked if the VEDC had undertaken any fundraising activity in their community. About 12.7 per cent members informed that the VEDC they represented had collected donations for organizing some sports events.

Activities for Incentives to Students

The VEDCs participate only in those activities which are sponsored either by the State or the Central Government. As regards the incentives to students, 82.5 per cent VEDC members informed that the VEDCs organized exposure visits for the school children whereas 79.6 per cent respondents told that free textbooks/notebooks schemes being monitored by these committees. As per 77.6 per cent respondents, the VEDCs were involved in giving cash prizes to the first three toppers of each class in every school. Other activities where the VEDCs participated related to vocational courses for girls like the course on computer literacy, embroidery and soft skills. There was no scheme/incentive known to have been launched by the VEDCs themselves, i.e. by generating their own funds.

General/Miscellaneous Activities

As regards the activities of general nature, a huge majority of respondents (85.4 per cent) were of the view that the VEDCs did not undertake any activity other than those mandated under government norms. Only about 14.6 per cent respondents told that the VEDCs they represented had undertaken one or the other activities for increasing enrollment and school results and reducing dropout. These activities were putting up of boards at various places within the village displaying the details of civil works and utilization of grants, making announcements from the gurudwaras from time to time regarding various school-related issues, organizing cultural programme and sports, holding door to door meetings, organizing lectures and speaking to local activists/community leaders about the problems at the school.

Conclusions

Overall, the contribution of VEDCs towards school-related activities other than those mandated under SSA norms is very poor. There is a general lack of initiative and motivation among the VEDCs members. The VEDCs, by and large, remain a male bastion and the personal merit of woman remains overshadowed by the patriarchal stereotypes and culture factors adverse to gender equality. Age still remains an important criterion in determining the leadership positions in rural areas particularly in the school-related activities. The VEDCs in Punjab continue to be dominated by the not so young people. In the absence of specific reservation provisions, the people of dominant castes tend to monopolize the leadership positions in villages with reference to community participation in the school-related activities. Nevertheless, in spite of the not so good scenario, the involvement of community through Village Education Committees in Punjab has given a good start in operationalizing the participatory decentralized model of development in all kinds of activities of the school governance.

Finally, it can be said that as envisioned by our policy planners the process of community ownership remains as prerequisite in the process of development and, as such, has created a space of its own with regards to school improvement and thus in accelerating the process of social development at the grassroots levels.

REFERENCES

Government of India (1986). *Programme of Action: National Policy on Education* 1986, Ministry of Human Resource Development, Department of Education, New Delhi.

Government of India (2005). *National Curriculum Framework 2005*, National Council of Educational Research and Training, New Delhi, December 2005.

Government of India (2010). *Compilation of 50 Years of Indian Education: 1947-1997*. Online available athttp://www. education. nic.in/cd50years/home.htm

Government of India (2000). *Sarva Shiksha Abhiyan: A Programme for Universal Elementary Education-Framework for Implementation*, Ministry of Human Resource Development, Department of Elementary Education and Literacy, New Delhi.

Government of India. Ministry of Education (1997). DPEP Guidelines. NCERT. New Delhi.

Government of India. Ministry of Human Resource Management (2002). "Janshala: Towards Empowered Community Schools". New Delhi. Online available at <http://www.education.nic.in/ Janshala/contents/pdf>

Govt. of Punjab. Sarva Shiksha Abhiyan Authority (n.d.). *Guidelines for maintaining accounts under Village Education Development Committees*. Chandigarh.

Govt. of Punjab. Sarva Shiksha Abhiyan Authority (n.d.). *How the Construction Works are to be done under Village Education Development Committees*. Chandigarh.

Govt. of Punjab. Sarva Shiksha Abhiyan Authority (n.d.). *Norms for Village Education Development Committees*. Chandigarh.

Govt. of Punjab. Sarva Shiksha Abhiyan Authority (n.d.). *Guidelines for Rural/Urban Education Development Committees*. Chandigarh.

Govinda, R. (2002). "Dynamics of Decentralized Management in Primary Education: Policy and Practice in Rajasthan and Madhya Pradesh". In R. Govinda and Rashmi Diwan (eds.), *Community Participation and Empowerment in Primary Education*, Sage Publication, New Delhi.

Govinda, R. and Rashmi, Diwan (Eds) (2007). *Community Participation and Empowerment in Primary Education*. New Delhi: Sage.

Govinda, R. and N.V. Varghese (1991). *The Quality of Basic Education Services in India: A Case Study of Primary Schooling in Madhya Pradesh*, National Institute of Educational Planning and Administration, New Delhi.

Noronha, Anjali (2003). "The Community in Charge: Shades of Experience from Madhya Pradesh", in R. Govinda and Rashmi Diwan (eds.), *Community Participation and Empowerment in Primary Education,* Sage Publication, New Delhi.

Wankhede, G.G. and Anirban Sengupta (2005). "Village Education Committees in West Bengal, India: Planned Vision and Beyond". *International Journal of Educational Development*, Vol. 25 (2005): 569-79.

8

ICT Development in Rural India

Manushi

ABSTRACT

Over the past few years, the information and communication technologies (ICTs) have developed spectacularly around the world. In recent time, India has also made great strides on national ICT policy. India is continually reforming and trying to maintain the growth and success it has already achieved. While many of its policies are enlightened and fostering environment that would allow for more ICT investment, India, still, has many other problems with ICT readiness. India carries a great disparity between users of ICT as there is a social and economic divide as well as there are disparities between urban and rural area. Limitations in electricity, telephony, Internet connectivity and other kinds of basic infrastructure in India's rural areas are key challenges. The country is going through an ICT revolution and this has become an enabling force for those living in rural India to become active participants in the growth of the country. In India, ICTs have impressive growth and have a bright future. A holistic development of India as a nation rests on a sustained and holistic development of rural India. This paper provides the status of ICTs in India, the recent trends, policy framework and rural development through ICT in India.

Introduction

ICT advances over the last few decades have led to the convergence of broadcasting, telecommunications, computing and content. It has impacted the way business is conducted, facilitated learning and knowledge sharing, and generated global information flows, empowered citizens and communities, resulting into a global information society. Increasingly, ICT is playing the catalytic role in pushing the development process forward and boosting the efficiency of the increasingly integrated global economy. In industrial countries, it is widely acknowledged to be the engine of economic growth and directly linked to productivity. Hence, countries that have harnessed the potential of ICT have attained significant social and economic development. The discussion that follows here will provide an account of the status of ICTs in India, specially the recent ICT trends and policy framework with reference to rural development.

ICTs: The Origin, Growth and Development

Over the past few years, the information and communication technologies (ICTs) have developed spectacularly around the world. ICTs have penetrated virtually every segment of society. In principle, ICTs have always been available since the advent of the printing press. The only difference is that from the late twentieth century, rapid advances in technology changed the traditional ways in which information was processed, communications were conducted, and services were available (Adu, 2002). These technological advances have changed business operations and the way people communicate. They have introduced new efficiency in old services as well as numerous new ones. One could even imagine to go as far as replacing the term "Post-Industrial Society" with "Information Society", that is, a society where the ability to access to, search, use, create and exchange information is the key for individual and collective well-being (Kaplan, 2001). Though distinctions are often made between new ICTs such as computers and mobile phones, and old ICTs such as radio, television, and landline telephony, the current technological convergences increasingly blur such divisions. Hamelink (1997) defines ICTs as encompassing "all those technologies that enable the handling of information and facilitate different forms of communication among human actors, between human beings and electronic systems, and among electronic systems". This broad definition includes both 'older' technologies such as radio, television and telephone, and 'newer' technologies such as mobile technology and computers (Wachholz and Meleisea, 2006). Hence, ICTs are those technologies that can be used to interlink information technology devices such as personal computers with communication technologies such as telephones and their telecommunication networks. ICTs are a diverse set of technological tools and resources to create, disseminate, store, bring value addition and manage information. The ICT sector consists of segments as diverse as telecommunications, television and radio broadcasting, computer hardware, software and services and electronic media, for example, the Internet and electronic mail (United Nations, 2005). So, ICTs are the technologies that enable recording, processing, retrieving and the transmission of information or data. Herselman and Hay (2003) describe ICT as technologies that support the communication and co-operation of "human beings and their organizations" and the "creation and exchange of knowledge". Furthermore, Yu (2010) considers ICTs as a range of technologies that allow the gathering, exchange, retrieval, processing, analysis and transmission of information. In other words, ICT can be described as any tool that facilitates communication, process and transmit information and share knowledge through electronic means. Rwashana and Williams (2006) state that ICT encompasses a range of electronic, digital and analog devices such as radio, television, telephones (fixed and mobile), computers, electronic media such as digital text and audio-video recording, and the Internet, but excludes the non-electronic technologies. Selwyn (2002) refers to ICT as "an umbrella term that includes computer hardware and software; digital broadcast and telecommunications technologies as well as electronic information repositories such as the World Wide Web or those found on CD-ROMs". According to Saewanyana (2009), ICT is a strategic tool that allows users to become more efficient and effective. Michiels and Van Crowder have defined ICTs as a "range of electronic technologies which when converged in new configurations are flexible, adaptable, enabling and capable of transforming organisations and redefining social relations". The range of technologies is increasing all the time and "there is a convergence between the new technologies and conventional media" (Michiels and Van Crowder, 2001). This rapid and ongoing convergence means that devices such as digital cameras, digital video cameras and players, personal digital assistants, slide projectors and mobile telephones are also compatible with more traditional mass media such as radio and television. Thus, most devices can now be linked to others to share and exchange information and allow it to be used in such a way that they can also be categorized as ICTs. Even books are being incorporated into ICTs either through the potential for informal web publishing or more formal digital book publishing with designated readers or 'e-books'. ICTs, therefore, are an expanding assembly of technologies that can be used to collect, store and share information between people using multiple devices and multiple media. Accelerated communication of information, in the interplay with other factors, can increase productivity; enhance access to services; widen markets; simplify transactions; substitute for physical transport; prevent crime; improve governance and create new socio-economic opportunities, among many other benefits. The linkage between mobile phones, livelihoods and poverty is also an echo of older discourses on development communication that expounded on the positive links between communications, access to information and development (Butner, 2003). Both traditional media and new ICTs have played a major role in diffusing information and have much more potential. Traditional media have been used very successfully in developing countries. Print, video, television, films, slides, pictures, drama, dance, folklore, group discussions, meetings, exhibitions and demonstrations have also been used to speed up the flow of information (Munyua, 2000). New ICTs, however, have the potential of getting vast amounts of information in a quicker, comprehensive and cost-effective manner and they could be used together with traditional media. In the 1990s with the rise of Internet many have seen ICT as a formidable tool to close the gap between the developing world and the developed world by skipping certain stages of industrial development and leapfrogging into the Information Economy (Negroponte, 1998). The revolution in the use of ICT has profound implications for economic and social development and has pervaded every aspect of human life (Shanker, 2008). The use of ICT is widespread and regarded as an essential tool for the efficient administration of any organization and in the delivery of services to clients. Schware (2003) states that ICTs are being integrated into procedures, structures, and products throughout businesses, governments, and communities. The use of ICT increases the supply of information as ICT plays a key role in information sharing and dissemination. According to Spanos et al. (2002), ICT removes distance and time constraint in accessing required information flows. ICT also reduces the cost of production as knowledge is produced, transmitted, accessed and shared at the minimum cost. There is a reduction in the degree of inefficiencies and uncertainty with the use of ICT because it enables businesses to interact more efficiently (Buhalis, 2003). Even if ICTs appear ubiquitous in this day and age, there still exists the growing presence of digital divide and social exclusion. It is also argued that inequalities have increased since the late 1970 both between countries, within countries and in both developed and developing nations (Thomas and Parayil, 2008). But detailed analysis of experiences around the world reveals ample evidence that used in the right way and for the right purposes; ICT can have a dramatic impact on achieving specific social and economic development goals as well as play a key role in broader national development strategies (Digital Opportunity Initiative, 2001).

ICT Scenario in India

In India, the path towards technology-induced development, especially associated with ICT, was given a vent in 1984 by the Congress Government under the Prime Minister Rajiv Gandhi. He assumed power and adopted informatization of Indian society as an effective route to development, with massive programme of computerization launched in the public sector as well in the commercial undertakings, and administrative departments. By 1985, large sectors had announced computerization plans, which included railways, banking operations, schools, etc. In the 1990s, the stress on IT for producing wealth and enabling development continued. A high power National Task Force on Information

Communication Technology and Software Development was set up in 1998. This Task Force prepared the blue print for making the adoption of IT as a national movement, by establishing a wide network of empowered taskforce at all governmental and non-governmental levels. In 1999, the Ministry of Information Communication Technology was established by bringing together government agencies involved in different aspects of IT for creating jobs to harness opportunities provided by convergence of communication technologies and to facilitate the use of IT in use of Electronic Governance. Taking into account the increasing convergence between telecommunication and IT, a Communication Bill was drafted by the Government of India, followed by the Information Communication Technology Act that was notified and brought into force on 17 October 2000. Moreover, the Information Communication Technology for Masses Working Group has been set up with an ambitious target of establishing at least 100 million Internet connections, opening up IT kiosks and cyber cafes for covering entire India. A Task Force on Human Resource Development in IT was set up for preparing a long-term strategy for increasing the number of well-trained IT professionals. There has even been a Task Force on Information Communication Technology as a Knowledge Super Power, which considers how India can become a knowledge economy and society (Bajwa, 2003).

Policy Framework in India

India has made great strides in recent time on national ICT policy. India is continually reforming and trying to maintain the growth and success it has already achieved. India has taken major steps since 1988 when a World Market Policy was developed. India has continually focused on software development for export, telecommunications policy reform and the privatization of the phone companies. While many of their policies are enlightened and fostering environment that would allow for more ICT investment, India, still, has many other problems with ICT readiness. India carries a great disparity between users of ICT as there is a social divide between many of the classes. As their old methods of social division have not been completely washed away, many people still believe in the caste system and treat others on the basis of their caste. These problems lead to a more closed off climate where ICT cannot flourish as greatly. India has long been tied down by government regulation. Recent liberalization of key industries has let market forces to take action, and swift change has proceeded in the ICT landscape of India. Throughout the change there have been published policies on the national level. The key published policies are as follows:

- National Telecom Policy (NTP) 1994
- New Telecom Policy (NTP) 1999
- Broadband Policy 2004
- National Policy on Information Technology (NPIT) 2011
- National Telecom Policy (NTP) 2012
- The ICT Policy in School Education 2012.

In 1994, the government announced the National Telecom Policy which defined certain important objectives, including availability of telephone on demand, provision of world class services at reasonable prices, ensuring India's emergence as major manufacturing/export base of telecom equipment and universal availability of basic telecom services to all villages. It also announced a series of specific targets to be achieved by 1997. NTP 1994 also recognized that the required resources for achieving these targets would not be available only out of government sources and concluded that private investment and involvement of the private sector was required to bridge the resource gap. The government invited private sector participation in a phased manner from the early nineties, initially for value added services such as Paging Services and Cellular Mobile Telephone Services (CMTS) and thereafter for Fixed Telephone Services (FTS). The government recognizes that the result of the privatisation has so far not been entirely satisfactory. The private sector entry has been slower than what was envisaged in the NTP 1994. The government views the above developments with concern as it would adversely affect the further development of the sector and recognizes the need to take a fresh look at the policy framework for this sector (http://www.trai.gov.in).

The New Telecom Policy of India was enacted in 1999. Due to the inability to fulfill many of the National Telecom Policy objectives and recent changes in the nature of technology, the New Telecom Policy was formulated, which further bolstered the government's mission to foster ICT development. The policy was enacted with the objective to provide the affordable and effective communications for the citizens; to provide a balance between the provision of universal service to all uncovered areas; to encourage development of telecommunication facilities in remote, hilly and tribal areas of the country and to create a modern and efficient telecommunications infrastructure taking into account the convergence of IT, media, telecom and consumer electronics.

The coming age of the Internet changed the ICT landscape, again. In order to maintain competencies in the new market, India enacted the Broadband Policy of 2004. Recognizing the potential of ubiquitous broadband service in growth of GDP and enhancement in quality of life through societal applications including tele-education, tele-medicine, e-governance, entertainment as well as employment generation by way of high speed access to information and web-based communication, government have finalised a policy to accelerate the growth of broadband services. Government envisions an accelerated growth in Internet penetration and PC as the success of broadband would largely be dependent on their spread. It decided framework of the policy. The Broadband Policy Framework visualises creation of infrastructure through various access technologies which can contribute to growth and can mutually coexist. Spread of infrastructure is a must for healthy competition and therefore it would be the endeavour of the government that the telecommunication infrastructure growth in the country is not compromised in any manner.

National Policy on Information Technology (2011) has been enacted with the vision to strengthen and enhance India's position as the Global IT hub and to use IT as an engine for rapid, inclusive and sustainable growth in the national economy. The National Policy on IT aims to maximally leverage the power of ICT to help address monumental economic and developmental challenges the country faces. It is rooted in the conviction that ICT has the power to transform India and improve the lives of all Indians (http://www.trai.gov.in).

National Telecom Policy (2012) is enacted with vision to provide secure, reliable, affordable and high quality converged telecommunication services anytime, anywhere for an accelerated inclusive socio-economic development. Telecommunication has emerged as a key driver of economic and social development in an increasingly knowledge-intensive global scenario, in which India needs to play a leadership role. National Telecom Policy, 2012 is designed to ensure that India plays this role effectively and transforms the socio-economic scenario through accelerated equitable and inclusive economic growth by laying special emphasis on providing affordable and quality telecommunication services in rural and remote areas. Thrust of this policy is to underscore the imperative that sustained adoption of technology would offer viable options in overcoming developmental challenges in education, health, employment generation, financial inclusion and much else. NTP-2012 is an initiative to create a conducive policy framework to address these issues and to touch lives of all citizens and transform India. By formulating a clear policy regime, NTP-2012 endeavors to create an investor-friendly environment for attracting additional investments in the sector, apart from generating manifold employment opportunities in various segments of the sector. Availability of affordable and effective communications for the citizens is at the core of the vision and goal of the National Telecom Policy, 2012 (http://www.trai.gov.in).

Notwithstanding the economic progress over the last decade, the digital divide in the country continues to be significant. On the one hand, expansion of telecommunications in the rural areas has been slower than urban areas, with the former accounting for only 34 per cent of the total connections. On the other hand, the ability of the poorer sections of the society, both, in rural and urban areas, to benefit from technology needs to be enhanced. NTP-2012 has the vision Broadband on Demand and envisages leveraging telecom infrastructure to enable all citizens and businesses, both in rural and urban areas, to participate in the Internet and web economy thereby ensuring equitable and inclusive development across the nation. It provides the enabling framework for enhancing India's competitiveness in all spheres of the economy. NTP-2012 envisages support to platform neutral services in e-governance and governance in key social sectors such as health, education and agriculture that are at present limited to a few organizations in isolated pockets. This will expand the footprint of these services and thus foster an atmosphere of participative democracy delivery model that is truly citizen-centric (http://www.trai.gov.in). The policy aims to address and enable the coordinated action to respond to the dynamic needs resulting from confluence of telecom, broadcasting and IT sectors.

The National Policy on Education, 1986, as modified in 1992, stressed the need to employ educational technology to improve the quality of education. The policy statement led to two major centrally sponsored schemes; namely Educational Technology (ET) and Computer Literacy and Studies in Schools (CLASS) paving the way for a more comprehensive centrally sponsored scheme—Information and Communication Technology at Schools in 2004. Educational technology also found a significant place in another scheme on upgradation of science education. The significant role ICT can play in school education has also been highlighted in the National Curriculum Framework (NCF) 2005. Use of ICT for quality improvement also figures in Government of India's flagship programme on education, Sarva Shiksha Abhiyan (SSA). Again, ICT has figured comprehensively in the norm of schooling recommended by the Central Advisory Board of Education (CABE), in its report on Universal Secondary Education, in 2005. With the convergence of technologies, it has become imperative to take a comprehensive look at all possible information and communication technologies for improving school education in the country. The comprehensive choice of ICT for holistic development of education can be built only on a sound policy. The initiative of ICT Policy in School Education is inspired by the tremendous potential of ICT for enhancing outreach and improving quality of education. This policy endeavours to provide guidelines to assist the states in optimizing the use of ICT in school education within a national policy framework. The ICT Policy in School Education aims at preparing youth to participate creatively in the establishment, sustenance and growth of a knowledge society leading to all round socio-economic development of the nation and global competitiveness (http://www.trai.gov.in).

The Recent ICT Trends in India

India is one of the fastest growing economies of the world and emerging as a testing ground for new technologies and business models that aim to narrow the digital divide between 'haves' and 'have-nots'. Limitations in electricity, telephony, Internet connectivity and other kinds of basic infrastructure in India's rural areas are a key challenge. The Indian Government has enacted several policies for the spread of ICTs; several universities have responded timely by introducing courses such as Information Technology; technology majors are keen to establish direct contact with potential customers in rural areas by establishing computer kiosks and CSOs are impacting the rural populace through innovative initiations. It is envisaged that with the growth of telecom infrastructure such initiatives would multiply and create an information society is not so distant in future. The country is going through an ICT revolution and this has become an enabling force for those living in rural India to become active participants in the growth of the country. Telecom Regulatory Authority of India (TRAI) has recently presented the trends of ICTs in India in their Annual Report 2011-12, which are discussed below (http://www.trai.gov.in).

Telecom Sector

TRAI publishes a quarterly report on "The Indian Telecom Services Performance Indicators". This report presents the key parameters and growth trends for Telecom & Broadcasting Services. For the Year 2011-12, TRAI has come out with four quarters' reports. Snapshot covering the key parameters for the four quarters is as follows:

Table 1: The Indian Telecom Services Performance Indicators June 2011-March 2012

Indicators	Quarter Ending June 2011	Quarter Ending Sept. 2011	Quarter Ending Dec. 2011	Quarter Ending March 2012
Telecom Subscribers (in Millions)				
Total Telephone Subscribers	885.99	906.93	926.53	951.34
Urban Subscribers	587.94	601.42	611.19	620.52
Rural Subscribers	298.05	305.51	315.33	330.82
Wireless Subscribers	851.70	873.61	893.84	919.17
Wire line Subscribers	34.29	33.31	32.69	32.17
Teledensity (in Millions)				
Total Teledensity	73.97	75.48	76.86	78.66
Urban Teledensity	163.13	166.01	167.85	169.55
Rural Teledensity	35.60	36.40	37.48	39.22
Internet & Broadband Subscribers (in Millions)				
Total Internet Subscribers	20.33	20.99	22.39	22.86
Broadband Subscribers	12.35	12.83	13.35	13.81

Source: TRAI

The Telecom Sector continued to register an impressive growth during the 2012. The number of telephone subscriptions increased from 846.32 millions to 951.34 millions, registering a growth of 12.41 per cent. The wireless subscriber base increased by 107.58 millions and the wireline subscriber base recorded a decline of 2.56 millions. The wireless segment continued to dominate with a total base of 919.17 millions connections. The overall teledensity in the country increased to 78.66 millions at the end of March 2012 from 70.89 millions at the end of 2011 recording an increase of nearly 7.77 millions. The rural teledensity increased to 39.22 millions from 33.79 millions. The urban teledensity increased to 169.55 millions from 157.32 millions.

Wireless: The wireless subscriber base was 919.17 millions as on 31 March 2012 in comparison to the subscriber base of 811.59 millions as on 31 March 2011. It added 107.58 millions subscribers in the financial year 2011-12 registering an annual growth rate of about 13.26 per cent. The total subscriber base of wireless services has grown from 165.11 million in March 2007 to 919.17 millions in March 2012.

Wireline: The subscriber base of wireline subscribers as on 31 March 2012 was 32.17 millions as compared to 34.73 millions subscribers on 31 March 2011 registering a decrease of 2.56 millions subscribers during the year 2011-12. Out of the 32.17 millions wireline subscribers, 24.62 millions are Urban Wireline Subscribers and the remaining 7.55 millions are Rural Subscribers.

Internet Subscribers: The Internet subscriber base in the country as on 31 March 2012 stood at 22.86 millions as compared to 19.67 millions as on 31 March 2011, registering an annual growth rate of about 3.19 per cent. The total broadband subscriber base has reached 13.81 millions as on 31 March 2012 as compared to 11.89 millions as on 31 March 2011 thereby registering a net addition of 1.92 million broadband subscribers during the financial year 2011-12 with growth of 16.15 per cent. The Internet subscriber base consisting of narrowband (< 256 kbps) and broadband (> 256 kbps) for the last six years (2007-12).

Broadcasting Sector

The broadcasting sector consists of Television and Radio Services. India has the world's third largest TV market after China and USA. As per industry estimates, of the 247 million households, around 150 million have TV as on March 2012 which are being served by cable TV systems, DTH services, IPTV services and the terrestrial TV network of Doordarshan (MPA Reports, 2012).

The pay TV universe consists of around 94 million (MPA Reports, 2012) Cable TV subscribers, including around 0.91 million subscribers (TRAI) in the notified CAS areas, 46.25 million registered DTH subscribers (TRAI) and around half a million IPTV subscribers. The terrestrial TV network of Doordarshan covers about 92 per cent of population of the country through a network of 1415 terrestrial transmitters. The broadcasting services TV sector consists of 26 pay broadcasters/ aggregators (TRAI), an estimated 60,000 cable operators, 6000 Multi System Operators (MSOs), six pay DTH operators, apart from a public service broadcaster—Doordarshan, having free-to-air DTH service—DD direct plus. There were 831 TV channels registered with the Ministry of Information and Broadcasting at the end of financial year 2011-12, out of which 168 (TRAI) were pay channels (Trai Annual Report, 2011-12).

India's TV industry grew from ₹ 29,700 cr. (FICCI-KPMG Report 2012) in the year 2010 to ₹ 32,900 cr. (FICCI-KPMG Report 2012) in the year 2011, thereby, registering a growth of around 11 per cent. The subscription revenue accounts for the major share of the overall revenue of the TV industry. The subscription revenue grew from ₹ 19,400 cr. (FICCI-KPMG Report 2012) in the year 2010 to ₹ 21,400 cr. (FICCI-KPMG Report 2012) in the year 2011 whereas the ARPUs remained almost flat at around ₹ 160 per month. The advertisement revenue in the TV sector in India registered ₹ 11,600 crore (FICCI-KPMG Report 2012) in the year 2011, up from ₹ 10,300 crore (FICCI-KPMG Report 2012) in the year 2010. In 2011, TV advertisement revenue recorded a growth of 13 per cent. Of the total advertisement volumes on television, 4,385 crore (FICCI-KPMG Report 2012) was contributed by regional channels of eight major languages, which is around 39 per cent of total advertisement revenue. The performance indicators of the broadcasting sector over the last four quarters (April 2011 to March 2012) are tabulated in Table 2.

Television: The broadcasting and cable TV services sector has shown a consistent growth over the years spanning last two decades. The sector comprises analogue and digital cable TV services, DTH services, terrestrial TV services, IPTV services, and radio services. The major component of the sector, i.e. pay television services sector, which emerged in the early 1990s, has experienced a rapid growth, with the number of subscribers

Table 2: Overall Status of Broadcasting and Cable TV Services

S. No.	Services	Total
1.	Number of households in country (estimated)	247 Million
2.	Number of TV households (estimated)	148 Million
3.	Number of Cable TV Subscribers (estimated)	94 Million
4.	Number of Cable operators (estimated)	60.000
5.	Number of Multi System Operators (estimated)	6000
6.	Number of pay DTH subscribers registered with private service providers as on 31 March 2012	46.25 Million
7.	Number of pay DTH Operators	6
8.	Number of Channels as on 31 March 2012	831
9.	Number of Pay Channels as on 31 March 2012	168
10.	Number of FM Radio Stations (excluding All India Radio) as on 31 March 2012	245
11.	Number of Licensed Community Radio Stations as on 31 March 2012	167
12.	Number of Operational Community Radio Stations as on 31 March 2012	130
13.	Number of Set Top Box installed in CAS notified areas of Delhi, Kolkata, Mumbai and Chennai as on 31 March 2012	0.91 Million
14.	Number of Permitted Teleports in the Country as on 31 March 2012	87

Source: TRAI

increasing from just 410,000 in 1992 to around 142 million (Cable + DTH + Other Platforms) by March 2012, an average growth rate of more than 34 per cent every year for the last 20 years.

DTH Services: Since its inception in the year 2003 in India, DTH services have had phenomenal growth, adding new subscribers at a rate of around one million per month, attaining a registered subscriber base of around 46.25 million subscribers of pay DTH services, catered to by six pay DTH operators by

March 2012. This is besides the viewership serviced by the free DTH services of Doordarshan. Over the period, apart from the increase in the conventional TV channels, the operators of DTH services have been adding several innovative offerings such as value added services (VAS), interactive services including movie on demand, gaming, shopping, etc.

Cable Services: The cable TV services sector is the largest pay television service sector with an estimated subscriber base of around 94 million subscribers. The cable TV services in India, at present, are mostly analogue (non-addressable cable TV systems) in nature. The evolution of technology paved the way for bringing about digitization with addressability in the cable TV sector. Accordingly, the authority, on 5 August 2010, gave its recommendations on implementation of Digital Addressable Cable TV Systems (DAS) across the country along with a roadmap to achieve the same.

Radio: In India, radio coverage is available in Shortwave (SW), Medium-wave (MW) and Frequency Modulation (FM) mode. There were 245 private FM radio stations operational by March 2012, besides the public service broadcaster—All India Radio (AIR) having a network of 237 broadcasting centres with 149 medium frequency (MW), 54 high frequency (SW) and 177 FM transmitters. With a view to further expand the spread of FM services to other cities, particularly in J&K, North Eastern States and island territories and to address certain other issues, the government, on 25 July 2011, issued consolidated policy guidelines on phase III of expansion of FM radio broadcasting through private agencies. The phase III is intended to extend FM radio's reach to 294 cities with additional 839 FM radio stations, thereby, boosting the regional growth of FM radio stations. It is expected that post-phase III, the FM radio will cover around 85 per cent of the territory of the country. The radio sector in the country witnessed another expansion with the opening up of Community Radio Stations (CRS). CRS is set up with the involvement of various educational institutions and civil society organizations. As on March 2012, out of the 167 licenses issued for the setup of community radio stations, 130 community radio stations have become operational.

In sum, the growth trends in telecom and broadcast sector experienced since mid-1990s continues to be on an upward swing. The Telecom sector continued to register an impressive growth during the year as the number of telephone subscriptions registering a growth of 12.41 per cent and the number of Internet subscribers registering an annual growth of about 3.19 million. The number of Broadband connections increased from 11.89 millions to 13.81 millions, whereas, in broadcast sector India's TV industry is registering a growth of around 11 per cent during this year. The FM radio sector has also shown impressive growth. The last decade has significantly changed the dynamics of the cable & satellite (C&S) TV market. The DTH subscribers are growing at a rate of around 1 million per month. India has emerged as the country with the largest DTH subscriber base. This clearly indicates the growing popularity and acceptability of digital addressable platforms which have a lot more to offer to all the stakeholders. In India, ICTs have impressive growth and have a bright future.

ICTs in Rural India

A holistic development of India as a nation rests on a sustained and holistic development of rural India. In post-Independence period, the government took upon itself the major responsibility of development in rural domain, many projects were implemented. The access to radio was supreme at that period, the use of radio for rural development was conceived first through rural radio forums. After radio it was television on which one of the biggest technological experiments SITE (Satellite Instructional Television Experiment) was launched for educational and rural development. The one year experiment (August 1975-July 1976) was aimed to provide direct broadcasting of instructional and educational programmes on television in 2400 villages in the states of Andhra Pradesh, Bihar, Karnataka, Madhya Pradesh, Odisha and Rajasthan. In post-media liberalization phase, Government of India announced the policy for Community Radio Broadcasting and Community radio is expected to focus on issues relating to health, education, environment, agriculture, rural and community development. For the last few years, the State Government, NGOs and some innovative companies have tried to overcome technologically barrier by developing pilot projects in a rural settings. Kiosk-based approaches to deliver e-governance have received considerable attention and finance. In recent times, ICT is playing a role of catalyst in rural development. It is used in every aspect of information, management and governance of development. ICT has emerged as a new way of reaching out to the people at grassroots level. ICT applications into the domain of Indian rural development dates back to 1986 when the Computerized Rural Information Systems Project (CRISP) was launched in 1986 by the Ministry of Rural Development. Under this project, every district in the country was provided with computers and a software called CRISP (now, re-named as Rural Soft) to help District Rural Development Agencies (DRDAs) to manage Ministry of Rural Development's programmes more efficiently. Indian Government has realized the role of the rural development and the contribution of IT in the development of rural markets. In recent years, information and communication technologies (ICTs) have been deployed in numerous initiatives in rural communities in the country. There are many projects underway that are using ICT to reduce poverty, overall rural development and promote good governance. A large number of projects are introduced in the rural area with many upcoming projects in pipeline; which are likely to be introduced by the government in the short span of time (Kapoor, Sindhi and Khosla, 2011).

Despite the huge potential to harness ICT for agricultural and rural development, only a few isolated projects have been initiated in India. Many of these projects were started by NGOs, private organizations, cooperative bodies and governmental organizations. There have been some initiatives in India, using ICT for agricultural and rural development. Indian experiences with IT projects are Gyandoot project (Madhya Pradesh); Warana Wired Village project (Maharashtra); Information Village project of the M.S. Swaminathan Research Foundation (MSSRF), Punducherry; iKisan project of the Nagarjuna Group of Companies (Andhra Pradesh); Automated Milk Collection Centres of Amul Dairy Cooperatives (Gujarat); Land Record Computerisation (Bhoomi), Karnataka; Computer-aided

Online Registration Department (Andhra Pradesh); Online Marketing and CAD in Northern Karnataka; Knowledge Network for Grass Roots Innovations—Society for Research and Initiatives (SRISTI), Gujarat and Application of Satellite Communication for Training Field Extension Workers in Rural Areas (Indian Space Research Organization). In addition, a few non-governmental organizations (NGOs) have initiated ICT projects such as Tarahaat.com by Development Alternatives (Uttar Pradesh and Punjab), Mahitiz-samuha (Karnataka), VOICES-Madhyam Communications (Karnataka), Centre for Alternative Agriculture Media (CAAM), etc. All these initiatives are about creating an IT-enabled rural market from scratch by first developing it, solving its basic problems, figuring out what it needs and then designing a product or service built around that one needs in rural areas (Kapoor, Sindhi and Khosla, 2011).

The potential impact of information and communications technologies (ICTs) on development has recently become a much contested issue within the development discourse. Proponents of ICTs (World Bank, 2002; UNDP, 2001; Pohjola, 2002; Braga, 1998) take an optimistic view and highlight the positive effects of the Internet and other forms of ICTs to create new economic, social and political opportunities for developing countries and the poor. Its critics, on the other hand, take a pessimistic view and claim that ICTs due to existing socio-economic inequalities will favour the privileged segments within society and not reach the economically and socially disadvantaged, thus, leading to a widening of the socio-economic gap within the society (Panos, 1998; Wade, 2002; Gumucio, 2001). India still breathes in villages and this becomes obvious when the fact is taken into consideration that more than 700 millions of its population resides in about 636 thousand villages of this country; but even after six decades of independence, rural India is characterized by severe poverty, illiteracy, lack of health services, lack of employment opportunities and overall backwardness. Rural areas are often regarded as information-poor, and information provision has always been a central component of rural development initiatives. Keeping in view these predominant features of rural India—Information and Communication

Technology (ICT) has earned its reputation to be the key to information-flow for intensifying the development efforts in rural India and is being considered as an imperative strategy for achieving the goal of sustainable rural development. Finally, the contextualized approach to ICTs underscores the importance of the socio-economic and cultural context, which is being considered crucial for better understanding of the potential effects of ICTs on development and the empowerment of poor communities (Avgerou, 2001; Walsham, 1993, 1998).

Information is critical to the social and economic activities that comprise the development process. Telecommunications, as a means of sharing information, is not simply a connection between people, but a link in the chain of the development process itself (Hudson, 1995). In the past decade (1991 to 2000), India has seen a veritable telecommunications revolution which is the result of effective regulatory and policy environment coupled with an enterprising telecommunications sector made of both public and private service providers. The growth of rural teledensity is remarkable as it has risen to 36 per cent as on 30 August 2011 from a mere 1.7 per cent in 2004. In fact, today rural teledensity is growing at a much faster rate than urban teledensity. At the beginning of 2011, there were 282.29 millions rural connections (most of which are wireless), as compared to a mere 4.84 million (only landline) phones in the year 2000. Practically, all growth has come from mobile telephony and the private sector has played a huge role in this expansion. With an average family size of five, it may be assumed that almost every rural household owns a mobile phone. If not, then there are Public Calling Offices and Universal Service Obligation Fund-sponsored Village Public Telephones in almost every inhabited census village in the country. Rural India is certainly well-connected through telephones though not to such an extent by the Internet. Yet, even in small towns and villages a good percentage of Indians do access the Internet regularly in shared spaces (public kiosks, offices, educational institutions, etc). The smart phone is the leading mode for individual Internet access suggesting a good market potential for wireless broadband services. Certainly, the growth of rural telephony, especially mobile telephony has brought about improved connectivity. However, much more needs to be done if the benefits of telecommunications connectivity are to translate into overall rural development. Improving broadband penetration is one key focus area and this is being addressed actively by the Department of Telecommunications. Thus, the Universal Service Obligation Fund has launched a Wireline Broadband Scheme in 2009 and is at an advanced stage of formulation of a Rural Wireless Broadband Scheme. It is also to fund the National Optic Fibre Network (NOFN) which shall connect 2,50,000 village panchayats and co-located Bharat Nirman Kendras [erstwhile Common Service Centres (CSCs)] with Optic Fibre, thereby, providing high speed broadband facilities. Bandwidth from NOFN will also be available to all licensed telecom service providers to provide broadband services in rural areas (Gulati, 2012).

India has achieved tremendous increase in rural teledensity and the government's focus is now squarely on rural broadband. Going ahead, apart from ubiquitous and affordable access to ICTs, greater emphasis must be placed on the availability and relevance of services and content in local language or multi-media/accessible format as per needs of target beneficiaries. Also, capacity building of various stakeholders to use ICTs is essential for the goal of ICT-enabled rural development to be achieved. This requires a shift in focus away from purely technology-related issues to the evolution of policies, strategies and schemes that ensure cross-sectoral and multi-stakeholder involvement and engagement including most of all the local communities and target beneficiaries themselves. The draft National ICT and Telecom Policies of the Indian Government and the recent Special Initiatives of the USOF are steps in the right direction (Gulati, 2012).

Conclusion

Both conventional traditional media and new ICTs have played a major role in diffusing information and have much more potential. Traditional media have been used very successfully in developing countries. Print, video, television, films, slides, pictures, drama, dance, folklore, group discussions, meetings, exhibitions and demonstrations have also been used to speed up the flow of information. New ICTs, however, have the potential of getting vast amounts of information in a more timely, comprehensive and cost-effective manner, and could be used together with traditional media. The revolution in the use of ICT has profound implications for economic and social development and has pervaded every aspect of human life. There is little question that the world is becoming more interconnected. The development of networks—and the services that run over them—has become a high priority in many countries as their importance for achieving economic and social objectives has been recognized. As a result, advanced broadband networks are being deployed around the world at an increasing pace. India has also achieved tremendous increase in rural teledensity and the government's focus is now squarely on rural broadband. Going ahead, apart from ubiquitous and affordable access to ICTs, Indian Government needs to give greater emphasis to the availability and relevance of the services and content in local language or multi-media/accessible format as per needs of target beneficiaries. Also, capacity building of various stakeholders to use ICTs is essential for the goal of ICT-enabled rural development to be achieved. This requires a shift in focus away from purely technology-related issues to the evolution of policies, strategies and schemes that ensure cross-sectoral and multi-stakeholder involvement and engagement including most of the local communities and target beneficiaries. In this regard, the recently drafted National I.T. and Telecom Policies of the Indian Government and the recent Special Initiatives of the USOF are steps in the right direction.

REFERENCES

Adu, B. (2002). *Building a national consensus for sustainable and business friendly ICT*. African Telecom Summit 2002, Accra, Ghana, 12-14 March.

Avgerou, C. (2001). "The significance of context in information systems and organisational change". *Information Systems Journal*, 11, pp. 43-63.

Bajwa, G.S. (1999). "ICT policy in India in the era of liberalisation: its impact and consequences". *GBER*, 3(2): 49-61.

Black, J. (1999). "Information rich—Information poor, bridging the digital divide". International Institute for Communication and Development. Available at: www.iicd.org

Braga, C.P. (1998). "Inclusion or exclusion, information for development (InfoDev)". The World Bank, http://www.unesco.org/courier/1998_12/uk/dossier/txt21.htm

Buhalis, D. (2003). "eAirlines: Strategic and tactical use of ICTs in the airline industry". *Information and Management*, 41: 805-25.

Butner, A. (2003). "Development communication theory and the various uses of radio in community development: A historical perspective and review of current trends". *Carolina Papers*. The University of North Carolina at Chapel Hill. http://cgi.unc.edu/uploads/media_items/a-presentation-of-development-communication-theory-and-the-various-uses-of-radio-in-community-development-a-historical-perspective-and-review-of-current-trends.original.pdf

Castells, M. (2000). *The Rise of the Network Society*. Malden and Oxford: Blackwell Publishing.

Digital Opportunity Initiatives (2001). Creating a Development Dynamics, July 2001. Accenture, UNDP & Markle Foundation.

FICCI-KPMG. (2012). Indian media and entertainment industry report 2012.

Gumucio Dagron, A. (2001). *Making waves: Stories of participatory communication for social change*. Rockefellèr Foundation.

Hamelink, C.J. (1997). "New information and communication technologies: Social development and cultural change". Discussion Paper No. 86. UNRISD.

Herselman, M.E. and Hay, H.R. (2003). "Challenges posed by information and communication technologies (ICT) for South African higher education institutions. *Informing Science*, pp. 931-43.

Hudson, H. (1995). *Economic and social benefits of rural telecommunications: A report to the World Bank*. University of San Francisco at http://www.usfca.edu/facstaff/hudson/papers/Benefits%20of%20Rural%20Communication.pdf

Human Development Report (2001). *Making New Technologies Work for Human Development*. UNDP. New York: Oxford University Press. I&B Ministry, India retrieved on 12-03-012 from http://mib.in/demo.aspx

ITDG (2001). "Enable people to make technologies work for them. ITDG's response to the Human Development Report 2001". Retrived on 8-10-2009 from http://www.itdg.org/html/advocacy/docs/itdg_response_to_hdr_june2.pdf

ITU (2013). *ICT facts and figures, the world in 2013*, International Telecommunication Union, Geneva, Switzerland.

ITU (2013). *Measuring the WSIS targets: A statistical framework (2013)*. International Telecommunication Union. Geneva, Switzerland.

Kaplan, D. (2001). *Defining the information society, initial preparatory workshop*. United Nations World Summit on the Information Society, 5-6 December. Coppet, Switzerland.

Kappor, B., Sindhi, V. and Khosla, A. (2011). "Impact of information communication technologies (ICTS) on marketing and development". *VSRD International Journal of Computer Science and Information Technology*, 1(6): 396-407.

Mansell, R. and When, U. (1998). *Knowledge Societies: Information Technology for Sustainable Development*. Oxford University Press.

Michiels, S.I. and Van, Crowder L. (2001). *Discovering the 'magic box': Local appropriation of information and communication technologies (ICTs)*. Rome: Food and Agriculture Organisation of the United Nations, Communication for Development Group, Extension, Education and Communication Service.

Munyua, H. (2000). "Application of information communication technologies in the agricultural sector in Africa: A gender perspective". *Gender and Information Revolution in Africa,* edited by Rathgeber, E. and Adera, E.O. IDRC/ECA. pp. 85-123. Verlaeten (2002).

Negroponte (1998). The third shall be first. *Wired Magazine*, Issue 6.1, January 1998.

Norris, P. (2001). *Digital Divide: Civic Engagement, Information Poverty and the Internet Worldwide*. John F. Kennedy School of Government (KSG), Harvard University.

Orlikowski, W.J. (2000). Using technology and constituting structures: A practice lens for studying technology in organizations". *Organizational Science*, 11(4): 404-28.

Panos (1998). "The Internet and poverty". *Panos media briefing,* no. 28. Panos Institute, London.

Pohjola, M. (2002). "The new economy: Facts, impacts and policies". *Information Economics and Policy.*

Richard, W. Oliver (999). *The Coming Biotech Age.* McGraw Hill.

Rwashana, A.S. and Williams, D.W. (2008). "Enhancing immunization healthcare delivery through the use of information communication technology". *International Journal of Education and Development Using ICT*, 4(2): 144-56.

Schware, R. (2003). "Information and Communications Technology (ICT) Aagencies: Functions, Structures, and Best Operational Practices". *Info*, 5(3): 3-7.

Selwyn, N. (2002). "Defining the digital divide: Developing a theoretical understanding of inequalities in the information age". *Cardiff School of Social Sciences Occasional Paper, 49.* School of Social Sciences, Cardiff University, Cardiff. [online] Available: www.cf.ac.uk/socsi/ict/definingdigitaldivide.pdf (March 2, 2013).

Shanke, R.D. (2008). "ICT and tourism: Challenges and opportunities". Conference on *Tourism in India—Challenges ahead*, 15-17 May 2008, IIML. [online] Available: http://dspace.iimk.ac.in/bitstream/2259/536/1/50-58.pdf (March 3, 2011).

Spanos, Y.E., Prastacos, G.P., and Poulymenakou, A. (2002). "The relationship between information and communication technologies adoption and management". *Information and Management,* 39, pp. 659-75.

Sewanyana, J.K. (2009). "ICT usage in microfinance institutions in Uganda". *The African Journal of Information Systems (AJIS),* 1(3): 5-28.

Thomas, J.J. and Parayil, G. (2008). "The capabilities to bridge the social and digital divides: Evidence from Andhra Pradesh and Kerala, India". *Development and Change*, 38(1).

Telecom Regulatory Authority of India (2012). *Annual Report (2011-2012).* Retrieved from http://www.trai.gov.in/WriteReadData/

Miscell/Document/201301150318386780062Annual%20 Report%20English%202012.pdf

UNDP (2001). "Making new technologies work for human development". *Human Development Report 2001*. UNDP. Oxford.

UNDP (2005). *Gender equality and empowerment of women through ICT*. United Nations Division for the Advancement of Women. New York, USA. www.un.org/womenwatch/daw/public/w2000-09.05-ict-e.pdf

Verlaeten, M.P. (2002). *Policy frameworks for the knowledge-based economy: ICTs, innovation and human resources—An OECD global forum*. OECD. Paris. [Online] Available: http://www.oecd.org/dataoecd/49/11/1961062.pdf [Accessed 16-9-2009].

Wachholz, C. and Meleisea, E. (2006). *Using ICT to develop literacy*. UNESCO: Bangkok.

Wade, R. (2002). "Bridging the digital divide: new route to development or new form of dependency?" *Global Governance*, 8(4). Oct-Dec.

Walsham, G. (1993). "The emergence of interpretivism in IS research". *Information Systems Research*, 6(4): 376-94.

Walsham, G. (1995). "Interpretative case studies in IS research: Nature and method". *European Journal of Information Systems*, 4: 74-81.

World Bank (1990). *World Development Report 1990*. New York: Oxford University Press.

World Bank (1995). *Harnessing Information for Development*. World Bank Group. Vision and Strategy.

World Bank (1999). "Knowledge for Development". *World Development Report*. New York: Oxford University Press.

World Bank. (2000). *The networking revolution, opportunities and challenges for developing countries*. Global Information and Communication Technologies Department.

Yu, E. (2010). "Information and communications technology in food assistance". [online] Available: http://home.wfp.org/stellent/groups/public/documents/newsroom/wfp225972.pdf (January 15, 2012).

9

Self-Help Groups and Rural Development

Manju Panwar

ABSTRACT

Programmes directly targeting poor families and supporting their livelihoods promotion hold a major promise to trigger pro-poor growth. However, the past record of implementation of these programmes has not been successful and the pro-poor growth that they were supposed to generate has actually not taken place. Despite efforts made over the past few decades, rural poverty in India continues to be significant. One of the main reasons of poverty is the lack of access to productive assets and financial resources for both individuals and communities. In recent years, the SHGs have become a very important tool for reducing poverty. In economic literature, credit has been assigned a docile and a passive role. It has been accepted as a lubricant or facilitator of trade, commerce and industry. But in reality credit plays a far more powerful social and political role than is generally admitted. It is, in fact, a powerful weapon. With appropriate credit institutions and credit policies, it is possible to drive the society towards a desired shape. In order to develop our villages, need of the hour is to DRDA, banks and other institutions which are involved in the promotion of SHGs should understand their responsibility towards society. They should participate in SHGs bank linkage programme with greater enthusiasm and dedication. The success of every programme depends upon the collective efforts. Hence, it is imperative that there is proper coordination and cooperation to fulfill the objectives of the rural development.

Introduction

Programmes directly targeting poor families and supporting their livelihoods promotion hold a major promise to trigger pro-poor growth. However, the past records of implementation of these programmes has not been successful and the pro-poor growth that they were supposed to generate has actually not taken place. Despite efforts made over the past few decades, rural poverty in India continues to be significant. While the anti-poverty programmes have been strengthened in successive years and while the percentage terms, poverty levels reduced from 56.44 per cent of India's population in 1973-74 to 37.27 per cent in 1993-94 and to 27.1 per cent in 1999-2000, the number of rural poor has more or less remained static and is estimated to be about 244 million persons. It is in this context that the self-employment programmes assume significance for; they alone can provide income to the rural poor on a sustainable basis.

To begin with Integrated Rural Development Programme (IRDP) was the only self-employment programme. Beginning with Training of Rural Youth for Self-Employment (TRYSEM), a number of allied programmes were added over the years such as Development of Women and Children in Rural Areas (DWCRA), Supply of Improved Tool Kits to Rural Artisans (SITRA) and Ganga Kalyan Yojana (GKY). The multicity of programmes, being viewed as separate programme in them, resulted in a lack of proper social intermediation, absence of desired linkages among these programmes *inter se* and the implementation being more concerned with achieving individual programme targets rather than focusing on the substantive issue of sustainable income generation. To rectify the situation, government decided to re-structure the self-employment programmes. A new programme known as "Swaranjayanti Gram Swarozgar Yojana" (SGSY) has been launched from April 1999. This is a holistic programme covering all aspects of self-employment such as organization of the poor into Self-Help Groups (SHGs), training, credit, technology, infrastructure and marketing. Keeping in view the fact the rural poor in general and rural women in particular suffer from inability to change their immediate environment on account of group solidarity on the one hand and the incapacity for action on the other hand. It is based on the group approach, i.e. organizing the rural poor into Self-Help Groups through social mobilization, their capacity building, training and provision of income generation assets through a mix of bank credit and government subsidy.

With the coming into force of SGSY, the earlier programmes IRDP, TRYSEM, DWCRA, SITRA, GKY and MWS are no longer in operation. The objective of SGSY is to bring the assisted poor families above the poverty line by ensuring appreciable increase in incomes over a period of time. This objective is to be achieved by *inter alia* organizing the rural poor into Self-Help Groups (SHGs) through a process of social mobilization, their training and capacity building and provision of income generating assets through a mix of bank credit and government subsidy.

An overview of the implementation of SGSY over the last ten years throws up a mixed picture. There is a widespread acceptance in the country of the need for poor into SHGs as pre-requisite for poverty reduction. In the last ten years about 250 lakh rural BPL households have been organized and brought under the SHG network. However, it has also brought into focus shortcomings like vast regional variations in mobilization of rural poor, insufficient capacity building of beneficiaries, insufficient investments for building community institutions, weak linkages with the banks leading to low credit mobilization, lack of repeat financing and lack of dedicated manpower to implement the programme. The focus on single livelihood activity has not met the multiple livelihood requirements of the poor.

Shylendra (1998) reported the experiences of the Shearhead Team from the Institute of Rural Management Anand (IRMA) in promoting eight women's SHGs from Bidaj village (Kheda district) during 1994-96. He identified three main reasons for the failure of SHGs to become stable and make any significant impact on the socio-economic life of women: (i) wrong approach in the formation of SHGs, (ii) misconceptions about goals of SHGs among both the members and the team, and (iii) failure in ensuring conditions necessary for their successful functioning.

Self-Help Group—Tool for Rural Development

One of the main reasons of poverty is the lack of access to productive assets and financial resources for both individuals and communities. In recent years, the SHGs have become a very important tool for reducing poverty. In economic literature, credit has been assigned a docile and a passive role. It has been accepted as a lubricant or facilitator of trade, commerce and industry. But in reality credit plays a far more powerful social and political role than is generally admitted. It is, in fact, a powerful weapon. With appropriate credit institutions and credit policies, it is possible to drive the society towards a desired shape. The more credit one can receive, the more resources one can generate. And, the more resources he can command, the more powerful he can be. Credit creates entitlement to resources, asserts Mohd. Yunus, the Founder of Grameen Bank (Yunus, 1993).

Since the 1980s, the field of microfinance has grown substantially and several experiments have taken place across the world. One of the most prominent and visible is the Grameen Bank in Bangladesh, that has developed highly effective techniques such as taking services to the village level, promoting and motivating groups of the poor, use of group guarantees, compulsory savings, mobilization, intensive supervision of borrowers and decentralized and cost-effective operations for lending to the poor (McGuire and Conroy, 2000).

Bangladesh is one of the Third World nations where women have a very low socio-economic status. The economy is poor and vast majority of the people still live below poverty line. The most vulnerable among the poor are the women. They are already in a disadvantageous position. So, the economic empowerment is the main way to uplift their pitiable condition. Since its inception, the Grameen Bank has been working for women empowerment by providing free collateral loans at their doorsteps.

In the late 1990s, SHGs as a concept had taken the shape of a movement in Andhra Pradesh. Today, it has become an integral part of all development programmes. A decade ago, cooperatives—which had evolved as institutions for self-help among common interest groups—played a major role in development across all sectors. Gradually, with changing national and developmental scenario, SHGs emerged as institutions for thrift and credit. At present, SHGs have become synonymous with women's groups. Evolved in the 1990s as an alternative to cooperatives, SHGs today account for one-third of the total customers in rural banks and hold about one-fourth of the rural banking business.

Many studies have been conducted to find out the impact of SHGs on women's status and it has been found by them that microfinance and self-help groups have resulted in positive changes in the economic lives of women folk. Ranjula Bali Swain and Fan Yang Wallentin (2007) tried to study the impact of microfinance and SHGs on women empowerment. They collected data from five states, namely Odisha, Andhra Pradesh, Karnataka, Maharashtra, Tamil Nadu, and Uttar Pradesh. They found a significant increase in women empowerment of the SHGs members. This research also noticed that there has been positive change in the attitude of beneficiaries. Consequently, several groups have according to them, become centres for initiating social actions against dowry system, alcoholism, illiteracy and divorce.

The SHGs can be built on social capital of the local community especially women to carry out thrift and credit activities to initiate micro-income generating activities for a sustainable livelihood (Moser, 1989). According to Kingree (1994), the concept of SHG can be traced to collection of people to informal groups with an aim to overcome the problems related to a particular negative status. Gregory and Marry have defined SHGs as being cost free, member governed, peer-led group made up of people, who share the same problems or situations. Kurtz, 1997 has defined SHG as a supportive, educational, usually change-oriented mutual aid group that addresses a single life problem or condition shared by all members.

The diversity of SHG has been summarized by Charles Zastrow in the following words:

> Self-Help Groups have been seen as support systems, as social movements, as spiritual movements and secular religions, as systems of consumer participation, as alternative care giving systems, as adjunct to professional helping systems, as intentional communities, as sub-cultural entities that represent a way of life, as supplementary communities, as expressive-social influence groups, and as organizations of the deviant and stigmatized.

Concept of SHG

SHG formation is a social mobilization process which enables the poor to build their own organization in which they participate freely, fully and directly and take decision on all issues concerning poverty eradication, employment creation and income generation. SHG has to pass through the various stages in its development, starting from group formation to stabilization, microfinance and micro-enterprise development, a stage in which the group takes up economic activity of its choice for income generating activities including entrepreneurship development as well as skill development training.

According to Meena (2003), an SHG is composed of about 10-20 members. Each homogenous group meets monthly or weekly close to members' home. At the designated meeting, all members save a commonly agreed amount. The group then lends these savings to its members, stores them in a cashbox, or deposits them in a group bank account in order to leverage a group loan. In cases of emergency or need, members can access a loan quickly from their group's fund. The basic philosophy lies in the fact that shortcomings and weaknesses at the individual level are overcome by the collective responsibility and security afforded by the formation of a group of such individuals. The collective coming together of individual members is also used for a number of purposes: education and awareness building, collective bargaining power and peer pressure, among others. As the group mature, the initiate income enhancement and entrepreneurial activities. These can be both individual and group activities. Groups also start connecting with other groups in the area and start the process of cluster formation, networking and federating, thus acquiring a larger status and becoming a larger pressure group operating in an enhanced sphere.

According to Kropp and Suran (2002), the members of SHGs make voluntary thrift on a regular basis and use the pooled resources to make small interest-bearing loans to their members on the terms decided by the group. The process helps them to imbibe the essential of financial intermediation, including prioritization of needs, setting terms and conditions, and account keeping. This gradually builds financial discipline and credit history for themselves, as the money involved in lending operations is their own hard earned money saved over time with great difficulty. They also learn to handle resources of a size that is much beyond their individual capacities.

Purpose of SHG

The SHGs act as a forum for the members to provide space and support to each other. These groups enable the members to learn to cooperate and work in a group environment by providing savings and an effective credit delivery mechanism that cater to the economic needs of their members.

- Provide the women a space for collective action for social and economic development; promote self-help and mutual cooperation through sharing, learning and acting.
- Inculcate the habit and promote savings among the poor and use of the same to meet the consumption and emergency credit needs to regulate household-level cash flows.
- Act as local financial institution to provide a range of financial services for the poor at the doorstep and leverage resources from bank thus reducing the transaction costs.
- Arresting leakage of income and get the poor out of the clutched of usurious moneylenders, provide credit to support livelihoods.

Structure and System

- All the members of the group constitute the general body. The membership of the group would be limited to primarily women. The size of the group could range from 10 to 20 members.
- Each group would elect/select 2-3 members as leaders for a specific period on a consensus basis to take greater role to lead and manage the activities. They could also act as signatories of the group and involve in responsibilities such as ensuring regular group meetings, attendance, implementation of norms, accountability, transparency, bookkeeping and represent the group at various forums. Rotation of leadership would be promoted to provide opportunities for all members to build their capacities.
- Each group would evolve a set of norms over a period of time by involving members. The norms could be on any of the following aspects based on their need and context:
    - o Membership related: Inclusion, cessation, withdrawal.
    - o Attendance related: Time, place, leave and absence.
    - o Saving related: Types of products, amount, frequency and interest/dividends on savings, sharing profits.
    - o Loans related: Types of products, eligibility criteria, prioritization, purposes, loans based on micro plans, quantum, number of loans/member at a time, installments, rate of interest, penalties, delinquency management, etc.
    - o Social development norms: Children's education, basic health and sanitation related.
    - o Leaderships related: Election/selection, tenure, required characteristics.
    - o Roles and responsibilities of leaders.
    - o Accounting system: Maintain prescribed books of accounts, bookkeeper—preferably paid and one among the group members, community auditing system.
    - o Representation and participation in federation.

Principles of SHGs

There are certain broad principles which govern the functioning of SHGs. These include (Srinivasan, 1996):

- The SHG is a network of members who fulfill locational criteria.
- They are resident in the area and are homogeneous.
- They have rules/norms regarding their functioning.
- Savings first, credit thereafter. Personalized services suiting the requirements of the members are ensured.
- SHGs hold regular meetings to ensure participation of members in the activities of the group.
- SHGs maintain accounts.
- Group leaders are elected by members and rotated periodically.
- Transparency in operations of the group and participatory decision-making ensure that the benefits to members are evenly distributed.
- Market rates of interest on savings and credit are charged.
- Group liability and peer pressure act as substitutes for traditional collateral for loans.

Challenges Faced by SHGs

No doubt, the SHGs approach to rural development is an innovative one as it lays emphasis on two important aspects that is group enterprise and key activity. From time to time, various workshops/conferences are being organized at the state, national and international levels in order to suggest measures to further strengthen the SHG movement for rural development. Dr. Raghuvansh Prasad Singh, former Union Minister of Rural Development has also emphasized that the SHG movement in the country should be intensified for generating self-employment with the countryside. He opined that facilitators/NGOs should be involved in a big way to ensure that a large number of SHGs are formed, nurtured and linked to economic activities. Despite of this, following challenges have been faced by SHGs:

Lack of Family Support

Development is not a smooth process; it is one step ahead, two steps backward and again two steps ahead. Women who are from the marginalized section need the family support in terms of their husband and in-laws in giving them moral support to go ahead. This problem is becoming more serious when joint families are breaking due to various reasons. If the women have full backing of family, they are able to overcome all their problems discussed in this chapter more confidently.

Faulty Below Poverty Line List

SGSY is specifically focused on the below poverty line households and poorest of the poor is expected to get the benefit from this. Below BPL households, identified through the BPL Census conducted in 2002 by Ministry of Rural Development, Government of India, and duly approved by the Gram Sabha will form the basis for identification of families for assistance under the SGSY. The guidelines further say that the rural poor such as the landless labour, educated unemployment, rural artisans and disabled persons should be covered under the scheme. But in real picture, it is the economically well-off sections of rural areas are getting the benefits of the scheme. On the other hand, the poor women who were eligible to harness the benefits of the scheme by becoming the members of SHGs could not get benefits because they did not have BPL card.

Conducting Regular Meetings

Holding of monthly meetings of the SHGs is a good indicator of showing that SHGs will be sustained for long time. The group should meet regularly at weekly/fortnightly or monthly intervals as per the rules decided by the members. Regular meeting help the members to come closer and discuss various common problems and their possible solutions. It helps them to understand each other in better way. The periodicity, venue and time for the meetings should be decided by the members. The groups should have a clear agenda for each meeting and discussion should be taken up as per the agenda. But in real sense, their monthly meeting is not taking place as per the rules of the SHG. Reason is that they are not trained to hold the meeting on their own. In the absence of holding regular meeting of the SHG, there is a lack of participation of the members in SHGs which resulted in the lack of interest in running their SHGs.

Lack of Marketing Facilities

Concerted efforts have to be made by administration to organize *melas* of the products of SHGs. These *melas* played a vital role in motivating women to strengthen the activities of their SHGs. These *melas* are organized by DRDAs half yearly and on regular basis. These *melas* or exhibitions are organized at district and block levels. The frequency of organizing these *melas* are very less and on account of that members could not have a regular link with markets for selling their products.

Lack of Cooperation from Bank Officials

SHGs have to face a number of problems in opening their saving account in the banks. First, the SHGs were formed hurriedly by the DRDA officials without any social mobilization and insult to injury was added by seeing the indifferent attitude of bank officials. Some of the bank officials felt that opening of account of the SHG is a cumbersome task and they felt uncomfortable as they found it difficult to cope with rural surroundings.

Reluctant to Provide Loan to SHGs

Credit linkages of SHG members with the bank is an important component of SGSY, as poor have difficulty in obtaining bank loan because of the cumbersome procedures of obtaining it. Bankers not only harass women in opening their accounts but also bother them while providing loan to them. The problem of the bank defaulters has further aggravated the problem. Because of this, poor women would not be able to get the benefits from bank and government agencies.

Recommendations

The SHGs have been able to get recognition in the entire world as an useful tool for poverty alleviation and for improving socio-economic status of rural poor. In India too, these have been making progress in the direction of reducing poverty and empowering rural women. Through a network of the cooperatives, commercial banks, regional rural banks, NABARD and NGOs, SHGs have so far been largely a supply driven and in providing financial services to the poor. Some of the recommendations are being given for strengthening SHGs movement in India.

(1) **Bank Officials Training:** SGSY needs to get a push from the banks. The indifferent attitude of bankers is the major constraint; they take much time in opening the accounts of the SHGs. As a result, some of them could not get loan on time. In this regard, efforts should be made to impart intensive training to the bank officials and make them aware of the importance of SHGs. They should be encouraged to take active interest in the project and reduce the duration of time which is taken for processing the applications and disbursing loans. Efforts should be made through training to change the attitude of bankers towards rural poor people, including the women so that they could treat them as potential business entrepreneurs. Their active involvement should also be sought in the selection of key activities, formation and grading of groups and follow up action after disbursement of loans.

(2) **Marketing:** Another area which needs proper attention is marketing. In general, the beneficiaries have to be made aware of the potential market for their products. They should also be given clear ideas on the various available marketing infrastructures from which they can get benefit. Need of the hour is that more and more marketing facilities be provided at the state and district levels for the sale of products of SHGs. There is need to evolve training packages for entrepreneurship development too to enable rural women to become successful business managers for sustaining micro-enterprises. In this task, role of NGOs, Panchayats, women's organizations, etc. may be enhanced to impart training, skill development and technical knowledge to the leaders and members of SHGs. They badly need marketing support and institutional capacity to handle marketing activities independently.

(3) **Personality Development Training:** It was observed that most of the SHGs disintegrate in the middle because of the lack of

trust among the members of SHGs. In order to be successful, the group requires good team work and active participation of all the members in its activities. Therefore, it is imperative that training should be provided on personality development programmes covering aspects like importance of team work, group dynamics and synergy effects to the beneficiaries so that they can get fullest benefit of the SHGs. In addition to this, training should also be given to the beneficiaries on topics like requirements and provisions, their entitlements and responsibilities under the scheme. Special attention needs to be paid for creating understanding and awareness about the financial aspects of the scheme. The women entrepreneurs should be given training for developing managerial and leadership skills to carry out their responsibilities effectively. The conveners and joint conveners of the enterprises should be rotated normally once a year. This may help in leadership development in all the entrepreneurs.

(4) **Wide Publicity:** The success stories of SGSY beneficiaries need to be given wider publicity. The DRDAs should document and circulate these among the SGSY beneficiaries. Documentaries may also be made to highlight the SHGs which were able to achieve the objectives of SGSY. Despite facing obstacles, while getting loans from the banks. These short films will inspire others to be more innovative and motivate them to continue their income generating activity.

(5) **Innovative Economic Activities:** It has been envisaged in the SGSY guidelines that the groups will move from livelihood to enterprise stage. The guidelines have further laid down that the focus should be on the identification of key activities and concentration on activity cluster. In fact, the very success of the SGSY is going to depend on the identification of the key activities. No doubt, these are identified block-wise, yet the traditional activities are being pursued for income generation instead of innovating new ones. For example, in the field, it was observed that majority of SHGs are opting for dairy loans. Therefore, it is suggested that the DRDAs should provide them help to identify such items which are required by the government departments in bulk and have market demand. Some of the key activities like duri making, soft toys, embroidery, knitting, stitching, pickle

making can be successfully adopted as these have local demand and market. Chalk making, candle making, file and files cover making are other activities which have market in the government offices. The SHGs should also be encouraged to undertake some innovative activities which can give them more earnings. NGOs, bank officials, government agencies should help them in this matter so that they can grab the market opportunities by coming out of traditional activities.

(6) **Not to be Treated as Targeted Approach:** Most of the SHGs are formed in haste. As a result, some of them disintegrate. The main reasons for their disintegration are the lack of attention and regular follow-up. It is, therefore, being suggested that the target approach for the formation of the group should be discarded. Once the names of members of the SHGs have been collected, adequate time should be given to 'nurture' them.

(7) **Involvement of Panchayati Raj Institutions (PRIs):** Gram Panchayats have an important role to play in the implementation of SGSY. There should be no bottlenecks in the communication between the beneficiaries and the implementing agency. The Sarpanch should arrange a meeting of villagers and the implementing authorities at the Gram Panchayat level. This will provide a platform to the people to clear all their doubts related to scheme. It will also create a sense of transparency in the minds of people and they will start trusting and participating in it.

(8) **Involvement of the NGOs:** The NGOs must be trained to form SHGs. They should make efforts to raise the groups to a level of self-managed entity. In addition to this, these should encourage SHGs to participate and to take active role in the social programmes, like family planning, literacy improvement, pulse polio, AIDS awareness, immunization programmes, health care schemes and other similar activities which are beneficial to the village community. Therefore, the NGOs should be given the needed interventions and support by the government to perform these roles.

Conclusion

In order to uproot the persisting poverty and improve the quality of life of people in general and women in particular, both Central and State Governments have been formulating various developmental schemes and programmes and to a large extent, they have been successful in achieving their objectives too. But the cause of concern is that the speed of development has been slow. Even today, millions of people continue to live below poverty line not knowing where the next meal is going to come from. The main problems of rural people are lack of employment, illiteracy, unavailability of clean drinking water, health facilities, etc. Implementation of different rural developmental schemes has helped people in certain areas but has also widened the disparity among the people in the society.

The multiplicity and duplicity of the schemes has also led to confusion to a large extent. One of the other important observations is that the approach still being followed in the implementation of the rural development schemes is top-bottom approach. The intended beneficiaries hardly have a say or a choice at any of the stages, be it planning, implementation, or anything else. On the other hand, this has led to a great mismatch of the interventions being provided with that of needs and expectations of the villagers. In order to develop our villages, need of the hour is to DRDA, banks and other institutions which are involved in the promotion of SHGs should understand their responsibility towards society. They should participate in SHGs bank linkage programme with greater enthusiasm and dedication. The success of every programme depends upon the collective efforts. Hence, it is imperative that there is proper coordination and cooperation to fulfill the objectives of the rural development.

REFERENCES

International Fund for Agricultural Development (2001). *India Country Strategic Opportunities Paper,* Rome.

Katz, A. (1965). Application of Self Help Concept in Current Social Welfare. *Journal of Social Work*, 68-74.

Kingree, J. and Rubac, B. (1994). Understanding Self Help Groups. In J. Thomas, and Powell, *Understanding the Self Help Organizations* (272). New Delhi: Sage Publication.

Kropp, E.W. and Suran, B.S. (2002). Linking Banks and (Financial) SHGs in India: An Assessment Paper presented at the Seminar on SHG-Bank Linkage Programme, November 25-26, New Delhi.

Mcguire, P.B. and Conroy, J.D. (2000). The Microfinance Phenomenon, *Asia Pacific Review*, 7(1): 1-19.

Meena, Z. (2003). Empowering Rural Women: An Approach to Empowering Women through Credit-based Self Help Groups, Delhi: Aakar Publications.

Moser, C. (1989). Gender Planning in the Third World: Meeting Practical and Strategic Gender Needs. *World Development,* 17.

Shylendra, H.S. (1998). *Promoting Women's Self Help Groups: Lessons from an Action Research Project of IRMA,* WP121, Anand: Institute of Rural Management, Anand.

Srinivasan, G. (1996). Financing of self help groups by banks, some issues, working paper 8, BIRD, Lucknow.

Working Group on Rural Poverty Alleviation Programmes for the Tenth Five Year Plan (2002-07). Government of India, New Delhi.

Yunus, M. (1999). Bankers to the Poors: Micro lending and the battle against World Poverty, New York: Public Affairs.

10

Role of Indian Women in Agriculture: An Overview

Rakesh Dwivedi

ABSTRACT

India is the fourth largest home to agriculture sector in the world. Agriculture is the main sector of economic activities because 70 per cent population is involved in this occupation for their livelihood. Women are the backbone of the Indian agriculture workforce. They play a significant role in agriculture and its allied fields but they are less paid worldwide and their contributions to agricultural and rural development are rarely acknowledged. Women have increased participation in agricultural workforce besides doing household activities. They play multidimensional role of wife, mother, homemaker and worker, these entire roles are equally important but women's role as a worker is unknown and unacknowledged. Women had touched all the fields of agriculture and forestry and their participation is also increasing. The government has also made provisions for safety and welfare of women but this is a long-run process for women to be acknowledged them as an active worker—producer in agricultural occupational activities. This paper aims to explore the participation of women in agriculture and its allied fields, this paper will also explore the major obstacles faced by women and provisions for upliftment of women in agriculture.

> "Women are the builder and molder of the nation's destiny. Though delicate and soft as lily, she has a heart, far stronger and bolder than man...she is supreme inspiration of man's onward march."
>
> —Rabindranath Tagore

Introduction

India is a global agricultural powerhouse and fourth largest home to agricultural sector in the world. Agriculture is the backbone of our country and regarded as largest sector of economic activity. India has an estimated 180 million hectares of farm land with 140 million of which are planted and continuously cultivated. The main occupation is agriculture because 70 per cent population is involved in this occupation for their livelihood.

Women are the molder and builder of the nation's destiny. They play a significant role in agriculture and its allied fields. Workforce of women is larger in rural areas than urban areas. The International Labour Organization (ILO) revealed that women are responsible for 50 per cent of production in developing countries. Rural women perform various tasks for their livelihood, and the agriculture is considered as the biggest unrecognized sector where large numbers of women take part actively. Since ages, women have been playing a key role in agricultural activities. Women participation in farm activities is increasing day by day because men are moving to cities for occupation and more income. This increased participation of rural women in agricultural is leading towards feminization of agriculture and contributing for economic growth and progress of the country.

This paper aims to explore the participation of women in agriculture and its allied fields, this paper will also explore the major obstacles faced by women and provisions for upliftment of women in agriculture. The famous agricultural scientist Swaminathan said that it was women who first domesticated crop plants and thereby initiated the art and science of farming. While men went out hunting in search of food, women started gathering seeds from the native flora and began cultivating and continue to play a key role in the conservation of basic life support systems such as land, water flora and fauna. They have protected the health of the soil through organic recycling and promoted crop security through the maintenance of varietal diversity and genetic resistance.

Women play multidimensional role in farm and domestic activities. Women cultivators and agricultural labourers perform about 70 per cent of all agricultural activities. Women bear responsibility of her family, children, household chores, etc. as well as she work on farmland also. On the farm land, she does all activities like land preparation, seed preparation, irrigation, etc. but it was observed that yet women performs these various responsibilities still her work is not acknowledged. They face extreme disadvantages in terms of payment of wages, land rights, decision-making in farm activities and representation as a farmer. Their valuable contribution is ignored and they are not identified as farmers. According to the Food and Agricultural Organization (FAO), there are only 9.21 per cent women own farm land in India. That is a major drawback for women identification as a farmer.

Women have dual responsibilities within and outside the home. She performs four distinct roles as result of biological and social factors, she plays role of mother, wife, home maker and worker. Her role as a worker is equally important as other three roles. But her role as an active worker and producers rarely acknowledged, though it is significant to family survival. Despite their importance in agriculture production, women face various problems, they are considered as unskilled workers, their work is unacknowledged and less paid as compare to men workers.

According to the Census of India (2011), there are 68 per cent of the total population lives in rural areas followed by 70 per cent of female living in rural areas having 58.8 per cent literacy rate. Women form an integral part of the Indian workforce. According to the information provided by the Registrar General of India, the work participation rate for women was 25.63 per cent in 2001. While there has been an improvement in the work participation rate of women, it continues to be less substantially less in comparison to the work participation of men. In 2001, the work participation rate for women in rural areas was 30.79 per cent as compared to 11.88 per cent in the urban areas. In the rural areas, women are mainly involved as cultivators and agricultural labourers. The NSS (National Sample Survey) 61st round survey on employment-unemployment and Census (2001) population projections revealed that women workers were 146.89 million or just 32.2 per cent of the total workers and 72.8 per cent of women worker were employed in agriculture. Table 1 shows some findings of Census of India (2001) regarding women participation in workforce of country.

Table 1: An Overview of Women Workforce in India

1.	Total women population (2001)	494.83 millions
2.	Total women workers (2001)	127.05 millions
3.	Total women main workers (2001)	72.65 millions
4.	Total women marginal workers (2001)	54.40 millions
5.	Total women owner cultivators (2001)	41.30 millions
6.	Total women agriculture wage workers (2001)	50.09 millions
7.	Total women household industry workers (2001)	08.08 millions
8.	Total women other workers (2001)	27.57 millions

Source: Census of India, 2001

Women play a significant and crucial role in agriculture and allied fields, women has maximum participation in cutting, clearing and drying of grains, storage, processing operations and major part of cleaning fields, raising nursery for seedling, weeding, shifting production to threshing floor, winnowing and grading operations whereas women participation was less in ploughing of fields, plant protection measures and marketing activities.

On the basis of activities performed by women on farmland and home, their role could be classified as following:

Agricultural Activities: Women perform all activities related to agriculture more or less. She does land preparation, seed preparation, storage of grains irrigation, etc.

Domestic Activities: Child rearing, household chores, etc.

Allied Activities: Cattle management, fuel and fodder collection, milking, etc.

Social Activities: Attending social gathering, ceremonies and following family rituals, etc.

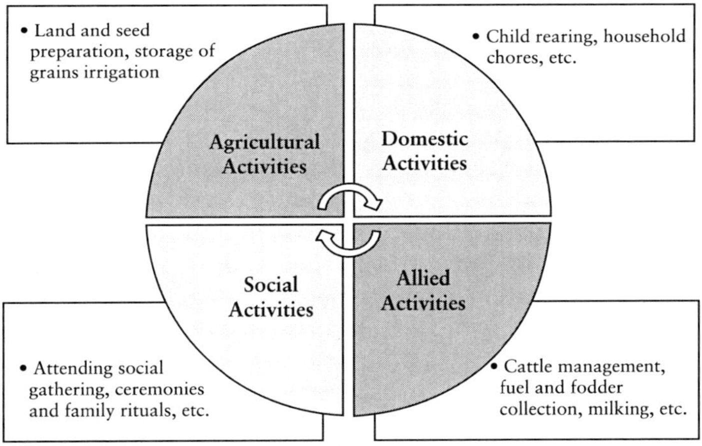

Fig. 1: Activity Performed by Women in Rural Areas

Women's Contributions in Agriculture

***Women as an Agricultural Labour*:** In India, majority of rural women workers are employed as labourers and cultivators, with the labour force participation rate of 31.56 per cent which is less than men's rate of 68.44 per cent. Women work for longer hours and participate in most of the field work related to crop production, and have a significantly higher involvement in livestock production, forest resource production and fishery. The Census of India (2001) shows that there are nearly 127 million cultivators, 107.50 million agricultural laborers and six million other farm workers engaged in livestock, forestry and plantation. Women workers account 38 per cent of total agricultural labourers, and 21 per cent of livestock, forestry and plantation workers.

Table 2: Share of Women in Agricultural Operations

S.No.	Activity	Involvement (Percentage)
1.	Land preparation	32
2.	Seed cleaning and sowing	80
3.	Inter-cultivation activities	86
4.	Harvesting, reaping, winnowing, drying, cleaning and storage	84

Source: Registrar General of India, New Delhi 2001

Involvement of women in agricultural activities widely depends on their farming system, caste, economic status and stages in the family cycle. Generally, poorer families have greater involvement of women as labourers in agricultural activities. Women belonging to higher socio-economic sections do not involve directly in cultivation or livestock they usually help in labour administration, supporting activities and accounting, etc.

Women have dual responsibility of farm operations as well as domestic activities such as collection of water, fuel for cooking and taking care of children, etc. This dual responsibility creates excessive workloads for women. Women work for longer hours and participate in most of the work related to crop production, livestock production, forest resource production and fishery. It was observed that in the peak season an active farm women work for five to nine hours per day on farm fields and their work responsibilities do not ends here, they also perform household chores simultaneously.

Despite women's significant and crucial role in agriculture development and allied fields, they have virtually no access to agricultural information, technologies, service or production assets and they have very limited control over their earnings. Here we are tried to explore various activities performed by rural women in agriculture:

Crop Production: India has a variety of crops grown in irrigated and rainfed areas. Rice, wheat, jowar, maize and bajra are the major food grains. Oilseed, sugarcane, cotton and jute are the important cash crops. Likewise, tea and coffee are important plantation crops. Women play a key role in process of crop production. Women are involved in all activities of crop production such as seed preparation, preparation of land, storage of food grains, applying manure and pesticides, etc.

Forestry: The Indian population, particularly the rural, is highly dependent upon forests. Fuel wood is major source of household energy consumption. Women are the major users of diverse range of forest products. Forest is also a large sector of their livelihood. They collect fuel for cooking, medicinal plants, building material for household items, etc.

Animal Husbandry: Seasonal unemployment is major problem in rural areas, in such conditions animal husbandry is a good source of income and it also ensures the economic stability of family. Women are taking part in poultry development, egg production, wool production, and meat production, etc.

Milk Production: According to Food and Agriculture Organization (FAO), India has become the world's number one milk producing country. The annual milk production of India in 2010 crossed the 110 million tonnes mark, meaning that India had more than trebled its production in the last three decades. India's white revolution backed by thousands of rural milk cooperatives covering 80,000 villages and over 10 million farmers is one of India's most celebrated success stories in development. The sector provides for about a third of Indian rural incomes and drives rural nutrition, employment and women's empowerment.

Obstacles that hinder active women participation in agriculture could be summarized as following:

1. Women have limited access to productive resources such as land, animal and machinery.
2. Limited participation in decision-making process either inside or outside home.
3. Limited access to training opportunities, which include extension services, literacy, and advisory services.

4. Most rural women suffer from a double burden, being engaged in several income-generating activities besides their household responsibilities which comes at the expense of their health, well-being and productivity.
5. Women do not know their legal rights.
6. Gender discrimination especially in work division, payment of wages, etc.
7. None or less access to technology related to agriculture.
8. No or limited rights over their earnings.

Women and Land Rights

India has deep patriarchal roots and this patriarchal structure offers an inferior position to women, denies them equal access and control over crucial resources that are responsible to enhance quality of life and one's potential to contribute to development of society. Even after 64 years of independence, women are considered as second-class citizens. Women are very vulnerable to exploitation and injustice from society. Agriculture is the major source of livelihood in India but very few women have land rights. The FAO report on land rights says that only 9.2 per cent women own their land. While in Hindu Law women are given a share of ancestral property but in other communities women do not have such rights.

Gender Issues

The concept of 'gender' was introduced during patriarchal system in which men are the decision-makers and hold positions of power and prestige, and have the power to define reality and common situations. Gender is seen closely related to the roles and behaviour assigned to women and men based on their sexual differences. Rural women work equal to men but their work is unacknowledged and they are being visible face of agriculture.

Women Health and Health Care

Biological Determinant of Health: Women face a number of biological risks. One is iron deficiency anemia related to menstruation. Other risks are associated with pregnancy and its complication. During pregnancy there are a number of conditions that can cause women to become ill or to die. Few factors like malnutrition, anemia, reproductive tract infections and hypertension are the leading cause of maternal mortality. Unsafe abortion in persuade of sex-selection leads to significant morbidity and mortality for women.

Women are also biologically more susceptible to some sexually transmitted infections than men including human immune-deficiency (HIV). There are also certain health conditions specific to women for biological reasons such as uterine cancer or ovarian cancer as well as breast cancer.

Social Determinants of Health: The social determinants of women's health are also very important especially in societies that favour males. These social determinants relate predominantly to gender norms, which assign different roles and values to male and female, usually to the disadvantaged to females in many societies, women's inferior status leads to social, health, and economic problems for women that men do not face. The social determinants of health begin even before young women are born and continued throughout her life. Son preference is one of the strongest manifestations of gender inequality in Indian society.

Intra Household Differences and Women's Health: Gender disparities in nutrition for women are evident from infancy to adulthood. Nutritional deprivation has two major consequences for women. They never reach their full growth potential, and suffer from anemia, which are risk factors in pregnancy. This condition complicates childbearing and results in women and infant deaths, and low birth weight infants. The tradition also requires that women eat last and least throughout their lives even when pregnant and lactating. Malnourished women give birth to malnourished children, perpetuating the cycle. Women receive less healthcare facilities than men. Many women in rural areas die in childbirth due to easily preventable complications. Women's social training to tolerate suffering and their reluctance to be examined by personal are additional constrains in their getting adequate services.

There are a number of social issues that relate to women's sexual experiences. The low social status of women in many societies is linked with the physical and social abuse of the women. Furthermore, male dominance means that women often have only a limited choice about when to have sexual relations, with whom, how to have them, and whether or not use protection. As a result, women are often forced to have sex, often at young ages, and often without any contraceptives. For these social reasons, women face heightened risk of becoming pregnant, having repeated pregnancies at close intervals, and getting sexually transmitted disease including HIV/AIDS.

Dowry system is also responsible for violence against women. "Dowry death" is the worst form of violence against women. Sometimes the husband's family forced her for suicide when they are not satisfied with the dowry that she brought from her parent's house. Poverty, lack or low level of education and social status of women in many societies seriously constrain the access of women to health services. There are also numerous instances in which women cannot use health services without the permission of her husband or male relative or without having male member to take them to the health services, which also constrains their attendance.

Provisions for Upliftment of Women in Agriculture

The Ministry of Rural Development runs various programmes to bring women in to main stream and to encourage their participation in the process of national development.

1. **Increased Participation of Women in Development Activities through Panchayati Raj Institution:** Panchayati Raj Institutions (PRI) have provision to increase their participation in rural development activities. PRI has encouraged women participation in political life in India through 73rd and 74th Amendments to the Constitution.
2. **Prevention of Harassment of Women Employees:** A complaint committee for prevention of sexual harassment of women at their workplace was reconstituted by the department. The committee is represented by five members, which comprises four women members, and one male member of the department. Three meetings of the committee were held during the year.

3. **Agricultural Extension and Mainstreaming Gender Concerns:** It is mandatary that minimum 30 per cent of resources on programme and activities are utilized for women farmers. Similarly, 30 per cent of resources meant for extension workers are to be utilized for women extension functionaries.
4. **National Gender Resource Centre in Agriculture (NGRCA):** This centre has been set up to reflect the national commitment of empowerment of women through 'strategy of mainstreaming and agenda setting'. The centre acts as a focal point for the convergence of gender-related activities and issues in agriculture and allied sectors addressing gender dimension to agriculture policies and programmes rendering advocacy or advisory services to the states to internalize gender specific interventions for bringing the farm women in to the mainstream of agriculture development.

Conclusions and Recommendations

Women are playing a significant role in agriculture and rural development process. They are broadening the horizons of agriculture and allied fields. Women are performing multitasks and making their footprints in each field of agriculture. Women are major contributors to the development of society. Despite this women's status is low by socio-economic-political indicators. It is necessary to acknowledge their work and their potential. Some recommendations to recognize women's work in agriculture and its allied fields are as following:

- Agricultural investments focused on women can raise their income and improve their lives.
- Ensuring access to free or low cost legal services, including legal literacy.
- Creation of awareness of the rights of women among the people in different spheres of life through various media of communication.
- Provision of equal wage payment and monitoring of payment methods.

- Training for cultivation using technology.
- Education opportunities for farm women to increase their knowledge regarding agricultural developments.

REFERENCES

Census of India (2001). Retrieved from http://censusindia.gov.in/census_and_you/economic_activity.aspx

Chayal, K., Dhaka, B.L., and Suwalka, R.L. (2010). Analysis of Role Performed by Women in Agriculture, *Humanity & Social Sciences Journal* 5(1): 68-72, retrieved on http//www.idosi.org/hssj5(1)10/9.pdf

Duvvury, N. (1989). Women in Agriculture: A Review of the *India Literature, Economic & Political Weekly*, Vol. 24, No. 43, pp. WS96-WS112. Retrieved on http://www.jstor.org/stable/4395526

India & FAO (Food & Agricultural Organization). Success Stories, Retrieved on http://www.fao.org/fileadmin/templates/rap/files/epublications/indiaedocFINAL.pdf

Lal, R. and Khurana, A. (2011). Gender issues: The role of women in agriculture sector, ZENITH *International Journal of Business Economics & Management Research*, Volume 1, Retrieved from http://zenithresearch.org.in/images/stories/pdf/2011/oct/ZIJBEMR/.zibemr_vol-1_issue-1.pdf

PTI (2010 February 21). Only 9.21% women own farm land in Country: FAO, dnaindia, New Delhi, Retrieved from http://www.dnaindia.com/india.com/india/1350710/report-only-9-21pct-women-own-farm-land-in-country-fao

Sulemaan, R., Jafery, T., and Ashok, M.S. (2003). Cafeteria for Women in Agriculture, National Centre for Agricultural Economics and Policy Research, Retrieved from http://www.ncap.res.in/upload_files/others/oth_4.pdf

11

Wither Away Panchayats: Two Narratives of Embedded Development

Chittaranjan Das Adhikary

ABSTRACT

Decentralization continues to attract considerable interest in the academics, particularly in the field of social work, sociology and socially-embedded political science. The superlatives used for democratic decentralization, however unsuccessfully, camouflage the need for course correction. The present paper, through two case studies, tries to capture two contrasting styles of governance in Odisha. It is divided into four sections. In the first section, the paper develops a distinction between liberal democratic, socialist and developmental models of democratic decentralization. In section two, a selective introduction to the political economy of Panchayati Raj in India is attempted. Third section presents two narratives of women functionaries in two backward districts of Odisha. In the concluding section, the findings of the study are discussed. The conclusions point to different ways in which these institutions are embedded in the colonial history, deficient political will and innovative use and misuse of power.

I. Indian Decentralisation in Perspective

Decentralisation seems to be an ideal political imperative for governments both in developed and developing countries. The need for some form of decentralisation appears to be universal.

All contemporary states must somehow meet this need (King, 1982: 125). The attraction for decentralisation is not merely that it is the opposite of centralisation and therefore can be assumed to be capable of remedying the later's defect. Decentralisation has a positive side. It is commonly associated with wide range of economic, social and political objectives in both developed and less developed societies.[1] Politically, decentralisation is said to strengthen accountability, political skill and national integration. It brings government closer to people. It promotes liberty, equality and welfare (Mass, 1959; D.M. Hill, 1974). Decentralisation provides a training ground for citizen participation. It has been elevated to the role of guardian of basic human values (Van Puttem, 1971). However, this is not to say that decentralisation, as a principle of governance is not without its critic, which is discussed in the next section of the paper.

In ordinary parlance, decentralisation refers to a process of reversing concentration of power at the centre and/or delegating more power to the territorial units of the state downward. Therefore, decentralized governance presupposes a territorial hierarchy implied in the delimitation of areas and division of power.[2] There are two underlying assumptions. The first is that the territorial subdivisions will have a measure of autonomy and these territorial subdivisions will be self-governing through political institutions. The second assumption is these institutions will be structurally organized along democratic lines (Smith, 1955: 18). As democratic decentralization is our concern here,[3] it is generally assumed that democratic decentralisation brings governments closer to people downward provides for citizen participation in the political process combined with responsiveness and accountability. These assumptions are based on only one model of decentralisation and there are as many models as the ideological and theoretical basis of the State. As the patterns of local government institutions will differ in different states according to their ideological basis, so the role of democratic decentralisation differ in tandem.

Political theorists of the liberal democratic tradition see democratic decentralisation or local government institutions as a precondition for national democracy and vehicle for political education, equality, liberty and responsiveness. Local government provides for extra opportunity for political participation, both in electing and being elected to the local office, for people who would otherwise have few chances to act politically between national elections.[4] A local government institution in the liberal political tradition is best represented by the English model of counties, parishes and boroughs. The local government institutions along side the ad hoc bodies continue to serve the objective of providing a platform for participation and a nursery for political education. Marxist thinkers see local government as a supportive infrastructure for renewing relations of production and reproducing the preconditions necessary for accumulation of capital. Therefore, states founded on socialist principle are found to follow different models of democratic decentralisation. One common thread that runs through all socialist models of local government is the extent of participation and the degree of centralisation and control. State socialism in China, for example, provides for local government at provincial, country, city, district and commune level through the revolutionary committees elected by People's Congress. However, these revolutionary committees consist of members who are frequently the party leaders at the respective level and therefore are bound to obey the commands of party committees in the center. Coupled with this is the elaborate integration of the economy through production teams and brigades at the commune level completes the socialist project and renders local government a façade.

Local government institutions in the developing countries represent another model of decentralisation. These countries have been British, French or other colonies in the past. After independence most of these countries have tried to renovate these local government structures and ascribed it a developmental role in their national reconstruction programmes. In fact, decentralisation has come to be seen as a precondition for social and economic development in the Third World countries (Smith, 1985: 185). It has come to be believed that (1) decentralization enables decision-making by the people (Conyers, 1981), (2) if development is to mean the eradication of poverty, inequality and material deprivation, it must engage the involvement of the poor (Rondinelli, 1983), (3) it can soften resistance to change and can secure a commitment to change through mass participation (Conyers, 1981), (4) decentralisation fosters speed and flexibility in taking decisions required by rural development, and (5) finally, it affords national integration in plural societies by accommodating diverse legitimate political aspirations.

The development of local government in India, like other Third World countries of Africa, Asia and America have to be necessarily seen in the above framework. The history of Panchayati Raj, traditional origin of the nomenclature not withstanding,[5] is rooted in the failure of community development programmes. Balwant Rai Mehta Committee was set up to find out the causes of the failure of the CD programmes and suggested effective ways to ensure mobilisation and participation of people in national development. The committee suggested, among other things, the strengthing of, unlike Gandhian village republic, three-tier Panchayati Raj system.[6] This three-tier structure of Panchayati Raj loosely fits into the name decentralisation in India. And this also partly explains many of the problems encountered by democratic units of self-government, which still continues to work as delivery agencies of national reconstruction programme started fifty years ago.

II. Locating Women in Local Government

Though local government in India had its genesis in the development imperatives in the period following independence, 73rd Constitution Amendment and the new Panchayati Raj point to a positive shift in approach. The Constitution 73rd Amendment Act, 1992 may be termed as historic one in the evolution of Indian policy since independence for variety of reasons. By this, an attempt was made to actualise the aspirations of the framers of our Constitution contained in Arts. 40 and 46 of the Constitution of India. A major step was taken in strengthening the democracy at grassroot level ensuring democratic decentralisation, local participation in development programmes and considerable devolution of functions, resources and powers to Panchayati Raj institutions; a structural change was made in the arrangement of institutions of democratic governance....[7] From mere delivery agencies of the government efforts at socio-economic development, local government institution were elevated to the status of statutory bodies by the blessings of 73rd Constitution Amendment. Another equally historic development was the creation of elaborate space for women and weaker sections in the local government institutions through the provision of one-third reservation.

Early evidence of women participation in politics in modern India can be found in India's struggle for independence from colonial rule. Credit goes to the clarion call from Gandhiji who said "As long as women of India do not take part in public life there can be no salvation for the country. I would have no use for that kind of swaraj to which women have not made their full contribution."[8]

Many outstanding names come up in the field of political engagement of women during freedom struggle, even under the shadow of imperialist excess. "During the nationalist struggle woman was essentially equated with nation and represented the value of self-sacrifice, benevolence and devotion...because women were representative of true India of its spiritual, traditional world. They were invited to participate in the independence movement, but only as long as their involvement did not threaten the prevailing notion of feminity."[9]

The issue of women participation in politics, especially local government institutions, was touched upon by Balwant Rai Mehta Committee which recommended that besides the 20 members of the panchayat samiti, there should be two women, who are interested in work among women and children, as co-opted members. Similar suggestion was made for the village panchayats also. Many states accordingly made provision for co-option of women members. But in practice women relatives of sarpanches, influential women from dominant castes or old obedient women adhering to traditional line of political patronage and having no experience in women and child welfare got co-opted into Panchayati Raj bodies. "Co-option as a principle was found to be highly questionable both in theory and practice. Not merely it is undemocratic but also smacks of protectionism as if women were weaker and incapable of fighting election. The women representation became one of tokenism and proxy and ended in a near total failure."[10]

Another attempt at giving space to women in local government institutions was made by the committee on status of women in India set up in 1971. The committee deplored the patriarchal domination and missing women-interest in the working of the panchayats. It recommended for fixing a quota for women candidates by political parties and allotting a block of seats to women in the municipal council. As a second transitional measure, it advocated the establishment of women panchayats (local council at the village level, directly elected by village women). These women panchayats would have autonomy and resources of their own for the management and administration of women and children welfare and development. Though all-women panchayats sprouted in some states, it remained as a matter coincidence due to lack of constitutional strength.

Some states like Odisha, Maharashtra and Kerala introduced 30 per cent reservation in panchayat bodies even before the 73rd Constitution Amendment came into force. After the 73rd Constitution Amendment in 1993, all states uniformly introduced one-third reservation for women in the local government bodies. According to one estimate, there were 31 per cent women members at the village panchayat level, 20.71 per cent at the panchayat samiti level and 31 per cent at the district panchayat level by the year 2000.

Participation of women in local government institutions for more than ten years has been subjected to critical scrutiny. It has been found that political participation of women comes in any of the four categories of (i) aspirant; (ii) hesitant; (iii) reluctant; or (iv) resistant. Election of women to PRI bodies produce in essence only token presence where the husbands or the male wards arrogate to themselves the power of their women who are termed as Pradhan Patis.[11] Thus, women in Panchayati Raj entail presence without empowerment where their political experience is mediated through a male figure. Others have constructed women participation as participation from a distance in the presence of men. It has been found in different studies that women PRI members lack experience in how to speak, what to speak, and whom to speak. They frequently depend on male family members for escorting them to meetings and even prompting them to speak in meetings.[12] Even after getting elected to panchayats, women remain tied to household work and their husbands discharge political responsibilities on her behalf. There is a strong sense of insecurity in women and deficiency in capacity for cent per cent participation in politics. An in-depth study of two cases in Odisha is presented in the next section.

A Case Study in Odisha

Odisha is one of the first States to introduce comprehensive law establishing rural government at the village level in 1948.[13] So village panchayats had been functioning in Odisha since 1950. Later on Gram Panchayats were reorganized and a new Gram Panchayat Act, 1964 was passed which replaced the 1948 Act. Odisha Gram Panchayat Act, 1964 was suitably amended in 1994 in conformity with 73rd Constitution Amendment and subsequently there had been two Amendments in 1997 and 2001. It should be mentioned in this context that Odisha is also one of the States to introduce women reservation even before the introduction of 73rd Amendment. Despite decentralised governance, which includes women, has been part of State politics for long, the two cases from the State cited below do not meet the expectations of matured democratic ethos.

The two cases in point consist of one panchayat samiti member in Thuamul Rampur block of Kalahandi district and another Naib-sarpanch in Kultajore Gram Panchayat of Boudh district in Odisha. Kalahandi is one of the most backward districts in western Odisha and has made headlines in National dailies several times due to hunger deaths. Thuamul Rampur block in Kalahandi is one of the poorest blocks in the district. Draupadi Majhi a young (25 years approx.) matriculate tribal lady gets elected to Thuamul-Rampur panchayat samiti for the first time. Draupadi didi, as others belovely call her, has been relatively better off than other women in her village. She is educated (has studied up to matriculation). Being unmarried and young, she has had past experience of mobilizing women in her panchayat for educational awareness. As we settle down in a charpoy near the anganwadi centre of her Gram Panchayat, she continued, "Initially I was hesitant to contest. But as our samiti constituency was reserved for women, I found an opportunity to enter into the politics." It has been generally argued that women lack political aptitude and are shy of public domain. But Draupadi's story negates the myth in toto. "Winning election really gave me a high" she revealed. "But my excitement did not last long. After few months I realized the futility of this panchayati raj. Though this block is predominantly populated by tribals, the post of samiti chairperson is reserved for schedule caste women" groans Draupadi. Being non-tribal, the chairperson turns deaf towards the concerns of the tribal people. Whether it is demand for information or on various development schemes or devolution of important responsibilities, there is non-cooperation from the chairperson. The block officials also do not listen to them. Being village women, they feel that they do not know anything. This is precisely because they know that samiti members are of no use once election of the chairperson is over. Back at the panchayat "how do you face people who ask did we elect you to do nothing?", reflects Draupadi. As a samiti member, Draupadi cannot do enough in the Panchayat samiti neither she has any say in Gram Panchayat affairs. Take the example of primary education in the panchayat. Draupadi has formed a co-ordination committee to encourage values of education among women. With this co-ordination committee Draupadi tried to persuade the teachers who were regularly irregular in schools of the panchayat and were playing truant since then. Repeated report in the block office was of no use. "Nobody listens you". Draupadi's plight does not end here. Now the teachers who are coming from Bhawani Patna, the district headquarter, have started threatening her physically. "Had the teachers been local people this would have never happened" laments Draupadi. On being asked how people see her as a women leader, she clarified "initially people use to feel being a girl I cannot do anything. But you know once you start asserting yourself everybody around you turn to you for help. There is visibly a change in attitude towards women among younger generation."

It is evident from the above case at the middle tier of the Panchayati Raj system that women leaders have began asserting their presence in the political space provided to them through 73rd Constitution Amendment. We can no more exclude them by pleading their underperformance in the male society. They are no more inhibited to lead and overcome the challenges of feminity. However, women lack adequate knowledge on process issues[14] (e.g. meetings, agenda setting, minutes of resolution). They face difficulty in getting information about development works, beneficiary details, budget and expenditure on different development works, etc. Panchayat functionaries are under pressure from people for more development, speedily and visibly. There are also hints of increase in expectation from the Panchayati Raj System to deliver the goods. People see PRI members as someone through which government help (Sorkari Sahayata) come to them. Another problem is that of apathetic bureaucracy. Women PRI members are treated as dirt in the hands of government officials.

Another case of Binodini (name changed given the sensitivity of information) in Chappra village of Kultajore Gram Panchayat presents a contrasting story. Chappra village comes in Kantamala block of Boudh district. Boudh was earlier a subdivision of Phulbani district. Development indicators of Boudh district present a pathetic picture with low literacy rate. Economy is based on forest, sporadic agricultural activity and migrant labour.

Binodini stands apart from rest of the womenfolk in more than one respect. She was introduced to politics for the first time. She won the election to Panchayati Raj bodies uncontested from a ward not reserved for women. And many such other distinctions continue. Binodini's husband who was a sarpanch in the last panchayat also contested from the same ward. But with the aim of making her naib-sarpanch, which is reserved for women, he withdrew from the contest. Binodini candidly confesses that because of power and scope for swindling money from the development programmes, she persuaded by her husband, reluctantly agreed to contest. She also agrees to have wasted lot of money in the election. After winning he or she would definitely like to recover the money. Though participation in Panchayati Raj bodies is to work for the development of the poor, social service has to be based on economically sound principle. "As one has to pay for the election so you have to pay for receiving benefits." Binodini informs that besides few male people no one comes to sabha. Many people do not know whether there is any sabha being held. Women are prevented by their male wards from coming to sabhas. They think women do not have anything to do where men are discussing. No one knows how beneficiaries are selected. Beneficiaries are selected much before Palli sabha or Gram sabha. Whoever agree to pay is included in the list. "You cannot be honest where everyone is dishonest", opines Binodini.

As the above case shows, it is apparently the wish of the husband who prefers the post of naib-sarpanch for his wife instead of the post of ward member for himself that cajoled Binodini to contest. It is a typical case of "instead of Ram Singh, Ram Singh's wife will be there."[15] Contrary to the popular image of women, women in this case is part of a corrupt nexus. It is also found that there is widespread benefit trading in developmental programmes. Consequently, panchayat members lack the trust of people and popular participation is missing from the developmental process. Women still prefer to take refugee in the security of four walls of their house and life within the confines of a male society. In essence, there is a failure of village community.

Conclusion

Indian experience of democratic decentralisation is a combination of colonial history, politics of struggle for independence and national identity and an urge for delivering development. While the very foundation of local government started by colonial rulers rests on adherence to or pretends to adhere to liberal democratic tradition of decentralisation, marked ambiguities are there to see for all in its grafting to developmental imperatives. The case in question here clearly strikes at the myths that have come to be associated with the models of Third World decentralisation. Taking the myths one by one, lets examine the proposition that decentralisation enables decision-making by people. As in the first case there are little or no decisions to make for the panchayat functionaries. The bottlenecks of red tapism, officergiri (officialdom) continues to hold sway. "Decentralisation facilitates speed and flexibility in decision-making" stands nowhere. The helplessness writ large in the conversation points to the poverty of democracy and is contrary to a democratic order where the last man is counted first.

In the second case, it is evident that Panchayati Raj bodies today are a mockery of fight against poverty and a means of mobilizing the poor. Poor remains in the periphery of this democratic drama. In a way, the poor remains away from these institutions by rational choice as they have nothing to loose by not participating nor they have anything to gain by participating. There is clearly lack of trust in these institutions. Also the large-scale political illiteracy among the people is in full display as a sign of colonial hang over. People largely remain political outsiders to Panchayati Raj Institutions. This is a pointer not to the failure of people but to the failure of these institutions to include them.

As a commentary on women in Panchayati Raj, it is evident that women face multiple handicaps in the face of patriarchy and democratic intrigue. While one of the women is an aspirant, the other one is a hesitant. Women participation in Panchayati Raj bodies is yet to mature. There is also proof of males capturing these institutions by encroaching their rightful space. Probably, it will not be fair to pronounce the demise of the gender agenda in Panchayati Raj Institutions. To be modest, the findings of this paper are more in the nature of birth pangs.

NOTES

1. Economically, decentralisation is said to reduce cost, promote better expression of local demand and effective utilization of human resource. Socially, decentralisation promotes individual values and protects culturally plural societies. For more see D.K. Hart, "Theories of Government Related to Decentralisation and Citizen Participation", *Public Administration Review*, Vol. 32, No. 4, October 1974.
2. Decentralisation should be distinguished from mere dispersal of headquarters or mere delegation of responsibility from the superior to the subordinate for it concerns with the extent to which power and authority are dispersed through the geographical hierarchy of the State and the institutions and processes through which such dispersal occurs. Also see B.C. Smith, *Decentralisation—The Territorial Dimensions of the State*, London, 1985.
3. Decentralisation does not automatically mean democracy for there can be decentralised state apparatus ruled by hereditary chieftains.
4. Also in addition local government extends such opportunities to the lower grades of society as local positions are rarely being sought by the higher ranks. For more see J.S. Mills, *Representative Governments*, London, 1931.
5. As a matter of fact the use of the title 'Panchayat' is false because the ancient panchayats were self-reliant and were controlled by the concept of Panch-parmeswar, i.e. detached Devine justice. In the process, by false use of the term Panchayat in the Constitution, a myth has been sponsored so irrelevant to our society. Also see Ramjee Singh, *Gandhi and the Twenty-first Century*, New Delhi, 1993.
6. The Balwant Rai Mehta Committee suggested that "without the agency at the village level which could represent the entire community, assume responsibility and provide the necessary leadership in implementing the development programmes, real progress in rural development could not come about at all". Also see C. Harichandran, *Panchayati Raj & Rural Development*, New Delhi, 1983.

7. P.D. Sharma, *Women Leaders in Panchayati Raj—A Case Study in Democratic Decentralisation and Panchayati Raj in India* (Ed.), New Delhi, 2002.
8. A. Kashyap, *Panchayati Raj*, 1989.
9. Partha Chaterjee, *The Nation and its Fragments—Colonial and Postcolonial Histories*, 1993.
10. Susheela Kaushik, *Women and Panchyayati Raj*, Har-Anand Publishers, New Delhi, 1993.
11. S.K. Singh and A.K. Singh, *Women Empowerment—Emerging Leadership in Uttar Pradesh*, pp. 181-82.
12. George Mathew, Will Reservation ensure Participation?, in Raj Singh (Ed.) *New Panchayati Raj—A Functional Analysis*, New Delhi, 2000.
13. B.C. Rout, *Orissa Administration*, Bhubaneshwar, 1991.
14. Poornima and Vinod Vyasuslu, *Women in Panchayati Raj—Grassroot Democracy in India: Experience from Malgudi*, 1999.
15. George Mathew, *op. cit.*, p. 47.

REFERENCES

Bottomore, T.B. *Sociology—A Guide to Problem and Literature*, Blackie and Sons, Bombay, 1975.

Dube, M.P. and Padalia, M. (Ed.). *Democratic Decentralisation and Panchayati Raj in India*, Anamika, New Delhi, 2002.

Kaushik, S. *Women & Panchayati Raj*, Har-Anand Publishers, New Delhi, 1993.

King, P. *Federalism and Federation*, Croom Helm, London, 1982.

Meenaskhisundaram, S.S. *Decentralisation in Developing Countries*, Concept, New Delhi, 1994.

Rout, B.C. *Orissa Administration*, Panchasheela, Bhubaneshwar, 1991.

Singh, R. (Ed.). *New Panchayati Raj—A Functional Analysis,* Anmol, New Delhi, 2000.

Singh, R. *Gandhi and Twenty-first Century*, Peace Publishers, New Delhi, 1993.

Smith, B.C. *Decentralisation—The Territorial Dimensions of the State*, London, 1985.

12

Marketing the Products of Self-Help Group—A Study of North 24 Parganas, West Bengal

Pradipta Dubey and *Atonu Chatterjee*

ABSTRACT

Self-Help Groups in West Bengal are trying their level best to eke out a distinct space for themselves in the overall milieu. However, while pursuing their economic activities they face an uphill task in terms of marketing their products. This paper tries to explore the efforts and procedures adopted by a specific district in West Bengal in marketing the products of SHGs operative under Swarna Jayanti Gram Swarojgar Yojana (SGSY). In course of discussion, the paper also traces the importance of group-based micro-financing and how SGSY programme is different in terms of ensuring forward linkage and imparting entrepreneurial skills and expertise among the SHG members.

Business has only two functions—marketing and innovation.
—Milan Kundera

Introduction

Irrespective of the fire and smoke generated by the recent debate on subsistence level, it is hard to conceal that, a sizable portion of the nation still languishes in abyss of poverty and that too despite a number of poverty alleviation programmes remaining in operation. The programmes, right from their inception operated at three fronts, viz. wage employment, self-employment and subsidizing the supply of certain essential commodities to the target group which in its present incarnation assumes the form of 'Cash Transfers'. While wage employment programmes as well as subsidizing the supply of essential commodities are more or less straightforward endeavours, where target group gets the return either in lieu of their work or by virtue of their position in the economic pyramid, self-employment programmes assume additional hue. Apart from the labour which goes into this component of self-employment, other three factors, namely the craftsmanship or the acumen, entrepreneurship ability and marketability of the product or service are absolutely vital for ensuring return, be it perennial or periodical.

Till 2012, in West Bengal, Swarnajayanti Gram Swarojgar Yojana (SGSY) is the single self-employment programme for the rural areas. The programme with an accent on the rural woman segment is handled by Ministry of Panchayats and Rural Development of the State. In this paper, we will make a modest attempt to delineate the efforts taken at different levels for inculcating skill (both craftsmanship and the entrepreneurial ability) among the rural Self-Help Group (SHG) members, operating basically through the SGSY programme and the efforts of marketing their products.

Incidentally, it can be mentioned that in addition to SHGs under SGSY programme:

1. There are SHGs promoted and nurtured by NABARD through their programme of 'NABARD—bank linkage programme'. Several government departments (viz. Co-operative Department, Forest Department, Backward Classes Welfare Department) and banks also promote SHGs through their own programmes.
2. A distinct difference, however, is apparent—while SGSY deals with the SHGs predominantly formed by the Below Poverty Line (BPL) members, groups of NABARD and other banks cater to members belonging to 'Above Poverty Line' (APL) strata. The groups promoted by Large-sized Multipurpose Societies (LAMPS) on the

other hand cater to solely tribal women and thrive on the loan provided by National Scheduled Tribe Finance and Development Corporation (NSTFDC) at a more sober rate of interest.

The area of our study will be the district of North 24 Parganas in the State of West Bengal. The district enjoys a seminal position owing to its proximity to Kolkata, the State capital. State's Human Development Report (WBHDR) published in 2004 ranks the district third in the composite "Human Development Index" (HDI). It is also in the epicenter of the recent trend of industrialization in West Bengal as well as undergoing a rapid spurt of urbanization (57.27 per cent of population lives in urban area as per 2011 census. It was 54.30 per cent as per 2001 Census; in 1991 it was 51.23 per cent). It also cuts a niche in terms of performance of SGSY programme. All these combine to give the district an edge and hence we go in for somewhat micro-level study of this district in context of the present issue. The performance statistics and the information about the district's show, if not otherwise mentioned, are taken from the 'Administrative Report' of DRDC, the monthly progress report (MPR) of DRDC and that of West Bengal Panchayats and Rural Development Department.

The Origin of SHGs

The problem of timely repayment of loans and their best possible utilization has long plagued the planners in regard to the self-employment programmes in India. The paradigm of group-based microfinance which gained considerable currency during the concluding years of the last century was conceived to be an appropriate tool to handle this problem. It was now being argued that when finance was provided to a close-knit group, the internal group dynamics would ensure optimal utilization and better repayment of the fund. This concept married with the neo-liberal approach of trimming down the state of some so-called unnecessary responsibilities sought to open a different vista in poverty alleviation programmes. Consequently, the idea of SHGs came into being. Certain developments within the country involving erstwhile failure of the individual microfinancing under the Integrated Rural Development Programme (IRDP) coupled with moderately successful experience with the Development of Women and Child in Rural Area (DWCRA), groups of nineties rendered it the status of 'magic potion' or panacea to all poverty-related problems. Eventually, Ministry of Rural Development, Government of India embarked upon a scheme called Swarnajayanti Gram Swarojgar Yojana (SGSY), on 1-4-1999 with an accent on group-based microfinance. The basic accent of the scheme thus was to organise the rural poor into SHGs through a process of social mobilization, enhance their capacity in the socio-economic domain and encourage them to take up some economic activities so that these poor families scale the all-decisive poverty line within three years of inception. Reserve Bank of India in its Master Circular on SGSY acknowledged the scheme as a 'holistic scheme covering all aspects of self-employment' where assistance to BPL families can be extended to initiate micro-enterprises in rural areas. Appropriate noise generated on the eve of Dr. Mohammad Younus winning the Nobel Prize in 2006 gave it further shot in the arm. The District Rural Development Cells (DRDC)/ District Rural Development Agencies (DRDA), thus with the active participation of the Panchayats leapt into the business of organising groups of women and men from BPL category, nurtured and trained them in group dynamics as well as in some economic activities as per their inherent natural tendency or the demand of the market, evaluated their performance and linked them up with the nationalised and other banks so that they get the adequate fund as soft loan to persue their economic activities. The bank loan consisting of 'term loan' and 'working capital' was again backed up by a provision of back-ended subsidy from the government where normally 0.125 millions is the highest limit a group can get. Therefore, the bank loan was considered an imperative to start the sojourn of the SHGs.

The programme thus was conceived as standardised supply-side solution addressing the credit and physical infrastructure needs of the ubiquitous Self-Help Groups, composed of members drawn from the BPL strata of the society. The groups thus formed, harped on mutuality and were integrally linked with both the community and the formal banking system. Here maturity rate of the SHGs was invariably slow, yet it yielded a strong edifice. The members of the group imbibed a sense of profound responsibility. They were dealing with their own collective coffer.

SGSY—A Perceptible Departure

The effort under SGSY was to ensure development of sustainable micro-enterprises in the rural areas so that the assisted families scale the all-important poverty line within a specific time frame, i.e. within three years. To ensure this, the programme envisages:

(i) **Adoption of Appropriate Technologies for the Entrepreneurial Success:** The crux here is not only espousal of appropriate technology but also identifying the entities responsible for technology management, its transfer, upgradation and monitoring. The SGSY guidelines published by Government of India, Ministry of Rural Development in 1999 (henceforth programme document) is absolutely pragmatic in this regard. It emphasizes that the technologies adopted:

1. Need to guarantee a comfort level for the SHG members. In fact, the programme document warns against indiscriminate adoption of new technologies.... "Any given activity there is a certain level of technology (*sic*). It is possible that introduction of certain technology may substantially alter the economics of working, in which case such new technology needs to be introduced. There could be in other cases where the technology can be upgraded to produce better economic results."[1]
2. Need to have a proven track record in terms of ensuring quality along with its commercial efficacy with a capital.
3. Inappropriate technologies are to be summarily shunned since the target group, i.e. the poor SHG members have scanty capacity to absorb the economic reverses if enterprises failed. We find that the document is adequately pithy against the rampant and predominantly urbane techno-bureaucratic tendency of approving all the technologies present in the market as the basic

saviour.... "In any case the technology introduction/ upgradation should be such as to suit the needs of rural poor for the given key activity."[2]

(ii) **Avenue for Proper Skill Training:** As a necessary precondition for adoption of apt technology, the programme document advocates proper skill training of the SHG members. Recognizing that training is a specialized acumen and that SHG members should possess 'Minimum Skill Requirement' (it is an imperative for securing loan for starting economic activities), the programme document prescribes networking with suitable training organizations such as "Government institutions like engineering colleges, polytechnics, universities and NGOs (Non-Government organizations)" for imparting training to SHG members. A distinct tilt, thus, is evident in favour of the reputed organizations with proven track record in regard to skill training.[3]

(iii) **Marketing Support:** Enlisting marketing support to the SHGs makes SGSY *sui generis* among other programmes of identical genre. The programme document is emphatic on this aspect. Traditionally, self-employment programmes have concentrated on backward linkages rather than outputs and their marketing. This essentially leads to adoption of production techniques totally divorced from marketing aspects and opportunities. As a remedy, the programme document suggests:

1. SHGs should adopt an income generating activity after proper market survey. This is an imperative not only because SHGs can hardly absorb business loss emanating out of lack of demand even if in the short run but also for having a realistic future income projection.
2. Through a rural market survey, the local demand can be assessed and productions can be suitably lined. However, production strategy must take into account locally available resources so that a reasonable profit margin is ensured. Further it must be kept in mind that it is neither feasible nor desirable to produce all goods in all places.

3. Finally, the existing and emerging markets in urban and peri-urban areas need to be explored to the hilt. Purchasers here have a test for value-added items. The emerging urban markets can be a good area for developing clientele for the rural products. Establishing marketing infrastructure in these areas can ensure an enabling atmosphere for the SHGs for marketing their products as well as establishing the identity of the products.[4]

A refreshing departure is imbued in SGSY programme. The departure is evident basically in the area of drafting a production strategy in sync with the available market and in the aspect of exploring urban and peri-urban market for the products. In this milieu of rapid urbanization, these programme strategies make SGSY hit the bulls-eye straightway.

II

As per the data available as on June 30, 2009, in the official website of Government of West Bengal '*banglarmukh*') total number of groups enrolled in Swarnajayanti Gram Swarozgar Yojana implemented by the Department of Panchayats and Rural Development is 2,59,615. NABARD handles roughly 4,13,293 SHGs. Besides these, there are 1,04,180 groups under the management of Small Industries Development Bank of India (SIDBI). However, the total count of groups including those run by government departments and non-governmental organizations exceeds 0.9 millions. Women constitute about 90 per cent of the total members of SHGs and as many as 0.56 million groups have received loans in some form or other to start their economic activities.

Initiatives of the State

West Bengal Government also took certain initiatives to cater to the growing number of SHGs.

In the year 2006, a completely separate department was created under a cabinet minister in the name of 'Self-Help Group and Self-Employment'. The mandates of the department involved:

1. Monitoring and supervising policy formulation and coordination of all activities pertaining to Self-Help Groups and Self-Employment Schemes operated by different departments of the State Government.
2. Arranging for and supervising skill-upgradation training to ensure functional improvement of Self-Help Groups and Self-Employment Schemes.
3. Coordinating delivery of institutional finance to these entities.
4. To consider such other matters relevant or incidental to the aforesaid terms of reference.
5. To coordinate marketing of products of Self-Help Groups through holding of different exhibitions and co-ordination with business houses.
6. Coordinating and synchronizing efforts of setting up of infrastructure in the districts for providing training and creating marketing outlets for the SHGs.[5]

Initially, hiccups were rampant! Duplication of works and trampling of areas of operation occurred between SHG and SE department, Panchayats and Rural Development Department (P&RD incidentally handles majority of SHGs). The matter sunk in gradually and later SHG and SE Department was successful in cutting its niche in the entire scenario. The department took significant strides in facilitating the SHGs nurtured by the banks and was also instrumental in tying up SHGs with fairs outside the state and with business houses for marketing of their products.

The procurement policy of the government also was given a facelift in the favour of SHGs. Two specific initiatives can be mentioned here:

(a) The Audit Branch of Finance Department, Government of West Bengal through its Notification No. 7369-F dated 23/9/2008 amended the West Bengal Financial Rules whereby the procurement base of stationery articles were enlarged to include the Self-Help Groups.

(b) SHGs through orders of Department of SHG and SE were entrusted with the task of paddy procurement from

2010. To facilitate the procurement, Government of West Bengal released a sum of forty thousand rupees as rolling fund to each identified SHGs who will return the sum in the Khariff season. The Central Government on its part has granted commission to SHGs @ 2.5 per cent on the price of paddy as incidental charges. Involving SHGs in the process of paddy procurement was also tried elsewhere. Andhra Pradesh is practicing this from 2005 and that of maize from 2004.[6]

Floccinaucinihilipilification! May be...one is definitely entitled to one's own judgment. Yet these small steps score on two counts. In fact, these orders spelt a fundamental change to the essential standing of the SHGs in the total milieu since:

1. This is perhaps for the first time the government acknowledged the status of SHG as viable economic unit akin to wholesale consumers' cooperative societies/ cooperatives and such similar organizations.
2. A bit of sociology went into the aspect also. These orders are the imprimatur on the entrepreneurial capacity and business acumen of SHGs, majority of whom are women-centric. This is a departure from the mere economic role as envisaged in the programme document.

Interpretations may galore but the point remains that these two orders brought the SHGs in the mainstream of activities.

III

Currently, employment opportunities in the country are at nadir. Recent report on unemployment by National Sample Survey (NSS in its 64th round) reveals an overcast sky. The situation becomes further depressing when the NSS report is juxtaposed with 'The Challenge of Employment in India: An Informal Economy Perspective'—a report by 'National Commission for Enterprises in the Unorganized Sector' (2009). In a nutshell, the employment scenario is—

(a) During 2005 and 2008 only 2.4 million employments were created, a mere 0.8 million per year. This is only a miniscule when compared to 12 million employments created per year between 1999-2000 and 2004-05.

(b) Total number of workers increased from 457.9 million in 2004-05 to 460.2 million in 2007-08, a growth rate of just 0.17 per cent per year. This is the lowest rate of employment generation in the last three decades, even lower than the previous spell of jobless growth of 1993-2000 when employment increased by less than 1 per cent per year.

(c) Overall, employment of males increased by 5.2 million per year but declined by 4.4 million per year for females.

(d) There was a decline in real wage rate and despite high economic growth there was no improvement in the quality of employment.

(e) Formal sector employees in several cases were able to latch on to their jobs only by accepting informalisation of their formerly secure and respectable labour standards.

(f) Informal sector gradually got bereft of their bargaining power whereas their employees consolidated themselves. The icing of the cake could not be more spectacular!

The district of North 24 Parganas divided into 22 blocks and 200 Gram Panchayats is no exception to this trend. The situation becomes starker since agriculture here has failed to absorb the growing workforce (DHDR 2010). One of the options available to this workforce is to migrate and we see that around 33.12 per cent of the families of the district migrated for employment. The District Human Development Report of the North 24 Parganas further reveals that:

(a) Migration is basically seasonal and is rampant in riverine and border areas of the district.

(b) And significantly out-migration involves only the male members of the household. An Indian woman, thanks to social obligations and taboo, scarcely have equal opportunities to migrate for wage work. SHGs therefore are the principal plank for women to improve employment and income opportunities *in situ*.[7]

District Rural Development Cell of North 24 Parganas, presented more sensitive face to the SHGs and the poor women of the rural areas at large. The sensitivity was revealed in the following indicators:

1. Total expenditure on SHGs in the district was 97.88 per cent and 98.30 per cent of the total allotment made on this count during the financial years 2009-10, and 2010-11, respectively. In the financial year 2010-11, the district recorded highest expenditure in the entire state on this count.
2. To ensure marketability of the products skill development trainings were organised. In the financial year 2010-11, total expenditure on this count was ₹ 1.257 million whereas in 2009-10 it was ₹ 3.509 millions. In the period 2008-09 again 7677 skill development training programmes were organised in the district at a total expenditure of ₹ 1.115 millions. Comparatively low expenditure in the financial years 2008-09 and in 2010-11 can be attributed to the Seventh panchayat general election and general Legislative Assembly elections respectively when normal developmental works in the district took a back seat.
3. There is a discernable effort on the part of the district administration to explore new areas to market the products of SHG along with retaining the older channels. The efforts basically involved tying up with the government departments for supply of materials.

Thus, it is apparent that the district is inclined to harness the full potential of SHGs as an alternative avenue of offering gainful employment to the BPL families of the district. DHDR of the district is emphatic on this "...there are reasons to believe that SHGs have come to stay in the life of the ordinary people of the district."

Marketing the Products of SHGs

"The aim of marketing is to know and understand customer so well (that) the product or service fits him and sells itself"— Peter Drucker.

Marketing is about identifying and meeting social needs and that too profitably. However, as Peter Drucker holds selling is only the tip of the marketing iceberg. The crux is to understand and conceive of the customer's wants so well that the products and service impels him to buy. Further there is a need of segregating markets into segments and identify distinct group of buyers, who may prefer varying types of products and services.[8] The aim of marketing therefore boils down to two specific actions, namely identifying the customer's wants and segregating these wants in different tiers and locale of markets. In a modest way, DRDC North 24 Parganas tried to accomplish these tasks through certain stages.

However, caveats need to be in place.

(i) Income from the economic activities of SHG is considered as an additional income along with some other source(s) which are the mainstay of the family income. An interesting example is that when 14.25 per cent of the three tiers panchayat members of the district are drawn from SHGs only 1.65 per cent of the members have income from SHG sources as the main source of income.[9]

(ii) Generally, the women after completing their household chores indulge into the economic activities of SHG.

(a) **Identifying the Local Acumen.** Initially, activity specific skills in the women members of relevant SHGs were identified. This was a task cut out in the scheme itself. "The success of SGSY will therefore depend, to start with, on the choice of activities. The key element is that the choice of activity should be based on the local resources, the aptitude as well as the skill of the people" (para 1.3 of programme document). And a cautionary note "The choice of key activities should not be an arbitrary or an ad-hoc decision but should be a careful thought out process" (para 1.4 of programme document). Consequently, under the guidance of SGSY committee and the Zilla Parishad, blockwise key activities were identified, to be modified after every three years. The exercise, needless to mention, has its own limitations. Instead of assessing the demand or want of the customers, this exercise emphasized the supply side. The logic was obvious. The scheme aimed at providing quick economic assistance/

supplements to the family income of BPL families so that they would scale the poverty line within a specific time period. Under this mandate assessing the needs of the customers was a bit problematic. So the approach was in a round about fashion. The effort was to identify the local existent acumen or expertise, do a market analysis on those specific products and then hone the members' skills in regard to those products so that quality products entice customers.

The DHDR of the district indicates a list of such activities which is given in Table 1.

(b) **Skill Upgradation.** A natural corollary to identification of key activities is, to upgrade the skills of SHG members in the relevant items. Skill development training in selected activities were imparted by local level 'Master Trainers' approved by DRDC and some selected organizations. Networking with organizations of repute with proven track record proved to be of immense help in this regard. Further, effort was taken to conduct residential training so that the group members inculcate among themselves a sense of cohesiveness, mutual sharing and exchanges in different aspects. Also interactions with the trainees and group members revealed that these residential trainings were a whiff of fresh air as the participants could stay away from their daily chores and related trials and tribulations. To many group members, it became the single case of so-called '*outing*'. Of course, the exercise had its own predicament. Mothers with toddlers and infants as well as unmarried girls in most cases could not attend these trainings or sometimes hit by family crises the members had to rush to their houses, abandoning the training midway.

The process of selection of trainees is done in the following process:

1. In the monthly monitoring meeting held by DRDC, the block representatives placed their demand of training in specific trade/activities. They in turn receive this demand from the Gram Panchayats who nurtures the SHGs. Alternatively, the demands are also received from SHG cluster members themselves.

2. After culling the demands the District Training Co-ordinator (an official posted in DRDC) interacts with the Master Trainers and the training organizations to determine the courses of training, duration and the availability of slots for training. In general, the non-residential courses are handled by DRDC approved Master Trainers and residential courses are conducted in training organizations.
3. The information is disseminated in the next monitoring meeting of DRDC.

Apart from normal skill enhancement trainings conducted by DRDC approved local master trainers, specialised trainings on specific activities were conducted by some important organizations.

1. National Institute of Fashion Technology (NIFT) Kolkata, conducted three months' training at 'ETC Rajarhat' West Bengal for two batches of SHG members drawn from the group members of Deganga block. Sixty participants were trained by the core faculty of NIFT. The trainees were trained in apparel designing with an accent on choice of fabrics, the specific cuts of the apparel, embroidery and its nuances as also the aspect of synchronising and balancing different types of fabrics and their colour. Traditionally, the women folk of the block were conversant with embroidery styles like 'Parsee stitch', 'Gujarati stitch' and 'Kantha stitch' and these skills were further spruced up. Programmes were launched to generate block-level Master Trainers who will be able to train other group members in their trade. The training was basically for secondary sector.
2. In the primary sector also several training programmes were held. These programmes were designed more to equip the group members with skills in animal husbandry, poultry and agri-horticulture. The trainings were held in Bidhan Chandra Krishi Vishwavidyalaya, Nadia and in West Bengal University of Animal & Fisheries Sciences, Kolkata.

3. Training on vermi-compost (organic manure) was another important programme organised by DRDC. The training was conducted by an NGO, namely "Consortium for Training Resource and Development" and DRDC had a buy back arrangement with them in the sense that the NGO bought back the organic manure produced by the trainees. The manure though was sold extensively in the peri-urban locality for their use in the private gardens and orchards and in the city of Kolkata, the trainees themselves also used it in their own agricultural fields which to a great extent reduced the cost of chemical manure and fertilisers. The NGO conducted the training in six blocks, namely Sandeshkhali-II, Hasnabad, Hingalgunj, Swarupnagar, Minakhan and Gaighata, in a span of three years.
4. SHGs under SGSY have been federated into clusters on the basis of their activities. In North 24 Parganas also there are several activity-based clusters. Training on "Market Orientation & Value Enhancement" for these cluster, SHG members was organised in the state in which seven participants from Dharampur Paddy Producers cluster and Sopan Kantha Stitch cluster of North 24 Parganas participated. The programme was devised to create 'District Level Master Trainers' in 'Market Orientation' and the programme was conducted in collaboration with Best Practices Foundation, an NGO of Karnataka state having specialization in this area. The participants were trained in skills of retailing, pricing mechanism, market survey, positioning of the product their distribution, etc. The language barrier was negotiated with the presence of facilitators having knowledge in English and extensive use of diagrams, pictures and field visits which banked upon Participatory Market Appraisal (PMA).

(c) **Marketing of Products:** A marketeer can hardly satisfy everyone in the market. Hence, they start dividing the markets into segments. They identify segment specific profile of distinct group of buyers preferring varying products basing on the demographic, psychographic and behaviour differences among buyers.

1. **Identifying Products for Specific Markets.** Without going into detailed and complex market analysis, SHGs of West Bengal following simple thumb rule and experience, carry embroidered *sarees* and dress materials with jute bags and other knick-knacks to the fairs held in metropolis. The products sold in Delhi Saras Mela held in IITF by the SHGs of West Bengal bear a testimony to this. In 2009, 23 SHGs of West Bengal participated in the fair and of them as many as sixteen SHGs carried embroidered *sarees*, dress materials and different types of women outfit, namely *silwar kameez* or *kurtis* and jute ornaments and bags. In that fair, three SHGs of North 24 Parganas participated and two of them carried embroidered *sarees* and dress materials. Identical approach was evident in 2010 in Delhi Saras. Out of 29 SHGs who participated from West Bengal, 21 carried embroidered *sarees*, dress materials and jute products and only one of the four participating SHGs of North 24 Parganas had a different item to offer.[10]

   This trend is evident in the fairs held in other metropolis also. In fact the products of primary sector are basically sold in village fairs rather than in metropolis. Rice is the only product which defies this logic and is sold in the fairs of Kolkata.

   In fact, this segmenting of the markets allows the SHGs to reap richer benefits in the sense that the groups which concentrate on the primary sector products target the rural and semi-rural markets while those with handicrafts, *sarees* and dress materials, etc. aim the urban markets.

2. **Marketing the Products-making it a Habit.** The main avenue of marketing the products of SHGs are the fairs organised either by the government or by private initiatives. Apart from that there are some sale counters in different districts and in North 24 Parganas the sale

counters are at Barasat, i.e. District HQ, Deganga block HQ and Swabhumi—The Heritage Plaza at Salt Lake.

It is a normal experience that the propensity to buy these SHG products can be discerned among the urban customers who apart from having disposable income attach the concept of 'freshness' with these products. Further the inevitable romanticism associated with buying products from rural women hailing from a far flung area who has either produced it or made it, is an undeniable factor in the psyche of urban customers. This gets further whetted when the customer identifies his rural moorings with the product. Further somewhat baseless notion that urban customers can squeeze better price deals from the SHG members also adds to this tendency. All these while shooting up the sale of products in fairs which are periodic affairs, fails to sustain the demand since the outlets are scarcely available in urban areas.

DRDC, North 24 Parganas had hit upon certain specific plans to handle this aspect.

(a) In the first regard an outlet was opened in 'Swabhumi' a mall-cum-entertainment park in Kolkata in the vicinity of Salt Lake. The outlet offers handicraft materials, embroidered *sarees* and apparels, junk and jute jewellery, jute slippers along with different spices. All the products are made by SHGs of North 24 Parganas operating under the SGSY scheme.

(b) Several offices, colleges and universities either hold training programmes or seminars in which it is customary to give a folder or a bag to the participants. SHGs of the district under active guidance of the DRDC and drawing upon the memo no. 7369F (cited above) approached different institutions, secured the orders and executed such orders. State Institute of Panchayats and Rural Development, West Bengal Industrial Development Corporation, University of Kalyani, CDPO's offices at different districts, Kolkata office of UNICEF are some of the customers of the SHGs of the district. It is a fact that these kinds of involvements are not incessant but they maintain a regularity of sorts. A plus point is that the organizations which once have placed orders with the SHGs tend to come back again. Kudos definitely goes to strong perseverance, quality consciousness and immaculate time sense of the SHG members in executing the orders.

(c) The branding of the products was also attempted. All the products of North 24 Parganas are marketed under the brand name 'Angana' (women working in the courtyard) save spices which is sold under the brand name 'Sanima'. This branding again, it is conceived will give a distinct identity to the products of North 24 Parganas.

3. **The Sale Figures:** The sale figures of different fairs in which the SHGs of the district participated are more or less impressive. The sale figures pertaining to the financial year 2008-09 and 2009-10 are detailed below in the tables. Further the sale proceeds at the sale counter at Swabhumi also registered an impressive figure. A novel attempt was made in supplying the materials to different offices in the district, universities and offices at Kolkata. The sale figure of the SHGs of the district under SGSY is given in Table 2 and Table 3 pertaining to the financial year 2008-09 and 2009-10. The sale figures are categorised in three distinct heads.

(a) Sales arising out of participation in national level fairs, viz. SARAS Mela conducted in several states.

(b) Sale figure of the products sold in the fairs within the state, viz. Poush mela at Santiniketan.

(c) Sale figure arising out of supply to different offices and organizations.

In 2008-09, supply of rice to 16 ICDS project of the district was a major breakthrough in office supply segment. 'Essential Commodities Supply Corporation' failed to execute the supply properly and the SHGs were called to step in. Two SHG activity clusters of Gaighata block, namely Dharampur Paddy

Producers Cluster and Dharmpur Chal Utpadak Swanirbhar Sangha consisting of ten SHGs each executed the supply. DRDC provided the clusters with a Tata Ace vehicle to carry rice to different ICDS centres under infrastructure fund of DRDC.

In 2012-13, the sale proceeds registered an upward trend also. Total sale figure adding all the sale figures of this financial year came up to ₹ 23,00,82191. This was really impressive and the SHG members were benefited by it and the incremental income registered a growth of around ₹ 6000 per year on an average. However, the increase in income remained skewed as some of the blocks who were urban in nature (viz. Rajarhat which is in the vicinity of Newtown did scarcely benefit by this SGSY) failed to benefit through this programme.

There are some exclusive sale counters of SHG products initiated by DRDC. The counter at Swabhumi—The Heritage Plaza (a mall-cum-entertainment park) is a prestigious outlet where different wares of SHGs are displayed for sale. It was started on 15/4/2008 and its sale proceeds for the 2008-09, 2009-10 and 2012-13 are given in Table 4. The entire sale proceeds are taken by the SHGs who have supplied the materials at the counter.

In Lieu of Conclusion

So far so good. Yet the flutter in the dovecot of SHG occurs when:

1. SHGs loose the battle of presence in market in face of stiff challenges posed by the branded and attractively packaged materials. Ideal example is that of honey, whose branded and packaged variety entice the customer more than the local one processed by SHGs.
2. As a corollary to this market presence, SHG products have to develop immaculate supply chains so that the products continuously occupy the shelves. To guarantee this, the flow of credit to the groups needs to be ensured which, unfortunately, is a sore spot throughout India. Alongside enabling environment has to be created by the people in power.
3. State should understand that the metropolis and newly emerging urban areas are prone to buying value

added items and secondary sector products of SHGs. Consequently more exclusive outlets for the SHG products in the metropolis backed up by a system of regular supply should be in place rather than setting up separate marketing outlets in the blocks.

A poverty alleviation programme, as J.S. Mill conceived way back, is basically a balancing act. It is a delicate balance between extending greatest amount of needful help to the deserving populace and at the same time discouraging them to be over reliant on this. SGSY, thus, as a poverty alleviation programme renders the initial 'push' to the entrepreneurial capacity of the rural populace, especially women, so that they come out of their proverbial morass. In this paper, we have seen that the concerned administering authorities have also tried to do their bit. The second part, i.e. to make the target group self-reliant is trickier and here one cannot establish a simplistic linear relationship between the demands of the beneficiaries and the nuances of the programme. A lamppost, it is ordinarily believed, precisely has two usages; a reveller uses it for support while sober understands it as a component of illumination! SGSY or for that matter all similar kind of programmes are akin to lampposts...it will be interesting to subsequently trace their usages.

Table 1

Sl.No.	Name of the Blocks	Major Activities Done by the Groups
1.	Amdanga	Tie and dye, paddy processing, mushroom cultivation, tailoring, block-printing, paper-bag production, goat rearing, fishing.
2.	Barasat-I	Hand-embroidery, goat rearing, fruit jam and pickles, tie-dye jute ornaments/bags/shoes and chappals, paddy processing, home decoratives/ idols like Laxmi Ganesh, Shiv Durga, etc. /dia/cup-plate/ornaments flower vase/pen stand/terracotta tiles/home decorative items.

3.	Barasat-II	Poultry, hand-embroidery, paddy processing tailoring, ari and jari work, nursing and attendant service, wood furniture making.
4.	Barrackpore-I	Animal husbandry, tailoring, sola-work, poultry.
5.	Barrackpore-II	Paper bag making, tailoring, house dairy, goat rearing, jute ornaments and jute products, ready-made garments, paddy processing.
6.	Bashirhat-I	Poultry, goat rearing, fishery and prawn culture, gauge bandage production, paddy processing.
7.	Bashirhat-II	Goat rearing, fishery, tailoring, paddy processing, jari work.
8.	Bonguon	Tailoring, poultry, animal husbandry, paddy processing, wool knitting, nursing and attendant service.
9.	Bagdah	Poultry, animal-husbandry, machine-embroidery, paddy processing tailoring.
10.	Gaighata	Vermi-compost production, paddy processing, paper bag making, house dairy, poultry, goat rearing.
11.	Swarupnagar	Animal husbandry, mat-making, paddy processing, tailoring.
12.	Habra-I	Spices, fruits and vegetable processing, mushroom production, crystal bag making, ready-made garments, paddy processing, ready food supply, fishing, floriculture.
13.	Habra-II	Poultry, tailoring, paddy processing.

14.	Haroa	Animal husbandry, fishery, goat rearing , ari and jari work.
15.	Deganga	Kantha-stitch, hand embroidery, vegetable-dye, paper bag making.
16.	Hasnabad	Honey production, piggery, horticulture-nursery, hand embroidery, jute works, mat making, vermi-compost production.
17.	Hingalganj	Fishing, poultry, paddy processing, vermi-compost production.
18.	Minakhan	Fishing, goat rearing, tailoring paddy processing, ready food supply.
19.	Rajarhat	Ari work, tailoring, catering service.
20.	Baduria	Bamboo works, tailoring, poultry, goat rearing, house dairy, paddy processing, pig rearing.
21.	Sandeshkhali-I	Fishery and prawn culture, goat rearing, paddy processing, poultry.
22.	Sandeshkhali-II	Fishery and prawn culture, goat rearing, poultry, paddy processing, vermi-compost production.

Table 2

Sl.No.	Financial year	Organization or office where supply has been made	Money value of the supply
1.	2008-09	National level fairs	₹ 1237455
2.	2008-09	State and district level fairs	₹ 724300
3.	2008-09	Office supplies	₹ 23022850

Table 3

Sl.No.	Financial year	Fairs and office where supply has been made	Money value of the supply
1.	2009-10	National level fairs	₹ 2597339
2.	2009-10	State and district level fairs	₹ 418335
3.	2009-10	Office supplies	₹ 511428

Table 4

Sl.No.	Financial year	Money value of the Sale
1.	15-4-2008-March 2009	₹ 85887
2.	2009-10	₹ 217000
3.	2012-13	₹ 208936

NOTES

1. Swarna Jayanti Gram Swarozgar Yojna, 1999, Government of India, Ministry of Rural Development-Guidelines-Para 6.2.
2. *Ibid.*
3. *Ibid.*, Para 6.4.
4. *Ibid.*, Section VII.
5. Self-Help Group and Self-Employment: Policies http://www.banglarmukh.com/portal/banglarMukh/Government/Departments/DepartmentListPortletWindow-Visited 3/9/2013
6. Letter from Principal Secretary, Department of SHG and SE addressed to District Magistrate, vide memo no-97/SH/o/2P-132/09, 17/2/2010 and 21(8)/SH/O/2P-132/09-25/1/2010. P. Purushotham (2006). In his 'National Study on SGSY: A Process Study Hyderabad: National Institute of Rural Development' traced the robust performance of SHGs of Andhra Pradesh regarding their rice and maize procuring activities.

7. District Human Development Report North 24 Parganas, Feb. 2010 Development & Planning Department, Government of West Bengal.
8. P. Kotler and K.N. Keller, (2009). *Marketing Management*, p. 5. Prentice Hall of India.
9. Information on West Bengal Panchayats. August 2010, Web-published by Panchayats & Rural Development Department, Government of West Bengal.
10. A Report on SARAS Mela, 2009 and 2010, CAPART.

13

Participation of Non-Governmental Organizations in Rural Development—A Social Work Perspective

V. Naveen Kumar and *V. Venkteswarlu*

ABSTRACT

To achieve the holistic vision of development, the state requires the constructive and collaborative engagement of the civil society in its various developmental activities and programmes. Non-governmental organizations as the operational arm of the civil society therefore have an important role in the development processes. NGOs are organizations within the civil society that work on the "non-for-profit" approach in the space which exists between the family (household), markets and state. It is made up of several types of formal voluntary organizations, where people based on community, neighborhood, workplace and other connections form their association to participate in actions for their own collective interests or for larger social good.

Introduction

In a democratic society, it is the state that has the ultimate responsibility for ushering development to its citizens. In India, through the progressive interpretation of the constitution and its laws and policies, the scope of development has been significantly broadened to include not just economic progress for citizens, but also promotion of social justice, gender equity, inclusion, citizen's awareness, empowerment and improved quality of life. To achieve the holistic vision of development, the state requires the constructive and collaborative engagement of the civil society in its various developmental activities and programmes. The objective of development is to enhance the quality of the living condition of people, more particularly the rural people and to mobilize the resources available at local level and to tackle the chief evils of the modern society such as unemployment, malnutrition, diseases, illiteracy and inequality so that social justice can be promoted. Therefore, the basic object of all developmental activities is to provide minimum needs to the marginalized sections of the society like food, shelter, health. Non-governmental organizations as the operational arm of the civil society therefore have an important role in the development processes. NGOs are organizations within the civil society that work on the "non-for-profit" approach in the space which exists between the family (household), markets and state. It is made up of several types of formal voluntary organizations, where people based on community, neighborhood, workplace and other connections form their association to participate in actions for their own collective interests or for larger social good.

Rural Development in India

Now, in India 70 per cent of people are living in rural areas. In India, the term 'rural development' is not a very old phenomenon. Early in the century there exist the British rule. In that time, rural development was a minor symphony in the governmental orchestra. The functions of the government were limited and even the spread of each function was narrowly restricted. Thus, development cannot but be of minor meaning and significance in the structure of the priorities of colonialism, which was also reflected in the rural areas. Since India is a country of diverse cultures with different languages, religions, castes, customs, traditions and more across different strata of different societies of various states, considerable achievement is not possible if the basics of development in terms of the socio-cultural aspects are ignored in the real development of people of a nation. Rural development means overall development of rural areas to improve the quality of life of rural people. It is an integrated process which includes social, economical, political and spiritual development of the poorer sections of the society. In most of the rural development programmes, human beings are the causes and consequences. Hence, the main objectives of rural development are:

- Food for all people and minimizing the malnutrition all over the country.
- Language for their ideas in the development of the individual.
- Free and compulsory education for children and adult education to all women.

Secondary objectives are:

- Agriculture and allied activities to increase the yield of crops.
- Development of villages and cottage industries and handicrafts is necessary to increase the production of goods.
- Socio-economic infrastructure which includes establishment of rural banks, schools, etc.
- Community services and facilities are necessary for rural community to provide drinking water, electricity rural and roads for transportation.

Census 2011 is the 15th Census of India since 1872. Government of India has released of provisional population 2011, as mentioned in Table 1.

Table 1: Total Population in India–2011

	Population in Crores	**Percentage in %**
India	121.0	100
Rural	83.3	68.84
Urban	37.7	31.16

Source: Census 2011 – Provisional Population Totals—India

Table 1 shows that 1210.2 million populations in India, the size of rural population is 833.1 million (or 68.84 per cent) of the total population, urban population 377.1 million (or 31.16 per cent). According to 2011 Census, highest, lowest population in rural area are occupied by Uttar Pradesh 155.11 million (or 18.6 per cent), Sikkim 0.45 million (or 0.1 per cent) simultaneously. In urban area highest, lowest places are occupied by Maharashtra 50.8 million (or 13.5 per cent), Sikkim 0.15 million.

Table 2: Sex Ratio in India–2011

	Overall	**0-6 Years age children**
India	940	914
Rural	947	919
Urban	926	902

Source: Census 2011, Government of India

Table 2 shows the overall sex ratio is largely in urban areas, though the urban child sex ratio is far worse than in the rural areas.

Table 3: Literacy Rate (in %) India-2011

	Literacy Rate (in %)	**Male (in %)**	**Female (in %)**
India	74.0	82.1	65.5
Rural	68.9	78.6	58.8
Urban	85.0	89.7	79.9

Source: Census 2011, Government of India

Table 3 shows that the improvement in female literacy is more than males in both rural and urban areas during 2001-11. The pace of increase in female literacy rate is perceptibly higher in rural areas.

Evolution of NGOs in India

In India, the rise of professional associations have paralleled the developments in the late 19th century. Voluntary organization or social service has been an integral part of socio-cultural and religious ethos in India right from ancient times, but modern indigenous forms of voluntary organization began to appear in the early colonial period during the renaissance of Bengal with the demands on the colonial state for social or religious reforms on issues like—polygamy, child marriages, promotion of women's education, widows, etc. Gradually, these issues mainly based on voluntary organization had spread to western India during the latter half of the 19th century. But secularist development-oriented voluntary movement got a new dimension after the advent of Gandhism in 20th century. During the freedom struggle, workers of Indian National Congress had undertaken the rural development activities besides freedom movement. The ashrams formed by Gandhiji were considered as the first generation of modern NGOs in India. In fact, Gandhiji was in favour of dissolving Congress after Independence rather than making it a political party.

Now NGOs today in India are found in almost all the areas of human activity. The activities are virtually multiplying in geometrical progression. They have taken up an array of roles; activists of environmental protection, strong advocates of human rights, consumer protectionists and the like. In the areas of welfare, education, health, sanitation, environmental protection, human rights and social justice, the sector has carved out a niche for itself. NGOs based on local inter-family, inter-household relationship addressing on various issues arising out of daily existence in those localities. In fact, the activities of the sector have influenced significantly the government policies and programmes. At local level, youth associations, women's organizations and neighborhood groups are operating in both rural and urban areas.

Participation of NGOs in Rural Development

NGOs are playing a promising interlocutors role in all development activities in existing academic as well as development studies. In recent times, responding to grassroots level initiative and voluntary action became necessary to develop the rural areas. The increasing demands for the NGOs are itself a response to recent trends relating to socio-economic issues and their corresponding development interventions in academic and policy-oriented research. NGOs are very vast and include poor, scheduled castes and schedule tribes, women and children, persons in need of medical aid, aged people, societies facing problems due to environment degradation and lack of infrastructure, people having lesser means to take up economic activity, etc. NGOs working with the rural poor have its own initiative, innovative intervention into the social development. NGOs work in close proximity with their target groups and hence, they have a distinctive advantage over other development agencies in the sense that on being successful in building the faith at initial stages, the NGOs are expected to carry their projects/ programmes smoothly in future. The successful NGOs gain stronger supporters and have emerged as an instrumental in the process of rural development and planning. That is why the NGOs are considered as mirror of the social life of the rural people and rural development. The constructive roles played by the NGOs in the field of rural development are explained briefly in the following points:

- Implementation of different rural development programmes.
- Securing people's participation which is very important for the success of rural development programmes as it increases acceptability and utilization of services.
- Given proper guidance to the illiterate and untrained beneficiaries in the use of advanced technology pertaining to agriculture and rural development.
- Acting as link between the administration and the people to bring about changes in the attitude of the people through education, persuasion, motivation and building up of awareness.
- Supplementing government programmes in rural areas by providing a wide range of choices and alternatives to the people.

- Providing direct services to the beneficiaries at individual level.
- Mobilizing financial and human resources from within the community and promoting self-reliance.
- To improve the condition of the rural poor, the status of women, preventing environmental degradation and promoting literacy.
- Providing facilities for education, health, drinking water, roads and communications, etc., to the rural poor.
- Studying the problems of rural areas and monitoring and evaluating different rural development programmes and documenting information relating to voluntary efforts.

Status of NGOs

Currently, the NGOs have emerged as a third sector in the country and the rest of the world, next to the government and the corporate sector. NGOs find a place in many government and semi-government policy and implementation bodies. With the failure of the state in reaching the poor and the marginalized, NGOs in India have come to play a very important role. As a part of civil society, the NGOs' role in micro-macro linkages and policy advocacy has become a dominant feature now. Now in India, there are many NGOs are there, also made sincere efforts to provide basic needs to the people like food, shelter, health and protection. Development in contemporary infrastructural facilities in the field of training, development of skills in specialized fields like primary education programmes, health services, malnutrition, unemployment programmes, marketing of rural produce, microfinancing, women and child development, etc., and demonstrating alternative methods suitable for the rural areas to improve the living conditions of the people.

Rural Development Programmes

The people who live in the rural areas are deprived of basic amenities such as food, shelter, education and health care. Skill formation and other basic services are inaccessible to most of the poor people. It is increasingly realized that improving the quality of life of the rural masses and removal of poverty should receive priority in the development process. For this, a number of innovative schemes were conceived and adopted to upgrade the poor. These were the Integrated Rural Development Programme (IRDP), Training of Rural Youth for Self-Employment (TRYSEM), Development of Women and Children in Rural Areas (DWCRA), Jawahar Rozgar Yojana (JRY), Indira Awas Yojana (IAY), Rajiv Gandhi National Drinking Water Mission, Central Rural Sanitation Programme (CRSP), Minimum Needs Programme, NREGA, MGNRDP, DRDA, SGSY, RADP, etc.

These schemes were designed to cover almost every aspect of rural development, including employment generation, health and sanitation. We have enough schemes and considerable budget allocations for the development of rural areas. But, due to lack of systematic approach, all our policies and programmes failed in this endeavour. During the initial planning periods, we neglected the participation of the rural people in policy formulation as well as implementation of different developmental programmes. It has been found that the majority of the schemes did not take into account the local needs and initiatives as well as feasibility of projects. In addition, there were political, social, bureaucratic and economic constraints which are hurdles in the path due to these lacunae the best-planned efforts could not bring about the process of development to the doorstep of the poor people. Poverty, squalor, inequality, exploitation and limited opportunities continue to the lot of the rural poor.

Rural Development under the Planned Era

Rural development as a process is complex and involves the interaction of economic, social, political, technological and other situational factors. These have to be integrated with government policies and plans with the objective of improving the quality of life of the people in the villages. The planning for rural development has been received utmost attention by the planners and policymakers along with the national plan for economic development. The rural development strategies were also adopted by planners as per the methods and strategies adopted for the economic development of the country. India adopted both the centralized and decentralized planning models in the process of its planned economic development.

The First Five-year Plan (1950-51 to 1955-56) adopted the Harrod-Domar model of capital accumulation and saving mobilization as its methodological approach towards planning. Under this approach, the process of economic development must start from the villages. In this context, the mobilization of people participation was required. In order to implement this ideology, the community development programme (CDP) was conceived. The block administration was created as a centre of rural development activities. This programme failed as blocks were quite big and left the weaker sections untouched.

The Second Five-year Plan (1955-56 to 1960-61) based on Feldman-Mahalnobis model of sectoral growth. This strategy emphasized investment in heavy industry to achieve industrialization, which was assumed to be the basic condition for rapid economic development. A good deal of reliance was placed on cottage and small industries with the aim of reducing rural underemployment, unemployment. In this respect, the need for viable institutional base was felt and the Panchayat Raj System was introduced during the plan period. Besides, specialized rural economic development programmes like Intensive Agricultural District Programme (IADP), Khadi and Village Industries Programme (KVI), Multi-purpose Tribal Development, Village Housing Projects/Schemes were also introduced in rural areas of the country.

The Third Five-year Plan (1960-61 to 1965-66) all-round agricultural development was envisaged. Increased agricultural production in the farm sector and activities allied to agriculture received top most priority during the plan period. The important agricultural programmes bringing green revolution strategy like Intensive Agricultural Area Programme (IAAP), and High Yield Varieties Programme (HYVP) were implemented in the country. Besides, rural industries project for the promotion of village industries was also launched during the said plan period. Health and nutrition is regarded as important inputs required for improvement in the quality of life.

The Fourth Five-year Plan (1969-74) in the name of "Growth with Social Justice" initiated efforts towards uplifting the vulnerable sections of rural society. In this connection a number of 'Area Development Oriented' and 'Target Oriented' programmes were introduced. Programmes such as Small Farmers Development Agency (SFDA), Small Farmers and Agricultural Labourers Development Agency (MFAL), Drought Prone Area Programme (DPAP), Tribal Area Development Programmes (TADP) were introduced as the important rural development programmes. These rural development programmes did succeed, but only in limited areas and numbers. This plan paved the path for a number of rural development and poverty alleviation programmes in the country. These programmes were implemented through the existing administrative apparatus at block and village levels. Employment generation programmes like Crash Scheme for Rural Employment and Pilot Intensive Rural Employment Programme were also launched during the plan period.

The most important objectives of the Fifth Plan period (1974-79) was: (a) removal of poverty and (b) achievement of self-reliance. In order to attain these objectives, the programmes like Command Area Development Programme (CADP), Hill Area Development Programme (HADP), Minimum Needs Programme (MNP), Food For Work Programme (FFW), were introduced during the plan period. Besides, in order to promote small-scale, village and cottage industries, the District Industries Centers (DICs) were set up in all districts of the country. The 20-point Economic Programme was also introduced during the said plan period.

The Sixth Five-year Plan (1980-85) aimed at the removal of poverty, growth, modernization, self-reliance and social justice. In order to attain all-round development in rural areas, one single integrated programme called Integrated Rural Development Programme (IRDP) was conceived. IRDP is regarded as a multi-level, multi-sector, and multi-section concept of rural development. Rural population such as small farmers, marginal farmers, landless and agricultural labourers, artisans, scheduled castes and scheduled tribes were given preferences. Besides IRDP, the employment generation programmes like National Rural Employment Programme (NREP), Rural Landless Employment Guarantee Programme (RLEGP), Economic Rehabilitation of Rural Poor (ERRP), Training of Rural Youth for Self-Employment (TRYSEM), Self-Employment for the Educated Unemployed Youths (SEEUY), Development of Women and Children in Rural Areas (DWCRA), etc. were also introduced during the said plan period.

The Seventh Five-year Plan (1985-90) focused on building an independent self-reliant economy, establishment of social system based on equity and justice, reduction of regional imbalance and adoption of advanced technologies. The plan intended to continue the rural development programmes launched/ implemented during the Sixth Five-year Plan. Besides, some rural infrastructural development programmes like Indira Awas Yojana (IAY), Integrated Rural Energy Planning Programme (IREP), Jawahar Rozgar Yojana (RJY), Million Wells Scheme (MWS), etc. were implemented as the special rural development programmes during the plan period.

The Eighth Five-year Plan (1992-97) aimed at generation of adequate employment opportunities, universalisation of elementary education, provision of safe drinking water and primary healthcare facilities, and strengthening the infrastructure. The special rural development and poverty alleviation programmes implemented in earlier plans were also intended to continue during the Eighth Five-year Plan. Intensified Jawahar Rozgar Yojana (IJRY), Employment Assurance Scheme (EAS), Operation Black Board (OBB), and District Primary Education Programme (DPEP) were introduced.

The Ninth Five-year Plan (1997-2002) aimed at generating employment opportunities in the secondary sector, all-round development of agricultural sector, strengthening the rural economy through development of agro-based industries, small-scale village and cottage industries and elimination of poverty. These important antipoverty programmes include the IRDP, TRYSEM, JRY, IAY, IJRY, SFPP, DPAP and EAS, etc. The IRDP, DWCRA, TRYSEM, MWS were in operation till the end of 1998-

99. The Government of India merged into a single new scheme called Swarnajayanti Gram Swarozgar Yojana (SGSY) with effect from 1-4-1999. In order to create adequate infrastructural development the Jawahar Gram Samridhi Yojana (JGSY) was also implemented on the same date.

During the Tenth Five-year Plan (2002-07), the strength of the fundamentals of the State economy was evident from a noteworthy transition to a high growth path during the 10th Five-year Plan period. The development of rural India is an imperative for inclusive and equitable growth and to unlock the huge potential of the population that is presently trapped in poverty with its associated deprivations. Irrigation Benefit Programme (IBP), Mid-Day Meals Act (MDM), Self-Help Group (SHG), Sarva Shiksha Abhiyan (SSA), Targeted Public Distribution System (TPDS), Small Scale Industries (SSI), Panchayat Raj Institution (PRI), Indian System of Medicine & Homeopathy (ISMH), Rural Livelihood Project (RLY), etc. were introduced and implemented during the plan period.

The Eleventh Five-year Plan (2007-12) had the opportunity to restructure policies to achieve a new vision of growth that will be more broad based and inclusive, bringing about a faster reduction in poverty and helping bridge the divides that are currently the focus of greater attention. It is clear that rapid growth will be essential to .reduce the number of the poor and for sustainable poverty reduction, but for growth to benefit the poor disproportionately; it will have to be accompanied by more rapid employment expansion than greater investment in health, education, water/sanitation, and child nutrition than so far, and directly targeted poverty-reduction programmes. Implemented Programmes are National Afforestation Pragramme (NAP), National Rural Employment Guarentee Act (NREGA): people in rural areas are guaranted 100 days of wage employment. National Rural Health Mission (NRHM), Swarnajayanti Gram Swarozgar Yojana (SGSY), District Rural Development Agency (DRDA), National Policy for Older Person (NPOP), National Social Assistance Programme (NSAP), Khadi and Village Industries (KVI), IAY, MSE, SME, Bharat Nirman and Flagship

Programme (BNFP), etc. was also implemented during the plan period on.

The Rural Development Programmes in India are based on various approaches and strategies. These very according to plan and the nature of the programme. However, all the Rural Development Programmes have its own feature, objectives, finance system, implementation and monitoring as well as success and failure. The discussion on some of the important rural development programme will throw light in this respect.

The Challenges before NGOs

Now the role of NGOs is very much a challenging one. In the current scenario of the 21st century, as observed by Anita Cheria and Edwin, the NGOs face the dual task of collaboration critically with the state and at the same time fighting against the anti-people/anti-marginalized policy. Such a dual task cannot be discharged effectively unless the NGOs are sustained, intervention will depend very much in future on their self-reliant capacity and local resource mobilization.

The paradigm of mainstream development indicates that such model is not sustainable in the ultimate analysis. Its anti-people, anti-women, anti-environment, anti-sustainable thrust has done irreversible damage and destruction. Yet, the process of globalization is pursued with alarming speed. While opposing this destructive approach, one cannot wait to see the reversal of this policy in the given global context. What is urgently needed is to develop and strengthen micro-level people centered and self-managed models. Grassroot level micro-banking systems, community resource management, collective and cooperative income generation activities, etc. are possible models. Though NGOs have promoted vast social infrastructure of the poor and marginalized, the Dalits, Adivasis, the Agri-labourers, etc. transforming them into reality depends very much on the political initiative of the people which, in turn, depends on the perspectives with which NGOs organize them.

NGOs Collaboration with Government

NGOs in India are working in collaboration with the Central and State Governments and a majority of the NGOs are receiving funds from the government and even implement government- sponsored schemes. NGOs have their own goals and pursue them independently of the government. Some were founded even before the formation of the independent Indian Government and continue working towards the fulfillment of their objectives without particularly bothering about the government's policy and programmes. The relation between the Government of India and the non-governmental sector is showing signs of an emerging partnership. This is because the government realizes and has reiterated in its official policy documents that the magnitude of the problem is far too large to be resolved by a single delivery system, be it public or private. The non- governmental sector also realizes and believes that the final and ultimate responsibility rests on the Indian Government. Even if the efforts of the government are critical, NGOs essentially perceive themselves in a partnership role with the government.

Conclusion

The overall objective of many NGO interventions is to enable disadvantaged groups to share more fully the benefits of development. They help the people to identify their wants and needs in rural development programmes and work effectively at satisfying themselves. It is evident that NGOs are able to mobilize and reach the rural people in their programmes. On the basis of the findings of the study, the following recommendations are made: (1) NGOs should create more awareness about their activities in their localities. (2) NGOs should be more flexible in their objectives to address the basic needs or felt needs of the people. (3) Training by NGOs should be complemented with provision of other assistance such as credit and infrastructure. (4) Development agencies should use the NGOs that have experience in field work and the needed manpower to execute the development programmes and activities. (5) They were instrumental in initiating, stimulating and accelerating the process of change in the tradition-bound rural society. They also created awareness among the people about the development programmes.

REFERENCES

Census of India 2011 (Relevant Issues).

Ganesh Babu, K. *NGOs and RD Programmes*, Discovery Publication House Pvt. Ltd., New Delhi.

Joel, S.G.R. Bhose (2003). *NGOs and Rural Development,* Concept Publishing Company, New Delhi.

Lalit, K. Sen (1951). Planning Rural Growth Center for Integrated Area Development, Institute of Community Development, Hyderabad.

Mukundan, N. (2004). *Environment, People's Participation and Sustainable Rural Development: An Overview,* Kurukshetra, June.

Pardon, M. *NGOs and Gross Roots Development: Limits and Possibilities*, The Hague, Institute of Social Studies.

Planning Commission, Various Five-Year Plans, New Delhi (First Five-year Plan to Eleventh Five-year Plan).

Rao, V.M. *Rural Development and Village Perspectives for Planning for Development,* Institute for Social and Economic Change, Bengaluru.

Raul, R.K. (2003). *Rural Development in India: Approaches and Applications,* Serial Publication, New Delhi.

Sahu, B.K. (2003). *Rural Development India,* Anmol Publication Pvt. Ltd., New Delhi.

14

Eco-Feminism and Dynamics of Gender Development in Rural India

A.V.V.S. Swamy, V. Subhashini and *Ch. Rani*

ABSTRACT

Women living in rural areas or mountain areas have special relationship with the environment. They are more close to the nature than men and this very close relationship makes them perfect managers of an eco-system. The life of mountain women is so much intertwined with the environment that whole ecosystem revolves around her and she can't even think of her survival without it. Through their practical experiences and managerial skills, they have acquired immense knowledge of the various types of plants. They know better than any scientist that what grass, herbs, shrubs, trees are best for them and should be planted to maintain a balanced eco-system and well-being of their families and communities. They always prefer a mixed forest, which can meet their demands of fuel, fodder, fruits and food as well as maintains the bio-diversity of the mountains. They are perfect in making an optimum use and conservation of natural resources.

Introduction

Traditionally, women have been responsible for subsistence and survival for water, food, fuel, fodder and habitat, though they rarely get the credit for nurturing these life-support systems. Added to these environmental destruction, exacerbates women's problems in a way very difficult from that of men (Sharma and Kaushik, 2011). The challenge is to re-establish the symbiosis between communities, women and natural resources and reverse the trend of the negative impact of existing developmental paradigms. Traditionally, women have dealt with non-monetized biomass-based subsistence economy of the household, i.e. firewood, cow dung, crop wastes, organic manure, etc. In comparison, men tend to destroy nature to earn cash even if it means creating hardship in their own families for their womenfolk to collect fuel and fodder, e.g. sale of herbs and wood. The important thing is that women work as unpaid labourers on family farms with a greater role than men in operational decision-making. The population pressure has increased male migration, which in turn adds to the women's work load. In effect, this means that women's responsibilities extend from the household duties to working in the fields as well. Women in our country have brought a different perspective to the environment debate, because of their different experience base. Poor women's lives are not compartmentalized and they see the issues in a broad and holistic perspective. They understand clearly that economics and environment are compatible.

Throughout history men have looked at natural resources as commercial entities or income-generating tools, while women have tended to see the environment as a resource support their basic needs. As an example, rural Indian women collect the dead branches which are cut by storm for fuel wood to use rather than cutting the live trees (Rodda, 1991). The dependence on nature and the environment for survival is common among Third World women. It has been argued by environmental feminists that this dependence creates a deeply-rooted connection between women and their surroundings. Jiggins (1994) suggested that the views women have on nature are unique in that they connect the land to immediate survival and concern for future generations rather than simply looking at the land as a resource with monetary value (Abuz, 1994). In developing areas like India, women are considered the primary users of natural resources (land, forest, and water), because they are the ones who are responsible for gathering food, fuel, and fodder. Although in many countries, women mostly can't own the land and farms outright, they are the ones who spend most of their time working on the farms to feed the household. Shouldering this responsibility leads them to learn more about soil, plants, and trees and not misuse those (Jiggins, 1994).

Women have always been the principal conservers of bio-diversity. Even today they perform duties such as seed selection, multiplication and conservation. The on-farm conservation traditions of rural and tribal women, with reference to agro-biodiversity were well-known. Unfortunately, current food security systems depend on too few crops. It is important to expand the basis of food security by including large number of species and variety of food plants. For this purpose, women can be trained in the revitalization of the on-farm conservation traditions of the older generation through bio-technological process. The training should also include equipping them for compiling bio-diversity inventories and for taking decision on issues like giving consent to using their genetic material by breeding companies/institutions (Jiggins, 2004).

Superiority of Women's Knowledge on Resources over Men

The dependence on nature and the environment for survival is common among Third World women. It has been argued by many environmental feminists that this dependence creates an deeply-rooted connection between women and their surroundings. The dependency women have on natural resources based on their responsibilities creates a specific interest that may be different from the interests of men (Tiondi, 2001). Jiggins (2004) suggests that the views women have on nature are unique in that they connect the land to immediate survival and concern for future generations rather than simply looking at the land as a resource with monetary value. Today in India women are playing pivotal role in conservation of natural resources and environment, men had degraded the physical environment abruptly while they had dominance over women and women's great investment in sustainability of environment. Whereas some other have theorized that women would protect the earth better than men if in power although there is no evidence for this hypothesis, recent movements have shown that women are more sensitive to the earth and its problems. They have created a special value system about environmental issues. Traditionally, women are responsible for resource mobilization and management. Fuel, fodder and water collections are the accepted responsibilities of women. As the environment degrades, these basic necessities become difficult to collect. The time a woman spends on gathering fuel, fodder and water, as well as attending to household work, agricultural work and animal care, reduces her competence. Dr. M.S. Swaminathan, former member of the Planning Commission stated, "If men had to fetch drinking water the 230,000 villages would not have remained without provision of drinking water after several years of planned development" (Agarwal, 1992). Thus, women's responsibilities extend from the household duties to working in the fields as well. A destructive chain reaction emerges. As the time required for fuel and fodder collection grows and firewood becomes scarce, cow-dung previously spread on the fields, is used in the kitchen, thereby depleting soil resources and causing a negative effect on the livelihood of local people and environment.

- Women view environment as the life-support systems of humanity. It is the source of all life, that people are dependent on the environment. Without good environment, our life will not be peaceful and healthy.
- Women's involvement on environmental protection and conservation work is crucial in the management and utilization of the natural resources. In general, the key informants are involved in the technical, policy, project proposal conceptualization, planning and programme designing, and supervising the implementation of the project.
- Women's commitment and dedication to work is a manifestation of their selfless love and concern for the environment; for their children; and for the future generation. While this work is not economically viable, they are aware and conscious that the only way to protect themselves and their family but to protect Mother Earth.

- Women's limited access and opportunities in the decision-making process constrain the implementation of their environmental conservation programmes.
- The lack of awareness, consciousness and commitment; how to change the attitude of the people towards environment; how to care for the environment; how to develop their love for livable environment; how to shift the paradigm of the local leaders on sustainable development and environment; and how to sustain the programmes and projects for the protection of the environment are among the challenges that confront the women groups in the implementation of environmental conservation programmes.
- Women play multiple roles in the family, community, and in the protection and management of the natural resources. Their multifaceted roles lead to their multiple burdens.
- Women's perspective on the connections of women and environment are linked to the domestic roles of women. Further, women's roles are directly affected by the state of environment because women are the main users of resources like coastal and water resources, forest resources and other land resources.
- Women viewed degradation of environment as equal to the degradation of women because it deprived them of a better life, better resources, and it makes motherhood.

Environmental Movements Led by Women

An example of female predominance in the defense of natural forests comes from India in 1906. As forest clearing was expanding, conflict between loggers and government, and peasant communities increased. To thwart resistance to the forest cleaning, men were diverted from their villages to a fictional payment compensation site and loggers were sending to the forests. The women left in the villages; however, protested by physically hugging themselves to the trees to prevent their being cut down, giving rise to what is now called the Chipko movement.

Chipko Movement

One of the first environment movements which were inspired by women was the Chipko movement (women tree-huggers in India). "Its name comes from a Hindi word meaning 'to stick'. The movement was an act of defiance against the state government's permission given to a corporation for commercial logging. Women of the villages resisted, embracing trees to prevent their felling to safeguard their lifestyles which were dependent on the forests. Deforestation could qualitatively affect the lives of all village residents but it was the women who agitated for saving the forests. Organized by a non-governmental organization that Chandi Prasad led, the Chipko movement adopted the slogan 'ecology is permanent economy'. The women embracing the trees did not tag their action as feminist activism; however, as a movement that demonstrated resistance against oppression, it had all the markings of such" (Grewal, 2008). It began when Maharaja of Jodhpur wanted to build a new palace in Rajasthan which is India's Himalayan foot-hills. While the axe men were cutting the trees, martyr Amrita Devi hugged one of the trees. This is because in Jodhpur each child had a tree that could talk to it. The axmen ignored Devi and after taking her off the tree cut it down.

Navdanya Movement

Navdanya also known as the 'Nine Seeds Movement' seeks to empower local Indian farmers to move away from growing any genetically modified organism (GMOs) on their land and return to organic, chemical-free practices. This movement has reached over 5,000,000 Indian farmers and created over 65 seed banks around India. Navdanya fights to eliminate the commercialization of indigenous knowledge also known as 'Biopiracy'. Navdanya addresses multiple other international issues including climate change, food security, misapplication of technology, food sovereignty, fair trade, and many others. This movement also created a learning center entitled Bija Vidyapeeth. Bija Vidyapeeth, in collaboration with Schumacher College in the United Kingdom, seeks to educate participants in sustainability and ecological principles.

Women Environmentalists

Vandana Shiva. An influential leader in developing national environmentalism is Vandana Shiva. Vandana Shiva is a world renowned environmental scholar and activist and she has made great strides for women in India as well as around the world (Vandana Shiva. Accessed 2012). Vandana Shiva has published numerous papers on the unequal burden placed on women by environmental degradation, stating that women and children "bore the costs but were excluded from the benefits" of development. Vandana Shiva is also an active voice for localized, organic agriculture and she began a movement entitled Navdanya where participating Indian farmers have created 'freedom zones' to keep their crops free of chemicals to revitalize an organic food market in India. She has received many honorary degrees awards. In 1993, she received the Alternative Nobel Peace Prize, also known as the Right Livelihood Award.

Medha Patkar. Medha Patkar is a well-known social activist of India. On 28 March 2006, Medha went on a hunger strike, in protest of the decision taken by the authorities, to increase the height of the Narmada dam. The strike continued for a long period of 20 days and finally came to an end on April 17, 2006. The Supreme Court rejected the plea of Narmada Bachao Andolan to stop the construction of the dam.

Awards and Honors Conferred on Medha Patkar

- She was a recipient of Right Livelihood Award (1991)
- M.A. Thomas National Human Rights Award (1999)
- Deena Nath Mangeshkar Award
- Mahatma Phule Award
- Goldman Environment Prize
- Green Ribbon Award.

Case Studies in India

Studies on participation of women in natural resource management in Sirmour district of Himachal Pradesh at Indian Institute of Himalayan Studies (IIHS), Shimla revealed that about 73.30 per cent women are engaged in agricultural as well as household work. 63.30 per cent women knew the meaning of natural resources. Majority of women (63.33 per cent) think that there is no proper utilization of natural resources whereas an appreciable number of respondents feel that the resources are used properly. Sixty-three per cent were of the opinion that all types of benefits could be derived by properly utilizing the natural resources. 66.66 per cent women think that they can participate in natural resource management. Further, they were of the view that 80 per cent of non-fertile land can be used as pastures. The study found that village women are affected by degradation of natural resources. In spite of age and health, the women are bearing victims of labour. As the sources dry up, the women have to walk/work more to meet their needs. The family system has much impact on the use of natural resources. Larger families use more natural resources and manage them more efficiently. Level of education is also important in managing the resources. In families, where more members are educated and level of awareness about the importance of conserving natural resource is high, the use of resource is quite judicious. A study on constraints and problems of women in tribal and hilly areas of Himachal Pradesh deals with asset ownership, labour contribution and women's participation in decision-making. Women are involved in decisions pertaining to farming, though not always in financial matters. This is higher in tribal districts than in hilly districts. The women contribute 50 per cent labour to all agricultural activities and their involvement in decision-making is directly proportionate to their labour contribution. Some important highlights of study are:

Studies in villages, i.e. Ichassar and Dev Nagar near Shimla town. The women of the village told that "some time ago, it took very little time to collect wood, but now the forest wood is scarce because of too much cutting. Now we have to go about two kilometers or more to find wood." The rural women interviewed by the author hardly went school, yet they talked about the importance of forest in their lives and how the deterioration of the environment, as a result of inappropriate and unsustainable development has made life difficult for them and their families. The rural women criticized the developmental projects implemented in their areas (Cranney, 2001).

Conclusion

Women are no longer viewed as mere victims, it is increasingly recognized that women can play key role in natural resources management as they have the knowledge and experience gained from working closely with their environment. To maintain the sustainable development, it is necessary to educate women regarding environmental problems, environmental degradation and impact on human health. Environment education should include the whole spectrum of women-nature relationships. It may be pertinent to add, that by educating a woman, a generation is educated. An alternative view of looking at the links between women and the environment acknowledges that if poor communities revert to traditional systems of natural resources management, they can manage their environment efficiently, or even improve it, despite being poor. Reducing poverty, decreasing the gap between the rich and the poor women and improving resource use can have a tremendous impact in fortifying these resources.

REFERENCES

Agarwal, B. (1992). The gender and environment debate: Lessons from India. *Feminist Studies*, Vol. 18, No. 1, Spring.

——. (1998). Disinherited peasants, disadvantaged workers: A gender perspective on land and livelihood. *Economic and Political Weekly*, Vol. 33, No. 13 (Mar. 26-Apr. 3, 1998): A2-A1.

Cranney, B. (2001). Local environment and lived experience: The mountain women of Himachal Pradesh (New Delhi).

Grewal, Jyoti. “Theorizing Activism, Activizing Theory: Feminist Academics in Indian Punjabi Society.” *NWSA Journal*. Volume 20, Number 1, Spring 2008.

Jiggins (2004). *Changing the Boundaries: Women-Centered Perspectives on Population and the Environment*. Covelo, Ca: Island Press.

Jiggins, Janice (1994). *Changing the Boundaries: Women-Centered Perspectives on Population and the Environment*. New York: Island Press.

Navdanya. Accessed March 5, 2012. http://www.navdanya.org/home

Sharma, Renu and Balajit Kaushik (2011). "Role of women in environmental conservation".

Shiva, Vandana. *The Impoverishment of the Environment: Women and Children Last*. Environmental Philosophy: From Animal Rights to Radical Ecology (Fourth Edition), 2005. Pearson Education Inc. Upper Saddle River, NJ.

Tiondi, T. (2001). Women, environment and development: Sub-Saharan Africa and Latin America. Theses and Dissertations, p. 1549.

15

Watershed Development Programme in Andhra Pradesh—A Study on Income and Employment Generation

Noorbasha Abdul, V. Tulasi Das and *Ch. V. Krishna Reddy*

ABSTRACT

Watershed Development Programme (WDP) has conventionally aimed at treating degraded lands with the help of low cost and locally accessed technologies such as soil and moisture conservation measures. Its broad objective was the promotion of the overall economic development and improvement of the socio-economic conditions of the resource poor sections of the society. The study revealed that SHGs formed and established under WDP has provided more benefits and facilities to the members to improve their economic standards resulting in the improvement of their living standards. Besides, WDP motivated all the communities in villages regarding credit and thrift. The respondents have stated that SHGs under WDP have been helping them by facilitating them with required loan for dairy development and management and other tiny business as like establishment of pan shops, laundries, etc. They have also stated that after the implementation of WDP they have been getting employment (labour) for more days with good remuneration.

Introduction

Efficient and sustainable use of natural resources has become the *sine qua non* for economic prosperity, especially in resource poor countries, and all the more so in agriculturally-dominated economies like India, where two-thirds of the cropped area is dependent on rainfall without any protective irrigation facilities. The promotion of appropriate technologies and development strategies in rainfed areas could potentially result in multiple benefits such as food security, and employment opportunities.

One such approach has resulted in watershed development programme which has conventionally aimed at treating degraded lands with the help of low cost and locally accessed technologies such as soil and moisture conservation measures. Its broad objective was the promotion of the overall economic development and improvement of the socio-economic conditions of the resource poor sections of the society.

About 66 per cent of area is rainfed even today. The productivity of crops in drylands is very low due to soil erosion, depletion of moisture resources, low soil fertility, denuding the plantation, bringing marginal soil under plough, etc. The soil erosion is a major problem in dry lands due to lack of ground coverage with grass or crops during the pre-monsoon period.

Though 33 per cent of geographical area should be under forests, at present 21 per cent of area is only under forest, the effective forest area is only about 9 per cent due to widespread deforestation. There are less water resources to meet the requirements of wild animals in summer season. The unemployment, seasonal unemployment, disguised unemployment, etc. are common in dry lands resulting in poverty, malnutrition and imbalanced diet.

Watershed management implies the best use of soil, water and vegetation to obtain optimum level of production with minimum hazards to natural resources.

Objectives

The major objective of this paper is to assess the impact of the Watershed Development Programme on the income and employment of the beneficiaries and also the non-beneficiaries. The study also attempts to elicit the opinions of the respondents on the implementation and the usefulness of the WSD programme in the study area.

Methodology

Prakasam District in Andhra Pradesh is selected purposefully for this study. Statistical evidence reveals that a remarkable progress has been achieved in Prakasam district after the implementation of watershed development programmes. Moreover being hailed from the district for a long time, the researcher has familiarity which has provided him an added advantage for analytical study. Further, there was no practical study of this type on this selected area.

Period of the Study

The present study covers a period of 10 years ranging from 2000-10.

Sampling Procedure

Prakasam district in Andhra Pradesh has been purposively selected for this study. This district comprises three Revenue Divisions, namely Ongole, Markapuram and Kandukur. From these three Revenue Divisions, one village each representing the largest number of watersheds has been selected, the three villages being Ammanigudipadu, P. Rallapalli and Naguluppalapadu. Next, from each village, 50 farmers are selected at randomly, which represent about one-fourth of the total beneficiaries of the Watershed Development Programme. Thus, in all, one hundred and fifty sample beneficiaries are covered by this study. Equal number of non-beneficiaries has been covered by this study as a control group.

Results and Analysis

Income and Employment Generation: A number of schemes have been initiated in the planning period for profiting employment to rural poor, namely National Rural Employment Programme (NREP), Rural Landless Employment Guarantee Programme (RLEGP), Jawahar Rozgar Yojana (JRY), Employment Assurance Scheme (EAS), Sampoorna Grameen Rozgar Yojana (SGRY), certain special programmes introducing the 1970s for the 'weaker sections' of the rural population and backward areas included the Small Farmers Development Agency (SFDA), the Marginal Farmers and Agricultural

Labourers programmes (MFAL), the Drought Prone Area Programme (DPAP), the Hill Area Development Programme (HADP), the Tribal Area Development Programme (TADP), the Crash Scheme for Rural Employment (CSRE) and the Food For Work Programme (FFWP). These programmes are aimed at attacking the problems of rural poverty and backwardness directly by helping the weaker sections so as to increase their income.

Table 1: Employment Generation of the Beneficiaries and Non-Beneficiaries in Sample Villages

Sl. No.	Employment (in Days)	No. of Respondents	
		Beneficiaries	Non-Beneficiaries
1.	Below 180	14 (9.3)	73 (48.7)
2.	180-210	31 (20.7)	26 (17.3)
3.	210-240	69 (46)	39 (26)
4.	Above 240	36 (24)	12 (8)
Total		150 (100)	150 (100)

Source: Computed by Collection of Primary Data

Employment of Agriculture Works

Table 1 shows the employment generation in agriculture for the beneficiaries and the non-beneficiaries in the sample villages. Among the beneficiaries, majority of the respondents, i.e. 69 (46 per cent) got employment for 210-240 days per annum and the lowest number of respondents, i.e. 14 (9.3 per cent) have got employment below 180 days.

Among the non-beneficiaries, the largest number of 73 respondents (48.7 per cent) have got employment for less than 180 days per annum and the lowest number of respondents, i.e. 12 (8 per cent) have got employment for above 240 days. From the above, it is evident that majority of the beneficiaries have got an employment opportunity of 240 days per annum, as against 180 days in the case of non-beneficiaries.

Table 2: Employment Provided by Beneficiaries and Non-Beneficiaries to Other Workers in Sample Villages

Sl. No.	Employment (in Days)	No. of Respondents	
		Beneficiaries	Non-Beneficiaries
1.	Below 15	46 (30.7)	82 (54.7)
2.	15-30	61 (40.6)	43 (28.6)
3.	30-45	22 (14.7)	14 (9.3)
4.	Above 45	21 (14)	11 (7.4)
	Total	150 (100)	150 (100)

Source: Computed by Collection of Primary Data

Employment Opportunities Provided to Other Workers

Table 2 shows the employment opportunities provided to other agriculture workers by the respondents for agriculture purposes in the selected villages. Sixty-one respondent beneficiaries (40.6 per cent) have provided employment opportunities for 15-20 days to the other workers. Only 21 respondents (14 per cent) have provided employment opportunity for more than 45 days to the other workers. Similarly, among the non-beneficiaries, the highest number of 82 respondents (54.7 per cent) has provided employment opportunity for below 15 days to other workers and the lowest number of 11 respondents (7.4 per cent) has provided employment opportunities for more than 45 days to other agriculture workers. From the above analysis, it is evident that most of the beneficiary respondents are providing more working days to other workers for agriculture purpose, as against the non-beneficiaries.

Income and Employment of Respondents Before and After Implementation of Watersheds

Table 3 shows employment opportunity of the respondents before and after implementation of watershed programme in sample villages of Prakasam district. Out of 150 respondents, majority of them, i.e. 70 (46.7 per cent) beneficiaries have got below 180 days of employment and the lowest number, i.e. 25 (16.6 per cent) beneficiaries have got employment for above 240 days before the implementation of watershed. Majority of beneficiaries, i.e. 66 (44 per cent) have got 180 to 240 days and the lowest number, i.e. 33 (22 per cent) beneficiaries have got employment for below 180 days after the implementation of watershed programme.

Table 3: Employment of Respondents Before and After Implement of Programme

Sl. No.	Employment (in Days)	No. of Respondents	
		Before Watershed	After Watershed
1.	Below 180	70 (46.7)	33 (22)
2.	180-240	55 (36.7)	66 (44)
3.	Above 240	25 (16.6)	51 (34)
Total		150 (100)	150 (100)

Source: Computed by Collection of Primary Data

It can be observed from the above table that majority of members are being provided employment for 180 days to 240 days after the implementation of watershed. So it is clear that employment opportunities are increased when compared to the pre-implementation of watershed.

Table 4 shows the per day income from agriculture works the beneficiaries gained before the establishment of watersheds. It shows that 53.33 percentages of the respondents have earned

Table 4: Per Day Income of Beneficiaries from Agriculture Works Before Watershed

Sl. No.	Income (in Rupees)	Before Watershed	
		No. of Respondents	Percentage
1.	Below 30	24	16
2.	30-40	80	53.33
3.	40-50	31	20.67
4.	Above 50	15	10
Total		150	100

Source: Computed by Collection of Primary Data

an income of between 30 to 40 rupees, followed by 20.67 per cent of respondents gained an income of between 40 to 50 rupees per day. The lowest percentage of respondents comprising 10 per cent fall within the average income of rupees 50 and above. From Table 4, it can be observed that majority of respondents fall within the income group of rupees 30 to 40 per day before the establishment of watersheds.

Table 5 shows the per day income from agriculture works of the beneficiaries after the establishment of watersheds. This table depicts that 36 per cent of respondents are in the income group ranging from 80 to 100 rupees. 28 per cent of respondents are in the income group of 60 to 80 rupees per day. 25.33 per cent of respondents have earned above 100 rupees per day and the remaining 10.67 per cent of respondents earned an income of below 60 rupees per day. This table envisages that majority of respondents earn high-income, i.e. 80-100 rupees per day after the establishment of watershed when compared to the time before the establishment of watershed.

Table 5: Per Day Income of Beneficiaries from Agriculture Works After Watershed

Sl. No.	Income (in Rupees)	After Watershed	
		No. of Respondents	Percentage
1.	Below 60	16	10.67
2.	60-80	42	28
3.	80-100	54	36
4.	Above 100	38	25.33
	Total	150	100

Source: Computed by Collection of Primary Data

Table 6 shows per day income of beneficiaries from dairy before and after the establishment of watershed. Out of total 150 respondents, 122 respondents earn income from dairy. Out of 122 respondents, 85 (69.67 per cent) beneficiaries have earned rupees 10 to 15 per day and only one (0.83 per cent) beneficiary has earned rupees 25 to 30 before the establishment of watershed. In

Table 6: Per Day Income of Beneficiaries from Dairy Before and After Watershed

Sl. No.	Income (in Rupees)	No. of Respondents	
		Before Watershed	After Watershed
1.	10-15	85 (69.67)	3 (2.46)
2.	15-20	31 (25.41)	41 (33.61)
3.	20-25	5 (4.09)	48 (39.34)
4.	25-30	1 (0.83)	30 (24.59
Total		122 (100)	122 (100)

Source: Computed by Collection of Primary Data

the same way, 48 (39.34 per cent) beneficiaries have earned rupees 20 to 25 per day and the lowest number, i.e. 3 (2.46 per cent) beneficiaries have earned rupees 10 to 15 per day after the establishment of watershed.

It is observed from the above table that per day income of beneficiaries from dairy is increased after the establishment of watershed when compared to the time before the watershed establishment. After the establishment of watershed, fodder is increased in lands. It shows that the dairy industry has projected to its zenith after the establishment of watersheds.

Opinions of Respondents

Table 3 shows the respondents opinion on benefits; they used to get from the Self-Help Groups under Watershed Development Programme in the sample villages. Among the beneficiaries, 125 (83.3 per cent) respondents are getting benefits from Self-Help Groups under Watershed Development Programme and the remaining 25 (16.7 per cent) respondents have responded negatively. Among non-beneficiaries, 91 (60.7 per cent) respondents are getting benefits from Self-Help Groups under Watershed Development Programme and the remaining 59 (39.3 per cent) respondents have responded negatively. Similarly, out of the 125 (83.3 per cent) positively responded beneficiaries, the highest number of respondents, i.e. 59 (47.2 per cent) have taken loan of between ₹ 5,000 to ₹ 10,000 and the lowest number of respondents, i.e. 21 (16.8 per cent) have obtained loan of more than ₹ 10,000.

Out of the 91 (60.7 per cent) positively, responded non-beneficiaries, the highest number of them, i.e. 46 (50.5 per cent) have obtained loan of less than ₹ 5,000 and the lowest number of respondents, i.e. 12 (13.2 per cent) have availed a loan of more than ₹ 10,000. It is observed that majority of the beneficiaries have taken loan of between ₹ 5,000 to ₹ 10,000 when compared to non-beneficiaries.

In the case of respondents with positive opinions, both beneficiaries and non-beneficiaries have availed loans for other purposes than agriculture, like purchase of cattle, establishment of pan shops and iron shops. Out of the beneficiaries, majority of the respondents, i.e. 105 (84 per cent) have availed loan for the purpose of purchasing cattle and very few of the respondents, i.e. 6 (4.8 per cent) have taken loan to establish laundries (Iron shops). Among the non-beneficiaries, the highest number of respondents, i.e. 59 (64.8 per cent) have taken loans for the purpose of purchasing cattle and the lowest number of respondents, i.e. 5 (5.5 per cent) have taken for the purpose of iron shops (laundries).

It is concluded that majority of the beneficiaries have taken loans for the purpose of purchasing cattle when compared to the non-beneficiaries. In the case of total respondents, who have positively responded both the beneficiaries and non-beneficiaries will pay interest on loans per annum. Out of the total beneficiaries, majority of the respondents, i.e. 55 (44 per cent) have paid more than ₹ 800 per annum towards interest on loans. And very few respondents, i.e. 34 (27.2 per cent) have paid interest of between ₹ 600 and ₹ 800 per annum. Out of the total non-beneficiaries, the highest number of respondents, i.e. 35 (38.5 per cent) have paid interest of less than ₹ 600 per annum and the lowest number of respondents, i.e. 27 (28.6 per cent) have paid interest of more than ₹ 800 per annum. It is concluded that majority of the beneficiaries have paid interest of more than ₹ 800 per annum when compared to the non-beneficiaries. The days of employment, the beneficiaries and non-beneficiaries get from cattle, pan shops and laundries are given hereunder.

Out of the total positively, responded beneficiaries, majority of the respondents, i.e. 55 (44 per cent) have got employment for more than 170 days and very few respondents, i.e. 26 (20.8 per cent) have got employment for less than 150 days on those works. Out of the total 125 positively, responded non-beneficiaries, the highest number of respondents, i.e. 51 (56 per cent) have got employment for between 150-170 days on those works and the lowest number of respondents, i.e. 19 (20.9 per cent) have got for more than 170 days on those works. It can be concluded that majority of the beneficiaries have got employment for more than 170 days on those works when compared to non-beneficiaries. The positively-responded beneficiaries and non-beneficiaries are getting the income as detailed below.

Out of the beneficiaries, majority of the respondents, i.e. 66 (52.8 per cent) have got income of between ₹ 25 to ₹ 30 and the lowest number of respondents, i.e. 20 (16 per cent) have got income of below ₹ 25. Out of the non-beneficiaries, the highest number of respondents, i.e. 36 (39.6 per cent) have got income of below ₹ 25 per day and the lowest number of respondents, i.e. 24 (26.4 per cent) have got above ₹ 30 per day. It can be concluded that majority of the beneficiaries have got income of ₹ 25 to ₹ 30 per day when compared to non-beneficiaries. From the above analysis, it is clearly observed that the majority of the beneficiaries are getting more benefits from the Self-Help Groups under the Watershed Development Programme when compared to non-beneficiaries.

Table 7 shows the statements of beneficiaries regarding their participation in watershed management and other activities of Watershed Development Programme. Out of 150 respondent beneficiaries, 48.67 per cent (73) have stated that they are participating in planning and management of watershed programme and 33.33 per cent (50) have given negative statement, whereas 18.0 per cent (27) haven't responded.

Table 7: Opinions of Beneficiaries on Watershed Development Programme

Sl. No.	Particulars	No. of Respondents			
		Yes	No	Not Respond	Total
1.	Participation in planning & management	73(48.67)	50(33.33)	27(18)	150(100)
2.	Voluntary organization participation in planning & management	18(12)	132(88)	–	150(100)
3.	Receive the training from watershed management	130(86.67)	10(6.67)	10(6.66)	150(100)
4.	Get any subsidy under programme	50(33.33)	100(66.67)	–	150(100)
5.	Increase of soil fertility	135(90)	5(3.33)	10(6.67)	150(100)
6.	Increase in the crop production	140(93.33)	10(6.67)	–	150(100)
7.	Increase in the ground water level	145(96.67)	5(3.33)	–	150(100)
8.	Groundwater level sustain	10(6.67)	135(90)	5(3,33)	150(100)
9.	Soil erosion controlled	139(92.69)	8(5.3)	3(2)	150(100)
10.	Decrease impact of drought conditions	145(96.7)	5(3.3)	–	150(100)
11.	Ponds getting recharge	68(45.3)	82(54.7)	–	150(100)
12.	Increase in the nutrition level of livestock	142(94.67)	8(5.33)	–	150(100)
13.	This programme any contribute for dairy development	122(81.33)	27(18)	–	150(100)
14.	Contribute for poultry development	1(0.67)	149(99.3)	–	150(100)
15.	Increase in economic conditions & living standards	138(92)	12(8)	–	150(100)

16.	NGOs working under this programme	50(33.33)	100(66.7)	–	150(100)
17.	Awareness about watersheds	140(93.33)	10(6.67)	–	150(100)
18.	SHGs and UGs working under this programme	145(96.67)	5(3.33)	–	150(100)
19.	Rainwater harvesting after prevailing this system	143(95.3)	7(4.7)	–	150(100)
20.	Corpus fund by the village watershed association	109(72.7)	41(27.3)	–	150(100)
21.	Participation in any activities under going in watershed	124(82.7)	26(17.3)	–	150(100)

Source: Computed by Collection of Primary Data.

Regarding the participation of voluntary organization in planning and management of watershed, majority of the respondents, i.e. 132 (88.0 per cent) has stated negatively and only 18 respondents (12.0 per cent) have given positive statement. Regarding training programmes, 86.67 per cent (130) of the respondents have stated that they receive training from watershed management and 6.67 per cent (10) haven't, whereas another 6.66 per cent (10) have given no response. Majority of the respondents, i.e. 66.67 per cent (100) are not getting subsidy under this programme and only the remaining 33.33 per cent (50) are getting subsidy facility. The respondents constituting 90.0 per cent (135) have opined that there is increase in soil fertility, only 3.33 per cent (5) have opined negatively whereas 6.67 per cent (10) of them haven't given any statement. The respondents accounting for 99.33 per cent (140) have stated that there is the crop production after the implementation of watershed programme, only 6.67 per cent (10) have stated negatively. Similarly, 145 respondents responded positively stating that there is increase in groundwater level and 5 (3.33 per cent) have stated against this.

Regarding groundwater level sustenance, 135 respondents (90.0 per cent) have given positive statement and 10 respondents (6.67 per cent) are against this, whereas only 5 respondents (3.33 per cent) have not given any response. Similarly, 139 respondents (92.69 per cent) have opined that the erosion of soil is controlled after the implementation of WDP and very negligible number, i.e. 8 respondents (5.3 per cent) are against this whereas 3 respondents (2.0 per cent) refused to answer.

According to the opinion of 96.7 per cent (145), there is decreasing impact of drought conditions after WDP implementation and only 5 respondents (3.3 per cent) are against this. As per the statement of 142 respondents (94.67 per cent), there is increase in the nutrition quantity to the livestock and 122 respondents (81.33 per cent) have stated that WDP has contributed more for dairy development. The respondents representing 92.0 per cent (138) are in favour of the opinion, that the WDP has improved the economic conditions and living standards of the members.

Regarding the participation of NGOs, 50 respondents (33.33 per cent) have stated that NGOs are working under the programme. 93.33 per cent (140) of the respondents are aware of the watershed. As per the statement of 145 respondents (96.67 per cent), SHGs and UGs are working under this WDP regarding the rainwater harvesting, 143 respondents (95.3 per cent) have stated that rainwater harvesting prevails, after the implementation of watershed development programme. Contribution of members through village watershed association in the form of corpus fund is made according to the statement of 109 (72.7 per cent) respondent beneficiaries. And 124 respondents (82.7 per cent) participate in other activities going on under watershed development programme.

As per the opinions and views presented in Table 7, majority of the respondents are participating in watershed management and getting benefited from it. It is also observed that most of the respondents have stated favourable and positive statements on watershed development programme, since their economic conditions and living standards are increased to satisfactory extent and so they are voluntarily contributing to the programme both financially and monetarily.

Conclusions

- Majority of the beneficiaries have got an employment opportunity of 240 days per annum, as against 180 days in the case of non-beneficiaries.
- Most of the beneficiary respondents are providing more working days to other workers for agriculture purpose, as against the non-beneficiaries.
- SHGs formed and established under WDP has provided more benefits and facilities to the members to improve their economic standards resulting in the improvement of their living standards. Besides, WDP motivated all the communities in villages regarding credit and thrift. The respondents have stated that SHGs under WDP have been helping them by facilitating them with required loan for dairy development and management and other tiny business as like establishment of pan shops, laundries, etc. They have also stated that after the implementation of WDP they have been getting employment (labour) for more days with good remuneration.
- Most of the respondents, i.e. 90.67 per cent (136/150) offer monitory contribution and very few, i.e. 9.33 per cent (14) only contribute voluntary labour to the watershed projects.
- As per the opinions acquired from survey, it may be concluded that almost all of the respondents are provided with all the required facilities and benefits through WDP. And thus all of them have expressed their satisfaction and have been contributing to the project whatever needed within their reach.

16

A Study on Micro-Credit through Self-Help Groups and Its Impact on Rural Development

V. Venkateswarlu

ABSTRACT

Women's empowerment can be viewed as a continuum of several interested and mutually reinforcing components. Awareness building about women's situation, discrimination, and right and opportunities as a step towards gender equality, collective awareness building, provides a sense of group identity and the power of working as a group. Capacity building and skills development, especially the ability to plan, make decisions, organize, manage and carryout activities, need to deal with people and institutions in the world around them. Participation and greater control and decision-making power in the home, community and society. Action to bring about greater equality between men and women. In this broad conceptual view of the above discussed approaches, there are certain prime and prominent aspects on which women need to be empowered, among which social empowerment, economic empowerment, political and psychological empowerment are considered as key aspects. Main objective of this paper is to study the socio-economic conditions of sample of 100 households of the SHG members and assess the impact of micro-finance programmes on income generation of the sample of 100 households in rural Krishna District of Andhra Pradesh. The main findings are: 34 per cent of households belong to backward classes while the other castes account for 28 per cent. Forty-seven per cent are in the income range of ₹ 10,000-20,000 per annum. Thirty-three per cent are below 14 years of age while 52.46 per cent are in the age of active economic participation, i.e. between 14-45 years. Major proportion of 22 per cent of sample households take up milk vending activity from the micro-credit. The average per household expenditure of ₹ 31,160.97 is worked out for the 47 sample households falling in the income group of ₹ 10,000-20,000. The study results indicate that 61.11 per cent of the members of Self-Help Groups who were below the poverty line before taking up micro-enterprises are able to cross the poverty line because of the micro-credit facility extended through SHGs. It has been observed that the Self-Help Groups are able to generate savings and they are able recycle the funds due to prompt repayment by members.

Introduction

'Empowerment' is a process and is not something that can be given to people. The process of empowerment is both individual and collective, since it is through involvement in group that people most often begin to develop their awareness and the ability to organize to take action and bring about change. So, women's empowerment can be viewed as a continuum of several interested and mutually reinforcing components.

- Awareness building about women's situation, discrimination, and right and opportunities as a step towards gender equality, collective awareness building provides a sense of group identity and the power of working as a group.
- Capacity building and skills development, especially the ability to plan, make decisions, organize, manage and carryout activities, to deal with people and institutions in the world around them.

- Participation and greater control and decision-making power in the home, community and society.
- Action to bring about greater equality between men and women.

In short, 'empowerment' is a process of awareness and capacity building leading to greater participation to great decision-making power and control, and to transformative power.

Types of Empowerment

In this broad conceptual view of the above discussed approaches, there are certain prime and prominent aspects on which women need to be empowered, among which social empowerment; economic empowerment, political empowerment and psychological empowerment are considered key aspects. An effort is made hereunder to define these four aspects precisely.

1. **Social Empowerment:** Achievement of social empowerment by women demands changes in their social mobility and interaction. Women who live in seclusion within the four walls of their homes, confining themselves to the domestic labour and subordinating themselves to the rights and decisions of their fathers/husbands or wards should come out getting rid of those conventional and patriarchal shackles and more out to the world outside to carryout the activities independently without anyone's assistance. They should have personal interaction with members of their widely spread society to take up and participate in the developmental activities not only for their own sake but also for the society.

2. **Economic Empowerment:** Economic empowerment, which is the hub for all dimensional empowerment, demands changes in two major aspects. The first and foremost demanding change is change in the pattern of women's labour and the other prominent change is the change in access of women to and their control over material resources which makes them economically viable.

3. **Political Empowerment:** Political empowerment is a prospective aspect resulting from the achievement of social

empowerment, which demands women's access to participation of women in decision-making at local, mandal, district, state and national level political and administrative organs. Women were deprived of their rights, due to gender discriminations, disparities and inequalities were excluded from politics and administration. Hence, they should have to make efforts to gain access to political and administrative powers where policymaking and implementation are resoled.

4. **Psychological Empowerment:** Psychological empowerment is to equip oneself with broad knowledge of various socio-economic political and cultural issue and strengthen one's intellectual faculty. Psychological empowerment is defined as a cognitive state characterized by a sense of perceived control, perceptions of competence, and internalization of the goals and objectives of the society to which the woman belongs.

Origin of Self-Help Group Movement

The origin of SHG is from the brain child of Gramin Bank of Bangladesh which was founded by the economist, Prof. Mohammad Yunus of Chittagong University in the year 1975. This was exclusively established for the poor.

Self-Help Group is a small economically homogeneous and affinity group of rural poor which is voluntarily ready to contribute to a common fund to be lent to its members as per group decision, which works for group's solidarity, self-group, awareness, social and economic empowerment in the way of democratic functioning. The Self-Help Group movement became a silent revolution within a short span in the rural credit delivery system in many parts of the world. It has been documented that nearly 59 developing countries including India, have taken up this on a large scale. In 1997, World Micro-Credit Summit at Washington converged the developed and the developing countries to tackle the serious problem of poverty by using micro-credit as tool to empower the poorest sections. A global movement has been launched to reach 100 million of the world's poorest families by the year 2005.

Concept of Self-Help Groups and Rural Development

The concept of SHG serves the principle "by the women (poor), of the women and for the women". Self-Help supplemented with mutual help can be a powerful vehicle for poor people's efforts in socio-economic upward migration. Poor people need not only credit support but also savings and services. The Self-Help Groups are small informal associations formed with the objective of enabling members to reap economic benefits out of mutual help, solidarity and group responsibility. These groups are composed of members, who are poor, having low savings capacity or no savings capacity and generally depending on moneylenders or private sources for meeting their consumption and emergent needs.

In a democratic society, it is the state that has the ultimate responsibility for ushering development to its citizens. In India, through the progressive interpretation of the constitution and its laws and policies, the scope of development has been significantly broadened to include not just economic progress for citizens, but also promotion of social justice, gender equity, inclusion, citizen's awareness, empowerment and improved quality of life. To achieve this holistic vision of development, the state requires the constructive and collaborative engagement of the civil society in its various developmental activities and programmes. The objective of development is to enhance the quality of the living condition of people, more particularly the rural people and to mobilize the resources available at local level and to tackle the chief evils of the modern society such as unemployment, malnutrition, diseases, illiteracy and inequality so that social justice can be promoted. Therefore, the basic object of all developmental activities is to provide minimum needs to the marginalized sections of the society like food, shelter, health.

Review of Literature

Vijay Mahajan (2005) studied the impact of micro-credit on poverty reduction and clearly explained the concept of micro-finance and certain limitations of micro-finance: Five fatal assumptions, risks of micro-credit by itself is enough strategy, micro-credit and economic growth and from micro-credit to livelihood finance.

Naila Kabeer (2005) explored in his study about the micro-finance strategies for poverty reduction: Markets and movements, economic impact of micro-finance, social impact of micro-finance, outreach of micro-finance and its wider social impact. He also analyzed the issues of poverty reduction, social change, poverty, vulnerability and social exclusion, micro-finance outreach, gender and power within households and alternative approaches to micro-finance.

M.S. Srirams (2005) reviewed the performance of formal institutional channels of micro-finance and discussed the emergence of new focus of collaboration in the delivery of micro-finance services.

Karmakar (2002) in his study on "Rural Credit and Self-Help Groups" explained the existing rural credit system in India. He analyzed its strengths and weaknesses and prescribed various strategies and innovations, which will enable the existing credit delivery system to emerge stronger and more viable. He reviewed the problems and prospects of rural credit in the context of its ascribed role in rural development and traced out the evolution and growth of the rural credit delivery system.

Objectives of the Study

The following objectives are formulated for the present study:

- To study the socio-economic conditions of sample households of the SHG members in rural Krishna district of Andhra Pradesh.
- To assess the impact of micro-finance programmes on income generation of the sample households.

Methodology

1. **Study Area:** Krishnaveni Gramina Bank spread in rural Krishna district has been identified and sample of SHGs under the bank has been selected for the study.

2. **Selection of Sampling:** The sample households for the study have been selected using random sampling procedure.

The study has been confined to the Self-Help Groups (SHGs) financed by the Krishnaveni Gramina Bank, which is a branch of Sri Venkateswara Gramina Bank, Krishna district. All the SHGs financed by the above branch have been considered for the selection of sample SHGs. There are 119 SHGs functioning under the jurisdiction of the above branch. Out of the 119 SHGs, 25 SHGs have been selected using simple random sampling method. Among the 25 SHGs have been selected as the first stage units, 100 members have been selected representing not less than two members from each SHG using random sampling procedure. Therefore, the study finally covered 100 sample households in Penamaluru, Kankipadu, Gannavaram and Agiripalle mandals. The main focus of this study is to assess the impact of the micro-credit extended through SHGs on the generation of income of the members and the extent the micro-credit programmes are viable to enable the poor to cross the poverty levels. Against this backdrop, thrust is laid on the sample households than SHGs. The net income generated from the micro-enterprise and also other sources of the sample households have been worked out to find the proportion of net income earned from micro-enterprise in the total income of the households.

3. Data Collection Methods: Primary data as well as secondary data has been collected for the present study. The secondary data has been collected from Census Reports, Economic and Statistics, Government of A.P., and *Handbook of Statistics*, Krishna district. The primary data on various aspects of the sample household was collected through personal interviews with the sample respondents with the support of a interview schedule specially designed keeping in view the objectives of the study. Pilot study was conducted so as to appraise the qualitative and quantitative aspects of the data. Sufficient crosschecks have been made to ensure reliability and accuracy information.

Statistical Techniques: Simple statistical techniques like percentages, frequencies are employed in this study to understand the association between various variables.

Table 1: Caste-wise Distribution of the Sample Households

Sl. No.	Caste	No. of Households	Percentage to Total
1.	Scheduled Castes	26	26
2.	Scheduled Tribes	12	12
3.	Backward Classes	34	34
4.	Other Castes	28	28
	Total	100	100

Table 1 shows that out of the 100 sample households covered by the study, 26 per cent belongs to scheduled castes and 12 per cent belongs to scheduled tribes. The percentage of households belonging to backward classes are 34 per cent while the other castes account for 28 per cent of the sample households. This shows that there is good participation of scheduled castes and tribes and backward communities in the micro-finance programmes.

Table 2: Distribution of Sample Households by Income

Sl. No.	Annual Income (Rs)	No. of Households	Percentage to Total
1.	0-10,000	12	12
2.	10,000-20,000	47	47
3.	20,000-30,000	14	14
4.	30,000-40,000	12	12
5.	Above 40,000	15	15
	Total	100	100

From Table 2, it can be observed that 12 per cent of the sample households have less than ₹ 10,000 income per annum while the major proportion of sample households, i.e. 47 per cent of the sample households are in the income range of ₹ 10,000-20,000 per annum. The sample households which fall in the income range of ₹ 20,000-30,000 per annum are 14 while 12 households have reported that they earn income in the ranges of ₹ 30,000-40,000 per year. The households which fall in the top income bracket of above ₹ 40,000 per annum are 15. The above trend shows that most of the households have a very poor economic background justifying the need for micro-credit for their economic improvement.

Table 3: Age and Sex Composition of the Population in the Sample Households

Sl. No.	Age Group (years)	Male		Female		Total	
		No. of Persons	Percentage	No. of Persons	Percentage	No. of Persons	Percentage
1.	0-14	76	36.36	55	29.44	134	33.00
2.	14-30	63	30.14	66	30.50	129	31.77
3.	30-45	39	18.66	45	22.85	84	20.69
4.	45-60	19	9.9	18	9.13	37	9.12
5.	Above 60	12	5.75	10	5.08	22	5.42
Total		209	100	197	100	406	100

Source: Primary Data

The data in Table 3 shows that there are 406 persons live in the sample households of which 209 are males and 197 are females. Out of the total population, 33 per cent are below 14 years of age while 52.46 per cent are in the age of active economic participation, i.e. between 14-45 years. The population in the age group of 45-60 years accounts for 9.12 per cent while 5.42 per cent of the persons are above 60 years of age.

Table 4: Micro-Enterprises Organized by the Sample Households

Sl. No.	Name of the Micro Enterprise	No. of Households	Percentage to Total
1.	Milk vending	22	22
2.	Tiffin centers	11	11
3.	Petty shop	8	8
4.	Leaf making	9	9
5.	Vegetable vending	8	8
6.	Laundry service	6	6
7.	Tailoring	8	8
8.	Wage labour	10	10
9.	Cultivation	12	12
10.	Other activities	6	6
	Total	100	100

Source: Primary Data

From Table 4, it is observed that out of 100 sample households covered by the study, major proportion of 22 per cent of sample households take up milk vending activity from the micro-credit taken from the SHG while 12 sample households took loan for meeting the expenses of cultivation.

Table 5: Expenditure Pattern of the Sample Households by Income Levels

Sl. No.	Income Category	No. of Households	Total Expenditure	Average Expenditure per Household
1.	Upto 10,000	12	1,42,324.88	11,860.41
2.	10,000 – 20,000	47	14,64,565.77	31,160.97
3.	20,000 – 30,000	14	4,55,498.10	32,535.58
4.	30,000 – 40,000	12	4,76,412.82	39,701.07
5.	Above 40,000	15	6,06,918.90	40,461.26

Source: Primary Data

Table 5 shows that out of the 100 sample households, 12 households have income of less than ₹ 10,000. But the average expenditure per household works out to ₹ 11,860.41. The average per household expenditure of ₹ 31,160.97 is worked out for the 47 sample households falling in the income group of ₹ 10,000-20,000. In this group, the average expenditure is significantly higher than the average income. In the income category of ₹ 20,000-30,000, there are 14 households whose average expenditure per household is worked out to ₹ 32,535.58. The average expenditure of ₹ 39,701.07 and ₹ 40,461.26 per household is worked out for the sample households that fall in the income group of ₹ 30,000-40,000 and above ₹ 40,000, respectively.

Conclusions and Suggestions

The result of the study indicates that 61.11 per cent of the members of SHGs who were below the poverty line before taking up micro-enterprises are able to cross the poverty line because of the micro-credit facility extended through SHGs. It has been observed that the SHGs are able to generate savings and they are able recycle the funds due to prompt repayment by members. The default rate in repayment has been very low. Among the different activities, some activities like tiffin centers, petty shops, laundry shops and tailoring units are high income fetching and some activities fetch low incomes. But, on the whole, it is to conclude that SHGs and micro-credit through SHGs have positive impact on poverty reduction. Considering the finding of the study, the following suggestions are prescribed:

- Literacy and numeric training is needed for the poor women to benefit from the micro-credit schemes.
- Training in legal literacy, rights and gender awareness are important complements to micro-credit for the empowerment of women. The members should be given necessary training and guidance for the successful operation of the group.
- The members of the SHG should be more active, enthusiastic and dynamic to mobilize their savings by group actions. In this process, NGOs should act as a facilitator and motivator.
- The office bearers managing the group should be given nominal financial benefits, which will enable them to be more involved in the activities of the group.
- The bank should advance adequate credit to the SHG according to their needs.
- Uniformity should be maintained in formation and extension of financial assistance to them by banks in all blocks.
- The procedure of the banks in sanctioning credit to SHG should be simple and quick.
- Marketing facilities for the sale of products of SHG may be created.
- Periodical exhibition at block level may be organized where the products of SHG can be displayed.
- Meetings and seminars may be organized where the members will get a chance to exchange their views and be able to develop their group strength by interactions.
- Active intervention by district administration, professional bodies and voluntary organizations is precondition for the successful conception of micro-

enterprises in terms of skill training, designing products, providing new technology and access to market.

REFERENCES

Ahluwalia, M.S. (1976). Inequality, Poverty and Development, *Journal of Development Economics*.

Chavan, Pavan and Rama Kumar, R. (2002). "Micro Credit & Rural Poverty". *Economic & Political Weekly*, Vol. XXXVII No. 10, March 9.

Indira Misra (2003). "Micro-credit for Macro Impact on Poverty", National Publishing House, New Delhi.

Karmakar, K.G. (2002). "Rural Credit and Self-Help Groups", Sage Publications India Pvt. Ltd.

Kunwar, Nagesh (2000). "Economic Reforms and their Macro-Economic Impact". *Economist and Political Weekly*, No. 10, March 4-10.

Maria, John. S., Jayabalan, R. and Krishna Murthy, S. (2004). "Rural Entrepreneurship", Discovery Publishing House, New Delhi.

Prasad, B.K. (2004). "NGOs & Development", Institute of Sustainable Development, Lucknow & Anmol Publications Private Limited, New Delhi.

Radhakrishna et al. (1998). *Levels of Living in State Setting*, Concept Publishing Co., New Delhi.

Sen, A. (1998b). "Theory and Practice of Development", In *India's Economic Reforms and Development: Essays for Manmohan Singh* (eds.) I.J. Ahluwalia and I.M.D. Little, Oxford: OUP.

UNDP, Human Development Report 1993 and EPW Research Foundation, "Three years of Economic Reforms in India, A Critical Assessment" (April 1994).

17

Mahatma Gandhi National Rural Employment Guarantee Programme in Andhra Pradesh: Its Social Audits

K. Madhu Babu and *P. Srinivasulu*

ABSTRACT

The rural employment guarantee scheme gives an opportunity for the country's poor to seek livelihood with dignity. It has the capacity to address debilitating hunger and poverty in the country. Poverty in India is the result of multiplicity of factors such as population explosion, unemployment, underemployment, low level of wages, low asset base, low educational standards, inequalities in income, underdevelopment, agrarian structure, low productivity of labour, unsatisfactory growth, high incidence of rural indebtedness, social factors, religious factors and political factors. Poverty alleviation is one of the prime objectives of planned economic development in India. Even after more than 66 years of Independence India still has the world's largest number of poor people in a single country. Of its nearly 1 billion inhabitants, an estimated 260.3 million are below the poverty line, of which 193.2 million are in rural areas and 67.1 million are in urban areas. More than 75 per cent of poor people reside in village. The government has initiated, and refined many programmes since independence to mitigate rural poor and unemployment. The central thrust of the "Eleventh

Five-year Plan is faster and more inclusive growth" and the plan strategy is "accelerated growth" combined with a steady expansion in schemes aimed at supporting incomes and welfare of the poorer sections, e.g. National Rural Employment Guarantee Scheme.

The scheme showed a better performance during 2010-11 than 2011-12 and 2009-10. A gradual improvement is observed in case of beneficiaries of land reform/IAY and disabled beneficiary households during the three years. Increase in the number of works completed from 2009-10 to 2011-12 is observed in case of water conservation and water harvesting and micro irrigation works while a decrease is noticed in case of land development works and provision of irrigation facilities. Viewing the performance of all ongoing projects from 2009-10 to 2011-12, a decrease in number is observed in almost all activities except in the case of rural connectivity activities. It is observed that about 33.25 per cent of increased amount was spent on complete projects during 2010-11 compared to the previous year. Between 2010-11 and 2011-12 the increase in the amount spent is reported around 72 per cent. The National Rural Employment Guarantee Scheme (NREGS) is one of the major landmarks in the process of formulation adopting the rights-based approach. A large number of workers in India are force to remain jobless both in rural and urban areas, Andhra Pradesh is not except from this situation. The experience of the recent economic reforms showed that economic growth above cannot guarantee creation of employment or livelihoods. In Andhra Pradesh, women have been the major beneficiaries of this scheme since its inception as scheme guarantees work for all those who demand it. This is a good single for economic prosperity of the state. Various studies have revealed that several lacunas in the NREGS. Particularly, misappropriation of funds, incomplete works and lack of follow up, leakages, poor quality of physical assets created under this scheme and poor wages are the important lacunas in the working and implementing process of the NREGS. Hence, it can be concluded that the Andhra Pradesh State Government should think seriously about these lacunas so that the NREGS can be implemented more effectively.

Introduction

The rural employment guarantee scheme gives an opportunity for the country's poor to seek livelihood with dignity. It has the capacity to address debilitating hunger and poverty in the country. Poverty in India is the result of multiplicity of factors such as population explosion, unemployment, under-employment, low level of wages, low asset base, low educational standards, inequalities in income, underdevelopment, agrarian structure, low productivity of labour, unsatisfactory growth, high incidence of rural indebtedness, social factors, religious factors and political factors. Poverty alleviation is one of the prime objectives of planned economic development in India. Even after more than 66 years of Independence India still has the world's largest number of poor people in a single country. Of its nearly 1 billion inhabitants, an estimated 260.3 million are below the poverty line, of which 193.2 million are in rural areas and 67.1 million are in urban areas. More than 75 per cent of poor people reside in village. The government has initiated, and refined many programmes since independence to mitigate rural poor and unemployment. These include, among others, the National Rural Employment Programme and the Rural Landless Employment Guarantee Programme. The National Rural Employment Programme evolved in Five-year Plan 1980 from the earlier food for work programme to use unemployed and under-employed workers to build productive community assets. The central thrust of the "Eleventh Five-year Plan is faster and more inclusive growth" and the plan strategy is "accelerated growth" combined with a steady expansion in schemes aimed at supporting incomes and welfare of the poorer sections, e.g. National Rural Employment Guarantee Scheme. In this background, the following are the main objectives of the present study.

Objectives of the Study

1. To examine the performance of National Rural Employment Guarantee Scheme in Andhra Pradesh.
2. To examine the social audit of MGNREGA in Andhra Pradesh.
3. To suggest suitable measures for better implementation of the programme for all round development of the state.

Data and Methodology

The study is based on secondary data, yet the main data source for the study website and NSS data collected during different rounds of NSSO on employment and unemployment for the period from 1973-74 to 1999-2001 and the census data for 2001. Comparable NSS quinquennial survey data on employment and unemployment are also available for various rounds. Statistical abstracts published by CSO and Economic Survey of India published by Government of India, CMIE reports and Andhra Pradesh at a glance 2012 are also utilized. The state was chosen as the unit of analysis. Taking into account the availability of data, the state seemed to be a more convenient unit of analysis. Simple statistical tools like percentages and growth rate techniques are used.

Mahatma Gandhi National Rural Employment Guarantee Scheme in Andhra Pradesh, 2012

Total Numer of Districts Underemployment Guarantee Scheme	22
Total Number of Mandals	1,098
Total Number of Gram Panchayats	21,858
Total Number of Habitations	68,983
Total Number of Job Cards Issued	1,19,34,068
Total Number of Adult Members Enrolled in Job Cards Issued	2,82,89,398

Table 1: Year-wise Progress

	2007-08	2008-09	2009-10	2010-11	2011-12
Total expenditure (₹ in crores)	587.4	2009.6	2507.2	4208.4	2952.2
Households employment provided (in lakhs)	21.7	46.8	57.1	61.6	56.3
Individuals employment provided (in lakhs)	31.7	74	99.88	116.1	104.1
Total number of person days generated (in crores)	6.6	20.0	22.7	40.1	24.0
Average wage rate per day per person (Rs.)	82.47	83.85	83.61	90.35	98.82
Average number of days employment provided per household	30.13	42.68	39.86	65.1	42.6
Total number of households completed 100 days of wage employment	67,242	4,10,517	4,81,004	13,93,734	4,69,482

Source: Commissioner, Rural Development, Government of Andhra Pradesh, Hyderabad

It is observed that there is a continuous progress from 2007-08 to 2010-11 and during 2011-12 there found a decline in the progress.

The Functioning of MGNREGA (in Three Phases)

The performance of MGNREGA among three phases is presented in Table 2 for the years 2009-10, 2010-11 and 2011-12. From the table, it can be observed that the percentages of households provided employment among the total number of households issued job cards are reported to be 50.23 in 2009-10, 52.45 in 2010-11 and 51.56 during 2011-12. Across the three phases, the percentages varied from 40.09 in third phase to 52.18 in second phase during 2009-10, 47.77 in second phase to 55.09 in first phase during 2010-11 and 49.06 in third phase to 52.92 in first phase during 2011-12. Glancing over three years of performance, higher percentage of households were provided employment during 2010-11 in case of districts of first phase with regard to second phase of districts higher percentage of households got employment during 2009-10. Similar percentage of households got employment, in case of third phase of districts during 2010-11 and 2011-12.

Table 2: Performance of MGNREGA—Phase-wise 2009-10, 2010-11 and 2011-12

Phase (Districts)	Cumulative No. of Households Issued Job Cards	Cumulative No. of Households Provided Employment*	Cumulative Person Days Generated	Cumulative No. of Households 100 days of Employment**	Expenditure (₹ In lakhs)	
					Completed (Works)	Ongoing (Works)
2011-12						
I	7167639	3793312	2117.24	593040	549664	203228
II	3322241	1651849	807.89	212938	234959	54318
III	1461031	716726	284.89	65742	73886	25470
Total	11950911	6161887	3210.02	871720	858509	283009
2010-11						
I	7120994	3922923	2598.2	956872	124688.28	119978.31
II	324847	1551932	987.9	333320	40354.04	34246.17
III	1372805	683638	329.1	105345	18676.24	13078.43
Total	11742646	6158493	3915.2	1395537	183718.56	167299.91
2009-10						
I	6924720	3543250	1879.17	349109	88823.47	80858.16
II	3168665	1653456	756.32	128349	35987.03	33358.24
III	1254430	502851	99.96	5600	5055.56	5118.90
Total	11347815	5699557	2735.45	483058	129866.06	119326.30

Source: Website – NREGS – AP

* Figures in parenthesis are the percentages to the total number of Households issued job cards.

** Figures in parenthesis are the percentages to total number of Households provided employment.

The scheme has succeeded in providing 100 days of employment to more number of households during 2010-11 than in the years 2009-10 and 2011-12. The expenditure on completed works are reported to be ₹ 129866.06 lakhs during 2009-10, ₹ 183718.56 lakhs in 2010-11 and ₹ 858509 lakhs during 2011-12. The expenditure on ongoing works is reported to be higher during 2011-12 than 2009-10 and 2010-11.

Performance of NREGS in Andhra Pradesh

The scheme has statutory support in the Andhra Pradesh Employment Guarantee Act, 2005, which was operated from February 2006. The works, which are undertaken under the scheme, are social forestry, canal works, irrigation works, percolation and storage tanks and underground bandharas. Another important feature of the scheme is that only productive works are permitted. Under this scheme highest priority is given to irrigation works, soil conservation, land development, rural rods and flood protection. Under the scheme the wages are fixed on a piece rate basis. The beneficiaries are provided drinking water, shelter, First Aid Box. The scheme is implemented through the State Government departments like agriculture, public works irrigation, forest, Zilla Parishads and Panchayati Raj. The performance of Employment Guarantee Scheme in Andhra Pradesh is presented in Table 3.

Table 3: NREGS Progress During the Year 2011-12 in Andhra Pradesh

Sl. No.	Item	2011-12 (upto October)
1.	Employment Provided households (lakhs)	53.7387
2.	Person-days (in lakhs) total	1838.04
3.	Expenditure (₹ in crores)	2062.46
4.	SCs as % of total beneficiaries	486.57 (26.47%)
5.	STs as % of total beneficiaries	239.36 (13.02%)
6.	Women as % of total beneficiaries	1067.68 (58.09%)
7.	Others	1112.11 (60.51%)
8.	Total Works taken up	578157

9.	Works completed	161112
10.	Works-in-progress	417045
11.	Labourwise pay order (No. of persons)	54631555 (3.8%)

Source: www.http://nrega.ap.gov.in

As can be seen from the above table, in the year 2011-12 the total employment generated under NREGS was 1838.04 lakh person-days. In the total employment the SC's employment was 486.57 lakh person-days which is 26.47 per cent and ST's employment was 239.36 lakhs person-days with 13.02 per cent. Another important interesting observation is the total employment the women employment was 1067.68 lakh person-days, i.e. 58.09 per cent. It means that female participation (women employment ratio) in the NREGS has above fifty per cent. This gainful employment has helped in raising the income and levels of living of the weaker sections in the state, particularly in the SCs and STs and women. It was observed that the total number of works completed were 161112. The labour-wise pay order in the state was 54631555 persons which is 3.8 per cent. Under the scheme upto October 2012, of the ₹ 2062.46 crore spent and of about 578157 works taken up 16112 were completed.

Performance of MGNREGA—Some Quantitative Indicators

Social Audit

Social audit is to make the planning implementation and evaluation of Employment Guarantee Scheme more participatory, transparent and accountable. Social audit is not retrospection but an ongoing process of participation to ensure that legal guarantees and entitlements flow to the workers in a legitimate way. Social audit will be done in three stages—pre, during and post-implementation. Social audit shall be integrated into the critical activities of Employment Guarantee Scheme.

Andhra Pradesh is the only state which established a full-fledged social audit at the state level with exclusive staff. The unit works independently and reports to the government. So far social audit has been conduced in 1088 mandals in 22 districts in the first round; 655 mandals covered in second round and 156 mandals in third round. This is an effective tool to check corruption and to enhance the accountability to people. So far more than 3991 functionaries have been either terminated from their services or disciplinary actions have been initiated. FIR was booked against 639 functionaries and departmental enquiry initiated against 1433 functionaries. The details of execution of social audit in Andhra Pradesh is furnished in Table 4.

Table 4: Execution of Social Audit

Sl. No.	Cadre	Dismissed	Suspended	FIR	Departmental Enquiry
1.	Post MPDOs	0	28	5	24
2.	Additional Post	29	15	7	3
3.	TAs	188	35	46	3
4.	Computer Operators	26	7	5	1
5.	FAs	2251	73	188	24
6.	Panchayat Secretary	0	2	11	6
7.	AEs	1	8	4	34
8.	WIS	11	1	3	91
9.	BPMs	3	2	61	1053
10.	Group Leaders	1326	36	35	28
11.	Others	156	1	274	166
	Total	3991	208	639	1433

Source: Office of the Commissioner, Rural Development, Hyderabad.

The district-wise performance of social auditory and inspection of MGNREGA works during three years, i.e. 2011-12, 2010-11, and 2009-10, is presented in Table 5.

Verification of Muster Rolls

The social audit starts with verifying the muster rolls used in each district. Of the total number of muster rolls (56.14 lakh) used, 91.71 per cent of the muster rolls are verified during 2011-12 in the state. Observing across the districts, eight districts, viz. Chittoor, Mahboobnagar, Medak, Nalgonda, Nizamabad, Rangareddy, Vizianagaram and Srikakulam have reported around 92 per cent of verified muster rolls. The percentage of verification of muster rolls ranged from 90.25 in Prakasam district to 92.80 in Mahboobnagar district. During 2010-11, a total number of 69.98 lakh muster rolls were used in the state, of which 91.71 per cent of muster rolls were verified. Glancing across the districts similar performance is observed during 2009-10 and 2010-11. Of the total number of 23.75 lakh muster rolls used in 2008-09 in the states of 88.16 per cent of them were verified. The percentage of muster rolls verified range between 70.17 in Kurnool and 92.95 in Vizianagaram across the districts.

Table 5: Social Auditing and Inspection of NREGA Work (2011-12)

(upto March)

Sl. No.	Name of the District	Must Roll Verified	Social Audit	Inspections Conducted		Gram Sabhas held		Complaints
		% of verified in No. of Muster rolls used	% of No. of GPs where social held in total Gram Panchayat	% of works inspected at district level in total works taken up	% of works inspected at block level in total works taken up	% of Gram Sabhas held in Total Panchayats	% of VMC meetings held in Gram Panchayats	% of Complaints Disposed in Complaints received
1.	Adilabad	91.90	99.77	9.15	92.45	78.06	1.26	99.73
2.	Ananthapur	91.35	96.92	9.25	91.10	84.39	0.80	100.00
3.	Chittoor	92.30	81.30	9.10	92.00	90.80	0.87	95.48
4.	Kadapa	90.85	98.78	9.30	91.00	98.41	1.22	99.70
5.	Karimnagar	91.30	85.75	9.28	91.60	91.95	1.09	99.17
6.	Khammam	90.50	90.69	9.18	92.00	94.95	1.42	98.34
7.	Mahboobnagar	92.80	85.41	9.20	92.00	95.26	1.41	100.00
8.	Medak	92.60	96.88	9.20	91.40	93.19	1.42	98.77
9.	Nalgonda	92.00	81.32	9.20	91.60	87.61	1.02	99.44
10.	Nizamabad	92.00	91.23	9.23	91.50	96.38	1.39	97.68
11.	Rangareddy	92.35	64.77	9.19	91.30	62.93	1.56	100.00

12.	Vizianagaram	92.55	88.74	9.14	91.50	88.42	0.96	91.13
13.	Warangal	91.85	93.80	9.21	93.00	96.85	0.79	99.39
14.	East Godavari	91.50	81.42	9.19	92.30	94.47	0.99	97.39
15.	Guntur	90.50	71.78	9.07	93.00	96.39	0.78	97.22
16.	Kurnool	91.50	88.52	8.90	91.00	92.75	1.34	99.63
17.	Nellore	91.35	72.56	9.20	91.50	95.11	1.14	98.87
18.	Prakasam	90.25	81.30	9.00	90.60	92.33	1.05	96.73
19.	Srikakulam	92.65	89.31	9.14	90.70	79.35	0.91	93.31
20.	Krishna	90.55	85.82	9.10	93.00	99.90	1.23	100.00
21.	Visakhapatnam	91.50	90.06	9.20	91.00	94.61	1.06	95.85
22.	West Godavari	91.35	89.30	8.90	91.30	99.32	1.01	98.89
	Total	91.71	86.47	9.15	91.65	91.28	1.11	98.17

Source: www.http//nrega.ap.gov.in

Table 6: Social Auditing and Inspection of NREGA Work (2010-11)

(upto March)

Sl. No.	Name of the District	Must Roll Verified	Social Audit	Inspections Conducted		Gram Sabhas held		Complaints
		% of verified in No. of Muster rolls used	% of No. of GPs where social held in total Gram Panchayat	% of works inspected at district level in total works taken up	% of works inspected at block level in total works taken up	% of Gram Sabhas held in Total Panchayats	% of VMC meetings held in Gram Panchayats	% of Complaints Disposed in Complaints received
1.	Adilabad	91.90	100.00	9.25	91.45	99.34	13.64	84.62
2.	Ananthapur	91.35	100.00	9.25	91.10	98.72	10.41	87.50
3.	Chittoor	92.30	100.00	9.00	92.00	98.08	9.79	84.62
4.	Kadapa	90.85	100.00	9.30	90.91	97.17	12.96	90.00
5.	Karimnagar	91.30	100.00	9.38	91.60	98.10	7.86	83.33
6.	Khammam	90.50	100.00	9.18	92.00	99.62	10.34	90.91
7.	Mahboobnagar	92.80	100.00	9.18	90.15	99.34	7.42	92.31
8.	Medak	92.60	100.00	9.20	91.40	95.58	8.00	100.00
9.	Nalgonda	92.00	100.00	9.20	91.60	93.07	10.39	90.91
10.	Nizamabad	92.00	100.00	9.23	91.18	98.75	14.56	100.00
11.	Rangareddy	92.35	100.00	9.19	90.85	99.44	13.43	90.91
12.	Vizianagaram	92.55	100.00	9.14	91.52	99.27	12.40	93.33
13.	Warangal	91.85	100.00	9.19	91.60	98.53	10.39	91.67
14.	East Godavari	91.50	90.61	9.19	91.30	99.70	9.39	90.00
15.	Guntur	90.50	59.59	9.07	91.70	98.64	10.56	100.00
16.	Kurnool	91.50	97.67	8.90	90.81	99.33	10.42	100.00
17.	Nellore	91.35	91.99	9.20	91.32	99.48	10.19	90.00

18.	Prakasam	90.25	77.86	9.00	90.60	98.67	9.06	90.00
19.	Srikakulam	92.65	93.75	9.14	90.30	98.37	9.24	88.89
20.	Krishna	90.55	67.82	9.10	90.51	98.88	10.93	88.89
21.	Visakhapatnam	91.50	73.22	9.20	89.61	99.16	11.30	100.00
22.	West Godavari	91.35	82.79	8.90	91.30	99.55	12.85	100.00
	Total	91.71	92.65	9.15	91.25	98.41	10.47	91.70

Source: www.http//nrega.ap.gov.in

Table 7: Social Auditing and Inspection of NREGA Work (2009-10)

(upto March)

S. No.	Name of the District	Must Roll Verified	Social Audit	Inspections Conducted		Gram Sabhas held		Complaints
		% of verified in No. of Muster rolls used	% of No. of GPs where social held in total Gram Panchayat	% of works inspected at district level in total works taken up	% of works inspected at block level in total works taken up	% of Gram Sabhas held in Total Panchayats	% of VMC meetings held in Gram Panchayats	% of Complaints Disposed in Complaints received
1.	Adilabad	92.40	100.00	9.20	90.45	100.00	90.83	98.21
2.	Ananthapur	90.35	100.00	9.18	90.10	99.21	94.60	91.11
3.	Chittoor	91.55	91.41	8.90	89.45	99.43	86.87	97.92
4.	Kadapa	90.35	98.59	9.30	90.91	97.53	86.57	95.56
5.	Karimnagar	92.35	100.00	9.16	92.60	95.78	86.19	93.48
6.	Khammam	89.85	100.00	9.25	92.00	100.00	91.17	93.75
7.	Mahboobnagar	92.35	100.00	9.18	90.15	100.00	78.99	98.53
8.	Medak	76.40	100.00	9.30	91.00	93.89	76.95	98.39
9.	Nalgonda	90.95	100.00	9.00	90.60	91.39	77.96	96.36
10.	Nizamabad	77.35	100.00	9.23	90.18	100.00	84.88	96.92
11.	Rangareddy	92.35	98.74	9.19	90.35	100.00	82.94	98.21
12.	Vizianagaram	92.95	97.40	9.24	90.50	95.10	82.60	94.74
13.	Warangal	91.35	100.00	9.19	91.10	100.00	88.73	98.11
14.	East Godavari	79.76	55.73	8.69	91.30	100.00	78.36	98.04
15.	Guntur	90.35	40.12	8.96	91.70	96.51	83.62	95.45
16.	Kurnool	70.17	70.95	8.73	90.31	100.00	88.14	100.00
17.	Nellore	90.35	50.43	9.20	91.32	100.00	86.90	95.65
18.	Prakasam	73.05	37.84	8.79	89.10	96.47	79.31	93.33
19.	Srikakulam	92.35	46.20	9.14	89.10	98.37	77.26	93.62
20.	Krishna	73.91	7.56	8.78	90.10	100.00	88.36	97.44
21.	Visakhapatnam	92.35	10.77	9.30	89.09	100.00	95.40	92.86
22.	West Godavari	93.35	6.59	8.90	91.00	100.00	88.60	97.06
	Total	88.16	73.76	9.08	90.58	98.22	84.94	96.26

Source: www.http//nrega.ap.gov.in

Social Audit Held in Gram Panchayats

The social audit was held in 18900 Gram Panchayats in the state consisting of 86.47 per cent of total Gram Panchayats during 2011-12. Across the districts, the percentage of Gram Panchayats in which Social audit was held ranged between 64.77 in Rangareddy and 99.77 in Adilabad districts. During 2010-11, the social audit was held in all the Gram Panchayats of 13 districts of first phase of MGNREGA. The percentage of number of Panchayats among the second and third phase of districts in which social audit was held ranged from 59.59 in Guntur to 97.67 in Kurnool district. About in nine districts out of 13 districts of first phase, the social audit was completed in all the Panchayats during 2009-10. On an average, about 73.76 per cent of Panchayats reported to have completed social audit during the year. Across the districts, the percentage of Panchayats in which the social audit was held ranged from 7.56 in Krishna district to 98.74 in Rangareddy district.

Inspections Conducted

About 11.41 lakh number of works were taken up in the state during 2011-12, of which 9 per cent of works were inspected at district level and about 91 per cent of works at block level. Across the districts, the percentage of works inspected ranged between 8.90 in Kurnool and West Godavari and 9.30 in Cuddapah districts. On the other hand, the percentage of number of works inspected at block level varied from 90.60 in Prakasam district to 93.00 in Warangal, Guntur and Krishna districts. During 2010-11, similar performance of inspections is observed as in the year 2011-12 at district level. But the percentage of inspections done at block level varied from 89.61 in Visakhapatnam district to 92.00 in Chittoor and Khammam districts.

Out of a total number of works 6.70 lakhs taken up during 2009-10 about 9 per cent of works were inspected at district level and around 90 per cent of works at block level. Observing across districts, the percentage of works inspected at district level varied from 8.69 in East Godavari to 9.30 in Cuddapah, Medak and Visakhapatnam districts. On the other hand, the percentage of works inspected at block level ranged from 89.09 in Visakhapatnam to 92.60 in Karimnagar district.

Gram Sabhas Held

Every year the Gram Panchayat shall convene a meeting of the Gram Sabha to estimate the demand for labour and to propose the number and priority of works to be taken up in the next financial year. The timing of the meeting will take into consideration of the work season and the migration time, in case the workforce in that area tends to migrate for work. Participation of likely beneficiaries should be ensured in the Gram Sabha so that their priorities and needs shape the Annual Plan. The time and date of the Gram Sabha meeting should be fixed well in advance and should be widely publicized so that people can participate in large number.

In Andhra Pradesh, out of a total number of 21857 Gram Panchayats, Gram Sabhas were held in 91.28 per cent of Panchayats during 2011-12. The percentage of Gram Sabhas held across districts varied from 62.93 in Rangareddy to 99.90 in Krishna district. On the other hand, the percentage of Village Monthly Co-ordination Committee (VMC) meetings held in Gram Panchayats is reported to 1.11 in the state. Across the districts, the percentage varied from 0.78 in Guntur district to 1.56 in Rangareddy district.

During 2010-11, of the total of 22109 Gram Panchayats in the state 98.41 per cent of the Panchayats held Gram Sabhas and about 10.47 per cent VMC meetings were held. Across districts, the percentage of Gram Sabhas held ranged from 93.07 in Nalgonda to 99.55 in West Godavari district. On the other hand, the percentage of VMC meetings held ranged from 7.42 in Mahboobnagar district to 14.56 in Nizamabad district. Of the total number of 22109 Gram Panchayats, 98.22 per cent of Panchayats held Gram Sabhas in the state during 2009-10. All the Panchayats of 12 districts in the state have conducted Gram Sabhas. These districts are: Adilabad, Khammam, Mahboobnagar, Nizamabad, Rangareddy, Warangal, East Godavari, Kurnool, Nellore, Krishna, Visakhapatnam and West Godavari. On the other hand, of the total Panchayats in the state, 84.94 per cent of Panchayats have conducted VMC meetings. The percentage of VMC meetings held ranged from 76.95 in Medak district to 95.40 in Visakhapatnam district.

Complaints

As per the guidelines in the Act of MGNREGA, any grievance shall be enquired and action initiated within seven days by the Panchayat Secretary/Field Assistant at village level, programme officer at the mandal level and district programme co-ordinator at the district level. Details of all the grievances received and disposed at each level should be maintained in the grievance register. Acknowledgement shall be given for any grievance received.

In Andhra Pradesh, the grievance redressal mechanism showed a significant performance in disposing the grievances during the years 2011-12, 2010-11, and 2009-10. Out of the total complaints received in each year 98.17 per cent in 2011-12, 91.70 per cent in 2010-11 and 96.26 per cent in 2009-10, were disposed.

Across the districts during 2011-12 in four districts, viz. Ananthapur, Mahboobnagar, Rangareddy and Krishna cent per cent of received complaints were disposed. In the remaining districts, the percentage of complaints disposed ranged between 91.13 in Vizianagaram and 99.73 in Adilabad district. During 2010-11, out of 229 complaints received in the state 91.0 per cent of complaints were disposed. Among the 22 districts, six districts have reported cent per cent disposal of the complaints. They are Medak, Nizamabad, Guntur, Kurnool, Visakhapatnam and West Godavari. Across the remaining districts, the percentage of complaints disposed ranged between 84.62 in Adilabad and Chittoor districts and 93.33 in Vizianagaram district.

Out of the total of 1097 complaints received in the state during 2009-10, 96.26 per cent of the complaints were disposed. Glancing over the districts, it is observed that only in Kurnool district cent per cent of the complaints were disposed. The percentage of complaints disposed among the other districts varied from 91.11 in Ananthapur district to 98.53 in Mahboobnagar district.

Unemployment Allowance

If a worker who has applied for work under Andhra Pradesh Rural Employment Guarantee Scheme (APREGS) is not provided employment within 15 days from the date on which work is requested, an un-employment allowance shall be payable by the State Government at the rate prescribed in the Act. The programme officer shall be responsible for the prompt payment of un-employment allowances throughout the Mandal. It is recommended that un-employment allowances should be paid on a fortnightly basis at the Gram Panchayat level. The payment of un-employment allowance shall be made not later than 15 days from the date on which it becomes due for payment. In Andhra Pradesh, no district has reported to have paid un-employment allowance during 2011-12.

Work Projection for 2011-12

The district-wise details of work projection under MGNREGA for the financial year 2011-12 in Andhra Pradesh are presented in Table 8. It can be observed from Table 8 that the number of spill over works from the previous year is accounted to be 729387, of which 13.22 per cent in Chittoor district and 11.39 per cent of works in Karimnagar district were reported. Among the remaining districts, seven districts have reported the spill over works between 5.22 per cent and 7.86 per cent. On the whole, the percentage of spill over works ranged from 0.54 in Krishna district to 13.22 in Chittoor district.

The total number of new works taken up in the present year are 847759, of which 48.51 per cent of works are taken up in Adilabad district only. The remaining 51.49 per cent works are spread over 21 districts and percentage of new works taken up in these districts varied from 0.99 in Rangareddy district to 4.03 in Kurnool district.

Moreover, out of total number of works taken up in the current year, 83.56 per cent of works are estimated to likely to be spill over from current financial year to next financial year. Of the total number of likely to spill over works, 56.75 per cent of works are reported to be spilled over to next financial year in Adilabad. The remaining 43.25 per cent of works are spread over 21 districts ranging from 0.98 in Rangareddy to 3.37 in Kurnool district.

Table 8: Work Projection under MGNREGA for 2011-12 Andhra Pradesh

(in %)

Sl. No.	Name of the District	Total No. of spill over works from previous year	Total No. of new works taken up in current year	No. of works likely to spill over from current financial year to next financial year	No. of new works proposed for next financial year	Benefit achieved unit	Person days to be generated	Estimated Cost (₹ In Lakhs)		
								On unskilled wage	On material including skilled and semi-skilled wages	Total
1	2	3	4	5	6	7	8	9	10	11
1.	Adilabad	6.42	48.51	56.75	2.77	–	4.97	5.18	4.56	4.94
2.	Ananthapur	7.43	3.31	2.58	17.10	–	6.32	6.30	6.36	6.32
3.	Chittoor	13.22	3.62	3.08	44.24	–	5.06	4.78	5.51	5.06
4.	Kadapa	3.70	2.68	1.91	1.34	–	4.85	4.82	4.92	4.85
5.	Karimnagar	1.80	1.56	1.01	2.29	–	0.68	0.73	0.60	0.68
6.	Khammam	6.64	2.99	2.79	1.65	–	4.37	4.61	3.99	4.37
7.	Mahboobnagar	11.39	2.63	2.51	2.76	–	5.72	5.21	6.54	5.72
8.	Medak	7.86	2.82	2.23	2.46	–	5.81	5.85	5.75	5.81
9.	Nalgonda	0.54	1.73	1.25	0.64	–	1.26	1.26	1.25	1.26
10.	Nizamabad	5.26	4.03	3.37	3.42	–	5.96	6.20	5.58	5.96
11.	Rangareddy	7.82	2.92	2.06	4.64	–	6.45	6.49	6.40	6.46
12.	Vizianagaram	3.62	2.28	2.22	1.22	–	4.55	4.55	4.55	4.55
13.	Warangal	5.22	2.67	2.14	4.15	–	5.97	6.17	5.65	5.97
14.	East Godavari	2.80	1.62	1.33	2.75	–	3.85	3.88	3.82	3.85
15.	Guntur	2.66	2.33	1.99	1.25	–	4.48	4.51	4.43	6.48
16.	Kurnool	1.47	0.99	0.98	0.44	–	2.39	2.53	2.16	2.39
17.	Nellore	2.51	1.66	1.27	0.84	–	2.74	2.55	3.03	2.74
18.	Prakasam	2.31	2.13	2.01	2.42	–	5.68	5.96	5.24	5.68
19.	Srikakulam	0.76	2.06	1.65	1.13	–	5.19	5.24	5.12	5.19
20.	Krishna	2.79	2.29	2.35	1.62	–	5.99	5.80	6.29	5.99
21.	Visakhapatnam	2.98	2.45	2.24	1.85	–	5.75	5.31	6.46	5.75
22.	West Godavari	0.80	2.72	2.26	1.02	–	1.96	2.08	1.79	1.96
Total		100.00 (729387)	100.00 (847759)	100.00 (708432)	100.00 (2782003)		100.00 (441862728)	100.00 (386867.09)	100.00 (244792.40)	100.00 (631659.49)

About 27.82 lakhs of new works are proposed for the next financial year with an estimated cost of ₹ 631659.49 lakhs and the person-days to be generated is about 4418.63 lakhs. Among the proposed new works, 44.24 per cent of works are

allocated in Chittoor district and 17.10 per cent of works in Ananthaputs district. The remaining 38.66 per cent of works spread over 20 districts ranging from 0.29 in Guntur district to 4.64 in Mahboobnagar district. The total number of person-days (4418.63 lakhs) to be generated is spread over 22 districts ranging from 0.68 per cent in Guntur district to 6.45 per cent in Mahboobnagar district.

The total estimated cost during 2011-12, for the execution of works is reported as ₹ 631659.49 lakhs. The distribution of the total estimated cost across the districts ranged from 0.68 per cent in Guntur district to 6.46 per cent in Mahboobnagar district. Out of the total estimated cost in the state 61.25 per cent of the amount is expected to spread on unskilled wage and 38.75 per cent of the amount on material including skilled and semi-skilled wages.

The total amount expected to spend on unskilled wage spread over 22 districts ranged from 0.73 per cent in Guntur district to 6.49 per cent in Mahboobnagar district. On the other hand, the amount which is expected to spend on material including skilled and semi-skilled wages spread over districts ranged between 0.60 per cent in Guntur to 6.54 per cent in Karimnagar district. On the whole, across districts, the larger amounts of the estimated cost are spent in the districts of Ananthapur, Mahboobnagar, Vizianagaram, Nalgonda, Kurnool, Warangal, Karimnagar and Srikakulam.

Main Observations

The scheme showed a better performance during 2010-11 than 2011-12 and 2009-10. A gradual improvement is observed in case of beneficiaries of land reform/IAY and disabled beneficiary households during the three years. However, the basic objective of the Act in providing at least 100 days of guaranteed wage employment is not achieved as expected. The number of projects undertaken in the state were increased from year to year. Increase in the number of works completed from 2009-10 to 2011-12 is observed in case of water conservation and water harvesting and micro irrigation works while a decrease is noticed in case of land development works and provision of irrigation facilities. Viewing the performance of all ongoing projects from 2009-10 to 2011-12, a decrease in number is observed in almost all activities except in the case of rural connectivity activities, harvesting works, land development works and provision of irrigation facilities. It is observed that about 33.25 per cent of increased amount was spent on complete projects during 2010-11 compared to the previous year. Between 2010-11, and 2011-12, the increase in the amount spent is reported around 72 per cent. Observing over the performance of the three years, larger amounts were spent on ongoing projects during 2010-11 than in the years 2011-12 and 2009-10.

Of the total number of muster rolls used, 91.71 per cent of the muster rolls are verified during 2011-12 and 2010-11 and only 88.16 per cent in the year 2009-10. The social audit was held in 86.47 per cent of Gram Panchayats in 2011-12, 92.65 per cent of Panchayats in 2010-11 and only in 73.76 per cent of Gram Panchayats during 2009-10 in the state. Out of the total works taken up, during the three years, 9.15 per cent of district level and 91.65 per cent of block level works during 2011-12, 9.15 per cent at district level and 91.25 per cent at block level during 2010-11 and 9.08 per cent at district level and 90.88 per cent at block level during 2009-10 were inspected. Out of the total number of Gram Panchayats in the state, 91.88 per cent of Gram Panchayats held Gram Sabhas and the VMC meetings were held in 2.11 per cent of Panchayats during 2011-12, Gram Sabhas in 99.41 Panchayats and VMC meeting in 10.48 per cent of Panchayats during 2010-11 and 98.32 per cent of Gram Sabhas and 84.94 per cent of VMC meetings were held during 2009-10. Out of the total number of complaints received in the state during the three years, 98.17 per cent in 2011-12, 92.80 per cent in 2010-11 and 96.26 per cent in 2009-10, were disposed.

Out of the total number of accounts opened in state in each year, 13.36 per cent of accounts in banks and 86.64 per cent of accounts in post offices during 2011-12, 14.04 per cent in banks and 85.96 per cent in post offices during 2010-11 and 8.34 per cent in banks and 91.66 per cent of banks and 91.66 per cent of accounts in post offices in 2009-10 were opened. Moreover out of the total amount disbursed in each year, 27.05 per cent of amount from banks and 72.95 per cent of amount from post offices during 2010-11, 19.98 per cent of the amount from banks and 80.02 per cent of amount through post offices during 2010-11 and 26.75 per cent of the amount from banks and 73.25 per cent through post offices in 2009-10 were disbursed.

In Andhra Pradesh, no district has reported to have paid unemployment allowance during 2011-12. Out of the total number of works taken up in the year 2010-11, 83.56 per cent of works are estimated to likely to be spilled over from current year to next financial year. About 27.82 lakhs of new works are proposed for the next financial year with an estimated cost of ₹ 631659.49 lakhs and the person-days to be generated is about 4418.63 lakhs. Out of the total estimated cost in the state 61.25 per cent of the amount is expected to spend on unskilled wage and 38.75 per cent of the amount on material including skilled and semi-skilled wages.

Conclusion

The National Rural Employment Guarantee Scheme (NREGS) is one of the major landmarks in the process of formulation adopting the rights-based approach. A large number of workers in India are forced to remain jobless both in rural and urban areas, Andhra Pradesh is not except from this situation. The experience of the recent economic reforms showed that economic growth above cannot guarantee creation of employment or livelihoods. Investment in labour intensive sectors coupled with direct initiatives by the government to generate employment is needed. In Andhra Pradesh, women have been the major beneficiaries of this scheme since its inception as scheme guarantees work for all those who demand it. This is a good single for economic prosperity of the state. Various studies have revealed that several lacunas in the NREGS. Particularly, misappropriation of funds, incomplete works and lack of follow up, leakages, poor quality of physical assets created under this scheme and poor wages are the important lacunas in the working and implementing process of the NREGS.

Hence, it can be concluded that the Andhra Pradesh State Government should think seriously about these lacunas so that the NREGS can be implemented more effectively.

REFERENCES

Bhalla, G.S. (2008). "Globalization and Employment Trends in India", *The Indian Journal of Labour Economics*, Vol. 51, No. 1, January-March, pp. 1-23.

Dev, S. Mahendra and C. Ravi (2003). "Macro-Economics Scene: Performance and Policies", in Rao, Ch. Hanumanth and S. Mahendra Dev (eds. 2003).

Eleventh Five-year Plan Document, 2007-2012, Vol. I, Inclusive Growth: Planning Commission – 2008.

Eleventh Five-year Plan, 2007-2012, Vol. II, Social Sector, Planning Commission – 2008.

Employment and Unemployment in India, 1993-94, Fifth Quinquennial Survey, NSS 50th Round (July 1993-June 1994), *NSSO Report* No. 409, March 1997.

Government of India, Employment and Unemployment Situation in India: 2004-05 (Part-I), NSS 61st Round (July 2004-June 2005), *NSS Report* No. 515, NSSO, June 2006.

Krishna Murthy, J. (2006). "Employment Guarantee and Crisis Response", *Economic and Political Weekly*, March 4, pp. 789-90.

Mehta, A.K. and Shah, A. (2003). "Chronic Poverty in India: Incidence, Causes, and Policies", *World Development*, Vol. 31, No. 3, pp. 491-512.

Popola, T.S. (2007). "Employment in the Development Agenda: Economic and Social Policies", Discussion Paper, DP/170/2007, The International Institute for Labour Studies, ILO, Geneva.

Rajakutty, S. (2004). "Self and Wage Employment Programmes for Poverty Alleviation in Rural India Overview", *Journal of Rural Development*, Vol. 23(2): 155-85, NIRD, Hyderabad, Andhra Pradesh.

Shah, Amita and Aasha Kapur Mehta (2008). "Experience of the Maharashtra Employment Guarantee Scheme are there lessons for NREGS?" *The Indian Journal of Labour Economics*, Vol. 51, No. 2, 198-212.

Srinivasulu, K. (2002). "Caste, Class and Social Agriculation in Andhra Pradesh, India: Mapping Different Regional Trajectories", Working Paper 179 Overseas Development Institute, London.

Various issues, Economy Survey of India.

Virmani, Arvind. *Economic and Political Weekly*, Vol. XLIII, No. 2, January 12, 2008: 54-62.

www.http://nrega.ap.gov.in

18

Fast Moving Consumer Goods Industry in Rural Market of India: A Case of Mutual Reinvigoration

Brajesh Kumar and *Mintu Gogoi*

ABSTRACT

The present study is undertaken to make an assessment of the growing eminence of FMCG industry in the era of enriching rural market in India. The Indian Fast Moving Consumer Goods (FMCG) industry began to shape during the last fifty years or so. The FMCG sector is a keystone of the Indian economy as it touches every aspect of human life. The FMCG sector, which offers tremendous growth prospects are food and beverage sector, health care and personal care. Presently, rural India accounts for 34 per cent of total FMCG consumption, but it accounts for more than 40 per cent consumption in major FMCG categories like as personal care, hot beverages, and fabric care. Moreover, 80 per cent of FMCG categories are growing faster in rural India as against urban India (Nielson, 2011). There is a huge growth potential for all the FMCG companies as the per capita consumption of almost all products in the country is amongst the lowest in the world. In recent years, rural markets have acquired significance in countries like China and India, as the overall growth of the economy has resulted into substantial increase in the purchasing power of the rural communities. On account of the green revolution in India, the rural areas are consuming a large quantity of industrial and urban manufactured products. Following the decades of opening of Indian economy to the outside world and the accompanying intervention in rural economy by the government in the form of various development schemes and programmes, i.e. SGSY, NREGA Sampoorna Swachchta Abhiyan, Gram Vikas Yojna, etc. and also decentralization of power through Panchayati Raj institutions have opened a new vistas of opportunities to the rural people. These together have made rural market attractive for FMCG industry in India. This relationship has grown over the years in a reinvigorating manner leading to the revitalization of the same.

Introduction

The Indian Fast Moving Consumer Goods (FMCG) industry began to shape during the last fifty-odd years. The FMCG sector is a keystone of the Indian economy as it touches every aspect of human life. "The FMCG companies are now encashing that opportunity. In rural India, this is the fact about the consumers that their income is increasing and the lifestyles are changing. There are as many middle-income households in the rural areas as there are in the urban. Thus the rural marketing has been growing steadily over the years and is now bigger than the urban market for FMCGs. With the increase in the rural literacy levels and the exposure to media, people in rural area are also becoming conscious about their buying decisions like their urban counterparts" (Gupta and Mittal, 2013). As a result of significant rise in the exposure level and brand awareness among the rural people they are becoming choosier and demanding than ever before. "The rural marketing environment also becomes more challenging for the companies to understand the buying behaviour, the consuming pattern, the need and wants of the rural consumer" (Gupta and Mittal, 2013).

"Indian rural market with its colossal size and demand base offers great opportunities to marketers. Two-thirds of India's consumers live in rural areas wherein almost one-third of the national income is generated. It is seen as a profusion of opportunities, whether for marketing durables, textiles and garments, personal care products or financial services" (Sathyanarayana, 2011). A rural marketeer is faced with an entirely different set of conditions and problems while marketing in rural area as with an urban area. For most marketeers planning to enter the rural markets, distribution poses a serious challenge. For the successful exploration of rural markets, a basic requirement is infrastructure. The absence of such an infrastructure is aggravating the distribution challenges in rural India. There are many other challenges that FMCG companies face in tackling rural markets, viz. geographically scattered nature of rural markets, their small size, remoteness, poor connectivity and tremendous heterogeneity. Low level of literacy, too many languages and dialects, cultural diversities, inadequate banking facilities, spurious products, low per capita disposable incomes, acute dependence on the monsoon; seasonal demand, and media darkness are some serious limitations.

Therefore, the real problem for the marketeers to penetrate into rural markets is in understanding heterogeneous rural consumers, reaching products to these remote locations, and communicating with media-dark rural spectators.

Statement of the Problem

The fast-moving consumer goods (FMCG) sector is an important contributor to India's GDP and it is the fourth largest sector of the Indian economy. "Globally, the FMCG sector has been successful in selling products to the lower and middle income groups, and the same is true in India. Over 70 per cent of sales are made to middle class households today and over 50 per cent is in rural India" (Kavitha, 2012). The sector is energized about an escalating rural population whose incomes are rising and which is willing to spend on goods designed to improve lifestyle. As the growth potential in urban markets is reducing, to sustain and survive, it is necessary for all companies to look, reach and serve the rural markets and the rural consumers, for volume-based growth. The same as the rural penetration increases in India, rural marketing has become the latest marketing mantra of most of the FMCGs companies in order to tap the unlimited opportunities and putting in place a parallel rural marketing strategy for capturing the rural consumers. The present study is undertaken to make an assessment of the growing eminence of FMCG industry in the era of enriching rural market in India.

FMCGs: An Overview

FMCG is the abbreviated form of fast moving consumer goods. In West, FMCG is also called consumer packaged goods. Any product that is used very frequently, sometimes daily and move relatively faster at the retailer end can be classified as FMCG. Examples are soap, toothpaste, batteries, beverages, cigarettes, etc. Thus, FMCGs are essential, low price goods which get repeat sales.

"FMCGs are also termed as non-durable goods—a tangible item that is quickly consumed, worn out or outdated and consumed in single use or few uses" (Majumdar, 1998). Consumer products used for personal, family or household use are further classified as three types: convenience, shopping and speciality categories. FMCG are also called as 'consumables' that are consumed by the consumer, typically sold in packaged form and generally branded.

"With respect to consumer behaviour towards this category, consumers tend to spend minimum effort in comparison and buying them. But much of astute marketing activities have evolved from these products, where consumers show low involvement, get wider choice and are allured by a host of inducements" (Majumdar, 1998).

FMCG Category and Products

Category	Products
Household Care	Fabric wash (laundry soaps and synthetic detergents); household cleaners (dish/utensil cleaners, floor cleaners, toilet cleaners, air fresheners, insecticides and mosquito repellents, metal polish and furniture polish).

Food and Beverages	Health beverages; soft drinks; staples/ cereals; bakery products (biscuits, bread, cakes); snack food; chocolates; ice cream; tea; coffee; soft drinks; processed fruits, vegetables; dairy products; bottled water; branded flour; branded rice; branded sugar; juices, etc.
Personal Care	Oral care, hair care, skin care, personal wash (soaps); cosmetics and toiletries; deodorants; perfumes; feminine hygiene; paper products.

Source: (ibef)

Characteristics of FMCG

FMCG industry is characterized by a few distinct factors:

- The sector touches every aspect of human life, looks to hygiene to palate.
- This industry is characterized by a strong focus on the four Ps, i.e. Product, Pricing, Place and Promotion.
- It is a high volume, low value driven industry in most categories.
- It is brand driven, rather than product driven.
- The capital investment required in plant and machinery is not high and any reasonably sized industrial house can enter the industry in manufacturing. The major area is the area of marketing: brand building and promotion. Distribution network is extremely vital for the success of an organization in the industry.

Distinguishing Features of Indian FMCG Business

FMCG companies sell their products directly to consumers. Major features that distinguish this sector from the others include the following:

1. Design and Manufacturing:

(a) ***Low Capital Intensity.*** Most product categories in FMCG require relatively minor investment in plant and machinery and other fixed assets. Also, the business

has low working capital intensity as bulk of sales from manufacturing take place on a cash basis.

(*b*) ***Technology.*** Basic technology for manufacturing is easily available. Also, technology for most products has been fairly stable. Modifications and improvements rarely change the basic process.

(*c*) ***Third-party Manufacturing.*** Manufacturing of products by third party vendors is quite common. Benefits associated with third party manufacturing include (1) flexibility in production and inventory planning; (2) flexibility in controlling labour costs; and (3) logistics—sometimes it's essential to get certain products manufactured near the market.

2. Marketing and Distribution: Marketing function is sacrosanct in case of FMCG companies. Major features of the marketing function include the following:

(a) ***High Initial Launch Cost:*** New products require a large front-ended investment in product development, market research, test marketing and launch. Creating awareness and develop franchise for a new brand requires enormous initial expenditure on launch advertisements, free samples and product promotions. Launch costs are as high as 50-100 per cent of revenue in the first year. For established brands, advertisement expenditure varies from 5-12 per cent depending on the categories.

(b) ***Limited Mass Media Options:*** The challenge associated with the launch and/or brand-building initiatives is that few no mass media options. TV reaches 67 per cent of urban consumers and 35 per cent of rural consumers. Alternatives like wall paintings, theatres, video vehicles, special packaging and consumer promotions become an expensive but required activity associated with a successful FMCG.

(c) ***Huge Distribution Network:*** India is home to six million retail outlets, including two million in 5,160 towns and four million in 627,000 villages. Super markets virtually do not exist in India. This makes logistics particularly

for new players extremely difficult. It also makes new product launches difficult since retailers are reluctant to allocate resources and time to slow moving products. Critical factors for success are the ability to build, develop, and maintain a robust distribution network.

3. Competition: ***Significant Presence of Unorganized Sector:*** Factors that enable small, unorganized players with local presence to flourish include the following:

(a) Basic technology for most products is fairly simple and easily available.

(b) The small-scale sector in India enjoys exemption/lower rates of excise duty, sales tax, etc. This makes them more price competitive vis-à-vis the organized sector.

(c) A highly scattered market and poor transport infrastructure limits the ability of MNCs and national players to reach out to remote rural areas and small towns.

(d) Low brand awareness enables local players to market their spurious look-alike brands.

(e) Lower overheads due to limited geography, family management, focused product lines and minimal expenditure on marketing.

Growth of FMCG Sector in India

The Indian FMCG market offers a level playing ground for both domestic and international players. All Indian brands and international brands enjoy higher acceptance in the urban market, the rural market is often dominated by the regional and local producers. The consumer market, especially Fast Moving Consumer Goods (FMCG), sector in rural and semi-urban India is estimated to cross $20 billion by 2018 and $100 billion by 2025 (AC Nielsen Survey, 2011). Some of the most popular consumer goods included fruit drinks, shampoos and biscuits are among the most bought items in rural and semi-urban India and will continue to be so. It also revealed that growth in the FMCG sector in rural India increased 3.5 times from 2000 to 2010, as compared to 3.2 times in urban India. Incomes in India are likely to grow three times over the next two decades and India will become the world's fifth largest consumer market by 2025 (McKinsey Global Institute Study, 2007). Market share movements indicate that companies such as Marico Ltd. and Nestle India Ltd., with domination in their key categories, have improved their market shares and outperformed peers in the FMCG sector. This has also been aided by the lack of competition in the respective categories. Single product leaders such as Colgate Palmolive India Ltd. and Britannia Industries Ltd. have also witnessed strength in their respective categories, aided by innovations and strong distribution. Strong players in the economy segment like Godrej Consumer Products Ltd. in soaps and Dabur in toothpastes have also posted market share improvement, with revived growth in semi-urban and rural areas. Penetration level and per capita consumption in many product categories is very low compared to world average standards representing the unexploited market potential. Mushrooming Indian population, particularly the middle class and the rural segments, presents the huge untapped opportunity to FMCG players. Growth is also likely to come from consumer 'upgrading' in the matured product categories like processed and packaged food, mouth wash, etc. A distinct feature of the FMCG industry is the presence of international players through their subsidiaries (HLL, P&G, Nestle), which ensures innovative product launches in the market from their parent's portfolio. The Rural FMCG Market of India is on the verge of registering substantial expansion across the country. The Indian Rural FMCG market is mostly unorganized and it is generally dominated by small time retailers. The organized FMCG market is only confined to the urban areas of India. Rural India mostly depends on agriculture, directly or indirectly for livelihood. Further, almost 68 per cent of Indian population lives in rural India in around 6,00,000 villages. Rural India offers tremendous growth prospects for the FMCG industry. Facilitation of better rural infrastructure like roads, telecommunication, electricity, supply chain, and transportation would propel the growth of Rural FMCG Market of India. The FMCG sector, which offers tremendous growth prospects are food and beverage sector, health care and personal care. Presently, rural India accounts for 34 per cent of total FMCG consumption, but it accounts for more than 40 per cent consumption in major FMCG categories like as personal care, hot beverages, and fabric care.

Rural Market in India

In recent years, rural markets have acquired significance in countries like China and India, as the overall growth of the economy has resulted into substantial increase in the purchasing power of the rural communities. On account of the Green Revolution in India, the rural areas are consuming a large quantity of industrial and urban manufactured products. In this context, a special marketing strategy, namely rural marketing has taken shape. Rural India, mostly termed as "high opportunity" market, is no longer just an opportunity, but is now yielding results. The concept of rural marketing in India Economy has always played an influential role in the lives of people. In India, leaving out a few metropolitan cities, all the districts and industrial townships are connected with rural markets.

Rural Consumer: The differences between rural and urban consumers always exist in India. Indian rural customer is large with illiteracy and poverty. Illiteracy leads to an inability to identify brand differences and read the basic text on packages. Poverty and dependence on vagaries of monsoon result into a low and unpredictable purchasing power. Moreover, products are sold lose, giving high competition to branded sealed products. Ignorance and illiteracy are accompanied by strong influence leaders like the local panchayat members, caste and religious leaders, etc. Since rural consumers are economically, socially and psychologically different from the urban counterparts and are definitely the rural consumers are price-sensitive.

Irregular income, dependency on the vagaries of monsoon induces the rural consumer to buy in small quantities. To address this issue, most FMCG companies have introduced products (such as tea, shampoos, biscuits, etc.) in smaller packs and sachets to make the product more affordable for rural consumers and obtain a share of wallet. Small Coke worth ₹ 5, Chick shampoo and Meera shampoo sachets has been credited with pioneering the sale of shampoos in sachets at ₹ 1 and ₹ 2, a trend that boosted in rural sales. Since rural population does not have the concept of storing goods and blocking too much capital into it is important for rural marketeers to provide products in small quantities as well as good credit systems for larger products. It is also important to induce first time purchase and trials so that customer is able to experience products he never has. Credit facility also needs to be extended to the wholesalers.

Rural customers have upgraded their lifestyles and as a result are purchasing lifestyle products like cosmetics, beverages, mobile phones, etc., which have become necessities for them. Urbanizations have become more of a lifestyle and are no longer bound to geographical areas.

Market Size for FMCG Sectors in Rural India

The rural market in India is not a separate entity in itself and it is highly influenced by the sociological and behavioural factors operating in the country. The total size of the rural market is estimated at about 83.3 crore people or 68.84 per cent of Indian population (Census, 2011). The rural market brings in bigger. Revenues in the country, as the rural regions, comprise the maximum consumers in this country. The rural market generates almost more than half of the country's income. Rural India contributes a big chunk to India's GDP by way of agriculture, self-employment, services, construction, etc. The rural population is empowered with rising income, improving education and awareness levels, enhanced contact with the outside world, evolving consumption patterns, emerging lifestyles and, most importantly, shift in occupation from agriculture to manufacturing, self-employment and construction.

The shift in rural income may not necessarily be happening due to rising food production, though it has a role to play, but the biggest change in the rural areas in the last few years has been the reducing dependence on farm income. The contribution of non-farm income to total rural income has increased.

Challenges Faced by FMCG Sectors for Rural Marketing

The peculiarities of the rural markets and rural consumers pose challenges to the marketeers in reaching them effectively.

While making out a case for opportunities that are rapidly developing in rural markets, one should not underestimate the several daunting problems in planning for growth. There are a large number of small villages which are not easily accessible because of all weather roads. Rural consumers are far less homogeneous than urban consumers. The main problems of rural marketing are discussed below:

Transportation Problems: Marketing activities require transportation facilities. Due to poor transportation facilities, farmers and marketeers find it difficult to reach markets. Transportation infrastructure is quite poor in rural India. Nearly 80 percentages of villages in the country are not connected by well-constructed roads.

Warehousing: In the rural areas, there are no facilities for public as well as private warehousing. Marketeers face problem of storage of their goods.

Packaging: It is the first important step of product processing. If the packaging cost is high, it will increase the total cost of products. It is suggested that the marketeers should use cheaper materials in packaging for the rural markets.

Media Problems: Media have lots of problems in rural areas. Television is a good medium to communicate message to the rural people. But due to non-availability of power, as well as television sets, majority of the rural population cannot get the benefits of various media.

Seasonal Marketing: The main problem of rural marketing is seasonal demand in rural areas, because 75 per cent of rural income is also seasonal. For example, the demand for consumer goods will be high during the peakcrop harvesting period, because this is the time at which the rural people have substantial high cash flow. Rural marketing depends upon the demand of rural people and demand depends upon income and consumer behaviour.

Low Per Capita Income: Per capita income is lower in rural areas compared to those in urban areas. Again, the distribution of rural income is highly skewed, since the landholding pattern, which is basic asset, it is skewed. Thus, the rural population presents a highly heterogeneous spread in the villages.

Low Level of Literacy Rate: The literacy rate is low in rural areas compared to urban areas. This again leads to the problem of communication for promotion purpose. Print medium becomes ineffective and to an extent irrelevant in rural areas, since its reach is poor.

Distribution: An effective distribution system requires village-level shopkeeper, mandal/taluka-level wholesaler or preferred dealer, distributor or stockist at district level and company-owned depot or consignment distribution at state level. The presence of too many tiers in the distribution system increases the cost of distribution.

Career in Rural Market: While rural marketing offers a challenging career, a rural sales person should require certain qualifications and specialized talent to deal with rural consumers.

Cultural Factors: Culture is a system of shared values, beliefs and perceptions that influence the behaviour of consumers. There are different groups based on religion, caste, occupation, income, age, education and politics and each group exerts influence on the behaviour of people in villages. There are several difficulties confronting the effort to fully explore rural markets. The concept of rural markets in India is still in evolving shape, and the sector poses a variety of challenges. Distribution costs and non-availability of retail outlets are major problems faced by the marketeers. The unique consumption patterns, tastes, and needs of the rural consumers should be analyzed at the product planning stage so that they match the needs of the rural people. Therefore, marketeers need to understand the social dynamics and attitude variations within each village, though nationally it follows a consistent pattern and each group exerts influence on the behaviour of people in villages.

There are several difficulties confronting the effort to fully explore rural markets. The concept of rural markets in India is still in evolving shape, and the sector poses a variety of challenges. Distribution costs and non-availability of retail outlets are major problems faced by the marketeers. The unique consumption patterns, tastes, and needs of the rural consumers should be analyzed at the product planning stage so that they match the needs of the rural people. Therefore, marketeers need to understand the social dynamics and attitude variations within each village, though nationally it follows a consistent pattern.

Factors Accountable for Upcoming Paradigms of Rural Marketing

Increase in Purchasing Power and Disposable Income: Projects from the private companies and the rural employment initiatives by the governmental schemes like NREGA (National Rural Employment Guarantee) have given the rural population an opportunity to meet their daily needs. The loan waver in the agriculture sector and an increasing demand for labour in the urban areas, has given a boost to the income levels in the rural sectors. Consequent lifestyle upgrade has added a new spectrum.

Accessibility of Market: Improvement in the road systems linking the villages has led to a systematic product distribution system. Earlier, there was a "trickle down" of the stocks observed to the buyers in the interior villages. These days, companies use delivery-cum-promotion vans that travel 8-10 haats/markets daily as a part of direct contact with villagers.

Competition in the Urban Market: The urban markets have got extremely saturated with the presence of all big players. This is very much evident in the automobile market. Motorcycles and scooters often find more acceptances in rural market as compared to urban market, since there is more proliferation of brands in the latter markets.

Reduction of Risk During Recession: It has been observed that the companies which cater to both urban and rural markets tackle the recession in a better way. The demand for goods in the urban market often follows a cyclic whereas in the rural market it is steady. The companies are bound to tailor the strategies depending on various factors to appeal to the rural market. For example, Hindustan Unilever Limited came out with the concept of "Shakti Ammas" (female social entrepreneurs) which was an innovative way of marketing products. This much needed transition can be weighed according to the 4 As model (Availability, Affordability, Acceptability and Awareness).

Availability: It deals with making the product reach the consumers. For this purpose, a highly integrated extensive distribution network is necessary and in rural context, the company incurs higher cost towards the logistics as compared to urban areas. In case of Shakti campaign, the local Shakti Ammas are selected based on their popularity which allows faster access to products.

Affordability: It involves pricing the product in such a manner that the people are attracted and at the same time it covers all the cost incurred.

Acceptability: It encompasses issues how the product or service could be made more acceptable to the rural consumers by incorporating attractive features. For example, Eveready came out with Jeevan-Sathi torches, with features like durable design and long life to make it more acceptable.

Awareness: It is linked to the issues of promotion of product in rural areas. The promotion needs to be adapted to the village environment, the local language and means of communication used. The best places to promote could be the frequently visited local haats and melas, the local festivals. Agricultural cycles require a major consideration too. As rural households form 72 per cent of total households and increasing levels of income coupled with more and more penetration to the rural markets is expected to take rural FMCG from the current ₹ 87,900 crore to a market size of ₹ 1,06,300 crore in 2012. Moreover, 80 per cent of FMCG categories are growing faster in rural India as against urban India (Nielson, 2011). There is a huge growth potential for all the FMCG companies as the per capita consumption of almost all products in the country is amongst the lowest in the world.

Conclusion

Following the decades of opening of Indian economy to the outside world and the accompanying intervention in rural economy by the government in the form of various development schemes and programmes, i.e. SGSY, NREGA Sampoorna Swachchta Abhiyan, Gram Vikas Yojna, etc. and also decentralization of power through Panchayati Raj institutions have opened a new vistas of opportunities to the rural people. These together have made rural market attractive for FMCG industry in India. This relationship has grown over the years in a reinvigorating manner leading to the revitalization of the same.

REFERENCES

Gupta, S.L. and Mittal, A. (2013). A Study of Consumer Behaviour Aspects and Brand Preferences in Rural India with Reference to FMCG Sector, *Journal of Small Business Management*, 35(2): 80-94.

Gupta, S.L. *Rural Marketing Text and Cases*.

Kashyap, P. and Raut, S. (2006). *The Rural Marketing Book*. New Delhi: Biztantra.

Kavitha, T.C. (2012). A Comparative Study of Growth, Challenges and Opportunities in *FMCG of Rural Market, Interscience Management Review* (IMR), Volume 2, Issue 3, 2012.

Kotler, P., Keller, K., Koshy A. and Jha, M. (2007). *Marketing Management: A South Asian Perspective*. New Delhi: Pearson Prentice Hall.

Krishnamacharylu, C.S.G. and Ramakrishnan, L. (2002). *Rural Marketing: Text and Cases*. Delhi: Pearson Education.

Majumdar, R. (1998). *Product Management in India* (2nd ed.), Prentice Hall India, 1998: 26.

Sathyanarayana, S. (2011). Trends in the Marketing of Fast Moving Consumer Goods (FMCGS) in Karnataka State, Dharana—Bhavan's *International Journal of Business* (5)1: 61-73.

Velayudhan, S.K. (2002). *Rural Marketing: Targeting the Non-Urban Consumer*. New Delhi: Response Books.

Websites

http://censusindia.gov.in/2011-prov-results/prov_results_paper1_india.html retrieved on 3/08/2013

http://www.ruralgov-ncaer.org

http://www.iseindia.com/ResearchPDF/FMCG_Update1.pdf retrieved on 15/02/2012

http://www.ibef.org/download/FMCG_sectoral.pdf

McKinsey Global Institute Study, 2007 retrieved from http://www.mckinsey.com/locations/india/mckinseyonindia/pdf/India_Consumer_Market.pdf on 4/08/2013

A.C. Nielson Survey, 2011 retrieved from http://www.thinkindia.net.in/2011/12/indian-rural-consumer-market-reaches-6-billion.html on 4/08/2013

19
Participatory Watershed Planning

Manish Dwivedi and *Surendra Singh*

ABSTRACT

The aim of this paper is to present the traditional "project" approach to watershed management. The technocrats and project administrators see themselves as key players. They keep to themselves the responsibility to plan, implement and manage the project, especially the power to make decisions. Moreover, invariably, the primary focus of watershed project depends upon the expertise of the project manager or the technical department that implements it.

Participatory approach is also different from a "project" approach which requires all activities to be predetermined in a tight jacket, sequential time frame. In the project approach, most decisions about the project are already made by the technocrats and administrators who "know" the solutions. They do not have to know the site-specific problems! In contrast, participation is a "process" that evolves from below and with people, and based primarily on their wisdom.

Participatory approaches are also a reverse of the conventional approaches in which technocrats and administrators control decision-making. Participation is a process of empowering the local communities. Therefore, when a project adopts a participatory approach, the staff should be prepared to accept a state of powerlessness. PRA (participatory rural appraisal) and GOPP (goal-oriented project planning) are tools which would facilitate the local communities to undertake appraisal, to make decisions and to prepare plans on their own using their knowledge and wisdom. The village communities have their own understanding of the problem, solutions for them, and, importantly, a vision for their village. The staff should be willing to learn from the local communities. Adoption for participatory approaches and tools would require changes in the attitude and outlook of the project authorities and technocrats, and in the systems and procedures they have established to control decision-making changes in behaviour in project staff, thus, is a critical prerequisite. "Ownership" by the local community and their taking of responsibility for the project management are critical prerequisites for project sustainability, and this condition could be achieved only when an authentic process of participation described below takes place. This is not an "ideal" situation to hope for, rather it is a minimum condition to be achieved.

Introduction

In the traditional "project" approach to watershed management, the technocrats and project administrators see themselves as key players. They keep to themselves the responsibility to plan, implement and manage the project, especially the power to make decisions. Moreover, invariably, the primary focus of a watershed project depends upon the expertise of the project manager or the technical department that implements it!!

(a) When the manager is a forester, the project starts from the top of the watershed, that is, the degraded forest areas or community lands in the catchment get the focus. For them a forest area is a jungle that is to be cleared and tress of their liking raised. Nurseries and plantations take center stage. Hectares of plantations raised become the target for monitoring and the indicators of project output and success. They have well-documented procedures to raise a plantation. The protection of the plantation commences by keeping people out.

(b) If it is an agriculturist, the project starts in the middle with the farm lands as the focus. Debates are on 'vegetative bunding' adopting of appropriate culture practices, ways of improving the productivity of the farm land, developing irrigation facilities, agro/farm forestry, etc., increased farm yield becomes the outcome indicator.

(c) With engineers managing the project, the intervention focuses at the lower areas: contour bunding, gully plugging, cross weirs, check dams and other engineering works or, broadly, 'land shaping' becomes the main project component. Thus, the starting, 'entry' point or the main focus becomes different with each of the experts!! and

(d) The basic difference between the above-mentioned traditional, technocratic approaches and participatory approach is that in the participatory approach "people" become the starting, entry or the central focus. This reversal in the starting point is critical to make the local community take responsibility for the project from day one, to develop in them ownership, and to make the project sustainable. Participatory approach is important because these aspects (local ownership and responsibility) are crucial to project success.

Participatory approach is also different from a "project" approach which requires all activities to be predetermined in a tight jacket, sequential time frame. In the project approach, most decisions about the project are already made by the technocrats and administrators who "know" the solutions. They do not have to know the site-specific problems! In contrast, participation is a "process" that evolves from below and with people, and based primarily on their wisdom.

Participatory approaches are also a reverse of the conventional approaches in which technocrats and administrators control decision-making. Participation is a process of empowering the local communities. Therefore, when a project adopts a participatory approach, the staff should be prepared to accept a state of powerlessness. PRA (participatory rural appraisal) and GOPP (goal-oriented project planning) are tools which would facilitate the local communities to undertake appraisal, to make decisions and to prepare plans on their own using their knowledge and wisdom. The village communities have their own understanding of the problem, solutions for them, and, importantly, a vision for their village. The staff should be willing to learn from the local communities. Adoption for participatory approaches and tolls would require changes in the attitude and outlook of the project authorities and technocrats, and in the systems and procedures they have established to control decision-making changes in behaviour in project staff, thus, is a critical prerequisite. "Ownership" by the local community and their taking responsibility for the project management are critical prerequisites for project sustainability, and this condition could be achieved only when an authentic process of participation described below takes place. This is not an "ideal" situation to hope for; rather it is a minimum condition to be achieved.

The above are the fundamental principles on which a participatory watershed project needs to be based. The first activity in a participatory approach should therefore be making the entire project organization, especially the administrative and finance sections, understand and accept the participatory approach by organizing orientation programmes on the concept, principles and techniques of participation. Because they are the first people who would rise objections and set rules that would almost entirely kill the participatory approach.

Authentic Participation

Participation is an empowering process, a process that progressively gives to the local communities, who have hitherto been excluded, (a) control over decision-making resource management and their own development, (b) responsibility, and (c) capability. Participation, thus, is a zero-sum game: increased power for the local communities would result in decreased power for the project authorities. Authentic participation leads to powerlessness of the project authorities!! Participatory rural appraisal (PRA) is a tool that enables the local communities to use their own knowledge and wisdom, and make decisions and plans/evaluation. It is not a method to collect data or to give effect to decisions which have already been made by technocrats and administrators. Apart from facilitations, the role of outsiders in PRA is almost nil. It is however possible that outsiders can share their knowledge, skills and experience as required by the local communities.

Participation becomes manipulation when the project authorities set the goal, purpose, objectives, activities and a time frame, i.e. prepare the entire project design and then make the people "fit" into their design. Ironically, these project authorities would want PRA undertaken in such projects as well!! Obviously, they have not understood the concept of both participation and PRA. Thus, there is an ideological contradiction between participation and PRA as empowering processes and the project authorities wanting participation and PRA undertaken in their projects in which they have already made most decisions and have set the terms for participation!! Therefore, authentic participation and PRA are impossible unless the project authorities change their attitude and the systems and procedures which they have established to give themselves control over decisions.

Inception Phase—Initiating the Process

The project inception phase in a people-centered project should be about initiating a participatory planning process and building capacity in the project staff and in the local communities. The inception phase must at least be for a period of twelve to eighteen months in large projects and a minimum on nine months in smaller project. This phase must be outside the preparatory phase in which the office and the administrative and financial systems are established, and the staff is appointed. The inception phase follows the preparatory phase, and all or most staff must be in position by then.

The outputs of the inception phase are: (a) a project management plan for the entire project period, (b) a detailed annual plan for the first year prepared 'jointly' by the project staff and people through a participatory process (the word 'participatory' is used to mean that 'the power to make decisions and control over resources, use lie with the local communities'; and the word 'jointly' is meant 'the knowledge and skills of the technocrats and the knowledge, wisdom and the skills of the local communities are put together'), (c) community level plans, (d) aware and capable local community, and (e) confidence and trust of the community.

The inception phase is also a period to win the trust and confidence of the local community on the project and the local staff, and to get the project concept accepted by them. A long planning process without any visible activities that would directly benefit the local communities could disappoint them, and they could quickly lose interest in the project. While making the project visible sooner is important, but undertaking during the inception phase activities which are not even remotely connected to watershed could give wrong signals to the local community, a waste of staff time, and more importantly, take the project to a different direction. Any activities undertaken during the inception phase should be simple and short duration in nature, and have direct links to the concept of watershed management.

As most interventions in a watershed project are geared towards the monsoon, the planning process should commence at least nine months ahead of the monsoon, in September-October if the monsoon is expected in June in the following year. Most of the staff members must be in place when the planning process starts, and the late comers must be inducted with appropriate orientation.

The first activity at the beginning of the inception phase is preparing an 'inception phase plan'. The aspects to be addressed to prepare the plan are: (a) staff orientation, (b) community awareness of the project concept, the cause-effect intra-relationship of resources and their inter-relationship with poverty, and the potential, (c) participatory appraisal, (d) inception phase activities, (e) involving women, (f) capacity building, (g) preparation of long-term and annual project and community level plans, (h) establishing project management and other communities, and (i) establishing monitoring/evaluation plans and database. If the project must be ready by March end, so the inception phase should start nine months before April 1.

Some critical questions which need to be asked in a participatory project during and at the end of the initial planning stage, that is, inception phase are:

- Does the local community have a clear understanding of the project concept? (Not just about what the project will given them and the extent of local contribution they have to give to get them!!)
- Is there a match between their understanding of the project concept and expectations from the project, and that is visualized in the project documents?
- Are the local communities aware of the issues, root-causes and effects of natural resource degradation, and their linkages with (effects upon) their quality of life?
- How was the planning made and by whom?
- What is the role of different stakeholders in planning?
- What are the social engineering process and its effects?
- Are there maps prepared by the local communities that reflect the current resource-use pattern and their long-term vision, and the result which they want to achieve? 'How does each intervention fit into the overall vision? What is the result-people linkage?'
- Who (which social/economic groups) made the decisions and how? Are local communities capable of making decisions; have they made informed decisions?
- Who is responsible for project activities? Do they have adequate skills to implement project activities?
- Is the project striving to adopt best and innovative practice?
- What is the local level institutional arrangement to execute the decisions? How do the members see their roles?

- What are the local contributions and how they were arrived at?
- 'What will be the direct effect of the project on women?' 'How do women relate themselves to the project?' What is their role in decision-making?'
- 'How does the project affect different social/economic groups?'

The inception phase is complete if, and only if, there are satisfactory answers to the above questions.

Staff Orientation on Participatory Approach

Participatory approach is a reverse of the conventional approaches. Thus, participatory approach is not about (a) educating and orienting the local communities, (b) forming various local organizations/associations/committees to implement the project activities, and (c) providing guidelines which define how the community should participate. It is very difficult, often impossible, for the traditional planners and decision-makers (technocrats and administrators) to give away the control and decision-making power to the local communities and to become learners and powerless. Staff orientation thus is an important first activity of the inception phase.

While technocrats may have a number of solutions to varied problems, they do not know the local condition and the site-specific problems which only the local communities know. The local communities have lived and worked with them. And they also have the wisdom as to how to go about changing the condition. The participatory approach recognizes this and seeks to build the programme upon this potential condition. So the outsiders become the learners in a participatory approach, and it is they who require education and awareness to change their outlook, attitude and behaviour towards the local communities. Changes in attitude in the technocrats and administrators are required: (a) to recognize and accept people's knowledge and wisdom to be superior than theirs and to learn from them, (b) to give decision-making and controlling power to the local communities, and (c) to see the local communities not as recipients and beneficiaries but as potential managers. Staff orientation has to address these aspects.

Outsiders should:

- Listen and learn, instead of lecturing;
- Try to understand the local condition and problems from the local communities than give out solutions;
- Facilitate the local communications to do the thinking and action; and
- Work with the whole community and with groups than on a one-to-one basis.

Community Awareness

Community awareness of the project concept, the cause-effect intra-relationship of resources and their inter-relationship with poverty, and the experiences of similar projects in other areas is important (a) to understand and appreciate the project concept and project efforts, (b) to focus their expectations, and (c) to know the potential their resources offer. This is because a number of government and NGO programmes may be going on in the project area, and their expectations could be very wide. Focused awareness opens their eyes and makes them think and want. The want creates demand from the local community for the project activities. Community awareness could be created through (a) orientation programmes, (b) using local traditional and electronic media, (c) exposure visits, and (d) PRA exercise, especially transact and historical analyses.

Community-level Participatory Appraisal and Planning

Participatory rural appraisal is a technique that enables the local communities to bring together their knowledge and wisdom, and to make decisions as they feel appropriate. It is not an expertise that is held by outsiders (experts), rather it is a way, a methodology of the local communities analyzing, appraising the information that they have. Thus, it is a simple method that ordinary people can use; it uses common sense and local materials. It is advised to not even use pen and paper which the local community might find it inconvenient because it is associated with the formally 'educated' people. There is a log of role for technocrats after the local communities have made the basic decisions; a role that would provide for technological options (the local communities) to choose from based on the local conditions which they are familiar with. The use of PRA method makes visible to all what is discussed, everybody can take part, and decision-making is broad-based. Conflicting interests come to light and consensus could be arrived at.

Six exercises, that would give a broader picture of the local situation, are very useful to begin with: (i) village/habitat resource-use mapping, (ii) transact analysis, (iii) historical resource-resource and resource-people linkages analysis, (iv) resource-social/economic groups linkage, (v) seasonality analysis, and (vi) local institutional analysis.

(a) Village resource-use mapping is a drawing that brings out how resources are currently used. (b) Transact analysis is undertaken by walling along all the resources studying their condition, and discussing the problems and the potential the resources offer. (c) Historical resource-resource and resource-people linkage analysis is made by stating how, over the past 50-70 years (time series data for every decade), (i) the condition of resources have changed, (ii) how changes in one resource have affected other resources, and (iii) how changes in resources have affected people, animals, etc. a number of factors can be studied: vegetative cover in the community lands, water in the streams in terms of the number of months it is available, water in the wells, land quality, grass/fodder/firewood availability, farm yield, number of cattle, human population, etc. based on this analysis, a problem tree can be constructed that would bring out the root causes for the problems which the local community presently faces. (d) Resource-social/economic groups' linkage brings out how different social and economic groups depend upon the resources. (e) Seasonality analysis is undertaken by drawing on a 12-month (January-December) scale: temperature, rainfall, crop pattern (sowing to harvesting of each crop), labour availability, water in the local streams/wells, fodder/firewood availability, etc. (f) Local institutional structure: drawing a circle for each local organization; the size of the circle representing the number of members, and if there are common members then the circles can overlap.

Family economy analysis can be undertaken as case studies of families representing different social and economic groups. The analysis will bring out the production, consumption (income and expenditure) and surplus in terms of both kind and money. Similarly, the village economy analysis can be undertaken by assessing the source and availability of various home/farm/non-farm inputs and marketing sources for various products.

Gender analysis can be undertaken: (a) how the time of women and men is spent on a day during farming and off seasons; (b) how the time of women and men is spent throughout the year; (c) gender-based discrimination of home/farm chores; and (d) gender-based discrimination in family, community decision-making in sources of income for women and men and in making expenditure decisions.

The awareness, exposure and the above analyses should contribute to the local communities developing a vision of how they would like to see the village natural resources become. What results they would like to happen in the village. These could relate to the habitat where they live as well as farming and community lands, and in the five, ten, fifteen, twenty years and longer. Vision building is an important activity, and it is only the local communities who could do this. It should be the local community's vision, not of the technocrats and the field staff. They do not need a lecture on this. This vision is the overall framework within which all the interventions should fit into. Thus, vision building is not a one-time activity; rather the interventions are constantly related to the vision. The vision is a dynamic concept. And interventions make sense when they are seen in the overall perspective of the vision. While the vision may seem a dream, the results and objectives must be clear, simple and achievable in a given time frame.

PRA is a planning and decision-making method. In this way, it is a management tool. PRA is a tool that enables the local community (a) to undertake a systematic appraisal of the resources they have and an analysis of the socio-economic and seasonal conditions, (b) to identify the problems and the potentials/opportunities the resources offer, and (c) to make their own choices and preferences. PRA should lead to preparation of a micro-level watershed management plan.

PRA is not just an "activity" listed in the annual implementations plan, to be undertaken and forgotten. It is continuously used to make planning and decision-making in respect of all activities. Every activity (for example, nursery raising, plantation, check dam, chula, etc.) is an independent project and hence participatory project planning (PPP) exercise will need to be done for each activity. The PPP lists all the activities that need to be undertaken, puts the activities in a time frame, works out the materials required and the cost, responsibility, etc.

When PRA for every activity has been completed and the people have made decisions, it is possible that the local community and technocrats can make planning jointly. The technocrats can provide technical options and designs for the local communities to choose from. The project plan for each activity can then be finalized based on the "joint" decision made.

Inception Phase Activities

The inception phase should not be just about establishing database, training, awareness generation programmes. It is also a confidence-building phase. Project vehicles and staff suddenly moving about would create in local communities anxious inquires as well as expectations. Three factors need to be considered while deciding which activities need to be undertaken during the inception phase: (a) activities that would provide a good entry point for the project and establish a good rapport with the entire community especially women, but these activities should form part of the overall vision. Activities that would give grants to individuals should be totally avoided as this would only create rivalry within the community, some becoming for and some becoming against the project; (b) as watershed management activities are geared towards monsoon, some preparatory activities such as nursery raising could be undertaken; and (c) some innovative practice could be tested.

Gender-Involving, Mainstreaming Women

Often this has not been properly understood in many projects. Under WID, women are nominated to committees, self-help groups are formed and income-generation programmes are undertaken. These are important but not sufficient. Just nomination of women to committees becomes ceremonial, and although self-help groups are formed exclusively for women, sometimes men do most decision-making. Income-generation programmes sometimes increase the drudgery of women or women from well-off families who have time to spare benefit than poor women who have to spend the whole day in wage labour.

Involving women is about mainstreaming women into the project: to make women take equal part along with men in every aspect of project decision-making implementation and management. 'Involving women' actually addresses the socio-economic and cultural issues which prevent women from taking equal part, and changing them.

Mainstreaming women would involve: (a) gender-sensitizing the project staff, (b) undertaking gender analysis, (c) preparation of a gender action plan, and (d) implementing the action plan.

Capacity Building

Capacity building is about developing skills in the project staff and the local community members so that they are able to perform certain activities. Every activity/project would require developing skills is, for example, participatory appraisal and planning, nursery raising, pit making, contour line marking, vermiculture, etc.

Once the community level plan has been finalized, capacity building can start. The crucial aspect is who should be selected for capacity-building training. The main factors are, the person: should have a genuine interest in the activities, should be one who will have free time, should have volunteer spirit, and who will remain in the village. Two to three persons from one village should be trained so that at least one trained person continues to be available in the village. An important factor is building capacity equally in women.

Establishing Local Organizations

The project normally forms watershed committees as a forum (and as an agency of the project) to give consent to the project activities proposed by the project authorities and to make the local community cooperate with them to implement the activities. Guidelines are first established how the committees should function and what they have to mobilize as local contribution.

Instead of being an agency of the project, the role of the watershed committees should be to take over, at an early stage of the project, the responsibility for the project at the community level to plan, implement, monitor, evaluate and manage the project, and continue to maintain the project outputs. The initial orientation and capacity building should be to make the local organization play this role.

Establishing Monitoring/Evaluation Plans and Database

Simple and clear outcome indicators must be established by the local communities facilitated by the project staff for every project activity so that (a) baseline data could be established, (b) appropriate records could be maintained, and (c) the impact could be evaluated.

NGO Roles

The roles that are presently assigned to the NGOs originate from the misconception of participation itself. Technocrats and administrators see participation as that the local communities do as defined by the technocrats and administrators. The roles of NGOs are to make the local communities do what the project authorities want them to do.

In contrast, the role of NGOs is to do social engineering to educate, organize and mobilize the community. The NGO roles are: (a) organize innovatively and using the local media awareness generation programmes, (b) facilitate the process of participatory appraisal and planning, (c) facilitate in the capacity-building programmes, (d) involve women, and (e) form and strengthen the local organization.

Preparation of Long-tem and Annual Project-level Plans

Every project, at the time of commencement of the project, has an "approved" project proposal. Legally, this is the project proposal which should be implemented in letter and spirit. If the funding agency had insisted upon a detailed project implementation plan before funding can be approved, then there would exist a detailed plan of operation with list of activities in a time frame. Alternatively, the funding agency might expect a detailed implementation plan immediately after the project commencement.

Some ambitious project managers fit the project area and people into this plan of operation which is implemented more in letter than in spirit. In this situation, the project staff go about "implementing" the activities already listed and decided. Sometimes, PRA is undertaken to "make" people do what has already been decided upon, which is not the role of PRA!!

Implementing an already approved project proposal would defeat the very purpose of participatory planning. Because (a) the push then comes from above, not from people and (b) the review (monitoring) by the project manager is based on how far the project activities listed already have progressed. The staff goes about achieving targets.

This paper argues that (a) the plan prepared at the community level, through a participatory process discussed above, should form the first level of reference to review the progress and (b) a monitoring plan and a monitoring system at the community level should be first established. Participation will be efficient and effective when planning, monitoring and evaluation are kept alive at the community level.

The overall project-level plan obviously can never by village-specific. This is the shortcoming of the GOPP exercise. However, it is an useful exercise to set a boundary to the overall project and overall goal, purpose, result/objectives and major activities. A detailed plan of operation would be implemented and results achieved. Thus, a project-level plan is also an important document as long as it performs the role of a reference document. It is also a dynamic document and it is revised on an annual basis. More importantly, the community-level plans should fall within the overall project-level plan perspective. The community-level plans are approved by the project management based on this fitness.

The community-level planning contributes to the preparation of the overall project-level plan; the reverse is not correct. The project-level plan is final output of the inception phase, and it will have evolved from "below".

There are important benefits in this approach: (a) the project staff having taken active part in the community-level planning and project-level planning would come to "own" the project plan and would know and understand the plan better, (b) there exists a direct link and fitness between the project and community-level plans, and (c) there are no targets for the project staff which they have to achieve in the villages.

Steps for Participatory Watershed Planning

- Organization of a PRA for the entire village;
- Demarcation of mini-watershed areas within the village boundary;
- Organization of a PRA for the mini-watershed areas;
- Organization of PPP at community level to prepare a mini-watershed management plan;
- Organization of PRAs for each intervention and preparation of plans including materials required, budget and persons responsible;
- Organization of GOPPP at the sub-project organization/ micro-watershed level;
- Organization GOPPP at the project organization level;
- Monthly/quarterly/annual review of the plans at the community level and make appropriate changes, additions; and
- Quarterly/annual review of the plans at the project level and prepare on an annual basis plans.

The above steps are based on the following five principles:

- Every village community in the project area should have taken active part in PRAs and in the preparation of the mini-watershed management plans and of plans for each activity;
- Every project staff member should have taken part, at least at the sub-project level, in GOPP exercise which defines the goal, purpose, results, activities, time frame and indicators;
- "Ownership" of the plans is crucial for the local communities and the project staff to commit themselves and material resources to the project;
- Taking part in decision-making and planning contributes to the feeling of "ownership"; and
- The local community takes responsibility to project implementation when it feels that the project is its own.

Conclusion

Participatory approaches are a reverse of the conventional approaches in which technocrats and administrators control decision-making. Participation is a process of empowering the local communities. PRA and GOPP are tools which facilitate them to undertake appraisal, make decisions and prepare plans on their own and using their knowledge and wisdom. Adoption of participatory approaches and tools would require changes in the attitude and outlook of the project authorities and technocrats, and in the systems procedures they have established to control decision-making. Changes in behaviour in project staff and in the system and procedures, thus is a critical prerequisite. Importantly, they should accept a situation of powerlessness. "Ownership" by the local community is a critical prerequisite for project sustainability and this condition could be achieved only when an authentic process of participation takes place that will empower and give control and responsibility to it. Capacity building is a crucial input that would make the local communities capable to make decisions and take responsibility for the project.

20

Contemporary Models of Gandhian Gramswaraj—The Story of Ralegan Siddhi and Hiware Bazar, the Ideal Villages in Ahmednagar District, Maharashtra, India

Jaimaon Varghese

ABSTRACT

Ralegon Siddhi and Hiware Bazar are two model villages in Ahmednagar practising Gandhian philosophy of rural upliftment or Gramswaraj. They are relatively small size villages in the district of Ahmednagar. Today, these villages have brought international fame to the district. The architect of Ralegon Siddhi is the visionary and the renowned social activist, Padmashri Anna Hazare. The founder of Hiware Bazar is Shri Popat Rao Pawar, a daring disciple of Shri Anna Hazare. There are several lessons the social workers, especially the community development professionals can learn from these contemporary models of Gandhian Gramswaraj.

Introduction

In a press release on 9 July 2009 (http://pib.nic.in, Release ID: 49796), the Government of India announced the launch of a new scheme called Pradhanmantri Adarsh Gram Yojana (PMAGY) for the integrated development of Scheduled Castes-dominated villages in the country. The scheme has already been launched in several parts of the country. As a pilot project, it would cover 1000 villages in the initial phase. Under this scheme, each village would receive ₹ 10 lakh over and above the allocations under various Rural Development and Poverty Alleviation Schemes. On successful implementation of the pilot phase, the PMAGY would be extended in more villages in the coming years. It may be recollected that there is a forerunner to this national scheme. It is Adarsh Gram Yojana (AGY), a Government of Maharashtra scheme launched in 1994. AGY is based on the lessons learned from Ralegan Siddhi, the ideal village in Ahmednagar district developed by Padmashri Anna Hazare on Gandhian principles. Implementation of AGY was successfully demonstrated in Hiware Bazar, another model village in Ahmednagar district.

Ralegan Siddhi and Hiware Bazar are two model villages in Ahmednagar practising Gandhian philosophy of rural upliftment or Gramswaraj. They are relatively small size villages in the district of Ahmednagar. Today, these villages have brought international fame to the district. The architect of Ralegan Siddhi is the visionary and the renowned social activist, Padmashri Anna Hazare, who is a hundred per cent Gandhian in words and deeds. The founder of Hiware Bazar is Shri Popat Rao Pawar, a daring disciple of Shri Anna Hazare. The study was conducted by visiting these model villages several times and discussing with various stakeholders of these villages. There are several lessons, the social workers, especially the community development professionals can learn from these contemporary models of Gandhian Gramswaraj.

Padmashri Anna Hazare and Shri Popat Rao Pawar have developed their villages as self-reliant communities through a systematic process of social change through people's participation. They have set role models of dynamic leadership and demonstrated to the world how to realise Gandhian models of Gramswaraj in the contemporary era. Among the methods implemented include participatory processes like social audit and micro-planning, the key strategies of rural reconstruction being practised in these villages are ban of drug abuse, ban of tree felling, control on free grazing of cattle, family planning and *shramdan*. By sustained cooperation and participation of the people, these villages have accomplished a successful water harvesting enterprise. Prosperity and community development were only the by-products of this endeavour. With this achievement, people's capacity for self-determination and self-governance improved. Finally, these model villages attained self-reliance in every sense. Their success stories will definitely contribute to the body of knowledge as well as the skill base of professional social workers who are committed to rural community development.

Gandhian Philosophy of Rural Development—The Literature Review

It is relevant to reflect over what Gandhiji wrote about the significance of rural development during 1920 to 1948. For Gandhi, Gramswaraj was more important than India's political freedom from the foreign rule. Gandhi believed that until and unless, autonomous, self-reliant and sustainable republics are founded in about 700,000 villages across the country, India cannot be considered as an independent nation in real sense. Therefore, Gandhiji wrote extensively on Gramswaraj and Adarsh Gram in *Young India* and *Harijan,* the two periodicals which published exclusively the Gandhian thoughts during the Indian National Movement. A review of Gandhian literature has been done in this section to deepen the understanding of Gandhian philosophy on rural development. There is much for social workers to ponder over Gandhi's invaluable thoughts on rural development. Gandhi's writings are simple and self-explanatory. They require little explanation and interpretations. They are simple in style and strong in spirit. The inspiration we get by reading the Gandhi's quotes cannot be substituted by any other verse. Soul of India is to be sought in the villages, Gandhi said, "I have belief and repeated times without number that India is to be found not in its few cities but in its 700,000 villages. We town-dwellers have believed that India is to be found in its towns and the villages were created to minister to our needs" (*Harijan,* 4-4-1936, p. 63). It is time for the city-dwellers to think about the village life and do something creatively.

There is a great need for rural development professionals who would stay among the villagers and spend time to educate and empower them. In Gandhi's opinion, the cities are capable of taking care of themselves. "It is the villages we have to turn to. We have to disabuse them of their prejudices, their superstitions, their narrow outlook, and we can do so in no other manner than that of staying amongst them and sharing their joys and sorrows and spreading education and intelligent information among them" (*Young India,* 30-4-1931, p. 94). Gandhi was aware of the fact that the cities are living on the prosperity of the villagers. The villagers are growing the food grains, fruits and vegetables and produce milk that are largely consumed by the city-dwellers. On the other hand, a large number of villagers live under utter poverty and starvation. "I have found that the town-dweller has generally exploited the villager; in fact he has lived on the poor villager's subsistence" (*Harijan,* 4-4-1936, pp. 63-64).

Gandhi believed that the cities enjoyed the benefits at the cost of villagers' sacrifice and hard work. It is through self-sacrifice and an option to work for the rural poor that the urban elite can repay the favours received from the rural sector. Here is Gandhi's counselling for rural development workers. "Hitherto the villagers have died in thousand so that we might live. Now we might have to die so that they may live" (*Young India,* 17-4-1924, p. 130). Shri Anna Hazare and Shri Popat Pawar are among those who have made sacrifices of their own lives towards the cause of rural prosperity and thereby contributed to the nation building.

Gandhi advised the youth of the nation to identify with the toiling villagers and learn the lesson of hard work from them. According to Gandhi, everyone should work for his or her own food. Are we willing to share the life of the villagers in true sense? "We must identify ourselves with the villagers who toil under the hot sun and see how we would like to drink water from the pool in which the villagers bathe, wash their clothes and pots, and in which their cattle drink and roll" (*Young India,* 11-9-1924, p. 300). It is not easy to follow the lifestyle of the majority of Indians who toil in the rural areas.

While identifying with the villagers, we must also appreciate the common sense and wisdom of the rural folk. Gandhi had staunch faith in the wisdom of the peasantry. There is so much to learn from the villagers. "The moment you talk to them [the Indian peasants] and they begin to speak; you will find wisdom drops from their lips" (*Harijan,* 28-1-1939, p. 439). Indian peasant is basically spiritual, non-violent, peaceful, tolerant and practical minded.

Gandhi had also believed that the villagers are wise enough to form Gramswaraj, a self-reliant village republic, if given the opportunity and encouragement. "Gandhi is regarded as the first social thinker in India who presented a complete picture of an ideal Indian society based on rural realities, giving thought to every aspect, such as nature of the State and its administration, defense, health, sanitation, housing, education, employment, development of weaker sections and eradication of various social problems such as untouchability, alcoholism, poverty, etc. (Billore, 2010: 338-39). While the world around is running after an urban-oriented development model, Gandhi advocated for a rural model of national development.

Gandhi has great faith in the villagers' ability for Gramswaraj and he had the vision of ideal development model for the nation based on rural reconstruction. He had a dream of village-based republic of India, where each of the country's village is politically free and economically prosperous and self-reliant. "If my dream is fulfilled, and every one of the seven lakhs of villages becomes a well-living republic in which there are no illiterates, in which no one is idle for want of work, in which everyone is usefully occupied and has nourishing food, well-ventilated dwellings, and sufficient Khadi for covering the body, and in which all the villagers know and observe the laws of hygiene and sanitation such a State must have varied and increasing needs, which it must supply unless it would stagnate" (*Harijan,* 30-7-1938, p. 200). Gandhi's dream has been realized in several villages across the country. Such realization is often considered as isolated and exceptional incidents. Ralegan Siddhi and Hiware Bazar are two such ideal villages where the Gandhian vision and dream about Adarsh Gram has been lived out.

It is interesting to note that Gandhi used the word Gramswaraj with a double meaning in the context of Indian National Movement. Gandhi promoted in the concept of *Swaraj*, or 'self-rule', advocating Indian independence from foreign domination. Simultaneously, he also discussed his belief in Gram Swaraj ('village self-rule'), asserting that the Indian village should be self-sufficient and autonomous. Considering that over two-third of Indians are still living in villages today, Gandhi's philosophy is still relevant. Gandhi termed his ideal society as 'Ramrajya', i.e. the kingdom of God on earth. "There will be neither paupers, nor beggars, neither high, nor low, neither millionaire employers nor half-starved employees, neither intoxicating drinks nor drugs. There will be the same respect for women as for men and the chastity and purity of men will be jealously guarded; where there will be no untouchability and where there will be equal respect for all faiths. They will be all proudly, joyously and voluntarily bread labourers". Gandhi's ideal society is predominately a rural society. "India is to be found not in a few cities but in its villages. The real India lies in the villages. If Indian civilization is to make its full contribution to the building up of a stable world order, it is this vast mass of humanity that has to be made to live again. I would say that if the villages perish, India will perish too. India will be no more India. Her own mission in the world will get lost". Gandhi had full faith in the wisdom of the rural people (Billore, 2010: 270-71).

Gandhi had worked out the minute details of a Gramswaraj. Hard work, cattle rearing, recreation, prohibition, education, irrigation, cooperation, *Satyagraha* and compulsory *shramdan* had their own place in Gramswaraj. "My idea of village Swaraj is that it is a complete republic, independent of its neighbours for its own vital wants and yet interdependent for many others in which dependence is necessary. Thus, every village's first concern will be to grow its own food crops, and cotton for its cloth. It should have a reserve for its cattle, recreation and playground for adults and children.... The village will maintain a village theatre, school and public hall. It will have its own waterworks ensuring clean water supply.... Education will be compulsory up to the final basic course. As far as possible, every activity will be conducted on the co-operative basis. There will be no castes such as we have today with their graded untouchability. Non-violence with its technique of *Satyagraha* and non-co-operation will be the sanction of the village community. There will be a compulsory service of village guards who will be selected by rotation from the register maintained by the village" (*Harijan,* 30-7-1938, p. 200). The *Panchasutri* (five-fold principles) of Adarsh Gram—*shramadan*, ban on tree cutting, ban on grazing of cattle in forest or in pasture land, ban on liquor and family planning) formulated by Shri Anna Hazare and implemented in Ralegan Siddhi and Hiware Bazar have their ideal base on Gandhian village Swaraj.

Gandhi's idea on village republic is bold and comprehensive. According to Gandhi, village panchayats should have full powers and little interference from the State. Emphasizing on autonomous village republic is the way to promote participatory model of rural development. "Independence must begin at the bottom. Thus, every village will be a republic or Panchayat having full powers" (*Harijan,* 4-1-1948, p. 500). Rural prosperity begins with the formation of all powerful village panchayat that would self-impose the rules and regulations for self-reliance and sustainable development. Such self-rule of the village panchayat has been demonstrated at Ralegan Siddhi and Hiware Bazar.

Gandhian thought on model village can be summarized by the 19-item constructive programme. The 19-item constructive programme is a unique contribution of Gandhi's ingenuity and imagination to the theory of social reconstruction and peaceful revolution (Parmeshwari Dayal, 2006: 269). Gandhi called his 19-point constructive programme a programme for construction of total or complete independence (*Poorna Swaraj*) consisting of not only political, but social and economic independence as well as through truthful and non-violent means. Social scientists look at it as a programme of social reconstruction aiming at eradication/mitigation of social problems like untouchability, alcoholism, unemployment through khadi and village industries, backwardness of weaker sections such as small farmers, labour, tribes, etc. through specific programmes for them and also aiming at bringing various sections of the society closer to one another through programmes on communal unity, economic equality, national language, etc. (Billore, 2010a: 304). The 19 items on the constructive programme can be classified into three categories, viz. (a) Economic Regeneration—khadi, village industries, cconomic equality, improvement of cattle, kisan and labour; (b) Social Reform—removal of untouchability, prohibition, uplift of women and adivasis, education in health and hygiene, and lepers; and (c) National Character Building—communal unity, village sanitation, basic education, adult education, provincial language, national language and students (Parmeshwari Dayal, 2006: 270-71). A detailed account of each programme has been given by Gandhi and other Gandhians in various contexts and at various times. All these constructive programmes are of course based on the twin Gandhian principles of truth and non-violence. The question of political and economic growth in India was thus intertwined with Gandhi's thesis of social development and of reconstruction of the fragmented rural communities on the basis of his concept of non-violence (Sugata Dasgupta, 1968: 119).

Peace and social harmony are by-products of an ideal Gramswaraj. Village republics are value based. Gandhiji contributed a new concept of non-violent socialism based on human values. The economic structure of Gandhian thought is based on the absence of exploitation, decentralization of producing units, cheaper defense organization, less inequality of income and self-sufficiency among the communities (Palsapure, 1972: 66). Gandhi was stern against corruption of the public offices. According to Gandhi, "a servant of the people cannot accept honours. One who has made service his religion, cannot lust for honour; the moment he does so, he is lost". When someone wanted to honour Gandhi, he exhorted, "I, therefore, beseech you that if you want really to do me a honour, do not give me a shower-bath of addresses and honours. The best way to honour me is to do my behest and to carry my principles into practice" (Tendulkar, 1951: 223-24).

'*Satyagrah*' may be regarded as the collective name of all the methods and techniques of Gandhian Social Work, namely persuasion, auto suffering, fasting, non-cooperation, boycott, civil disobedience, picketing, strikes, etc. All these methods are based on Gandhian values and principles of truth and non-violence (Billore, 2010: 325). A *satyagrahi* is always ready for an honourable settlement with the opponent but he has not to arrive at a compromise with issues which are not moral. As a *satyagrahi* has to be ready even to fight injustice, he is to welcome peace in an honourable manner. He cannot surrender his moral principles. Gandhi believed that in the path of *Satyagraha*, negotiations and compromise are essential at some stage or the other because if they are attempted in the very beginning, the conflict may be avoided (Gaur, 1977: 63). While analyzing Gandhian thought, one can understand that he has staunch belief in the goodness of human nature. According to him, goodness and honesty are essential to human nature. Ignorance and greed often block our perception of our own basic good nature. The effectiveness of *Satyagraha* lies in his unflinching faith in good human nature. "The exploitative attitude is not human but one conditioned and fostered by bourgeois materialism and greed, while the quiescent attitude is of the rebel who tries to escape the bourgeois world and voices his idealist protest against bourgeois greed" (Raj Kumar and Vijendra Kumar, 1999: 104). A *satyagrahi* can change the mind of the oppressor by removing his ignorance at the cost of own suffering.

Rural development which is concerned with economic growth and social justice, improvement in the living standard of the rural people by providing adequate and quality social services and minimum basic needs becomes essential. The present strategy of rural development mainly focuses on poverty alleviation, better livelihood opportunities, provision of basic amenities and infrastructure facilities through innovative programmes of wage and self-employment. Modern concept of Adarshgram refers to sustainable and self-reliant Gramswaraj. The idea of sustainability is relative to the time and space. Some discourse is required to understand the concept of sustainable rural development that Gandhiji envisaged and relevant in modern context. "In recent years, the notion of sustainable development has emerged as a reaction to the highly technological and centralized processes that have governed thinking on development, the green revolution being a classical example. The process of sustainable development envisages that people should not merely participate, but be in charge of their own development. Some initiatives in India (experiments in Ralegan Siddhi and Hiware Bazar in Ahmednagar) have grappled successfully with this complex process, and different models of people-driven development have emerged. Village economy and its development are based on its natural resource and their management of production. Natural resource management, therefore, has to be the key pin for an effective strategy for rural development. Most of the rural development models have therefore considered natural resource management as the means for rural transformation" (Shahaji and Arya, 2004: 208-09). In this regard, sustainable rural development is essentially economic development in tone with the ecological and environmental conservation.

Ahmednagar—The Context of the Study

Ahmednagar District is the largest district in the state of Maharashtra having 5.66 per cent of the area of the state (www.ahmednagar.nic.in). Due to scarce rainfall, Ahmednagar often suffers from drought. The district has a rich historical heritage. Ahmednagar is named after its founder, Ahmed Shah Nizam Shah (1494 A.D.). Numerous Mughal-era buildings dot the environs of the city. Ahmednagar Fort, once considered the second most unimpregnable fort in India, was used by the British to house Jawaharlal Nehru (the first Prime Minister of India) and other Indian nationalists before Indian independence. During his confinement by the British at Ahmednagar Fort, Nehru wrote the famous book *The Discovery of India*.

Ahmednagar has made significant contribution in the field of rural development in the past. Ahmednagar is the birth place of National Social Service Scheme, a Government of India programme for the student community of the higher education. In the year 1961, Prof. S.K. Hulbe, the founder director of CSRD, Ahmednagar, member of Planning Commission and member of Kothari Education Commission recommended to the Government of India regarding National Service Scheme for the students at college and university level. Based on his experience

Table 1: Basic Statistical Information about Ahmednagar District

Item	Unit	Ahmednagar	Maharashtra
Rural population	"000"	3284	55778
Urban population	"000"	804	41101
Total population	"000"	4088	96879
Scheduled Caste population 2001	"000"	485	9881
Scheduled Caste percentage	Percentage	12	10.20
Scheduled Tribe population 2001	Numeric "000"	303	8577
Scheduled Tribe percentage	Percentage	7.5	8.9
Total population percentage:			
Male	Numeric "000"	2106	50401
Female	Numeric "000"	1982	46478
Ratio Male/Female (Female for 1000 Male)		941	922
Density (per sq. km area)	Population	235	315
Literacy (as per census 2001)			
1.Total	Percentage	75.82	76.90
2.Male	Percentage	86.21	86.00
3.Female	Percentage	64.88	67.00
Tahsil	Number	14	353
Panchayat Samities	Number	14	347
Town (as per 2001Census)	Number	18	378
Villages (as per 2001Census)	Number	1581	43711
1. Desert	Number	2	2616
2. Habitated	Number	1579	41095
Area	Sq. KM.	17412	307583
Municipal Corporation	Number	1	22
Nagarparishad	Number	8	222
Cantonment Board	Number	1	7
Gram Panchayat	Number	1310	27949
Police Stations	Number	24	926

Source: www.ahmednagar.nic.in

of implementing the Rural Life Development Project with the support of the students of Ahmednagar college and CSRD in about 100 villages in the district of Ahmednagar, Prof. Hulbe prepared the basic guidelines of the scheme and the National Service Scheme was implemented by the Govt. of India in 1969 as a nationwide programme where hundreds and thousands of students of colleges and universities render their voluntary services towards rural reconstruction activities. Upon the successful implementation of Employment Guarantee Scheme (EGS) of the Government of Maharashtra in various villages in Ahmednagar district such as Hiware Bazar, the scheme has been adopted as a nationwide programme in 2005. With a view to alleviating poverty by providing gainful employment to the poorer sections of the community in rural areas as well as 'C' class municipal councils in Maharashtra State, the Employment Guarantee Scheme (EGS) was started in the year 1972. The State Government has given the statutory support to the guarantee of employment through the enactment of the Maharashtra Employment Guarantee Act, 1977, which has been brought into force from 26 January 1979. The EGS guaranteed that every adult who wanted a job in rural areas were given one, provided that the person was willing to do unskilled manual work on a piece-rate basis. The projects to which EGS employment contributed included moisture conservation and water conservation works (e.g. percolation and storage tanks), soil conservation and land development works, afforestation, roads, and flood protection schemes. Successful demonstration of EGS is visible in several villages in Ahmednagar. EGS had a significant role in the path of transformation of Hiware Bazar the model village in Ahmednagar. In December 2004, a bill was tabled in the Indian Parliament, the National Rural Employment Guarantee Bill, which proposed to extend the EGS to the poorest 150 districts of the country. It became National Rural Employment Guarantee Act in 2005 and today it has become a highly popular and successful scheme under the name of Mahatma Gandhi National Rural Employment Guarantee Act.

Adarsh Gram Yojana is yet another Government of Maharashtra scheme under implementation since 1994 based on the lessons learnt from Ralegan Siddhi, a model village in Ahmednagar transformed by Padmashri Anna Hazare. The transformation of his village Ralegan Siddhi began in the year 1975 based on Gandhian ideals of 'Panchasutri for Adarshgram' such as *shramdan*, ban on tree felling, ban on drug abuse, ban on free grazing and family planning. Since 1989, Hiware Bazar village in Ahmednagar district followed this Gandhian path for rural transformation and in five years, they demonstrated its success. Adarsh Gram Yojana is being implemented in phase by phase by the Government of Maharashtra in various parts of the state. Padmashri Anna Hazare and Shri Popat Rao Pawar are in the steering seats of this scheme. Training centres established at Ralegan Siddhi and Hiware Bazar for imparting training for local body functionaries are the nerve centres for the implementation of this scheme. Government of India has realized the scope of this scheme and adapted the same for national level implementation. A comprehensive idea of Adarsh Gram has been conceived by Government of India in 2010 while launching Pradhanmantri Adarsh Gram Yojana (PMAGY). A model village in the context of Pradhanmantri Adarsh Gram Yojana (PMAGY) is one which has adequate physical and institutional infrastructure, in which minimum needs of all sections of the society are fully met. Sustainability is the key factor of model village. Here are the success stories of both the model villages—Ralegan Siddhi and Hiware Bazar from where the social workers can draw up the practical tips for rural transformation.

Ralegan Siddhi, the Gandhian Model Village

The process of sustainable development envisages that people should not merely participate, but be in charge of their own development. The model for self-reliant and sustainable development has been set at Ralegan Siddhi, the Adarshgram in Ahmednagar district, by its dynamic leader, Padmashri Annasaheb Hazare. When Shri Annasaheb Hazare, a retired army man, first returned to his village in 1975 it was an extremely degraded village. There was a large-scale outward migration, ill health, low productivity and a flourishing business in the illegal distilling of alcohol, resulting into violence especially against women.

Today Ralegan is transformed completely. There is a sense of community living, cooperation and sharing among all the people, and complete self-sufficiency in food grains. Ralegan just demonstrated what village people can do when they take control of their own development. It shows what can be achieved when community interest takes over self-interest. The success formula was *Panchasutri* the five-point programme—ban on open grazing; ban on tree felling; ban on consumption of liquor; family planning; and donation of labour (*shramdan*). Annasaheb began the task of rural reconstruction with his intervention to manage rainwater runoff through watershed development by cheap, local, and maximized use of local resources especially labour. Having started with water management, he went on to include community work to prevent erosion and to promote widespread afforestation. The villagers have been working continuously on this process for about 20 years to demonstrate the tangible output. Thus, long-term continuity is a vital ingredient in the strategy for sustainable development. The role of local body is very important for sustainable development. All major decisions were taken in the Gram Sabha, which has institutionalized a democratic style of functioning.

Village Profile

Ralegan Siddhi is a small village with an area of 982 ha in Parner taluka of Ahmednagar district, Maharashtra, India. It is situated on latitude 19°22′ N and longitude 74°27′ E at an altitude of about 755 m AMSL. It is 87 km of Pune city towards north-east, 5 km away from Pune-Ahmednagar State Highway. It is a drought-prone and resource poor area with annual rainfall ranging between 50-700 mm and temperature varying between 28°C and 44°C. The village is surrounded by small hillocks on the northeast and southern sides. The land is undulating and slopes vary from 3-15 per cent. The soils are shallow. In lower areas, patches of black soils mixed with pebbles are seen but towards the higher areas the soils are inferior and unsuitable for cultivation. In about 70 per cent of the area, the soils are light to medium in structure.

The population of the village is 1,982 living in 310 households (presently estimated to be around 325). The sex-ratio is 902 females per 1,000 males (1,029 in 1971; 1,013 in 1981). The continued decrease in the ratio is explained as the return of male folk to the village with improvement in the socio-economic conditions of the village. Backward classes (Scheduled Castes and Scheduled Tribes) constitute 14.23 per cent of the total population. The level of literacy has gone up from 30.4 per cent in 1971 to 39.65 per cent in 1981 and further to 50.95 per cent in 1991. As of now, according to the villagers, no one in the 15-35 year age group is illiterate.

Marathas of Khatri caste outnumber other castes and constitute nearly two-third of the families. Among others are the backward castes including Mahar, Chamar, Bharhadi, Pardi, Sutar, Barber, Fishermen, Matang, etc. There are only five landless and 13 artisan households in the village. Most of the landholders are small. 51 per cent of the landholders own 1-3 ha land which is about half the total area as well as population of the village. There are only 12 farmers (about 3 per cent) owning more than 6 ha, who own about 18 per cent of the total area. Though the average size of landholding (2.5 ha), appears to be relatively large, considering the poor quality of soils and low productivity levels, the holdings are quite modest. Occupation-wise cultivators are in majority, followed by agricultural labour. Agriculture is the mainstay for majority of the people. Others like grocers, drivers, cobblers, barbers, blacksmiths, broom makers, health workers, teachers, shopkeepers, flour mill operators, welder, and bank workers represent the services and rural artisans.

Problems

Till 1975, prior to intervention by Anna Hazare, the village presented the profile of a poverty-stricken and debt-ridden society. The water level was below 20 m, most of the wells used to dry up during summer and the drinking water had to be fetched from the neighbouring villages. The high rate of surface run off, due to the slope and lack of vegetative cover washed away the top fertile layer of the soils. Barely

20 ha of the village area were under irrigation. As a consequence the agricultural production was too meagre to support and sustain the livelihoods of the people. About 45 per cent of the villagers had a single meal per day and about one-third of the households missed their meals every alternate day. The poor farmers and agricultural labourers forced by their poor economic conditions had only two options—either to migrate to nearby cities of Pune and Mumbai or join the army of labourers working under Employment Guarantee Scheme of the government by commuting a distance of about 22 km daily. Any shortfall in the earnings had to be met by borrowing from the moneylenders (*Sahukars*). The inability to repay the loans often led to further indebtedness and bondage.

An enterprising villager being depressed by his impoverished condition went to the neighbouring village and mastered the technique of distilling liquor by using *'Shindi'* grass which grew in abundance in the area. His success attracted many more in the trade and by 1975 as many as 40 illicit liquor distilling houses came up. The combination of poverty, unemployment, alcoholism, indebtedness, mutual suspicion, use of money and muscle power for malpractices, not only shattered the village economy but also degraded the social and community life. Majority of children were denied access to education—hardly 10 per cent children attended schools and dropout rates were high. It was difficult for girls to step out in village streets which were full of rogues and drunkards. Social strife and tension became routine, conflicts and crimes were common. The devastating drought of 1972 made the situation from bad to worse.

In 1970s, this was the scenario in most of the villages including Hiware Bazar in Ahmednagar district. There was an air of hopelessness and worthlessness in rural life and the educated and the elite youth always desired to migrate to the prosperous cities in the state and the other states. Most of the villages in Ahmednagar district witnessed a sort of brain-drain in 1970s and 80s. Even the parents did not want their educated youth to remain in the village, but encouraged them to look for their fortune in the cities. No one seemed to have faith in Gandhian ideals of Gramswaraj. In this context, in 1975, Shri

Anna Hazare returned to his ancestral village, Ralegan Siddhi after the completion of his tenure in the service of Indian Army.

Anna Hazare and the Rural Reconstruction

Hazare's house was in a hamlet just half a kilometre away from the centre of the village. Hazare avoided going to the heart of the village due to its pathetic condition. In 1975, when he returned from military service, he felt helpless, as he could not do anything to change the conditions prevailing in the village. Having decided to dedicate his life for social cause after his retirement from military service, thanks to his miraculous escape from death during Indo-Chinese war (1962), Hazare taxed his brains on how to solve the manifold problems of his village. He remembered that Late Mr. Vilasrao Salunkhe had started experiments in watershed development and water management in some villages near Saswad in Pune district in 1972. His work used to be frequently discussed in informal gatherings everywhere. So, Hazare visited his project and was inspired. On his return from Pune, he made up his mind to begin his mission of rural transformation by starting water harvesting projects.

Shri Anna Hazare started his work alone. Gradually, the villagers understood the sincerity and selflessness of his work and joined hands with him. On undertaking of the watershed development work in the village, Hazare started supervising the work at sites from dawn to dusk, without taking any remuneration. He considered it as social work; and day by day his experience and knowledge was building up. Shri Anna Hazare was convinced of the value of *shramdan* and continuously motivated the villagers by his own example of *shramdan*. He remained unmarried and lived in a small room attached to the village temple (Yadav Baba). Gradually, Shri Anna Hazare rose to the leadership of the village who insisted the Gandhian principles of rural development. *Panchasutri* was his formula for village transformation. He trained every villager to follow *Panchasutri—shramdan*, ban of drug abuse and alcohol, ban on tree felling, ban of free grazing to protect newly growing vegetative cover of the village and family planning. Most of the water harvesting structures was acquired by the villagers through 100 per cent *shramdan*.

With his experience and knowledge, Shri Anna Hazare constructed many water harvesting structures with people's participation, such as 48 *nallah* bunds, 5 cement check dams and 16 Gabion structures. The villagers under Hazare's guidance also undertook fodder development, continuous contour trenches and loose boulder structures on 500 acres of land. The watershed development work helped in conserving each drop of rainwater in the village itself and in recharging the groundwater aquifers. This ultimately raised the water level. In the same village where earlier it was not possible to cultivate more than 300-350 acres of land for one crop, now the villagers are harvesting two crops in 1500 acres of land.

Earlier only 300 litres of milk was sold from the village. Now the milk production has gone up to 4000 litres. This milk is purchased by cooperative and private dairies. This brings in ₹ 1.3 to 1.5 crores (13 to 15 million) annually to the village. The dairy business has flourished as a subsidiary to agriculture which has provided a new income generation avenue to the unemployed youths of the village. The per capita income of the villagers has increased from ₹ 225 to ₹ 2500. After the economic transformation of the village, villagers constructed buildings worth ₹ 1 crore (10 million) for school, hostel and gymkhana and renovated the old village temple through financial contributions and *shramdan*. Today the villagers have completely given up brewing of liquor. Nobody sells liquor in the village. Further, the shopkeepers do not sell cigarettes, *beedies* and tobacco too. Mass marriages are arranged in the village in order to curb expenditure. This has helped in removing caste barriers and promoting social cohesiveness.

Like any other village in India including Ralegan Siddhi, there was a social problem of untouchability. Today people of all castes and creeds live together in peace like members of the same family. The consecutive droughts led to non-payment of bank loans taken by the Dalit community for agriculture purposes. The bank decided to sell their mortgaged land to recover the loans. At this critical time, rest of the villagers decided to toil on the farmlands of Dalits and repay the loan by harvesting crops. The villagers cultivated their land in 1983-84 and

1984-85 through *shramdan* (voluntary labour), repaid the bank loan, and saved their land.

In the last 35 years, many institutions and cooperatives like Gram Panchayat, Cooperative Consumer Society, Cooperative Credit Society, Cooperative Dairy, Educational Society, Women's Organization and Youth Organization, with different mandates are operating in Ralegan Siddhi. Some critics of Ralegan Siddhi complain that till date no elections were held for the selection of members of Panchayat Raj institutions. Shri Anna Hazare says that the members were selected unanimously by the villagers in the Gram Sabha. The Gram Sabha has emerged as a powerful forum for taking collective decisions at the village level. All the developmental programmes are implemented in the village after taking consent of the Gram Sabha.

Since last 25 years, thousands of visitors, Indian as well as foreign, have been visiting Ralegan Siddhi to study the impact of watershed development. They include researchers, academicians, farmers, government officials, people's representatives and students. A training institute to impart training in watershed development has been established at Ralegan Siddhi. So far, about 17-18 thousand people from different states of India have been trained at the Training Centre on Watershed Development. After the success of watershed development programme in Ralegan Siddhi, Hazare endeavoured to replicate his model in the neighbouring four villages. The results were encouraging. Now the same project is being replicated in 80-85 villages of Maharashtra under aegis of Adarsh Gram Yojana. Shri Popat Rao Pawar of Hiware Bazar is the ally of Padmashri Anna Hazare in this enterprise.

Achievements

Achievements of Ralegan Siddhi can be summarized as successful abolition of social evils like alcoholism, dowry, corruption and the caste system; successful implementation of voluntary code of ethics, the *Panchasutri* of Adarsh Gram; social acceptance of the use of public toilets for biogas; successful implementation of development schemes through cooperatives with the support of government and bank loans (no aid is taken either from national or foreign agencies); regeneration of watershed resources through people's participation, a living example of watershed development and management; successful involvement of the people in formation of development schemes in a democratic way through village meetings showing that participatory sustainable development is possible; non-degrading and sustainable utilization of natural resources as well as generating alternative sources of income to enhance the economy at family and village levels; development of agriculture and allied sectors by better farming practices and cropping patterns, judicious use of water by introducing drip irrigation system, yield enhancement, etc. as a result the village where nearly three-fourth population was below poverty line, has become self-sufficient and is surplus in food grains. The quality of life of women and people belonging to backward classes improved appreciably because of special attention and focus.

The case study shows the success of Gandhian approach to people's participation in watershed management (*shramdan*). Since 1975, this has resulted into participation of all the 325 village families in renovation of a temple and stopping illicit liquor distillation. Ingenious water harvesting enterprises in four small watersheds by construction of many check dams, plantation of five hundred thousand forest trees and controlled grazing raised the groundwater level from 20 m depth to 6.5 m. The success has made the Government of India to request the leader Padmashri Anna Hazare to take up the programme in 300 talukas of Maharashtra state.

The major elements responsible for the successful people's participation in watershed management at the Ralegan Siddhi village were the involvement of all sections of society, holistic and sustained development over long time (10-20 years), use of simple, appropriate but efficient technology for watershed management and the primacy of village assembly in decision-making. The salient feature of this model of people's participation in rural reconstruction is that it is driven by a strong and highly motivated local leader which is the case of most Gandhian models of development. Padmashri Anna Hazare has set the role model for Gandhian social workers. His greatest investment was his own honest, hardworking, genuine and positive personality. His involvement in various social issues and mass movements in the nation is nothing but his natural reaction as a responsible citizen of the country.

Success Story of Hiware Bazar Village

The Gandhian ideal of Gramswaraj has also been achieved at Hiware Bazar 20 years after the success of Ralegan Siddhi. Hiware Bazar, the 'Adarsh gaon', is a unique model based on the twin principles of self-governance and self-reliance. At these places, the most vulnerable rural communities were made aware of their rights and choices as Indian citizens. People were enabled to control local bodies as policymakers at the grassroots level. "The Gram Sabha was the force behind village regeneration. It took decisions consensually and people listened." "Villages and the government should be partners in development; but villages must be in the driver's seat", says Pawar. Hiware Bazar's strong, participatory institutional set-up has facilitated success. The Gram Sabha has the power to decide on a range of issues, including identifying sites for water and types of crops to be cultivated. The village voluntary body is its arm. The village's biggest innovation is its water budget. During 2003-04, there was a drought in the district and there was a drinking water scarcity. Hiware Bazar was the only village in Nagar block, which did not need tankers. "That year, our village did not cultivate any major crop like wheat, bajra and had to switch to drip irrigation for crops like tomatoes and onions", Pawar says (Neha Skhuja, 2008: 30-31). State got its first National Productivity Award due to the works done in Hiware Bazar.

Village Profile

Hiware Bazar is situated in the Ahmednagar district of Maharashtra in the rain shadow area of the Sahyadri Range. The average annual rainfall in the district is 579 mm, though this is both erratic and uneven [Government of Maharashtra, 1991]. Out of the total geographical area of the village which is 976.84 hectares, 795.23 hectares is cultivable. Pasture land is 6.75 ha and irrigated land is 100.40 ha. Number of functioning wells is 190. Slope of the watershed is 3 to 25 per cent. About 500 ha is arable and it is divided into three micro watersheds. Of this 70 ha is the forest and, which has been developed while working with close cooperation with the forest department. Presently, its entire management is village's responsibility. The department even does not have their guard to protect the reserves. In 1994, joint forest management (JFM) programme was brought to the village and the results are evidently visible to everyone. Under JFM and EGS water and soil conservation works were taken up in the upper reaches.

The population of Hiware Bazar is 1,150 (2001). The population is relatively homogeneous in terms of caste, an important factor in facilitating collective action. As in other regions of western Maharashtra, Marathas constitute the dominant caste (185 out of the 205 households). Out of 217 households only 12 are landless.

Problems

Drought and famine of the region affected very badly the village. Unrestricted grazing removed the green cover of the available forest land. There was no water harvesting structures to prevent rain drain in the hills. The wells got dry and the water table went down due to continuous exploitation of the ground water through borewells. Continuous draught and famines made the agricultural activities unprofitable. The direct adverse impact was visible in the form of migration of families to meet their basic survival needs. Those who did not have any urban skills for a successful migration to the cities remained in the village incurring heavy debts and land mortgages. 22 liquor shops and the bad habits of gambling and fighting eclipsed the village and its progress restricting the inhabitants. Soon the village earned the title of criminal village. All the government functionaries as well as the government school teachers considered posting at Hiware Bazar as punishment transfers.

Educated youth never remained in the village. After completing post-graduation, the parents did not wish Shri Popat Rao Pawar to come back to Hiware Bazar, but compelled him to settle down in Pune or Mumbai. However, some of his friends, who had faith in his leadership qualities, invited him to come back to the village and contest the Panchayat election.

Shri Popat Rao Pawar and the Rural Reconstruction

In 1989, Shri Popat Rao Pawar completed the Master of Commerce Degree from New Arts College, Ahmednagar. He spent his leisure in playing cricket, where he excelled up to state level. In 1989, the State Govt. declared elections for village Panchayats in which he was elected and became the Sarpanch for five years. Popat Pawar is the force behind all the changes that transformed Hiware Bazar since 1989.

On 26 January 1990 when the Gram Sabha met for the first time under the chairmanship of Shri Pawar identified several crucial needs of the village. Improving the educational facilities of the village, providing fodder for cattle, providing irrigation for agriculture, providing safe quality drinking water, providing health facilities, improving village roads, providing electricity for farm pumps, and increasing local employment were those needs identified for time-bound action.

"The Villagers decided to give priority to Education. One Educated girl or boy could change the home. One educated home could change the village. And one educated village could change the management of its water resources and agriculture", says Shri Pawar. The school in the village was not functioning well in the beginning. Teachers appointed by the education department were not sincere and dedicated. They seldom come regularly and attend the classes punctually. They considered transfer to Hiware Bazar as punishment posting. In order to improve the quality of teaching, the villagers decided to close down the school, until the education department appointed good teachers. Government bent to the villagers' demands. Gradually, the educational status of the village improved. The Primary school was extended into a High School from 5th class to 10th class. 18 villagers donated their own land for school building and playground. Eventually, coupled with adult education programme, the ratio of literacy in the village grew from 30 per cent to 95 per cent by 1994.

On 15 August 1994, the Hiware Bazar village Gram Sabha established the "Yashwant Krishi Gram and Watershed

Development Trust" for implementing watershed development programmes in the village. Funds were drawn from employment guarantee scheme and joint forest management to manage the water harvesting programmes. Twelve agencies were engaged in water harvesting projects. However, the Gram Sabha's plan was implemented. Entire monitoring of the programmes was done by the Gram Panchayat. Voluntary labour of the villagers augmented to the project activities. The total cost of watershed programme sanctioned by Govt. of Maharashtra state was ₹ 6.60 million and the villagers of Hiware Bazar contributed ₹ 2.10 million through *shramdan*. Activities undertaken included contour bunding, continuous contour trenching on hill slopes and planting of local, hardy trees, bushes and grasses over the watershed. Under these schemes, about 52 earthen bunds, two percolation tanks, 33 loose stone bunds were constructed. About nine check dams have also been constructed in a series on the downstream *nallah*. New constructions and repairs of loose boulder bunds, cement bunds, farm bunds, farm tanks and percolation tanks have also been undertaken from time to time.

Along with the implementation of water harvesting project, in 1995, the Adarsh Gaon Yojana was launched. Hiware Bazar was selected as the village that could be developed as the model village in the taluka. The village then started implementing the programmes and activities of Adarsh Gram Yojana (Ideal Village Scheme). Acceptance and implementation of *Panchasutri* (five Gandhian principles of rural development) was the essential aspect of Adarsh Gaon Yojana. *Panchasutri* is important for self-reliance and sustainability of the village. They are *shramadan*—ban on tree cutting; ban on grazing of cattle in forest or in pasture land; ban on liquor and family planning. The Gram Sabha added to *Panchasutri* five more principles based on consensus. The additional five rules for village development were ban on using a borewell for irrigation, ban on cultivating water intensive crops such as banana and sugarcane, ban on selling of land to outsiders, ban on any feeling of full and private ownership of groundwater occurring in individual farms and use of borewells only for drawing drinking water. In fact, these additionally self-imposed rules have made Hiware Bazar distinct village and on the fast track to become *Adarsh Gram* in a very short period.

In the process of village transformation through the implementation of Adarsh Gram Yojana, the community experienced positive changes. There was an increase in the employment opportunities available for the unemployed and the underemployed villagers, productive use of leisure and lean seasons, improvement in the hardworking nature of the villagers, reduction in soil erosion (no silting in reservoirs), improvement in the ecology of the village, availability of more water for irrigating high value crops, economic stability and corresponding improvement in living standard, better housing, positive social change and thrift. Increased cooperation and mutual trust among the villagers were demonstrated in women's thrift groups (SHG), women's dairy society, *Bhajini Mandal* (singing *kirtans*), youth clubs, cooperative societies and cooperative farming. Common crematorium, common drinking water source and adoption of 'one family, one child' concept were other achievements.

The spirit of cooperation and sharing grew among the villagers. During the 'Ganpathy Utsava', instead of many idols, the entire village got one idol and saved about ₹ 21,000, which were gifted to the wife of a Kargil martyr living in the neighbouring village. Attitudes of the villagers have significantly changed. Solidarity and cooperation of the villagers were demonstrated in *'Samodayik Kheti'* (cooperative farming). Shortage of agricultural labour was solved through cooperative farming. People stopped employing agricultural labour from outside. Instead, two or three families work collectively in each others farm. While solving the problem of labour, this kind of farming created an environment of social cohesion, where people readily come together and work together.

During the Adarsh Gram Yojana decade (1995-2004), the village witnessed significant progress in various sectors. Hiware Bazar started reaping economic harvests of water conservation. Water table rose from 70-80 ft to 20-25 ft. One can draw water through a hand pump in any part of the village from 20-25 ft from beneath the earth. Crops grown are jawar, bajra, wheat, onion, potato, and vegetables along with floriculture and horticulture. The village is witnessing a change in cropping pattern from millets like jowar and bajra to onion, potato and horticulture. The village is maintaining a patch of land where 100 different species of plants are duly preserved.

Area under irrigation during season increased 3.18 times (250 to 795.23 hectares). During summer, it increased 10.28 times (7 to 72 hectares). Use of improved seeds increased 10 times (53 to 548 hectares). Number of wells increased 2.4 times (97 to 318). Use of electric pumps increased 2.25 times (87 to 280). Grass production has gone up from 1500 metric to 6000 metric tonnes. The diary sector has also registered a remarkable improvement. Milk production increased 21 times (140 to 5000 litres per day). Each village resident earns almost double of most of the country's rural population. Annual Per Capita Income increased from ₹ 832 to ₹ 30,000 ($ 600), i.e. about 30 times. According to recent press coverage, there are 54 millionaires in this village. Thirty-five families, who have migrated to Mumbai and Pune, have returned.

Today people from every corner of the country visit Hiware Bazar to learn the lessons of Adarsh Gram on Gandhian model. People from far and wide have also paid visit to the village. Delegates from 122 nations have so far visited Hiware Bazar. The village and Shri Pawar its Sarpanch have won several honours and awards so far, including the National Agricultural Award, National Productivity Award and AGRI GOLD Award and "Certificate of Honour" from the International Association of Hydrogeologists (I.A.H.). The Government of Maharashtra has now appointed Shri Popat Rao Pawar as the Chief of its "Ideal Village Programme" (Adarsh Gram Yojana) under which 300 villages are to be developed on Ralegan Siddhi and Hiware Bazar's pattern. Selection of 100 villages has already done to replicate the Adarsh Gram. Along with Padmashri Anna Hazare, the founder of Gandhian model, Adarsh Gram, Shri Pawar is busy making concrete plans to implement Adarsh Gram Yojana in the selected villages. Meanwhile the Government of India has come up with National programme of Adarsh Gram in the pattern of Ralegan Siddhi and Hiware Bazar in 2010.

Pradhanmantri Adarsh Gram Yojana

A comprehensive idea of Adarsh Gram has been conceived by Government of India in 2010 while launching Pradhanmantri Adarsh Gram Yojana (PMAGY). A model village in the context of Pradhanmantri Adarsh Gram Yojana (PMAGY) is one which has adequate physical and institutional infrastructure, in which minimum needs of all sections of the society are fully met; they live in harmony with each other, as also with the environment, and a village which is progressive and dynamic. These villages should be covered with all the facilities necessary for dignified living, creating thereby an environment in which all its residents are enabled to utilise their potential to the fullest.

Pradhanmantri Adarsh Gram Yojana is in its implementation phase. It is an ambitious project covering most of the aspects of the Gandhian 19-point rural reconstruction. PMAGY consists of 24 points. Unless it is successfully implemented in some villages as per the guidelines, and the impacts are evaluated after its completion, we cannot rightfully criticize its conception and implementation. It will take not less than three to five years to document any tangible impact of the scheme. For, the scheme is just introduced in five states in India. It can be seen that the scheme is being implemented by the Ministry of Social Justice and Empowerment focusing the SC-concentrated areas of the country. It would have been better if the scheme was monitored by the Ministry of Rural Development. Convergence is a fundamental feature of the scheme. Since a gap funding of ₹ 10 lakhs is involved in the implementation of the scheme, this is just another scheme that consider the recipient a beneficiary who is dependent on the donor. Does it really empower the community? Since Gramswaraj is the ideal which is relevant to all the villages in India, it may be tried with more prosperous villages also, where the real issues are people's participation in local governance, social auditing, micro planning, etc.

Learning for Social Workers from Ralegan Siddhi and Hiware Bazar

Ralegan Siddhi and Hiware Bazar have demonstrated participatory model of rural community development. Rural development professionals should believe in participatory development and promote the same in the villages where they choose to work. Involvement and participation of the people is possible provided there is a committed and sincere leadership to educate, organize and motivate the people for the attainment of a common goal. Voluntary action either by an individual or people is an extremely vital factor to promote, facilitate and catalyze people's participation in sustainable village development. A mix of commitment with flexibility, sensitivity, innovativeness and autonomy are essential for success. Holistic approaches to people's participation in sustainable development are necessary for involving people wholeheartedly. The approach being employed must have the potential to generate the spirit of cooperation, caring and sharing, adjustment, harmony, self-help, self-reliance and special emphasis on the resource poor farmers and women. Need-based planned initiatives and their proper prioritization by the people themselves through democratic decisions with focus on the poorest and weakest and proper consideration for gender issues ensures better and fuller participation. Once they come together, they talk, discuss, plan and act collectively and share the costs and benefits in a just manner.

Rural reconstruction and transformation must begin with positive interventions in the environment and ecology of the villages. The basic components of environment, particularly land, water and vegetation are the vital links to bring rural people together as their livelihoods are closely dependent on these natural resources.

Leadership has no relationship with educational qualifications. Anna Hazare is a 7th pass retired military truck driver. Shri Popat Rao Pawar, an M.Com drew inspiration from Padmashri Anna Hazare. Rural leadership essentially demands a high degree of selflessness, egalitarian attitude, foresight and humane virtues to win the trust of the people. Moral cleansing is a necessary step to remind people of their moral and social obligations as well as to sensitize them for community/collective action. Rich and poor, high and low, men and women can cooperate with each other if there is a sound reason and shared concern. Secular and sincere leadership has a creative role in this regard. Under such leadership, people themselves can develop their moral codes for cooperation. *Shramdan* is a no cost method to bring people together for common good.

Community organization must depend on the expertise of the local community. People understand their environment much better than anybody else from outside. Hence, people's participation is an essential element and pre-requisite for, any development initiative to be successful. Hence, it needs to be designed into development programmes from the beginning. The initiatives to mobilize people should be people/community and place specific. Any kind of generalization may be harmful. The weak, poor and women need special consideration and concessions for their fuller participation. The efforts for participatory watershed development must aim at the improvement in the quality of life of the people and should be designed for people first.

Conclusion

Gandhiji had the dream of Adarsh Gram. Ralegan Siddhi and Hiware Bazar are the two model villages in Ahmednagar district, Maharashtra that have realized the Gandhian dream in a way relevant today. *Panchasutri* is the five-fold strategy devised by Padmashri Anna Hazare for rural reconstruction in Ralegan Siddhi. *Panchasutri,* based on Gandhian ideal of rural reconstruction, is important for self-reliance and sustainability of the village. They are *shramadan*, ban on tree cutting, ban on grazing of cattle in forest or in pasture land, ban on liquor and family planning. While Ralegan Siddhi achieved the excellence through *Panchasutri,* the Gram Sabha of Hiware Bazar added to *Panchasutri* five more principles for a fast track success. The additional five rules for village development were ban on using a borewell for irrigation, ban on cultivating water intensive crops such as banana and sugarcane, ban on selling of land to outsiders, ban on any feeling of full and private ownership of groundwater occurring in individual farms and use of borewells only for drawing drinking water. These are the rules hard to follow, but surely lead to success, if sustained. Both the villages sustained their efforts in the right direction for over 10 years before reaping the concrete benefits. Finally, they achieved self-reliance and the path of sustainability which could be replicated in other villages. The greatest lessons that we learn from Ralegan Siddhi and Hiware Bazar are the lessons of sustained efforts towards sustainable development through participatory governance. They are models of participatory development. The faith in the wisdom of peasants is to be emphasized. What social workers need to concentrate is their participatory approach to rural development.

REFERENCES

Billore, S.R. (2010). Gandhi's Perception of an Ideal Society in Gracious Thomas (Ed.) (2010), *Origin and Development of Social Work in India,* New Delhi: IGNOU, School of Social Work.

——. (2010a). Gandhi's Charter of Social Reconstruction in Gracious Thomas (Ed.) (2010), *Origin and Development of Social Work in India,* New Delhi: IGNOU, School of Social Work.

——. (2010b). Gandhian Social Work: Methods and Techniques in Gracious Thomas (Ed.) (2010), *Origin and Development of Social Work in India,* New Delhi: IGNOU, School of Social Work.

——. (2010c). Gandhian Social Work: The Historical Perspective in Gracious Thomas (Ed.) (2010), *Origin and Development of Social Work in India,* New Delhi: IGNOU, School of Social Work.

Dasgupta, Sugata (1968). Gandhian Concept of Nonviolence and its Relevance today to Professional Social Work, *The Indian Journal of Social Work*, XXIX, 2, July, Mumbai: TISS Dept of Publication.

Dayal, Parmeshwari (2006). *Gandhian Theory of Social Reconstruction,* New Delhi: Atlantic Publishers and Distributors.

Gaur, V.P. (1977). *Mahatma Gandhi A Study of His Message of Nonviolence,* New Delhi: Sterling Publishers Private Ltd.

http://en.wikipedia.org

http://gandhiphilosophy.blogspot.com/2009/08/rural-development.html retrieved on 14 November 2011.

http://hiware-bazar.epanchayat.in

http://nariphaltan.virtualave.net/gandhiseminar.pdf retrieved on 14 November 2011.

http://nrega.nic.in

http://nrsl.wordpress.com/2005/04/04/hiware-bazaar retrieved on 14 November 2011.

http://pib.nic.in/newsite/erelease.aspx?relid=49796 dated 9 July 2009.

http://rural.nic.in

http://socialjustice.nic.in/pdf/pmagyguidelines.pdf

http://www.annahazare.org/Ralegan-siddhi.html retrieved on 14 November 2011.

http://www.breds.org.in/gandhi.html retrieved on 14 November 2011.

http://www.indiavideo.org/text/gandhi-for-rural-reconstruction-95.php retrieved on 14 November 2011.

http://www.lifepositive.com/spirit/masters/mahatma-gandhi/gandhi.asp retrieved on 14 November 2011.

http://www.maharashtra.gov.in/pdf/tenthPlan/Chapter20.pdf retrieved on 17 November 2011.

http://www.mkgandhi.org

http://www.mkgandhi-sarvodaya.org

http://www.nariphaltan.org/gandhitalk.pdf retrieved on 14 November 2011.

http://www.ncri.in/html/gramsevakendra.html retrieved on 14 November 2011.

http://www.nextindia.org/index.php/2009/07/04/swaraj-story-of-hiware-bazar retrieved on 14 November 2011

http://www.rainwaterharvesting.org/rural/Hirve.htm retrieved on 14 November 2011.

http://www.rainwaterharvesting.org/rural/Ralegan.htm retrieved on 14 November 2011.

http://www.telegraph.co.uk/earth/earthcomment/geoffrey-lean/8081883/Hiware-Bazar-putting-a-price-on-nature.html retrieved on 14 November 2011.

http://www.thebetterindia.com/2264/hiware-bazar-model-village-india retrieved on 14 November 2011.

http://www.yehhailife.com/2010/10/26/hiware-bazar-an-indian-villages-journey-from-poverty-to-riches retrieved on 14 November 2011.

Mishra, B. (1993). *People's Participation in Sustainable Use and Management of Agriculture Resources: A Case Study of Ralegon Siddhi*, PCSD/FARM, RAS/93/067, ANGOC, Manila, Philippines.

Palsapure, P.Z. (1972). Gandhiji's Ideas on Social and Economic Life and its Progress, *Proceedings of the Seminar on Gandhian Thought*, Pune: Pune University Press.

Raghav, Gaiha (2006). *The Maharashtra Employment Guarantee Scheme* in Policy Brief February 2006, Inter-Regional Inequality Facility-sharing ideas and policies across Africa, Asia and Latin America, New Delhi: University of Delhi, Faculty of Management Studies and Katsushi Imai, School of Economic Studies, University of Manchester, UK (www.odi.org.uk/inter-regional_inequality).

Raj Kumar and Vijendra Kumar (1999). *Mahatma Gandhi: Life, Ideology and Thoughts—A Vision for 21st Century*, Jaipur: Mangal Deep Publication.

Shahaji Phand and Arya, H.P.S. (2004). Adarsh Gaon Yojana—Way towards Gandhi's dream village: self-sufficient, prosperous and peaceful, *Journal of Rural Development*, Vol. 26, No. 2, Hyederabad: National Institute of Rural Development.

Skhuja, Neha (2008). *Hiware Bazar Calling, Down to Earth*, January, New Delhi: Centre for Science and Environment.

Tendulkar, D.G. (1951). *Mahatma Life of Mohandas Karamchand Gandhi*, Vol. I, Govt. of India: Ministry of Information and Broadcasting (rev ed. 1960).

21

Satisfaction Motives of Pilgrim Community

Sameeksha Sharma

ABSTRACT

Pilgrimage is one of the oldest and most basic forms of community mobility and its political, social, cultural and economic implications have always been, and continue to be, substantial. This study aims to examine the key conceptualisations and gaps in the scholarship on satisfaction motives of pilgrim community. The present paper is a literature review of researches done on social psychological and economic motives of satisfaction of community sentiments. The 'pilgrim' and 'pilgrimage' as subject matter covers the interest areas of how community over the period of time has changed and what are the present-day requirement of the society and culture. The detailed analysis presents the trends of past and present focus of research-literature on pilgrim-motive and satisfaction. It has also put forth the gaps and potential areas where the scholars have to ponder.

Introduction

A pilgrimage is a special journey made to some sacred place as an act of religious devotion. It also gives opportunity to travel across the boundaries of culture and geography. For this it is considered to be a false friend of tourism. The triad of religion, tourism and occupation is an important business gateway of tourism industry. In fact, the modern reality has demonstrated the increasing importance of phenomena such as 'multifunctional journeys' in which the same displacement has several aims including religious-social journeys and cultural-historical pilgrimage in the packages offered by travel agencies. However, the debate of faith that who is a better pilgrim may sometime devalue the idea of multifunctional journeys and the pure spiritual motive of tough-travel or pilgrim-suffering may lead. Sometimes it depends upon the socio-cultural factors of the pilgrim place and pilgrim both (Murthy, 2008). The business world has a continuous need to understand the expectations and demands of the stakeholders. Then it becomes important, to understand the motivation of pilgrim and to know the factors leading to pilgrim satisfaction in the changing scenario. The academic researches on pilgrim-satisfaction have put forth various dimensions, which in turn points towards issues of changing and continuing concepts, their operationalisation and methodology as gaps and areas for further exploration. As a part of study on Motives of Pilgrim Satisfaction, this paper aims to review the key conceptualisations and gaps in the related scholarships.

Review of Literature

The paper examines the previous and present trend of literature available from 1958 onwards by reviewing the objectives, methodology and findings on motives of pilgrim satisfaction. The reviewed literature is multidisciplinary, where pilgrim and pilgrimage as subject matter covers geography, psychology, consumer behaviour. Religious places or destinations are the interest areas of sociology, cultures studies, history, marketing and also geography. Published researches on tourism studies have also been examined, as they bridge for religion and occupation.

The broad objective of the review of studies is to understand the key assumptions, methodology-adopted and the findings for the basic question of "why people go for pilgrimage?" in order to frame the design of future research problem. For that the sub-objectives are required for in-depth inquiry.

The sub-objectives of the literature-review are as follows:

(a) To understand the need of study on motives and satisfaction of pilgrim.

(b) To understand the key concepts and their standardization for the purpose of operationalization.

(c) To know the past and present trends by analyzing theoretical framework, objectives, findings and methodology over the period of time.

(d) To find out gaps in the present literature and the scope of future researches.

Need of Study on Motives and Satisfaction of Pilgrim

Emphasizing on the need of researches on pilgrim satisfaction, scholars have argued that if the organizers realize and identify the critical factors that influence satisfaction of pilgrims they can take appropriate action in the present and future researches. Many agencies like government, organizing committees, private players involved in organizing and marketing religious events spend huge amount of money every year. If organizers have to judiciously spend the money, imperative is the knowledge of pilgrim satisfaction. If they can identify the key factors which influence the pilgrim satisfaction, resources can be diverted accordingly. Also, many agencies would like to organize events on regular basis at the behest of the pilgrims. For this, they need to ensure that the arrangements for the current events are satisfying. If pilgrims are satisfied with the arrangements, positive word of mouth spreads and the propensity of the pilgrims' recommendation of the events to others would increase. Satisfaction of pilgrims is an indication of the quality of services rendered by the event organizers. It acts as a yardstick for measurement of the success of the event by the organizers. The responsibility of organizing and managing mega religious events to some extent remains on the government. If government fails to provide adequate facilities at the events, then it has to face a wrath of the public and it may affect government popularity. In fact, worldwide, understanding key variables influencing the pilgrim satisfaction is still inadequate in spite of a large body of literature available on tourist satisfaction like Pizam and Taylor

(1993); Ryan, C. (1997); Choi and Chu (2000), and Ibrahim and Gill (2000), suggesting scope of future researches.

Conceptual Framework in the Literature Definitional Issues

In order to understand motives of pilgrim satisfaction, studies have put forth the standardized as well as the operational definitions of pilgrimage. Though emphasizing on standard definition to promote clarity in communication and for establishing relationships among phenomena of pilgrimage studies, scholars have been facing lot of ambiguous issues. These difficulties were highlighted in the studies done in the decade of 80s.

Consider the following three definitions:

Definition 1: A journey to a sacred place as an act of religious devotion (Skyes, 1982: 776).

Definition 2: Pilgrimage involves three factors: a holy place; attraction of individuals or crowds to this place; a specific aim, i.e. to obtain some spiritual or material benefit (Bradon, 1970: 501).

Definition 3: The term pilgrimage is used in at least three senses. (1) There is first the "interior pilgrimage", "the journey of the soul" in a lifetime of growth from spiritual infancy to maturity. (2) There is, second, the literal pilgrimage to some sacred place as a paradigm of the intent of religion itself. This literal journey may be called "extroverted mysticism" (Turner, 1973). (3) Finally, every trek to one's local sanctuary is a pilgrimage in miniature insofar as it acts out on a small scale and new community which pilgrimage in general affords (Crim, 1981: 569).

These definitions possess some common and individual concepts such as—distance of movement and motivation.

Distance of Movement

One of the most basic concepts in a definition of pilgrimage is movement. However, the concern for the minimum distance required for the movement is the primary definitional problem. Certainly, the popular conceptualization of pilgrimage regards the movement as being longer than the local travel. Furthermore, most pilgrimage scholars including the Turners have insisted that going on a pilgrimage involves movement away from the 'local' environment (Turner and Turner, 1978). Excluding local journeys from the definition of pilgrimage is consistent with the general meanings of "procession" and "circumambulation". Conceptually, however, long processions and circumambulations seem to merge into short pilgrimages. This poses a question that whether the movements from Mecca to Mina and Arafat and back to Mecca be called processions or short pilgrimages?

Therefore, studies suggested that the goals of definitional standardization at this issue could be achieved best by "pilgrimage" defined as movement that is "longer than local" (Stoddard, 1997).

Motivation

A second element in the definition of pilgrimage, where the main focus of this paper lies, concerns the motive for the movement. The motive is usually religious. Nevertheless, there is general agreement that the motivation of the traveller must be religious for the event to qualify as pilgrimage. However, the term "religion" is as vague and lacking standardization as the phenomenon being defined here. Even with an assumed working definition of "religious", the actual separation of motives is virtually impossible. Neither observers nor travellers themselves can differentiate motives that are primarily religious from a magnitude of other reasons for making a journey to a place where pilgrims congregate. At a popular pilgrimage sites where fairs, festivals, sporting events and markets concurrently attract pilgrims, tourists, vacationers, excursion groups, traders and hustlers, the true religious pilgrims cannot always be identified (Stoddard, 1997).

Furthermore, even if the "true motives" of travellers to pilgrimage sites are known, some conceptual problems remain. One is the fact that motives change. If a person decides to visit a pilgrimage place because of curiosity but experiences a religious conversion while at the site, has the journey become a personal pilgrimage?

Another conceptual problem results from the fact that trips are taken for multiple reasons. If a person travels to a foreign area as a tourist but while in that vicinity also makes a religious journey to a sacred site, is that person a pilgrim? The issue is well illustrated by the uncertainty about whether the large number of participants in commercial tours to religious sites should be counted as pilgrims (Nolan and Nolan, 1989). However, the pilgrims and tourists are distinct actors situated at two opposite ends of Smith's continuum of travel that first appeared in 1992 proved as a resolution. The polarities on the pilgrimage-tourism axis are labelled sacred vs. secular; between them ranges an almost endless list of possible secular-sacred combinations, with the central area now generally termed 'religious tourism'. These positions reflect the multiple and changing motivations of the traveller whose interests and activities may switch from tourism to pilgrimage and vice versa, even without the individual being aware of the change. Jakowski and Smith (1992) use the term 'knowledge-based tourism' as synonymous with religious tourism.

The literature shows that new interest of scholars in pilgrimage emerged in 1990s and especially in 2000s. They raised some interesting political, cultural, behavioural, economic and touristic research subjects. In current usage, the term 'pilgrimage' connotes a religious journey, 'a journey of a pilgrim; especially one to a shrine or a sacred place' (*Webster's Dictionary*) but its derivation from the Latin perigrinus allows broader interpretations, including foreigners, wanderers, exile and traveller, as well as newcomer and stranger. The term 'tourist'—'one that makes a tour for pleasure or culture' (*Webster's Dictionary*) also has latin origins, namely tornus, one who makes a circuitous journey, usually for pleasure, and returns to the starting point. Smith (1992), an anthropologist claims that the contemporary use of the terms, identifying the 'pilgrim' as a religious traveller and the tourist as a vacationer, is a culturally constructed polarity that veils the travellers' motives.

The Pilgrim

A traveller can be called a pilgrim if the purpose of travel to a destination or event is to perform rituals driven by religion or spirituality and not any activity remunerative in nature. A pilgrim can visit any of the four types of attraction: natural attractions, manmade attractions, man-made objects created for purpose other than attracting pilgrims and eventually become attractions, sights constructed from the beginning as attractions and cultural events and religious events (Sridhar, 2008). The available literature has classified pilgrims in terms of the attributes such as their age, life-stage, gender, family status, occupation, income and religious affiliations (Stoddard, 1997).

Pilgrim Satisfaction of Religious Events

Pilgrim satisfaction can be defined as the outcome of the pilgrims' subjective comparisons of the expectations and achievements. In consumer researches, this conceptualization is similar to consumer or tourist satisfaction of a product or destination which is the outcome of consumer's subjective comparison of expected and received product or destination attribute levels (Oliver, 1980; Vavra, 1997; Pizam, 1999; Ibrahim, 2005).

In terms of religious events, the quality of services rendered by the event organizers, prevents negative evaluation and unfavourable word of mouth of the events. This is similar to a tourist future behaviour as observed by Gyte and Phelps (1989); Hair (1998); Kozak (1998); Malhotra (2002).

Pilgrim satisfaction as tourist satisfaction is widely researched in the marketing domain (Crompton, 1995; Swarbrooke, 1995; Anderson, 1994; Cho, 1998; Baker, 2000; Foster, 2004). Much of this satisfaction literature in tourism is drawn from the theories propounded in consumer behaviour. Consumer satisfaction is considered as a major issue in post purchase period (WTO, 1995). It determines the quality delivered to customers through the product or service and the accompanying services (Vitterso, 2000). Broadly, there are two paradigms of satisfaction research observed in consumer behaviour literature, which include Expectancy Disconfirmation Approach (EDA) and Emotional perspective. However, in the recent past, theories which are in the mid-way between these two paradigms are also proposed.

As per Expectancy Disconfirmation Approach, a consumer is considered as rational and that he/she evaluates his experiences with an attraction against and ideal standard or comparative standard or minimal standard or to his/her expectations (Westbrook, 1981). As a result interaction between the consumers' prepurchase expectations and post-purchase expectations, consumer would be either satisfied or dissatisfied (Vavra, 1997; Engel, 1990). If outcomes match expectations conformation occurs, lest disconfirmation.

Emotional perspective scholars raise their eyebrows against EDA approach and question if a consumer is always rational. Scholars in this paradigm define consumer satisfaction as consumer's emotional response to use of a product or service. (Oliver, 1993; Baker, 2000). Many do not agree completely to either the first or second paradigm as they believe that consumer satisfaction is a complex human process that involves cognition and effective process, psychological and physiological influences (Oliver, 1980; Anton, 1996) defines consumer satisfaction as a state of mind in which the customer's needs, wants and expectations throughout the product or service life have been met or exceeded resulting in subsequent repurchase and loyalty. WTO (1995) also considers consumer satisfaction as a psychological concept that involves the feeling of well-being and pleasure that results from obtaining what one hopes for and expects from an appealing product and/service.

Review of literature also suggests that satisfaction measurement (whether consumer or pilgrim) has broadly followed two perspectives, viz. transaction and cumulative (Fornell, 1992; Boulding, 1993; Olshasky, 1972; Anderson, 1994; Kandampully, 2000; Andreassen, 2000). With regard to pilgrim satisfaction measurement, transaction specific satisfaction is a post experience evaluative judgement of specific occasion that pilgrim would have encountered in their entire event. Cumulative satisfaction on the other hand is the overall evaluation based on the entire experience of the visit to the event (Sridhar, 2008).

Studies on Motives of Pilgrim Satisfaction and their Trend-Analysis

This section deals with the research questions of what motivates people to go for pilgrimage and what are the factors leading to pilgrim satisfaction? These issues have been addressed from different perspectives which are extended from religious and spiritual, to sociological and psychological, to cultural and leisure and to tourism and business, as human behaviour has been emphasised by Ryan and Bates (1995) as services are to humans and satisfaction from services can be improved by understanding human behaviour. However, 'visitor-experience' and the psychosocial dynamics have been studied as drive of pilgrimage by Maccannell (1973), Turner and Turner (1978), Cohen (1979, 1992, 1998). The religious motives literature was initiated primarily by Lickorish and Kershaw (1958) who argued that the decision of religious tourists to visit a destination is initiated by forces beyond their control often based on sentiment of great personal interest, or family ties.

People are motivated to go for pilgrimage for personal reasons like to see and touch holy places and objects, hope for forgiveness, for self-realisation, to know possible selves, people go for pilgrimage. It is a feeling of physical nourishment and spiritual well-being which gives satisfaction to pilgrim. People want to believe in some invisible supernatural power, which is miraculous and by visiting such sacred, incredible, apart places, they get satisfaction. They feel that they have approached something which is beyond the reach of common minds and mundane routine. Feeling of having this special diet out of routine gives them lot of satisfaction (Christen, 1983; Gitelson et al., 1995; Frohlick, 2005, Gursoy et al., 2006; Karlson and Brandstorm, 2008; Liang et al., 2008; Lim et al., 2008).

People go for pilgrimage also for social reasons. Man has worshipped nothing but society, throughout the history. Thus, accepting and respecting the social norms confirms the group membership and then gives satisfaction. Also, by following community sentiments, one harmonises co-existence and solidarity. In addition people go to pilgrimage for 'identity and existence'. People also go for pilgrimage to support 'religious territory', 'exclusive ownership satisfaction' (Greenwood, 1972; Buck, 1977; Heenan, 1978; Ritche, 1984; Cohen 1988; Eder et al., 1995; Pritchard et al., 1998; Dwyer et al., 2000; De Bres and Davis, 2001; Xiao and Smith, 2004; Snowball and Wills, 2006a; Rooney-Brown, 2008).

The assumption that religious elements were at the core of pilgrimage seems to get changed in recent years. There has been a growth in the number of researchers dealing with various aspects of pilgrimages and in their diverse backgrounds like emphasizing on historical and cultural reasons of pilgrimage, unifunctional journey to multifunctional journeys, religious tourism and sacred pilgrimage. According to Kreiner (2010), pilgrim destinations direct people to travel across the country, to come out of their own boundaries to see distinct cultures and places is the focus of current researches. However, in such motives of pilgrimage, the 'basic facilities' is the key factor, which influences pilgrim satisfaction, followed by enhancers (Sridhar et al., 2008). In 1973, MacCannell, a sociologist, was the first to claim that tourism is a quest for the 'authentic' and that it presents the pilgrimage of modern man. He went further, asserting that contemporary tourism embodies many of the same characterstics as pilgrimage. He claimed that the tourism is perceived as pilgrim in the current modern secular world.

According to Turner and Turner (1973), travellers expect a spiritual experience and a chance to meet with other travellers, in a classless society called "communitas" (Turner and Turner, 1978).

In the 1990s, researches started to deal with the complicated relationship between pilgrimage and tourism. This connection is the subject of Eade's (1992) article, which describes the interaction between pilgrims and tourists at Lourdes, in Bowman's (1991) work on the place of Jerusalem in the various Christianities, and in Rinshede's (1992) typology of tourist uses of pilgrimage sites.

Cohen (1992) maintains that the pilgrimage and tourism differ in terms of the direction of the journey undertaken. The "pilgrim" and the "pilgrim tourists" peregrinate toward their sociocultural centre, while the "traveller" and the "traveller-tourists" travel from it toward the periphery. Tourists and pilgrims are similar, if not one and the same, for "even when the role[s] of tourist and pilgrim are combined, they are necessarily different but form a continuum of inseparable elements" (Grabun, 1983: 16). Sousa (1993) argues that people can switch from being a pilgrim to a tourist without the individual being aware of change from one to another. However, Smith (1992) identifies tourists and pilgrims as two distinct actors situated at opposite ends on a continuum of travel. This shows that the difference of tourist and pilgrim is narrowing down, giving way to dedifferentiation.

Often a journey to sacred sites may have several motivations, interests and other subordinate goals some of which have nothing to do with religion directly, but are closely connected with holiday making and with journeys undertaken for social, cultural or political reasons as is emphasised in the works of Andriotis (2009), Nolan and Nolan (1992), Rinschede (1992). Likewise, Timothy and Boyd (2003) observed that many people travel to a widening variety of sacred sites not only for religious purposes or to have experience with the sacred in the traditional sense, but also because they are marked and marketed as heritage or cultural attractions to be consumed.

Secular pilgrimage is another important sector of the tourism industry. Harman and Hyde (2011) have identified five distinct motives for visits to the pilgrimage sites—spiritual, nationalistic, family pilgrimage, friendship and travel motives. These motives share some commonality with the motives for religious pilgrimage, and conversely, with the motives for leisure tourism; yet other motives are unique to the secular pilgrimage. Over the years, this discussion expanded especially in the decade of 1990s when various researchers such as Reader and Walter (1993), Seaton (1999, 2002), Digance (2003) and many more added knowledge regarding secular sites and secular aspects of pilgrimage research. Sites experiences and terms such as 'dark tourism', 'thanatourism', 'popular culture' and 'New Age Pilgrimage' have added to the transition of research toward the experience of individual and dedifferentiation. However, the secular pilgrimage and the other terms needs more critical analysis or in other words they are the upcoming research focus.

The overall analysis of the studies suggests that there are personal, social, cultural, historical, and secular travel motives. It is observed that differentiation is giving way to dedifferentiation. Earlier researches have kept pilgrimage and tourism apart from each other. There had been the issues of sacred vs. secular, pure pilgrim vs. visitors. Some researchers claim that the differences between tourism, pilgrimage and even secular pilgrimage is narrowing (Bilu, 1998; Kong, 2001).

Discussion and Conclusion Concepts, Gaps and Priorities

The definition of pilgrim and pilgrimage plays very important role in understanding the motives and satisfaction issues. The review of researches analyses that in place of one standard definition, operational definitions are required, so that the new findings of future researches can be accommodated. The core phenomenon is actually the pilgrimage experience and meanings attached to it. As well, pilgrim motives and satisfaction have importance and multiple meanings within societies and cultures that transcend experiences. To fully understand and create knowledge about motives and pilgrim satisfaction, all aspects social, personal, cultural, historical and also modern and global changes have to be considered. As far as satisfaction of services are concerned, the management of services have to be understood for who produces them and why, how they are planned and managed, what are the dynamic forces shaping individual experience and collective experience.

The Methodological Gaps and Priorities

The current trend of literature covered has over emphasized consumer motivations. This approach is firmly situated within a positivistic, quantitative research paradigm in which consumer behaviour approaches prevail, leaving little room for socio-cultural antecedents and constraints, especially in different cultures and for specific social groups. Thus, researches based on interpretative methods should be done in order to fill this gap. More and more cross cultural studies should be increased.

Applying phenomenological (hermeneutics) and experiential assessment methods is a real need and open to both experimental and participant observation method. Cross-cultural comparisons of destinations, festivals and pilgrimages will be useful in generating new ideas from an artistic perspective, as well as in revealing much more in theoretical terms about motives of pilgrim satisfaction and meanings.

The analysis of trend found in the literature, can be categorised as follows:

1. The transformation is from differentiation to dedifferentiation.
2. There is an expansion of areas of researches, since new issues such as secular pilgrimage, dark-tourism, thanatourism, New Age spiritual travel, modern secular pilgrimage have been raised but still inadequately studied.
3. There is a shift from 'External' and 'General' elements to the 'Individual Inner Experience'. Many past works presented pilgrimage as a general phenomenon (Turner, 1969; Nolan, 1989; Vukonic, 1996). Over time, in a gradual process a shift has taken place, first towards typologies, for example, Cohen's (1979, 1992, 1998) typology of the different experiences of a visitor. The second stage evolved deconstruction of the typologies, including classification of visitor experiences into sub-types, for example, pilgrims being placed along the pilgrimage experience (Collins-Kreiner, 2000). The next stage in research was to understand that a visitor may have different experiences and may switch from one to another. The experience and mental state of the visitor can change in time and intensity according to his/her different characterstics.
4. Movement from 'objectivity' to 'subjectivity'. In earlier works, the emphasis was placed on the way the objective, namely the pilgrimage, provided one kind of experience or another. In later researches, the experience is shown

to depend on the visitor and how he or she perceives his or her visit and experience.

5. From the 'Either-or' Approach to a 'Both-And' Approach. Researchers speak of 'interpretations' instead of 'true' or 'false'. Every researcher has his or her own assumptions and perceptions with which they interpret the world and its various phenomena. Individual experiences can change from moment to moment and there are no clear-cut distinctions between pilgrimage sites and tourist attractions. The major implication of 'Both-And' approach is that contradictions do not matter, since everything is acceptable. This means the trend shows that current researches are still based on the existing theories, and the transformation is still perceived as an expansion and not contradiction. However, it seems that allowing a multiplicity of interpretations and interpreters, none of which are exclusive, has offered a way out of competing explanations and research agendas.

REFERENCES

Andreason, E.W., Fornell, C., and Lehmann, R.R. (1994). Customer Satisfaction, market share, and profitability: Findings from Sweden. *Journal of Marketing*, 58: 53-66.

Anton, J. (1996). *Customer Relationship Management: Making Hard Decisions with Soft Numbers*, New Jersey. Prentice Hall.

Baker, D. and Crompton, J. (2000). Quality satisfaction and behavioural intentions. *Annals of Tourism Research*. 27(3): 785-804.

Bilu, Y. (1998). Divine Worship and Pilgrimages to Holy Sites as Universal Phenomena, In: R. Gonen, ed., *To the Holy Graves: Pilgrimage to the Holy Graves and Hill Out in Israel*, 11-26. Jerusalem: The Israel Museum.

Bowman, G. (1991). Christian ideology and the image of a holy land: The place of Jerusalem in the various Christianities. In: Sallnow and Eade, eds., *Contesting the Sacred: the Anthropology of Christian Pilgrimage*, 98-121. London: Routledge.

Bradon, S.G.F. (1970). *A Dictionary of Comparative Religions*. London: Weidenfeld and Nicholson.

Buck, R. and Mules, T. (2001a). Reconciling cost-benefit and economic impact assessment for event tourism. *Tourism Economics*, 7(4): 321-30.

Cohen, A. (1979). Authenticity and commodification in tourism. *Annals of Tourism Research*, 15(3): 371-86.

——. (1992). A polyethnic London carnival as a contested cultural performance. *Racial and Ethnic Studies*, 5(1): 23-41.

Cohen, E. (1998). The postmodernisation of a mythical event: Naga fireballs on the Mekong River. *Tourism Culture and Communication*, 7(3): 56-71.

Kreiner, C.N. and Kliot, N. (2000). Pilgrimage Tourism in the Holy land: The behavioural characterstics of Christian Pilgrims. *Geo Journal*, 501: 32-52.

Crim, K., gen. ed. (1981). *Abingdon Dictionary of Living Religions*. Nashville: Abingdon.

Christensen, R. and Dowrick, P. (1983). Myths of mid-winter depression. *Community Mental Health Journal*, (3): 177-86.

Crompton, J. and Love, L. (1995). The predictive validity of alternative approaches to evaluating quality of a festival. *Journal of Travel Research*, 34(1): 11-24.

Choi, Y. Tat and Raymond, Chu (2000). Level of satisfaction among Asian and Western travellers. *International Journal of Quality and Reliability Management*, 17(2): 116-31.

De Bres and Davis, J. (2001). Celebrating group and place identity: A case study of a new regional festival, *Tourism Geographies*, 3(3): 326-37.

Digance, J. (2003), Pilgrimage at contested sites. *Annals of Tourism Research*, 301: 143-59.

Dwyer, L., Mellor, R., Mistills, N. and Mules, T. (2000). A framework for assessing tangibles and intangible impacts of events and conventions. *Event Management*, 6(3): 175-89.

Eade, J. (1992). Pilgrimage and Tourism at Lourdes, France. *Annals of Tourism Research*, 19: 18-32.

Engel, J.F., Blackwell, R.D. and Miniard, P.W. (1990). *Consumer Behaviour*, 6th Edition. Illinois. Dryden Press.

Foster, D. (2004). Measuring Customer Satisfaction in tourism industry. Paper presented at Third International and Sixth National Research Conference on Quality Management Research, RMIT University.

Frohlick, S. (2005). That playfulness of white masculinity: Mediating masculinities and adventure at mountain film festivals. *Tourist Studies*, 5(2): 175-93.

Gatrell, J. and Reid, N. (2002). The cultural politics of local economic development: The case of Toledo jeep. *Tijdscrift voor Economiche en Sociale Geographic*. 93: 397-411.

Gitelson, R., Kerstetter, D. and Kiernan, N. (1995). Evaluating the educational objectives of a short-term festival. *Festival Management and Event Tourism*, 3(1): 9-14.

Gursoy, D., Spangenberg, E. and Rutherford, D. (2006). The hedonic and utilitarian dimensions of attendees' attitudes towards festivals. *Journal of Hospitality and Tourism Research*, 30(3): 279-94.

Gyte, D. and Phelps, A. (1989). Patterns of destination repeat business: British tourists in Mallorca, Spain. *Journal of Travel Research*. 28(1): 24-28.

Harman, S. and Hyde, K. (2011). Motives for a secular pilgrimage to the Gallipoli battlefields. *Tourism Management*, 32(6): 1343-51.

Hair Joseph, E., Jr, Roph E. Anderson, Ronald, L. and William, T.C. Black (1998). *Multivariate Data Analysis*. Fifth Edition. New Jersey Prentice Hall International Inc.

Ibrahim, E. Essam, Jacqueline, Gill (2005). A positioning strategy for a tourist destination, based on analysis of customer's perceptions and satisfactions. *Marketing Intelligence and Planning*, 23(2): 172-88.

Jackowski, A. and Smith, V.L. (1992). Polish pilgrim tourists. *Annals of Tourism Research*, 19: 92-106.

Karlsen, S. and Brandstorm, S. (2008). Exploring the music festival as a music educational project. *International Journal of Music Education*, 26(4): 447-65.

Kong, L. (2001). Mapping new Geographies of religion: Politics and Poetics in Modernity. *Progress in Human Geography*, 25: 211-33.

Kozak, M. (2001). Repeaters' behaviour at two distinct destinations. *Annals of Tourism Research*, 28(3): 784-807.

Liang, Y., Illum, S. and Cole, S. (2008). Benefits received and behavioural intentions of festival visitors in relation to distance travelled and their origin. *International Journal of Event Management Research*, 4(1): 12-23.

Lim, M., Hellard, M., Hocking, J. and Aitken, C. (2008). A cross-sectional survey of young people attending a musical festival: Associations between drug use and musical preference. *Drug and Alcohol Review*, 27(4): 439-41.

MacCannell, D. (1976). *The tourist: A New Theory of Leisure Class*. New York: Schocken.

Malhotra, N. (2002). *Marketing Research: An Applied Orientation*. New Jersey. Prentice-Hall.

Murthy, N.G. (2008). Pilgrim satisfaction of religious event. *Interscience MR*, 1, 1-10.

Oliver, R.L. (1981). Measurement and Evaluation of Satisfaction Processes in Retail Settings. *Journal of Retailing*, 75: 25-48.

Oliver, R.L. (1980). A cognitive model of the antecedents and consequences of satisfaction decisions. *Journal of Marketing Research*, 17: 460-69.

Pizam, A. and Taylor E. (1999). Customer satisfaction and its measurement in hospitality enterprises. *International Journal of Contemporary Hospitality Management*, 11(7): 326-39.

Pizam, A. and Milman, A. (1993). Predicting satisfaction among first time visitors to a destination by using the expectancy disconfirmation theory. *International Journal of Hospitality Management*, 12(2): 197-209.

Prichard, A., Morgan, N., Sedgely, D. and Jenkins, A. (1998). Reaching out to gay tourist: Opportunities and threats in an emerging market segment. *Tourism Management*, 19(3): 273-82.

Reader, I. and T. Walter (1993). *Pilgrimage in Popular Culture*. London: The Macmillan Press.

Rinschede, G. (1992). Forms of religious tourism. *Annals of Tourism Research*, 19(1): 51-67.

Ritchie, B. and Beliveau, D. (1974). Hallmark events: An evaluation of a strategic response to seasonality in the travel market. *Journal of Travel Research*, 14(2): 14-20.

Rivera, M., Hara, T. and Kock, G. (2008). Economic impacts of cultural events: The case of the Zoral Festivals. *Journal of Heritage Tourism*, 3(2): 121-37.

Rooney-Browne, C. (2008). Changing the way we look at libraries? An evaluation of Renfrewshire's look at libraries festival. *Library Review*, 57(1): 50-66.

Ryan, C. and Bates, C. (1995). A rose by other name: The motivations of those opening their gardens for a festival. *Festival Management and Event Tourism*, 39(2): 59-71.

Ryan, C. and Cliff, A. (1997). Do travel agencies measure up to customer expectations? An empirical investigation of travel agencies' service quality as measured by SERVQUAL. *Journal of Travel and Tourism Marketing*, 6(2): 1-31.

Nolan, D. (1989). *Christian Pilgrimage in Modern Western Europe*. The University of North Carolina Press: Chapell Hill.

Stoddard, R. (1997). Defining and Classifying Pilgrimages, from University of Nebraska, Website: http:// digitalcommons.edu/ geographyfacpub/2

Skyes, J.B. (1982). *The Concise Oxford Dictionary of Current English*, 7th ed. Oxford: Clarendon Press.

Smith, V.L. (1992). Introduction: The quest in guest. *Annals of Tourism Research*, 19: 1-17.

Snowball, J. and Wills, K. (2006a). Building cultural capital: Transforming the South African National Arts Festival. *South African Journal of Economics*, 74(1): 20-33.

Sridhar, G. Ravindranath, M. Murthy, and G. Narasimha (2008). Pilgrim Satisfaction of Religious Event. *Interscience MR*, 1, Issue 1-10.

Swarbrooke, J. (1995). *The Development and Management of Visitor's Attractions*. Butterworth-Heinemann, Oxford Publishers.

Timothy, D.J. and Olsen, D.H. (2006). *Tourism, Religion and Spiritual Journeys*. London/New York: Rutledge.

Turner, V. (1973). The centre out there: Pilgrim's goal. *History of Religions*, 12: 191-230.

Turner, V. and Turner, E. (1978). *Image and Pilgrimage in Christian Culture: Anthropological Perspectives*. New York: Columbia University Press.

Vavra, T.G. (1997). *Improving Your Measurement of Customer Satisfaction: A Guide to Creating*. Milwaukee, WI. ASQ Quality Press, pp. 430-40.

Vitterso, J., Vorkinn, M., Vistad O.I. and Vaagland, J. (2000). Tourist experiences and attractions. *Annals of Tourism Research*, 27(2): 432-50.

Westbrooke, R.A. and Oliver, R.L. (1981). The dimensionality of consumption emotion pattern and satisfaction. *Journal of Consumer Research*, 27(2): 432-50.

Xiao, A. and Smith, S. (2004). Residents's perceptions of kitchener-Waterloo Oktoberfest: An inductive analysis. *Tourism Management*, 8(3): 161-75.

www.cummingsstudyguides.net/guide/Canterbury

www.sciencedirect.com/science/article

www.sacredsites.com/middle_east/jewish-pilgrimage

www. Tourism-review.com/travel-tourism-magazine-sacred-destination

22

Mainstreaming Mal Paharia Primitive Tribal Groups of India

Kumar Satyam

ABSTRACT

This paper reviews the mainstreaming of Mal Paharia Primitive Tribal Groups in the background of Indian Tribes and also make an attempt to understand the consequences they have been facing in their different domain of life. Mainstreaming is a fuzzy term and it brings more ambiguity when it uses for Primitive Tribes of India. There are seventy-five Primitive Tribal Groups in India. Among these seventy-five Primitive Tribal Group, Mal Paharia has a distinct mark and attribute. This Primitive Tribal Group is found in Middle Eastern part of India more particularly in the state of Jharkhand. Mal Pahariya has been living in the multi-ethnic parish having different castes and tribal communities. Their main occupation is agriculture with some allied work like basketary, livestocks and fishery. Despite making so many affect for fortifying and enriching their social, economic, political state, the Mal Paharia Primitive Tribal Group still is in underdevelopment and underprivileged in every walk of life. So here it is urgent to know and intervene vigorously what the means of mainstreaming for them. It also needs to revisit and re-evaluate our deliberative intention for mainstreaming of Mal Paharia Primitive Tribal Group.

Introduction

Mainstreaming is a notion which has been always talked about under the background of social, cultural and economic status of any group, community and society which is less privileged and developed comparatively with others. The concept 'mainstream' appeared in Indian anthropology apparently after postcolonial period particularly in relation to the integration of tribes. But it acquainted much earlier in the colonial period. They wanted to develop tribal populace and bring them with conventional society. Though it was not taken as for upholding the aboriginal population, yet the real intention of Britisher was to take over the resources which were spread massively in the locale of tribal habitat of Jharkhand (which was undivided Bihar that time). Thus, Britisher introduced Francis Buchanan[1] who was professionally a physician. He had asked to survey for accumulating vast knowledge and information about capital and resources. This territorial space was untouched till the moment Buchanan infiltrated. In the early nineteenth century, Buchanan travelled through the Rajmahal hills.[2] The term 'tribe', like similar terms, such as 'primitive', 'savage', 'barbarous', 'uncivilized', 'preliterate', 'non-literate', 'little community', 'native', etc. was copiously used by the colonial masters for the communities under their control. So it's clearly reflecting the oxymoron of colonial leaders particularly for the tribes of Jharkhand.

Tribes or Indigenous: Mal Paharia Primitive Tribal Group

Although much has been written and spoken about the tribes or indigenous population by numerous authors and academicians. During the discussion on the Indigenous Labour Organization (ILO) Convention 169 of 1989, the Indian representative objected to terms such self-determination and sovereignty and rejected the indigenous status. In the absence of official recognition, indigenous has become the status that the tribes assign to themselves with their as the first inhabitants of India. Some political parties of Tamil Nadu in South India state that the Dravidians are indigenous to India and that the Aryans came from outside and imposed Brahminism on them. Some fundamentalist groups claim that the Aryans too are indigenous to India (Lal, 1996: 190-92). Risley defined, "The tribe represents a collection of families, or group of families, bearing a common name, which as rule does not denote any specific occupation; generally claiming common descent from a mythical or material ancestor and occasionally from an animal, but become parts of the country they are held together rather by the obligation of blood feud than by the tradition of kinship, usually speaking the same language; and occupying or claiming to occupy a definite tract of country. A tribe is not necessarily endogamous, i.e. it is not an invariable rule that man of a particular tribe must marry a woman of that tribe." The meaning of the word tribe according to *Oxford Dictionary* is a race of people; now applied specially to a primary aggregate of people in a primitive or barbarous condition, under a headman or chief. Evan Pritchard's opinion about the word 'primitive' is worth quoting:

> The word 'primitive', in the sense in which it has become established in anthropological literature does not mean that the societies it qualifies are either in time or inferior to other kinds of societies.

Kuper precisely points out, the myth of the 'primitive' was created by the Europeans of the nineteenth century, in order to understand their own selves, because industrialization has shaken the foundations of their own belief in the feudal order as being the natural unchangeable order of things. In the Article 342 of Indian Constitution, procedure to be followed for specification of Scheduled Tribe is prescribed. However, it does not contain the criterion for the specification of any community as scheduled tribe. A well-established criterion being followed is based on certain attributes such as:

- *Geographical isolation*—They live in cloister, exclusive remote and inhospitable areas like hills, forests.
- *Backwardness*—Livelihood based on primitive agriculture, low cost closed economy based on low level of technology which leads to their poverty. They have a low level of literacy and health.

- *Distinctive culture, language and religion*—They have developed community-wise distinctive culture, language and religion for their own.
- *Shyness of contact*—They have margin degree of contact with other cultures and people.

According to the United Nation, the most fruitful approach is to identify, rather than define indigenous peoples.

Review of Invasion in Their Life in Different Timeline

According to P.O. Bodding, before the arrival of Santhals[3] in this area a very primitive tribe Sauria Paharia and the Mal Paharias were already living in the hill tracts of Rajmahal hills. Whatever their origin and from wherever they might have come, it remains a fact that the wild Paharias had always maintained their independence before the British came because of their geographical isolation. The inhabitants of Rajmahal hills were never in subjection to the Mughal Government. It is presumed that the Mughal administration failed to penetrate into this area as it is vast hilly tract covered by deep forest and by that there it might have remained hill locked completely cut off and isolated from the outside world. They were also never in any way subordinate to the British Government till the arrival of Captain Browne in 1774.

Buchanan in his report portrayed the detail account of the life of Paharias. He characterized the PTG as hunters, shifting cultivators, food gatherers, charcoal producers, silkworm rearers was thus intimately connected to the forest. To the British, porch of settled agriculture was necessary to enlarge the sources of land revenue, produce crops for export, and establish the basis of settled, ordered society. So in this regard, in the 1770s the British embarked on an atrocious policy of extermination, hunting the Paharias down and killing them. Afterward, by the 1780s, Augustus Cleveland, the Collector of Bhagalpur,[4] came out with a policy of pacification. As the pacification campaigns continued, the Paharias withdraw deep into mountains, insulting themselves from hostile forces, and carrying on a war with outsiders. And for these entire efforts Britisher had taken a help from Santhal. The Santhals performed to be great settlers for clearing forests and ploughing the land with vigour. Britisher has given the land and persuaded to stay in the foothills of Rajmahal. By 1832 a large area of land was demarcated as Damin-i-koh and this land was declared to be land of the Santhals. The Santhals of *Damin-i-koh* did not come in direct confrontation with the original settlers of the Rajmahal Hills region. Though from the very beginning, the Paharias never welcomed the entrance of the Santhal in their forested regions. Now, Paharias people amalgamated with the persuading concerns of preserving their own tribal norms, traditions and folk centering round their freedom in the Rajmahal region and their incessant consumption of the forest-resources and thereby they raised the protest against the deliberate foreign people. They did not submit to the British power at the cost of their sovereignty. The protest and revolt of Paharias against the Britisher were developed due to their strong ethnicity and sense of existence of autonomous life. Cleveland got to know the gravity of these troubles and tried to initiate a separate administration for self-governance. In this regards, he made an arrangement for the local judiciary system. All the disputes and cases of Paharias were judged by the newly constituted Hill Assembly where the hereditary hill headman was given all the obligatory power to judge. So this entire narrative was proved to be a novel one in establishing a non-violent relation with the chaotic Paharias tribe.

Indian Administration for Primitive Tribes

Constitutional Provision: Part X and Article 244 deals with the scheduled and tribal areas. The term Scheduled Areas has been defined in the Indian Constitution[5] as such areas as the President may by order declare to be scheduled areas. The architects of Indian constitution were serious about the development and the way of living of tribes. They kept in mind of these all issues and subjects related to tribes and as a result of all those discussions and deliberations Part X of Constitution came as administration of Scheduled Area and Scheduled Tribes. Some pockets fall under the Schedule V of the Constitution which clearly indicates for special provision for the tribal population. Jharkhand is one among nine states which fall under Schedule V. Panchayat (Extension to Schedule Area) Act, 1996 is an Act to provide for constitution of Panchayat Raj[6] in the state of Jharkhand. There is a provision of Tribal Advisory Council in the fifth Schedule of the India Constitution. It is the duty of Tribal Advisory Council to advice on such matters pertaining to the welfare and advancement of the Scheduled tribes in the state as may be referred to them by the governor. In addition to this, National Commission for Scheduled Tribe came into existence in 2004 for investigate and monitor all matters relating to the constitutional and legal safeguards for the Scheduled Tribes and inquire specific complains with respect to the deprivation of rights and their safeguarding. Apart from all these constitution provisions, Indian Constitution provides many welfare remedies and policies especially for the tribal population in which this indigenous tribe also covers. Indian Government allots a consolidated fund from the union budget for tribal people. For that there is provision for tribal sub plan in Indian five-year plans for the country in which welfare programmes and schemes have been promoting and sponsoring by the ruling government.

An Overview

Jharkhand state was formed on 15 November 2000 after the great struggle of local people demanding their own identity and land. It was also considered before separating it from Bihar that it will review and give high priority to the indigenous population before making any policy and planning for the state. It is the 28th state of Republic of India. The Jharkhandi identity and the demand for autonomy was not premised solely on the exclusivity of its tribal cultural heritage but was fundamentally a fallout of the complete breakdown of development policy to intervene in socio-economic situation and circumstances of the tribal and non-tribals in the region.

Despite being one of the most richest interms of resorces states, Jharkhand has been identified and discussed infamously as one of the most underdeveloped and politically unstable states of the country. After its formal separation state of Bihar, Jharkhand rose to existence with its own set of opportunities and challenges. The newly constituted state since then has been struggling to establish its own growth model together with synchronizing the existing practices of development. The unique territorial features, traditional practices, ethnic identities, political experience and diverse social composition have been greatly in conflict with the larger idea of the Jharkhand identity. Whereas the political instability added pains to the desired growth process the multiple vulnerabilities of the various social sections particularly that of Mal Paharia Primitive Tribe therein have been at the forefront of concerns. So, here it became more appealing to know that what the intensity and impact of all these spoiled situation of State which ruined the life of Mal Paharia Population.

Sufferings of Mal Paharia

Mal Paharia Primitive Tribe has been facing many problems and difficulties in this existing system of governance. A biggest problem of this tribal area is that of acquiring land for development purposes since the British period. The people have their well intention for developing all curves in their life. But their real need and demand are differing with regards to what they have getting with periods of time. Their real identity and uniqueness is hidden in their original own forms life. But the westernization and globalization has been greatly piercing and destroying the origin folk and customs of this primitive tribe. Another major problem is that of poverty. Majority of people of this primitive tribe live under poverty line. Most of them live under abject poverty and are in debt in the hands of local moneylenders and agents. In order to repay the debt they often mortgage or sell their lands (which is not legal according to Santhal Pargana Tenancy Act).

Their Real Needs and Demands

They need the uninterrupted social and geographic space where they can live with their own culture, customs and folk. The nature loving people are very close to hills, rivers and woods where they have been getting enough life surviving bits and pieces. They are the actual protector of natural resources and we should give value and respect to it. Policymakers have to revisit and rethink whether these programmes and schemes are really upto their requirements. What is the actual self-governance for this tribal people? If we closely observe there is nothing as self-governance in the local rule. Instead they have been imposing the Western notion tangentially.

Conclusion

It is time to look and revisit our implemented strategy very critically for the sake of Mal Paharia Primitive Tribal Group very precisely. In colonial period, Paharias of this region was always considered as robber and assaulter because they were infiltrate with an intention of capturing the resources and restrain those areas. Nowadays this notion is typically use for the non-tribal population. It is utterly true that non-tribal population has been sucking from difference ways and means since after India got freedom from the British. They have internalized and accepted these all continuous suppression and aggravation throughout generation to generation as their faith. These also made huge impact in their psychology and things became as worse that they are not in position to defend and shield themselves. The circumstances and representations are different but the actions are still same what it had been practicing in colonial period.

NOTES

1. Francis Buchanan was also known as Buchana-Hamilton.
2. Rajmahal hill is presently situated in district of Sahebgunj in the State of Jharkhand, India.
3. This was also belongs to indigenous population but they had been regularly being the contact of other social groups. They had started coming Rajmahal hills around 1780s. The local Zamindars engaged them to snatch the geographical land purposefully.
4. Bhagalpur was the part of undivided State of Bihar.
5. The Constitution of India is the lengthiest of all the written constitutions of the world.
6. Local Self-Governance.

REFERENCES

Béteille, A. (1986). "The Definition of Tribe with Special Reference to India". *European Journal of Sociology*, Vol. 27.

Barth, Fredrik (1969). *Ethnic Groups and Boundaries*. London: George Allen & Unwin.

Cernea, Michael M. (1991a). *Putting People First: Sociological Variables in Rural Development*. New Delhi: Oxford University Press.

Chattopadhyay, K.P. (1994). *History of Indian Social Organization: An Essays in Social Anthropology*. Calcutta: K.P. Bagchi & Co.

Dalton, E.T. (1872). *Descriptive Ethnology of Bengal*. Calcutta: Superintendent of Government Printing.

Elwin, V. (1943a). *The Aboriginals*. London (1943b). *Maria Murder and Suicide*. London: OUP.

Kuper, Adam (1988). *The Invention of Primitive Society*. London: Routledge.

Kluckohn, Florence R. and Strodtbeck, Fred L. (1961). *Variations in Value Orientation*, Row, Peterson, Illinois.

L.H. Morgan, *Ancient Society* (Cambridge, Mass., Belknap Press, 1964, first publish 1877).

Lal, A.K. (1996). Implications of fundamentalist revival for dalit identity. In W. Fernandes (ed.), *The Emerging Dalit Identity: The Re-assertion of the Subalterns* (New Delhi: Indian Institute), pp. 184-97.

Madan, T.N. (1982). *Culture and Development*. Delhi: Oxford Univesity Press.

Mandelbaum, D.G. (1963). "The Cottage in their Social Sitting", in Milton Singer (ed.), *Introduction to the Civilization of India*. Chicago: University of Chicago Press.

Oran, Martin (1965). *The Santhal: A Tribe in Search of a Great Tradition*. Detroit: Wayne University Press.

Sahlins, M. and Elmon Service (eds.) (1960). *Evolution and Culture*. Michigan: University of Michigan Press.

Tomei, M. (2005). Indigenous and Tribal Peoples: An Ethnic Audit of Selected Poverty Reduction Strategy Papers (Geneva: International Labour Organization).

23

Revisiting Women's Participation in Agriculture

Nagaraju Battu

ABSTRACT

India is developing country. The main occupation is agriculture, as 70 per cent of the population is involved in this occupation. Agriculture can be an important engine of growth and poverty reduction. The women are the backbone of agricultural workforce and are a vital part of Indian economy. The purpose of this study was therefore to evaluate the activities of women and their participation in agricultural production to fulfill the food security of their family. More specifically to answer the question's "what is the role of women in agriculture?". In view of the current agrarian crisis facing the country, it is important to recognize women's role in agriculture to ensure agricultural growth so as to (a) eradicate poverty, (b) ensure food security for the majority, and (c) promote the well-being of women themselves. Over the years, there is a gradual realization of the key role of women in agricultural development and their contribution in the field of agriculture, food security, horticulture, dairy, nutrition, sericulture, fisheries, and other allied sectors. Women form the backbone of agriculture, in India, comprising the majority of agricultural labourers; women have been putting in labour not only in terms of physical output but also in terms of quality and efficiency.

Many women in developing countries are occupied in agriculture. Women occupation in agriculture in low income countries in Asia is between 60-80 per cent. In almost, Asian countries, the number of women employed in agriculture as a percentage of the economically active population is higher. Long-standing obstacles faced by rural women in terms of limited access to productive resources (Land, Credit, Inputs, Transport, Extension Services, Storage and Technical Assistance) prevent them from adopting new technologies. Although women are more than ever finally employed, differences in wages earned by women and men persist in all countries. Women also have less access to productive resources especially in developing countries. Due to these reasons and women's lower education level compel them to have a greater tendency to remain in subsistence agriculture. Though they are part of farm households, women's role in agriculture necessitates special inputs from our policies and programmes. With various targeted efforts, her enlightenment will change the face of rural India.

Introduction

Women have played a significant role in traditional agricultural production technology.[1] Because women's contribution was so central in both the agricultural division of labour and its reproduction, traditional structures of resource allocation have provided them access to the basic factors of production in agriculture. Despite the fact that they remained socially subordinate to men, they participated in resource control, decision-making, and production. However, in programmes for improvement of agricultural technologies, women are seldom recipients of the benefits, although they no doubt are capable of using them. In the cases cited in the literature where women either could not obtain the new technology nor were adversely affected by it, underlying social, cultural, and economic conditions were primarily responsible. This was usually compounded by insensitivity in programme design and implementation. Development programmes can produce drastic changes within households by altering the perceived value of women's contribution and the traditional structures of authority and resource allocation.

The Role of Women in Agriculture and its Allied Fields

Women performs numerous labour intensive jobs such as weeding, hoeing, grass cutting, picking, cotton stick collections, separation of seeds from fiber. Women are also expected to collect wood from fields. This wood is being used as a major fuel source for cooking. Because of the increasing population pressure, over grazing and desertification, women face difficulties in searching of fire wood. Clean drinking water is another major problem in rural areas. Like collection of wood, fetching water from remote areas is also the duty of women. Because a rural woman is responsible for farm activities, keeping of livestock and its other associated activities like milking, milk processing, and preparation of ghee are also carried out by the women.[2] Livestock is the primary subsistent activity used to meet household food needs as well as supplement farm incomes. The majority of farms own some livestock. The pattern of livestock strength is mainly influenced by various factors such as farm size, cropping pattern, availability of range-lands including fodder and pasture. It is common practice in the rural areas to give an animal as part of a women's dowry. Studies have revealed rural women earn extra income from the sale of milk and animals. Mostly women are engaged in cleaning of animal, sheds, watering and milking the animals. Rural women are also responsible for collection, preparing dung cakes an activity that also brings additional income to poor families.

Evidently, rural women are involved in almost all livestock-related activities. Except grazing, all other livestock management activities are predominantly performed by females. Majority of women are involved in shed cleaning and collection of farm yard manure. Males, however, share the responsibility of taking care of sick animals. It is evident that the women are playing a dominant role in the livestock production and management activities. Poultry farming is one of the major sources of rural economy. The role of women in poultry farming at household level is the central in poultry industry. Even though rural women are not using modern management techniques such as vaccination and improved feed, but their poultry enterprise is impressive. Every year, income from poultry farming has been rising. In order to generate more and more income, rural women often sell all eggs and poultry meat and left nothing for personal use. Due to poverty and lack of required level of proteins most of women have got a very poor health. Most of women suffer from malnutrition. The study also noted that majority of the rural women are uneducated, unskilled and tradition-bounded therefore their productive capacities are also low, and counted as unskilled labour. Though rural women also help to produce the staple crops like rice, wheat, and maize, yet her contribution is secondary in staple crop production, however, in legumes and vegetables, her role is instrumental.

Women's Contribution to Agricultural Production

As seen above, women play a significant role in the agricultural labour force and in agricultural activities, although to a varying degree. Consequently, their contribution to agricultural output is undoubtedly extremely significant, although difficult to quantify with any accuracy. It has often been claimed that women produce 60-80 per cent of food. However, assigning contributions to agricultural outputs by gender is problematic because in most agricultural households both men and women are involved in crop production. It can be attempted to allocate output by gender by assuming that specific crops are grown by women and others by men and then aggregating the value of women's and men's crops to determine the share grown by women.

Time Spent in Agricultural Activities

Time use surveys attempt to provide a more complete account of time use by men and women than are available from the labour force statistics. Such studies usually are not nationally representative and are not directly comparable because they usually cover small samples, report on different types of activities (that are not always clearly specified) and use different methodologies. Despite these caveats, a summary of the evidence from studies which specify time use by agricultural activity suggests interesting patterns.[3]

Time-use surveys[4] that cover all agricultural activities reveal considerable variation across countries, and sometimes within countries, but the data are broadly similar to the labour force statistics. In Africa, estimates of the time contribution of women to agricultural activities ranges from about 30 per cent in the Gambia to 60-80 per cent in different parts of Cameroon. In Asia, estimates range from 32 per cent in India to over 50 per cent in China. The range is lower in Latin America, but exceeds 30 per cent in some parts of Peru. Two separate studies are reported each for Zambia and Peru, and differences reflect different time periods and locations within the countries.

Multi-Dimensional Role of Women

(a) ***Agricultural activities:*** Sowing, transplanting, weeding, irrigation, fertilizer application, plant protection, harvesting, winnowing, storing, etc.

(b) ***Domestic activities:*** Cooking, child-rearing, water collection, fuel wood gathering, household maintenance, etc.

(c) ***Allied activities:*** Cattle management, fodder collection, milking, etc. Mainly rural women are engaged in agricultural activities in three different ways depending on the socio-economic status of their family and regional factors. They work as:

- Paid labourers.
- Cultivator doing labour on their own land.
- Managers of certain aspects of agricultural production by way of labour supervision and the participation in post-harvest operations.

Gender Differences in Roles and Activities

Gender[5] refers to the socially determined differences between women and men such as roles, attitudes, behaviours, and varies across gender roles are learned and vary across cultures and overtime. They are, thus amenable to change. Gender is a relational term that includes both women and men. Gender equality focuses on changes for both women and men.

Another issue is the problem-ridden conceptualization of women's and men's work in rural environments, in particular, the failure (by census-takers and researchers who are not gender-aware, for example) to recognize the importance of their differing roles. Analysis of the gender division of labour has revealed that women typically take on three types of roles in terms of the paid and unpaid labour they undertake. These three roles can be described as follows:

(i) ***The productive role:*** This refers to market production and home/subsistence production undertaken by women which generates an income.

(ii) ***The reproductive role:*** This refers to the child-bearing and child-rearing responsibilities borne by women (which are essential to the reproduction of the workforce).

(iii) ***The community management role:*** This refers to activities undertaken by women to ensure the provision of resources at the community level, as an extension of their reproductive role.

An understanding of these three roles can inform gender-aware planning that takes into account the differential impact of programmes and projects on women and men because of women's triple role. When under-estimations and under-valuations of rural women's work are found, as they so often are, in the sphere of development planning, the consequences are serious. Failure to acknowledge the importance of women's multiple contributions to rural survival means that practical policy interventions are frequently detrimental both to women themselves and to their communities. Another factor that needs to be taken into account is that certain tasks, activities or enterprises may be regarded as "male" or "female". For example, women typically gather forest products for fuel, food for the family, fodder for livestock and medicinal uses. Men more often cut wood to sell or use as building materials. In order to secure sustainable and equitable management of forest resources, therefore, both women and men need to be consulted in the design and implementation of forestry projects. Similarly, where livestock is concerned, women and men often own different animal species and use different animal products, and any policies or programmes would need to address the needs of both.

The Gender Demographics of Agriculture and Rural Areas

The preceding sections discussed gender differences in labour market participation and type of employment in agriculture and in rural areas, with the data available revealing a significant amount of regional diversity. This section concentrates on demographic gender[6] imbalances in rural areas. In this respect numerous studies find that agriculture and rural areas are becoming "feminized". Not all authors have the same understanding of the meaning of this word, although two concepts are generally considered: women predominate in the agricultural sector or women are rapidly gaining a predominant position. The opposite is true in Latin America, Eastern Asia and countries in developed regions. These patterns reflect different economic and social norms, which have produced different migration trends for men and women. We note that feminization is also frequently observed in certain sectors such as unskilled labour in the fruit, vegetable and cut-flower export sector.

Women play a crucial role in all farm-related activities from land preparation to marketing. They contribute a higher proportion of labour in agricultural sector than men. However, they are not active in decision-making. This research note discusses the impact of Green Revolution and mechanization on farm women in India. It stresses the need for a new agricultural research and extension agenda which integrates gender analysis into the process of technology generation and dissemination. It also comes up with future strategies to make women a more active part of important farm decisions both at the household and legislature level. This research note emphasizes the importance of balancing agricultural research systems, extension education, and policy-making bodies to attain women empowerment in agriculture.[7]

Rural Women's Rights Over Land

The recognition of rural women's rights over land is more crucial because, women have more limited access to alternative sources of livelihood for instant to wage employment. Another reason is that, women's rights over land and forests tend to be more insecure and deprived. The lack of secure land rights further curtails the women's access to other inputs, especially credit, necessary for carrying out productive activities. The limited access to credit and to extension services further erodes women's capacity to maintain control over their land.

Women's land rights, like men's land rights, are affected by the socio-economic status of the household in a given society. But, in addition, women's rights are determined by the lines of gender authority and subordination within the household and community in specific cultural settings. Women's access to land is limited, deprived and insecure. Land rights are closely tied to inheritance and marriage customary laws. Customary laws usually vests rights of land allocation in certain men of landholding group like lineage. Women drive rights of access and use by virtue of their relationship to these men mainly as wife, though also as mother. For rural women, land is perhaps the most important household asset to support their families and provide for food, nutrition, and income security. Less than 20 per cent of all landholders are women because of legal and cultural constraints in land inheritance, ownership, and use.

Women in the Agricultural Labour Force

Two types of data can contribute to measuring the contribution of women in the agricultural labour force: statistics on the share of women in the economically active population in agriculture and time use surveys, which document the time spent by men and women in different activities. In most countries, women in rural areas who earn an income are more likely than men to hold seasonal, part-time, and low-wage jobs. Women receive less pay for the same work. The estimates for changes in the last 5-7 years show declines in employment ranging from 20 per cent to as much as 77 per cent. Employment in agriculture is thus available for fewer days per year. It is, therefore, becoming essential for men to migrate in search of better-paid work. Women are filling this vacuum. Women are forced to accept work in agriculture in their own village under very bad conditions because they cannot migrate as easily as men. The dependence of women's labour on family farms, especially during the peak periods of sowing and harvesting has become very common. About 15 years ago, agricultural work was considered acceptable for poor tribal women. Muslim women today even, who were traditionally bound by rules of purdah, go out to work for wages in the fields in certain areas. Farmers, on the other hand, also seem to prefer women as agricultural workers. The farmer is faced with the increasing costs of production required for modern agriculture. He finds that he can squeeze his labour costs by using lower-paid women workers. Similarly, the work of women within family-based agriculture is preferred because it is cheaper than hiring labour. Women agricultural workers, although they represent a big proportion of all women workers, continue to receive lower wages than men. The Ministry of Labour puts the difference at 60 per cent of men's wages, while the *Indian Labour Journal* showed that women received 75 per cent of men earnings.

Economically Active Population in Agriculture

Data on the economically active population in agriculture are available for many countries, and provide the most comprehensive measure of the participation of women in agriculture. In this measure, an individual is reported as being in the agricultural labour force if he or she reports that agriculture is his or her main economic activity. However, these data may underestimate female participation in agriculture for reasons discussed below, and caution is advised in interpreting changes over time because improvements in data collection may be responsible for some of the observed changes.[8]

Women's Constraints in Farming

The low economic status of women limits their opportunities for broader participation in society. This is compounded by the trouble women experienced in child-bearing and rearing. African culture discriminates a lot against women and girls, especially in the area of inheritance (land). Culture is not static and in modern-day Nigeria, it is subject to pressure and influences. Modern education and the development of technology and information have introduced Nigerians to new cultural concepts and norms.

Since culture is not static, the forces of social change may be expected to lowering the barriers against women's economic opportunities. Many women took to prostitution due to poverty and inadequate information and education. Access to education, extension services, information, land, credit facilities and other relevant agricultural innovations will entice many women to agricultural productions and will reduce poverty among women farmers. Women have little access to capital and other assets that make agricultural production easy and profitable. In the study area, majority of the women farmers have financial problem and lack financial assistance (88 per cent), similarly women have to beg (83 per cent) for farmlands from husbands and relatives. In Nigeria culture controls many aspects of the life of women. Famoriyo (1979) stated that land is the vital possession of the people, without land, farming cannot take place. Searching for the way out of poverty, majority of women take to farming, but the constraints limit their performance. They also complained about inadequate extension contact, high cost of farm input and late delivery of farm input especially fertilizer.

Women farmers here also have little access to capital or credit facilities. They do not have collateral this is probably why it has traditionally been difficult for them to obtain bank loan or other forms of credit, only 13 per cent were able to obtain bank loan and as high as 33 per cent got loan from their cooperative societies, 23 per cent got money from their former farm output, while others got money from other available sources.[9]

Main Obstacles for Women Growth in Agriculture Sector

- Few women holding of agricultural[10] productive resources such as land, animals, and machinery.
- Women absence from decision-making process, either inside or outside home.
- Women perform all un-mechanized agricultural tasks and perform multiple tasks, which add more burden to them.
- Women workers in agriculture suffer from high illiteracy rate among them and drop-out of schools.

- Women earn less wages, especially in joint, informal and private sector.
- Women do not know their legal rights.
- Miss application of some laws and regulations in favour of women such heritage legislation.

Factors Affecting the Role of Women in Agriculture

There are four important factors that affect the women participation of women in agriculture. They are:

1. Personal factors
2. Situational factors
3. Psychological factors
4. Socio-economic factors

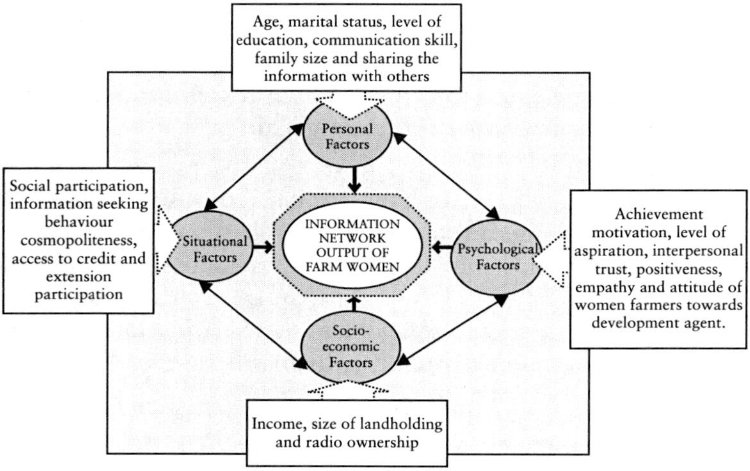

Fig. 1: Factors Effecting Role of Women in Agriculture

Source: Agricultural information networks of farm women and role of agricultural extension: the case of dale woreda, southern nations, nationalities and peoples' region

Steps for the Women Empowerment in Agriculture

Following are the key points, which will help in creating respectable role of women in Indian agriculture:

1. **Skill empowerment:** (a) By training in the area of various operations: (i) Field operations. (ii) Conservation of biodiversity. (iii) Nutritional bio-security. (iv) Vocational training. (v) Organic farming.
2. **Technology development for women:** (a) Designing of tools for various field operations. (b) Animal husbandry: (i) Artificial insemination. (ii) Veterinary knowledge. (c) For side income: (i) Mushroom cultivation. (ii) Floriculture.
3. **Creation of self-help groups:** (a) For financial support. (b) For generation of employment.
4. **Projection of contribution of women by collecting and analyzing data:** (a) Collection and display of data. (b) Projection of successful women in agriculture. (c) Representation of their contribution in economic terms.
5. **Providing Financial Powers:** (a) Giving representation in landholdings. (b) Accessibility to bank loans.

Infrastructure and Information and Communications Technologies

When women don't have access to education or information, they cannot influence research agendas that benefit women. As a result, they are less likely to adopt new practices and technologies.[11]

- Access to new technology is crucial in maintaining and improving agricultural productivity for women.
- Gender gaps exist for a wide range of agricultural technologies, including extension services, machines and tools, improved plant varieties and animal breeds, fertilizers, pest control measures, and management techniques.
- In Ghana, only 39 per cent of female farmers adopted improved varieties, compared to 59 per cent of men.
- The differences are largely explained by women's unequal access to land, labour, and education, which reduces the likelihood of women's awareness of new

technology or practices, and limits women's resources for obtaining them.

Women can change their economic status. This, in turn, will transform the economic life of the communities and countries in which they live. The effort to combat poverty and ignite economic development can only come to pass if women are an integral component of the solution—if not the motor. The economic empowering of women in agriculture will translate into healthier and better educated families. It also helps lift their countries out of poverty. Women make essential contributions to the agricultural and rural economies in all developing countries. Their roles vary considerably between and within regions and are changing rapidly in many parts of the world, where economic and social forces are transforming the agricultural sector.

Rural women often manage complex households and pursue multiple livelihood strategies.[12] Their activities typically include producing agricultural crops, tending animals, processing and preparing food, working for wages in agricultural or other rural enterprises, collecting fuel and water, engaging in trade and marketing, caring for family members and maintaining their homes. Many of these activities are not defined as "economically active employment" in national accounts but they are essential to the well-being of rural households.

Women Role in Farm Production with Technological Change

In general, the literature suggests that failure to incorporate women's roles in implementing technological change has three interrelated consequences.[13] First, there is a loss of adaptive efficiency from not taking their operational knowledge into consideration. Second, there is a reduction in women's household bargaining position accompanied by an increase in their work. Third, there are lower adoption rates due to women's lack of access to technology and training and to a failure by the proponents of the technology to address women's time constraints.

National Research Centre for Women in Agriculture

The National Research Centre for Women in Agriculture (NRCWA) has been functioning at Bhubaneshwar, Odisha, for developing methodologies, for identification of gender implications in farming systems approach and to develop women specific technologies under different production systems. There are 16 ongoing research projects in the areas of gender study on agriculture and household economy, management of coastal agro-ecosystem, extension methods for farmwomen, standardization of women specific field practices, occupational health hazards, reducing drudgery of women in agricultural operations, improvement of farming system suited to farmwomen, eco-friendly pest management technologies for vegetables among farmwomen, evaluation of interactive learning modules, technological needs in empowering women in rural aquaculture, and improvement in storage practices of seeds and grains. Under the project on development and testing of extension methods for farmwomen in eastern India, the extent of participation of farm women in different farming systems and farm enterprises and the role of change agents in that context were studied. Contrary to the situation at coastal tract the male extension agents maintained higher contacts with farmwomen than the lady extension agent.

The studies under "identification and improvement of farming systems suited to farmwomen in Eastern India", the project revealed that there is intense involvement of farmwomen in vegetable cultivation necessitating to take follow up supportive activities and interventions in the area of vermin composting, natural plant pesticides, biological control and IPM. Under the project "Standardization of women specific field practices in rice in Odisha data were collected from women heads of 50 farm families on participation of women in relation to varying operations in rice cultivation. Women of family contributed highest hours per season (61.66) in harvesting and post-harvesting operations and participated lowest in land preparation. Same pattern was observed from the paid women and total women (family + paid labour). Under project on "Occupational health hazards of farm women in coastal Odisha" the health hazards faced by women in household activities, farm activities; post- harvest activities and livestock management were assessed. Under the project identification and evaluation of interactive learning modules for dissemination of homestead technologies ergonomic assessment was carried out on the traditional and improved method of paddy parboiling procedures. During paddy parboiling using improved technology (paddy parboiling unit) the heart beat rate and energy expenditure were significantly reduced and the output also increased from 35 kg per batch to 75 kg per batch. The time duration of carrying out this activity also reduced from two days to six hours. Considering the significant utility of paddy parboiling unit, an interactive learning module is being developed on paddy parboiling unit, which will be useful for trainers in disseminating the technology.[14]

International Development Community for Agriculture

The international development community has recognized that agriculture is an engine of growth and poverty reduction in countries where it is the main occupation of the poor. But the agricultural sector in many developing countries is underperforming, in part because women, who represent a crucial resource in agriculture and the rural economy through their roles as farmers, labourers and entrepreneurs, almost everywhere, face more severe constraints than men in access to productive resources. Efforts by national governments and the international community to achieve their goals for agricultural development, economic growth and food security will be strengthened and accelerated if they build on the contributions that women make and take steps to alleviate these constraints.[15]

Three major sets of interrelated concerns characterize the literature on this subject. First, development programmes can change the distribution of resource control by allowing those already favoured in traditional and evolving structures to benefit disproportionally from growth. In the past this has largely been addressed as a problem between households. However, it is becoming increasingly evident that similar changes may also affect distribution of resources within households. Second, if changes lead to the marginalization of women in production decision-making, they may result in both welfare and efficiency losses. Third, the higher labour intensity usually accompanying technological change for small farmers is increasing labour demands on already overburdened rural women.

Perhaps the most pervasive factor in these changes is the ease with which women's roles can be overlooked; this frequently occurs. The usual theoretical or analytical models and agricultural statistics tend to be gender neutral; at best they are of limited value in analyzing women's role. Another problem is the usually unstated assumptions of farm management—that a single manager farmer supervises the labour and use of other resources on all household fields by "his" paid workers and "unpaid family workers". Examination of the consequences of this myth and a better analytical framework are needed. The primary and most obvious consequence of adopting an inadequate farm management model is the loss of efficiency from having a wide array of institutions—including legal ones—develop and deliver input packages and services for improving farm productivity. These packages and services do not reach all farm decision-makers and hence do not address all the relevant constraints. Illustrations of this are readily found in adaptive research, development of technology packages, and in extension services and education. Equity losses for women also stem from failure to reach women; these losses result from the reduction in women's contribution to management of family farms and the consequently greater potential for women's economic and social marginalization. Despite the failure in recent development efforts to take stock of women's role, it was precisely this role that made feasible the past strategies for export and urban-led growth in both the non-agricultural and the commercial agricultural sectors. Women's subsistence production in agriculture facilitated male outmigration to mining and commercial farming areas at lower cost than would otherwise be possible. At the same time, the already large role of women in subsistence agriculture and food production has probably expanded.

Conclusion

The contribution of women to agricultural and food production is clearly significant. Women comprise half or more of the agricultural labour force in many African and

Asian countries, but the share is much less in some. Time use surveys, which provide a more comprehensive assessment of how men and women spend their time, further emphasize the heterogeneity among countries and within countries in women's contribution to agriculture. Women comprise about 43 percent of the global agricultural labour force and of that in developing countries, but this figure masks considerable variation across regions and within countries according age and social class. The labour burden of rural women exceeds that of men, and includes a higher proportion of unpaid household responsibilities related to preparing food and collecting fuel and water. However, it is impossible to verify empirically the share produced by women because agriculture is usually a venture among household members and involves a range of resources and inputs that cannot be readily assigned by gender. Women's participation in rural labour markets show much heterogeneity at the regional level, but women are over represented in unpaid, seasonal and part-time work, and the available evidence suggests that women are often paid less than men, for the same work. We conclude that accurate, current, regionally specific information and analysis is necessary for good gender-aware agricultural policy-making. Data collection has improved substantially over the last decades, as has our understanding of the complexity of women's roles and the need to collect data not only on primary activities but on all women's activities. Data are needed to better understand gender roles in agriculture and how they change over time and in response to new opportunities. We have shown that women's roles are diverse and that they vary across regions and countries. These roles cannot be understood properly, and interventions targeting cannot be designed effectively, without also understanding their differential access to land, capital, assets, human capital, and other productive resources.

NOTES

1. B. Agarwal (1981). Agricultural Modernization and Third World Women: Pointers from the Literature and an Empirical Analysis. Geneva: ILO.
2. Food and Agriculture Organization (1999).

3. Ferocious Hannan and AKM Abdul Hannan Buiyan (1994). *Role of Women in Agriculture: Some Conceptual Issues*.
4. Lynn R. Brown and L. Haddad (March 1995). Time Allocation Patterns and Time Burdens: A Gender Analysis of Seven Countries, *The Gender CG Newsletter*, International Food Policy Research Institute (IFPRI), Vol. 1, No. 2.
5. Gender Mainstreaming in Education: A Reference Manual for Governments and Other Stakeholders. London: Commonwealth Secretariat.
6. S. Razavi and C. Miller (1997). Conceptual Framework for Gender Analysis within the Development Context. New York: UNDP Gender in Development Programme.
7. J. Betts Beoku (1990). Agriculture Development in Sierra Leone: Implications for Rural Woman in the Aftermath of the Woman's Decade, Africa Today.
8. Jositske Hulsebosch and Doris Ombara (1995). Towards Gender Balance in Irrigation Management: Experience in Kenya South West Karu Project Irrigation and Drainage System, Vol. 9: 1-14.
9. www.fao.org/Gender/en/agrib2-e.htm
10. ncw.nic.in/pdfreports/Impact%2520of%2
11. www.cge.org.za/index.php%3Foption%3Dc.
12. Knowledgecentre.drwa.org.in/women agriculture.
13. Khushk Ali M. and S. Hisbani (2004). *Rural Women at Work*.
14. www.wikigender.org/index.php
15. censusindia.gov.in/Tables Published/S

24

An Analysis of Theoretical Context of Implications of Development Discourses

Mukul Srivastava

ABSTRACT

In this analytical discussion, we shall restrict the use of the term economic development to widespread, widely shared, sustainable economic growth accompanied by significant structural change in production patterns and in economic and political institutions and by generalized improvement in living standards. This definition distinguishes economic development from economic growth that is narrowly based; dualistic in production and distribution; cyclical; grounded in the exploitation of natural resources; and unaccompanied by systematic changes in production structure, institutional development or improvement in the living standards of the poor.

Development Theories Contrasted

Both the modern pioneers of development economics (Rosenstein-Rodan, Chenery, Hirshman, Leibenstein, Lewis, Myrdal, Nurkse, Rostow, Scitovsky and Streeten) and the neoclassical development theorists (Bhagwati and Krueger) view economic development as a growth process that requires the systematic reallocation of factors of production from a low-productivity, traditional technology, decreasing returns, mostly primary sector to a high-productivity, modern, increasing returns, mostly industrial sector. But while neoclassical development economists assume that there are few technological and institutional impediments to the requisite resource-reallocation, the development pioneers assumed that the resource reallocation process is hampered by rigidities, which are both technological and institutional in nature. Investment lumpiness, inadequate infrastructure, imperfect foresight, and incomplete and missing markets impede smooth resource transfers among sectors in response to individual profit maximization and provide the bases for the structuralist approaches to economic development of the modern development pioneers. The modern development pioneers emphasized that long-run economic growth is a highly non-linear process. This process is characterized by the existence of multiple stable equilibria, one of which is a low-income-level trap (Leibenstein, Rosenstein-Rodan and Nurkse). Developing countries are caught in the low-income-level trap, which occurs at low levels of physical capital, both productive and infrastructural, and is maintained by low levels of accumulation and by Malthusian population growth. Industrial production is subject to technical indivisibilities, which give rise to technological and pecuniary externalities (Rosenstein-Rodan and Scitovsky). However, coordination failures lead to the realization of systematically lower rates of return from investments based on *ceteris paribus*, individual, profit maximization than from those that could be realized with coordinated, simultaneous investment programmes. Uncoordinated investments do not permit the realization of the inherent increasing returns to scale and, together with low incomes, which restrict levels of savings and aggregate demand, and Malthusian population growth, ensnare an economy starting at low levels of income and capital in a low-income-level trap (Rosenstein-Rodan, Nurkse). Hence, the need for government action to propel the economy from the uncoordinated, low-income, no-long-run-growth static equilibrium to the coordinated, high-income, dynamic-equilibrium, golden-growth path. Neoclassical development theorists emphasize that international trade can provide a substitute for low domestic aggregate demand. They argue that the only things government need to do to position an economy on an autonomous; sustained-growth path is to remove barriers to international trade in commodities.

Comparative advantage, combined with the Hecksher-Ohlin theorem, will then do the rest. Subsequent amendments to this position add the requirement of removing price distortions in domestic factor and commodity markets ("getting prices right") to the list of government actions required to induce suitable movements of factors among sectors, encourage the adoption of appropriate technology, and increase capital accumulation. In this view, domestic and international liberalization programmes suffice to bring about sustained economic growth and structural change. The modern development pioneers were not unaware of the potential of international trade for stimulating economic growth.

Their first counterargument against the "trade will do the job" view was elasticity and terms-of-trade pessimism, based on the cyclical growth process induced by the Industrial Revolution in the overseas territories prior to World War II (Prebish and Nurkse). The proponents of the "trade is not enough" view also argue that even if, in principle, trade could expand sufficiently to provide the necessary growth stimulus, trade by itself will not do the job because: (1) non-price barriers militate against the smooth transfer of resources among sectors in response to individual profit maximization (Chenery and Hirshman); (2) in the absence of government action, the divergence between rates of return from uncoordinated and coordinated investments entangles the economy in the low-income trap (Rosenstein-Rodan, Leibenstein and Nurkse); (3) the necessity to learn-by-doing implies the need for some initial infant-industry protection; and (4) non-tradable, in the form of physical and social infrastructure, are required to enable competitive domestic industry to emerge. Both the physical infrastructure, in the form of transport and energy, and the social infrastructure (Abramowitz), in the form of property rights, market institutions, social and political structures, and economic and political cultures are lumpy, and hence subject to increasing return to scale. Neither form of infrastructure will therefore emerge spontaneously in response to uncoordinated, market-oriented incentives. In the view of the classical development economists, the conjunction of these factors leads to the need for government actions to initiate the process of economic development. In the absence of appropriate government intervention, the Hecksher-Ohlin theorem will not prevent the emergence of a low-income equilibrium trap.

A different, more recent, underdevelopment theory associated with the Chicago endogenous-growth school identifies low-human capital endowments as the primary obstacle to the realization of the potential economies of scale inherent in the industrialization of developing countries. The productivities of raw labour and capital are assumed to be magnified by factors that reflect the levels of human capital and knowledge. There are different potential dynamic growth paths open to countries: At one extreme, identified with low levels of human capital and knowledge, economic growth is characterized by low degrees of economies of scale; the corresponding growth path is therefore a low-factor-productivity, low-growth one that tends to a stationary state characterized by low per capita income levels in the long run. At the other extreme, identified with high levels of human capital and knowledge, economic growth is subject to significant increasing returns to scale; the corresponding growth path is a high-factor-productivity, high-growth one that tends to a stationary state characterized by high levels of per capita income. According to this view, investments in human capital and knowledge are therefore all that governments must undertake to propel developing countries from a low-growth trajectory to a high-growth one.

The "human capital is enough" development theory is open to objections which are analogous to the ones raised against the "trade is enough" development theory: (1) non-price barriers militate against the smooth transfer of resources among sectors that is necessary to take advantage of potential scale economies; (2) missing and incomplete markets, especially for capital, are likely to impede private individuals from undertaking the investments necessary to take advantage of potential scale economies; (3) appropriate trade policy is required to bring about the realization of the potential economies of scale inherent in industrialization: the necessity of learning-by-doing implies the need for some initial infant-industry protection, while the low aggregate demand induced by low income levels implies the need for export-led growth; and, last but not least, (4) physical and institutional infrastructures are required to enable competitive domestic industry to emerge. Both forms of infrastructure must be provided by modernizing governments if the economies of scale posited by the Chicago production function are to materialize.

Comparative Development History and Comparative Development

To help evaluate the relative merits of alternative development theories we shall devote the rest of this essay to synthesizing the major implications of development history for development theory. For this purpose, we shall draw upon our work *Comparative Patterns of Economic Development 1850-1914* (Morris and Adelman, 1988) and *Society, Politics and Economic Development—A Quantitative Approach* (Adelman and Morris, 1967). These works apply systematic econometric analyses to the study of interaction patterns among social, political, and economic institutions, economic policies, and various aspects of economic development. In these studies, countries are grouped into relatively homogeneous groups, defined by either a common process or common initial conditions (Morris and Adelman, 1988) or by a range of institutional development (Adelman and Morris, 1967). Comparative history and comparative economic development provide the following four major lessons: First, the process of economic development has been highly non-linear and highly multifaceted. Our research into patterns of growth during the two eras of accelerated global economic development, contradicts the proposition that all countries have undergone similar patterns and sequences of economic and institutional change.

Historically, one can discern at least four distinct development paths: (1) The autonomous export-led industrialization path followed by the first comers to the Industrial Revolution, Great Britain, Belgium and France, in which successful industrialization started from high-productivity agricultural systems, highly developed market institutions, and political institutions that limited the power of agricultural elites. (2) The government-led, inward-oriented industrialization path followed by the large latecomers to the Industrial Revolution in which success with industrialization in past varied greatly. These countries were institutionally less advanced than the first comers, started with significant impediments to labour mobility and incompletely unified commodity markets; had less productive, sometimes even backward, agricultures and land tenure institutions less favourable to the diffusion of agricultural innovations; and had political institutions in which modernizing indigenous entrepreneurs, businessmen and workers, at best, shared power with landed elites. During the 19th century, these economies thus resembled today's developing countries. (3) The balanced-growth, open economy, limited-government-intervention path pursued by some countries. In these countries, agricultural productivity growth kept pace with industrialization and there was rapid growth of skill-intensive, internationally competitive exports. These countries started with unusually favourable market institutions and human resources; well-functioning parliamentary systems; high-productivity agricultural sectors; and favourable land-tenure systems that provided for a well-distributed agricultural surplus and farmer-incentives. (4) The agricultural, primary-export oriented, sharply dualistic path, pursued by both land-abundant and densely populated countries. The countries in this group varied in ultimate development success according to their natural resource endowments and degrees of government autonomy from domestic traditional elites and colonial powers. The land-scarce countries with low-productivity in food agriculture attained very little modern industrial growth, and experienced negligible increases in per capita incomes and massive poverty. The land abundant countries in which the political power of expatriates, landed elites and export-interests remained strong had cyclical, dualistic growth, with little structural change and generalized improvement in living standards. Only those land abundant countries in which small farmers, domestic manufacturers and labour eventually attained political power accomplished some economic development before industrial revolution. There, the impetus from export expansion also spread to the domestic economy; a domestic market for the growth of small industry emerged; the economic and political institutions of modern capitalism evolved; and the growth of exports and average incomes ultimately reduced poverty.

Along the same lines, in contemporary developing countries we found that the interaction patterns among economic and institutional changes differed sharply among countries characterized by different institutional, social, and economic initial conditions. In the developing countries that were at the lowest end of the spectrum in socio-economic development, the economic growth process principally entailed an interrelated process of economic and social transformations. This group of countries has been characterized by minimal degrees of development of market institutions and political systems and by a preeminence of social tribal influences over the economic activity of the predominantly subsistence agrarian economy. The process by which economic growth was induced in this low-development group of countries has entailed the dualistic development of a modern, export-oriented, primary sector which provoked significant transformations of social structure, the diffusion of the market economy and the reduction in the sway of traditional tribal customs over economic activity. In the next group of transitional economies, that were intermediate in socio-political and economic degrees of institutional development, the process of social, economic and political modernization had proceeded far enough to profoundly disturb traditional customs and institutions without progressing far enough to set them on the path of self-sustained economic development. Dualistic industrialization, the buildup of economic institutions, particularly financial systems, and of physical infrastructure has dominated the explanation of intercountry differences in rates of economic growth for this group of countries. There was no longer evidence of a direct systematic impact of changes in social structure upon rates of economic progress; and neither the precise form of the political system nor the extent of the leadership's commitment to economic development played an important role in influencing growth rates in this transitional group, perhaps because the specific patterns of socio-political progress varied substantially among clusters of countries in this transitional group. Finally, in the third most developed group of developing countries, the crucial forces accounting for intercountry differences in economic performance were the effectiveness of economic institutions and a cluster of variables indicating the extent of national mobilization for economic development. This cluster combined the extent of leadership commitment to development, the rate of industrialization, the investment effort and the extent of technological modernization in agriculture and industry.

Thus, both contemporary and historical development experiences suggest rather strongly that different economic, institutional and political processes are important in countries characterized by different economic and institutional initial conditions. Corollaries of this proposition are that: (1) a single theoretical framework, unless highly non-linear, is not likely to offer an equally good explanation of the development process over the entire range of development experience; (2) a single-factor theory of underdevelopment is likely to apply moderately well to only a small range of countries; (3) there is a strong presumption that all developing countries cannot be combined together into a single sample for purposes of econometric analysis, since observations at different levels of institutional and economic development are drawn from different universes; and (4) policy prescriptions based on generalizing across countries at very different levels of socio-institutional and economic development are likely to be seriously misleading. The second lesson of comparative history and development is that institutions (a) matter most in explaining which transitional became developed economically and which did not; (b) matter greatly in explaining which countries among those having similar initial conditions perform much better than others; and (c) affect development in a very non-linear fashion.

Domestic institutions have been the most important differentiators between those countries that have ultimately succeeded in attaining widely spread and widely shared economic development and those that have-not. Countries that industrialized first had the most developed market institutions, very favourable land tenure systems, considerable human resources and political systems responsive to capitalist interests. Among the late-comers to the Industrial Revolution during the second half of the 19th century, the Industrial Revolution technology spread faster where market institutions were more developed. Primary education was significantly more widespread, land was more widely farmed by independent owner-cultivators as opposed to small-holder, short-term tenants; and the government played a much more aggressive developmental role and unified the system economically through the creation of a customs union and extensive investment in inland transport; and it subsidized, owned or directly participated in a considerable number and variety of transportation, financial, and industrial enterprises.

During the golden era of economic development those developing countries that had the most advanced economic and political institutions were the major beneficiaries from the strong growth-impetus imparted by trade with developed countries. A corollary from this is that building institutions is one of the critical tasks of government.

The impact of most individual domestic institutions on development appears to be best described by an S-shaped curve. There are both ceilings and thresholds to the effectiveness of specific institutions in inducing either economic growth or economic development. For instance, we found that, the impact of further development of market institutions on economic progress became negligible once market institutions had reached development levels characteristic of the 19th century first comers to the Industrial Revolution or of today's top institutionally most advanced, developing countries currently. By the same token, it was not until countries attained political and economic development levels characteristic of current semi-industrial countries and degrees of political autonomy characteristic of moderately dependent countries in the 19th century that parliamentary institutions started exerting significant impact on growth and distribution. In our contemporary results, for example, the ceiling for the impact of various types of socio-institutional development was reached first, probably because social development starts very early and proceeds most rapidly. In contrast, we found no ceiling to the impact of further development of financial systems on development in the range represented by even our institutionally most advanced countries. As to thresholds, countries had to proceed to the pre-semi-industrial stage before political leaderships or representative parliamentary institutions could exert a systematic influence on economic growth or before the degree of development of tax institutions could affect development.

The third lesson of comparative history and comparative development is that the process of development has involved a significant variety of substitutions for incomplete, missing or underdeveloped domestic institutions, inadequate domestic factors supplies, and deficient domestic aggregate demand.

The institutions conducive to economic development during transition were neither immutable nor unique. Both historically and in contemporary transitional economies, there have been three major sources of substitution for inadequate or missing domestic elements: domestic governments, foreign institutions, and international factor and commodity flows. These provided temporary substitutes for missing or incomplete domestic capital markets, internal factor mobility, or underdeveloped domestic commodity markets. Governments in moderately backward countries evolved a variety of substitutes for deficient domestic elements: they substituted government demand for manufactures for deficient domestic aggregate demand; engaged in direct investment and provided investment finance as substitutes for deficient private domestic savings and as a mechanism for overcoming coordination failures; and subsidized industrial development both directly and by sheltering infant industries from premature international competition. Foreign international institutions have provided investment finance, balance of payments support and, during the contemporary period, policy advice for restructuring the economy and its institutions and for achieving macroeconomic stability. International trade has been a substitute for low domestic aggregate demand thus permitting economies of scale to be realized in small or poor economies; trade provided a mechanism for importing modern technology thus substituting for domestic R&D, and, at later stages, trade has increased efficiency by imposing the discipline of world market prices on domestic industry. Finally, direct foreign investment, capital flows and immigration of skilled workers and entrepreneurs have substituted for domestically underdeveloped capital markets and institutional cultures, trading networks and skills.

The precise mix of substitutes has varied among countries at similar levels of institutional development, both historically and on the contemporary scene. Governments, international trade, foreign institutions and factor imports have not played the same role in all countries. Thus, for example, the contemporary development pattern has entailed a process of: government-led capitalist development; high government investment and ownership of industry, with initially substantial foreign aid and little direct foreign investment; high private and public investment in human resources and almost no reliance on foreigners; and a short period of generalized infant-industry protection followed by export-led growth combined with selective import-substitution and government promotion of those industries that would become the core export industries in the next phase of dynamic comparative advantage; and has resulted in very fast, widely shared, equitable development. By contrast, the rather less successful pattern has involved a process of government intervention which is less developmental and more responsive to pressures emanating from powerful, tradition-oriented economic elites; a lengthy period of import substitution, starting with consumer goods and extending to capital-intensive producer and consumer goods, and combined with subsidies to non-traditional exporters and constraints upon the sourcing of inputs; moderate investment rates; moderate levels of human-capital development and substantial reliance on foreign investment and entrepreneurship in both agriculture and industry; extensive agriculture, characterized by the predominance of large owner-absentee commercial farms or plantations; and has led to moderately dualistic and rather inequitable development.

Nevertheless, the eventual domestic evolution of: complete domestic markets; land tenure institutions which provide for the wide distribution of the marketable surplus; educational systems which provide for widespread access; financial systems which are effective in mobilizing domestic savings and channeling them into investment; tax systems which are moderately equitable and adequate to the provision of government finance; and fully functioning political systems based on wide representation, have been critical to sustained long-run economic development. Unless the incomplete or missing domestic institutions were eventually developed, their absence ultimately led to economic stagnation. Institutional development and institutional flexibility and adaptability have therefore been crucial to the continued long-term growth of follower countries and overseas territories during the nineteenth century, as well as to contemporary growth. Indeed, it is the very lack of institutional flexibility, imposed by political dependence, which was responsible for the growth without development which characterized the evolution of the land abundant colonies during the Industrial Revolution period. The fourth lesson of comparative history and comparative development is that, among countries similar in institutional development, economic policies with respect to trade, agriculture, international factor movements, and investment were critical. However, the critical policies and governmental actions required in each of these spheres and their relative effectiveness have differed by development level.

In the description of critical policies and how they change with the level of institutional development we focus primarily on our results for contemporary developing countries, for the sake of brevity. The initiation of development in severely underdeveloped countries entails. Investment in social, physical and institutional infrastructure as well as in export-centered industrialization. These investments are critical to the generation of external economies and to the advancement of this set of countries to higher levels of economic and institutional development. Significant social development that helps break down traditional societies, customary behaviour patterns and the sway of traditional cultures and leads to the enlargement of the domain in which market-oriented behaviour guides economic activity. The important processes for this purpose were: reductions in the size of the subsistence economy and increases in narrowly-based, dualistic, industrialization; the spread of literacy and primary education; increases in the size of the middle class and rural-urban migration. Foreign skills and foreign capital inflows are needed as substitutes for underdevelopment of human capital, technology, and domestic capital markets. Expatriates, foreign advisors, foreign aid, foreign investment, and turnkey industrial projects could play a critical role in industrialization and in the management of the development process in this most underdeveloped set of countries.

In trade policy, primary exports are needed to provide the foreign exchange and savings required to fuel industrialization. At the same time, a process of import-substitute industrialization is required to permit the initiation of industrial development. Historically, there were very few countries that industrialized without tariffs during the Industrial Revolution period; inability to adopt import-substitution policies in the developing economies/countries because of domestic and international political constraints has resulted in their remaining underdeveloped until today. No contemporary developing country has been able to start industrialization without an initial period of infant-industry protection, though there are a few examples of specific industries in particular countries that entered export markets without first producing for domestic markets. To maintain the development momentum requires: Adopting a dynamic approach to comparative advantage by successively moving the economy from resource-intensive, to first labour-intensive, and then to either skill or capital-intensive industrial and export structures and fostering the requisite accumulation patterns in education, savings, and financial institutions (Balassa, 1979). Implementing the dynamic approach to comparative advantage by shifting trade policy from general import-substitution to selective import substitution within an export-oriented trade and incentive regime. First expanding the enclave-based, narrow, dualistic industrialization process and then reducing the productivity gaps among and within sectors by extending reliance on modern technology throughout the economy. Raising both private and public investment rates in industrial and infrastructural capital in order to expand the scope of the modern industrial sector, take advantage of scale economies through coordinated investments, and change the industrial structure in accordance with the country's dynamically changing comparative advantage. This entails continued developing of domestic financial and tax institutions, maintaining appropriate interest rates, as well as raising rates of return to private investment through technological modernization and selective, temporary, incentives. Raising the productivity of agriculture while decreasing the size of the agricultural sector, in order to provide food for the cities, earn and save foreign exchange and, later, reduce dualism, release labour and provide a mass market for domestic manufactures. Land tenure institutions must be adapted to enable agriculture to perform its dynamically changing functions in support of industrialization. Specifically, initial land tenure conditions must hasten the creation of a marketable-surplus through agricultural commercialization and technology diffusion, while later land tenure patterns should favour the widespread distribution of the agricultural surplus. Continued foreign investment, foreign technology import, and foreign capital inflows to supplement domestic savings and effect transfers of technology to industrial sectors according to the country's phase in the hierarchy of dynamic comparative advantage. Providing a fairly stable economic setting by controlling inflation and setting realistic exchange rates and adopting a pattern of social-infrastructure investment that is relatively balanced among regions, ethnicities, economic sectors, and socio-economic strata to avoid crippling social tensions, internal wars, and political instability. Active and capable governments that pursue national medium-term economic goals with respect to industrial policy, investment allocation, market-intervention, and provide substitutes for incomplete or missing markets and market failures. Governments with sufficient autonomy so that they can shift policies and forge the institutions needed for continued development, and, towards the end of this phase, engineer the institutions and policies required to effect transition into the next phase.

Emphasis on productivity growth through technology and price policies including not only industry but also agriculture. Emphasis on the competitiveness of the domestic industrial structure through opening up the economy to international trade, dropping subsidies to mature industries, generating appropriate industrial organization, and un-repressing financial markets.

Emphasis on fostering domestic competition through changes in industrial organization, removal of impediments to entry, and neoclassical trade policy. Shifting to a more balanced growth process that provides for the wider sharing of benefits to reduce economic and social instability and generate mass domestic markets for manufactures. Establishing governmental structures that allow for wide political participation, power sharing, and middle class and labour interest representation. Shifting the functions of government away from industrial policies to watchdog functions that: correct the excesses of unfettered capitalism, through enforcement of antitrust and worker-safety legislation; shelter the population from excessive risks through safety-net provision; ensure civil safety and punish anti-social behaviour; ensure a modicum of equal opportunity through educational policies, taxation and anti-discrimination measures; guarantee civil liberties and provide for a judicial and law-enforcement system that protects individual rights and fair treatment to all; and maintain a stable macroeconomic environment.

Implications for Development Theories

Development theories, both old style and new, have suffered from misplaced universality and from tunnel vision. The menu of institutions and policies is extensive. And different institutions, different policy priorities, and different policies are applicable to countries in different phases of economic and socio-institutional development. Development theories must therefore be changed to take full cognizance of historical and situational relativism and of the multifaceted nature of the development process. The most appropriate theoretical description of the economic aspects of the development process for the least developed 40 per cent of countries that are engaged in constructing the economic, social and political institutions and infrastructure required to initiate a development process is offered by the Lewis model. But the Lewis model must be restated so that it becomes an open-economy model with trade in primary goods used to collect potential primary-sector savings and transform them into ingestible resources in dualistic industrialization. Moreover, at this stage, anthropologists have much to teach economists about how the penetration of markets affects and is affected by traditional societies. The subsequent, early phase of building development-momentum in the next more developed third of developing countries is best described by Rosenstein-Rodan and Nurkse type, big push models. These models center on raising investment rates significantly and directing the investment to the creation of both economic and institutional, infrastructure and to the coordination of investments in externality-generating industries. The important economic institutions in this phase are the financial ones, which enable aggregating savings and directing them towards appropriate investment channels. The important actors in this process are governments whose primary function is to build up economic and institutional infrastructural capital; coordinate investment activities; provide finance for investment; raise incentives for private savings and investment; develop human resources and entrepreneurship; and maintain checks upon the divisive socio-political processes which persistent dualistic development engenders. At this stage, international trade continues to promote the aggregation and redirection of savings and the accumulation and redirection of foreign exchange. Appropriate trade policy is generalized infant-industry protection, which is required to enable the creation of an industrial base and lead to structural change away from an economy centered on a primary sector. Thus, neoclassical development theory is plain wrong for this stage.

Once economic, institutional, and social development have proceeded to the point at which countries are ready to enter the semi-industrial stage, our experiences and development discourses suggest that continued development requires: a big-push on the buildup of institutional and human capital, with emphasis on broadening access; continued emphasis on high investment rates; the extension of the scope of modernization to encompass agriculture and the expansion of technological modernization within the industrial sector, thus widening the spread of benefits. This phase entails a shift in trade policies away from generalized import substitution to export promotion combined with selective import substitution centering on fostering the industries needed to climb the next rung of the ladder of comparative advantage. It also entails continued buildup of financial institutions, tax systems, removal of institutional barriers and buildup of the institutions needed to complete markets, "get prices right", and increase competitiveness. And it also entails a shift in government activity away from generalized finance of direct investment and generalized coordination of investment towards selective finance and selective industrial promotion. Developmental governments are essential at this stage both to promote institutional and social development and to engineer the requisite shifts in trade policy and in the government-business balance. All development theories have some limited applicability to this relatively advanced stage. Neoclassical theories that stress open-economy growth, tariff and subsidy reductions, more uniform tariffs and less generalized bias towards imports, have substantial validity for this stage with an important proviso: selective targeting and protection for the buildup of industries which are either skill or capital-intensive or a combination of both. Selective subsidies, protection, and credit and foreign exchange targeting are needed if the economy is not to be locked into static comparative advantage that blocks further development. Chicago school theories centering on the buildup of human capital and knowledge are also appropriate to this stage, especially if they are reinterpreted to include the buildup of the necessary institutional capital required for human capital and knowledge to be translated into increasing economies of scale (thereby becoming non-endogenous growth theories), and if they are made multisectoral. Also important are the development theories formulated by the pioneers that stress the importance of governments for increasing the productivity of private resource-use by undertaking steps aimed at generating externalities, especially if greater stress is placed on building the economic-institutional infrastructure for externality-creation and rather less on direct government investment.

Thus, no development theory is completely irrelevant in this late phase nor is any theory completely applicable to it without serious amendment. We are least likely to go wrong in policy formulation for countries in this phase if we: (1) study each transitional country's initial conditions, including size, natural and human resources, economic structure, and institutional features; (2) form some ideas of the country's economic potential and the most important barriers to its realization, based on formal quantitative analysis applying a system-wide conceptual framework which describes how its institutions work and encompasses all three major development-theory contenders; and (3) tailor our policy prescriptions accordingly. The "have-policy-will-travel" approach to policy formulation is least applicable to this phase. Finally, the purely neoclassical Washington-consensus theories apply fully mainly to the handful of developing countries currently engaged in the final process of transition.

The only universal prescription is that it takes strong, able, public-spirited, far-sighted, enlightened and committed governments to forge the institutions and adopt the policies appropriate to each development phase and engineer the substitutions and transitions in institutions and policies required to shift between phases. The very fact that this is a tall order which may explain why the development process has not been monotonic at any stage; why it took about one generation of development and why only few developing countries have so far been able to graduate to higher status in the development process.

The other major reason for the limited development success is the nature of the guidance developing countries have received from development economists and international institutions committed to the principles of "universality-of-theory-and-policy" and "simplicity-of-theory-and-policy". Inappropriate institutions and policies cannot avoid delaying or altogether blocking development. As we have seen, development history suggests that policies and institutions are context specific and do not transfer well across development levels characterized by very different institutional settings and initial conditions. The principle of Occam's razor may help illuminate certain facets of development within well-defined ranges of institutional development, but it generally constitutes an impediment to the formulation of appropriate development policy in specific countries characterized by particular institutions and particular initial conditions. Various researches have demonstrated that there are a multiplicity of development paths and a multiplicity of aspects of institutional and social change, with different interaction patterns among institutions and policies along each path and at each development level. Our studies have also demonstrated the importance of institutions to the development process. All modern development theories, except the informal ones of Hirshman and Myrdal, either neglect or underemphasize institutions. (The 19th century classical economists, who lived through an era of rapid institutional change, are, incidentally, not subject to this criticism. Their writings are littered with institutional analysis and with recommendations for changes in domestic and trade institutions.)

Economic growth has been at best stalled for the overwhelming majority of developing countries since 1981. But there is hope. The last decade and a half has been one of substantial institutional restructuring in a large number of economies/countries and the beginnings of restructuring of the global trading environment. It is hoped that there will be a resumption of economic growth and development in the near future. Such resumption will require: (1) a better understanding of the need to tailor institutions and policies appropriately to the particular country's moment in history. Situational relativism must become commonly accepted by academic development economists as well as by policymakers, both within developing countries and in the international development-policy community; (2) the restructuring of the global trading regime and international payments system so they become more appropriate to the development and growth needs of all countries, developed or developing; and (3) an acceleration of economic growth in the developed and developed countries both.

REFERENCES

Adelman, Irma (1958). *Theories of Economic Growth and Development*, Palo Alto: Stanford Press.

Adelman, Irma and Cynthia Taft Morris (1967). *Society, Politics and Economic Development—A Quantitative Approach*, Hopkins Press.

Balassa, Bela (1979). "A 'Stages' Approach to Comparative Advantage" in Vol. 5, Irma Adelman (ed.) *Proceedings of the Fifth World Congress of the International Economic Association*, London: Macmillan: 121-56.

Morris, Cynthia Taft and Irma Adelman (1988). *Comparative Patterns of Economic Development*, 1850-1914, Hopkins Press.

Skott, Peter and Jaime Ros. The 'Big Push' in an Open Economy with Non-Tradable Inputs. *Journal of Post Keynesian Economics.*

Thomas, Brinley (1973). *Migration and Economic Growth: A Study of Great Britain and the Atlantic Community*, Cambridge: Cambridge University Press.